D0557204

The Cambridge Companion to
Shakespeare Studies

CAMBRIDGE COMPANIONS TO LITERATURE

The Cambridge Companion to
Shakespeare Studies

Edited by
STANLEY WELLS

CAMBRIDGE
UNIVERSITY PRESS

Published by the Press Syndicate of the University of Cambridge
The Pitt Building, Trumpington Street, Cambridge CB2 1RP
40 West 20th Street, New York, NY 10011–4211, USA
10 Stamford Road, Oakleigh, Melbourne 3166, Australia

First published 1986
Reprinted 1991, 1992, 1994, 1996

Printed in Great Britain at
the University Press, Cambridge

British Library cataloguing in publication data

The Cambridge companion to Shakespeare studies.
1. Shakespeare, William–Criticism and
interpretation
I. Wells, Stanley, *1930–*
822.3'3   PR2976

Library of Congress cataloguing in publication data

Main entry under title
The Cambridge companion to Shakespeare studies.
includes index.
1. Shakespeare, William, 1564–1616–Criticism and
interpretation–Addresses, essays, lectures.   I. Wells,
Stanley, W., 1930–
PR2976.C29 1986   822.3'3   85–29066

ISBN 0 521 26737 4 (hardback)
ISBN 0 521 31841 6 (paperback)

WV

Contents

Illustrations

Contributors

EDWARD BERRY, University of Victoria, British Columbia
DAVID DANIELL, University College, London
LAWRENCE DANSON, Princeton University
ALAN C. DESSEN, University of North Carolina at Chapel Hill
ROBERT ELLRODT, University of Paris III, Sorbonne Nouvelle
W. R. ELTON, City University of New York
INGA-STINA EWBANK, University of Leeds
ROBERT HAPGOOD, University of New Hampshire
TERENCE HAWKES, University College, Cardiff
G. K. HUNTER, Yale University
MACD. P. JACKSON, University of Auckland
RUSSELL JACKSON, The Shakespeare Institute, University of Birmingham
HARRY LEVIN, Harvard University
DIETER MEHL, University of Bonn
KENNETH MUIR, University of Liverpool
S. SCHOENBAUM, University of Maryland
R. L. SMALLWOOD, The Shakespeare Institute, University of Birmingham
PETER THOMSON, University of Exeter
ROGER WARREN, University of Leicester

Preface

This volume owes much – including its first two chapters, before revision – to its predecessor, *A New Companion to Shakespeare Studies*, edited by Kenneth Muir and S. Schoenbaum and published in 1971. I am grateful to the editors of that volume, and to several of the contributors, for their contributions to this one. In restructuring the *Companion* I have tried to take into account the needs of a new generation of readers and students of Shakespeare. Some topics have reluctantly been omitted; others (such as Shakespeare's reading) are subsumed under new headings; and new ones are added. Each chapter has its own selective reading list except for those on twentieth-century Shakespeare criticism and on Shakespeare reference books, whose principal concern is to draw attention to useful secondary literature. Readers wishing to keep abreast of current developments in Shakespeare criticism and scholarship may do so through the regular review articles in *Shakespeare Survey*, published annually by Cambridge University Press.

S.W.W

1   The life of Shakespeare

'ALL that is known with any degree of certainty concerning Shakespeare, is – that he was born at Stratford upon Avon, – married and had children there, – went to London, where he commenced actor, and wrote poems and plays, returned to Stratford, made his will, died, and was buried.' Thus wrote a great Shakespearian scholar of the eighteenth century, George Steevens. His remark has been often quoted, and others have made essentially the same comment in less memorable words. But Steevens exaggerated, and since his time much has been learned about the poet, his ancestors and family, and his Stratford and London associations. These facts, it is true, are of a public character, and are recorded in official, mainly legal, documents – conveyances of property, tax assessments and the like; as such, they afford no insight into the interior life of the artist, wherein resides the chief fascination of literary biography. Yet we know more about Shakespeare than about most of his fellow playwrights. John Webster, for example, the author of two great tragedies, remains little more than an elusive ghost. And, however impersonal, what we know about Shakespeare is not without interest or meaning.

The parish register of Holy Trinity Church records his baptism on 26 April 1564. Tradition assigns his birthdate to the twenty-third. An interval of three days between birth and christening is not unlikely, and supporting evidence is provided by the inscription on the dramatist's tomb, which states that he died on 23 April 1616, in his fifty-third year. But the date of Shakespeare's birth is not precisely known, and behind the conventional assignment lurks the urge to have the National Poet born on the day of St George, patron saint of England; the wish is father of many a tradition. The register of Stratford Church records also the baptism of seven brothers and sisters. Of these, three – Margaret, Anne, and the first Joan (another Joan was christened later) – died in childhood. The infant William may himself have narrowly escaped mortality, for the plague gripped Stratford in 1564, carrying off over 200 souls in six months. Of the surviving siblings, most interest attaches to the playwright's youngest brother Edmund, christened on 3 May 1580; he became an actor in London, where he died young. He was buried in December 1607 in St Saviour's Church in Southwark.

The name of Shakespeare is of great antiquity in Warwickshire: as far back

I

as 1248 a William Sakspere of Clopton was hanged for robbery. John Shakespeare, the dramatist's father, was probably the eldest son of Richard, a husbandman of Snitterfield, a village some three miles north of Stratford. This Richard Shakespeare held lands as a tenant on a manor belonging to Robert Arden, a gentleman of worship in the hamlet of Wilmcote, north-west of Stratford. Arden's youngest daughter Mary inherited from him the Asbies estate of fifty acres when he died in 1556. Shortly thereafter she married John Shakespeare.

He had by 1552 migrated to Stratford, and there set himself up as a glover and whittawer (curer and whitener of skins), an occupation requiring a seven-year apprenticeship. He prospered. In addition to his glove business, he is known to have had dealings in barley, timber, and especially wool. In 1556 he bought a house, with garden and croft, in Greenhill Street, and a house adjoining the one he already occupied in Henley Street. Tradition identifies the double house in Henley Street as the poet's birthplace. Civic recognition came to John Shakespeare: first appointed to minor offices – inspector of ale and bread, constable, affeeror (assessor of fines not determined by the statutes) – he became, in turn, chamberlain, member of the town council, one of the fourteen aldermen privileged to wear a black cloth gown trimmed with fur, and finally, in 1568, high bailiff (the equivalent today of mayor). Yet he was probably illiterate, for no signature exists for him. He signed documents with his mark, a pair of glover's compasses, or with a cross.

Between 1570 and 1572 John Shakespeare four times faced prosecution in the Exchequer: twice for lending money at interest, and twice for illegally buying wool. (Although, in the sixteenth century, trade required credit, the law anachronistically forbade the taking of interest; the purchase of wool was restricted to manufacturers or merchants of the staple.) Some time in the mid-seventies John Shakespeare initiated application for a grant of arms, but nothing came of it, apparently because he had fallen on hard times. After 1575 he purchased no more property. The aldermen excused him, in 1578, from paying his 4d weekly tax for poor relief. He stopped attending council meetings, and in 1586 was deprived of his alderman's gown. He contracted debts, and had to mortgage part of his wife's inheritance. In 1592 he appears in a list of persons 'heretofore presented for not coming monthly to the church according to Her Majesty's laws'; the document has been interpreted as offering evidence of John Shakespeare's recusancy, but a note appended to it indicates that he avoided services 'for fear of process for debt', arrests by sheriff's officers being then permitted on Sunday. (That he subscribed to the old faith is, however, possible, and is supported by a Spiritual Last Will and Testament, a Catholic profession attributed to 'John Shakspear' and purport-edly found in the roof of the Henley Street homestead in the eighteenth century; however, this document, since lost, is of doubtful authenticity.)

John's straitened circumstances forced him, before 1590, to part with his house in Greenhill Street, but he never became so desperate that he had to sell his Henley Street dwelling. The grant of arms that in 1596 conferred the status of gentleman on John Shakespeare was probably instigated by his son, who had by then succeeded handsomely in the London theatrical world.

Fortunately the education of his children cost him nothing. According to Nicholas Rowe, who published the first connected life of Shakespeare in 1709, the dramatist's father bred him 'for some time at a free school'. Although records for pupils at the King's New School of Stratford-upon-Avon in the sixteenth century have not come down, there is no reason to doubt Rowe. It was a superior institution of its kind: the masters during Shakespeare's boyhood held bachelor's and master's degrees from Oxford University, and received better remuneration – £20 a year plus a dwelling – than their counterparts at Eton. A child entering at about the age of five probably passed his first two or three years at an attached petty school where, under the tuition of the usher, he mastered the alphabet and learned the rudiments of reading and writing. Then, at the grammar school proper, he spent long hours – from seven until eleven in the morning, and one to five in the afternoon – memorizing by rote his Latin grammar, an experience perhaps ruefully recalled in *The Merry Wives of Windsor* when the Welsh pedagogue Sir Hugh Evans puts little William through a model interrogation for the benefit of his disgruntled mother:

Evans. Show me now, William, some declensions of your pronouns.
William. Forsooth, I have forgot.
Evans. It is *qui, quae, quod*; if you forget your *qui's*, your *quae's*, and your *quod's*, you must be preeches [i.e. flogged].

Having survived Lilly's *Grammatica Latina*, the scholars moved on to their Latin axioms and phrases, then to *Aesop's Fables* and the *Eclogues* of Baptista Spagnuoli Mantuanus ('Old Mantuan, old Mantuan!' ecstatically declares Holofernes the schoolmaster in *Love's Labour's Lost*, 'Who understandeth thee not, loves thee not'). There followed literary classics – Virgil, perhaps Horace, Plautus or Terence (sometimes acted by the children), and especially Ovid, who would remain the dramatist's favourite – as well as training in rhetoric (Cicero) and history: Caesar or Sallust. Thus Shakespeare acquired the small Latin with which Jonson credits him; possibly in the upper forms he obtained his 'less Greek'. How long Shakespeare attended the free school we can only guess. Rowe, whose information derives from Stratford traditions, reports that the father was forced, because of 'the narrowness of his circumstances, and the want of his assistance at home . . . to withdraw him from thence'.

For the next episode in Shakespeare's life better documentation is available. On 28 November 1582 the Bishop of Worcester, in whose diocese Stratford lay, issued a bond authorizing the marriage of 'William Shagspere' and 'Anne Hathwey of Stratford' after one asking of the banns, rather than the customary three. (Pronouncement of the banns in church allowed members of the congregation to come forward if they knew of any hindrance to the match.) Fulk Sandells and John Richardson, the friends of the bride's family who signed the bond, obligated themselves to pay the Bishop or his officials £40 should any action be brought against them for issuance of the licence. The licence itself is not preserved, nor is any record of the ceremony.[1] Of Anne Hathaway we know little, except that she was probably the eldest daughter of Richard, a husbandman living at Hewlands Farm in Shottery, a hamlet a mile west of Stratford; on this property stands the thatched farmhouse today known as Anne Hathaway's cottage. In his will, dated 1 September 1581 and drawn up shortly before his death, Hathaway mentions no daughter Anne, but the names Anne and Agnes were used interchangeably, and the latter is bequeathed ten marks (£6 13s 4d) to be paid to her on her wedding day. At the time of the marriage she was twenty-six, and the groom eighteen. An entry in the Stratford register recording the baptism on 26 May 1583 of Susanna daughter to William Shakespeare may help to explain why he married so early. On 2 February 1585 his twins, Hamnet and Judith, were christened at Holy Trinity. They were named after lifelong family friends, Hamnet and Judith Sadler; years later Hamnet, a baker of Stratford, witnessed the poet's will and was remembered in it.

Between the birth of the twins in 1585 and the first reference to Shakespeare in London in 1592 the documentary record is a virtual blank, the only extant notice being a Bill of Complaint, *Shakespeare v. Lambert*, 1588, in which John Shakespeare refers to his eldest son William ('Johannes Shackespeare et Maria uxor eius, simulcum Willielmo Shackespeare filio suo'). This phase – the so-called 'lost years' – has occasioned much speculation. The seventeenth-century gossip Aubrey reported, on the authority of the actor William Beeston (whose father knew Shakespeare), that 'he had been in his younger years a schoolmaster in the country' – a suggestion that has met with unsurprising favour on the part of academic biographers. The possibility of a Lancaster connection for Shakespeare during the Lost Years has been suggested on the basis of a will devised in 1581 by the wealthy recusant landholder Alexander Hoghton of Lea, Lancashire, in which he bequeathes all his musical instruments and play-clothes to his half-brother Thomas. If Thomas does not intend to keep players, Hoghton wishes his friend Sir Thomas Hesketh to have the same instruments and play-clothes; 'and I most heartily require the said Sir Thomas to be friendly unto Fulk Gillom and William Shakeshafte now dwelling with me and either to take them unto his service or else to help them to some good master.' Could this Shakshafte be our William Shakespeare? Lancashire is a long way from Stratford, but John Cottom – Shakespeare's schoolmaster – hailed from there, and might have provided an entrée. Such a speculation, while not novel, has recently been vigorously reasserted by E. A. J. Honigmann, who suggests that, through

Cottom's good offices, the young Shakespeare worked as an assistant teacher in a Catholic household in which interludes and other shows were occasionally performed. It is a fact, however, that Shakeshaftes (including some named William) were thick on the ground in sixteenth-century Lancashire and adjoining Cheshire.

The circumstances of the poet's departure from Stratford are the subject of a celebrated legend which Rowe included in his life:

He had, by a misfortune common enough to young fellows, fallen into ill company; and, amongst them, some that made a frequent practice of deer-stealing engaged him with them more than once in robbing a park that belonged to Sir Thomas Lucy of Cherlecot, near Stratford. For this he was prosecuted by that gentleman, as he thought, somewhat too severely; and in order to revenge that ill usage, he made a ballad upon him. And though this, probably the first essay of his poetry, be lost, yet it is said to have been so very bitter, that it redoubled the prosecution against him to that degree that he was obliged to leave his business and family in Warwickshire for some time, and shelter himself in London.

A somewhat earlier version of the same story recorded by Richard Davies, rector of Sapperton, has Shakespeare 'much given to all unluckiness in stealing venison and rabbits, particularly from Sir — Lucy, who had him oft whipped and sometimes imprisoned and at last made him fly his native country, to his great advancement'. For centuries accepted unhesitantly by most biographers, the deer-poaching tradition has certain inherent improbabilities (Lucy, for example, did not then have a park at Charlecote) and is now consigned to the Shakespeare mythos, although a few responsible scholars – notably Sir Edmund Chambers and G. E. Bentley – are willing to allow it a possible grain of truth.

Shakespeare may have joined one of the touring companies – Leicester's, Warwick's, the Queen's – that played at Stratford in the eighties. By 1592 he had established himself in the London theatrical world as actor and playwright, for in that year he was subjected to a venomous attack by another dramatist, Robert Greene. In his *Groatsworth of Wit, Bought with a Million of Repentance*, written as he lay dying, Greene warns his friends – fellow playwrights trained up (unlike Shakespeare) in the university – against 'those puppets ... that spake from our mouths, those antics garnished in our colours', and particularly against one: 'an upstart crow, beautified with our feathers, that with his *Tiger's heart wrapped in a player's hide*, supposes he is as well able to bombast out a blank verse as the best of you: and being an absolute *Johannes fac totum*, is in his own conceit the only Shake-scene in a country.' The punning reference to a Shake-scene and the parody of a line from *3 Henry VI* ('O tiger's heart wrapp'd in a woman's hide!') identify the victim unmistakably. Less clear is the purport of the attack, couched as it is in obscurely allusive language; but Greene seems to be sneering at a mere player, one of the 'antics garnished in our colours', who deigns to set himself up as a universal genius (*Johannes fac totum*) and to rival his betters by turning out plays in stilted blank verse. The notice, however hostile, pays tribute to a successful competitor.

The *Groatsworth of Wit* stirred protest which, Greene being dead, fell on the head of the man who had prepared the manuscript for the printers. Before the year was out Henry Chettle had included, in the prefatory address to his *Kind Heart's Dream*, a handsome apology to the actor-playwright: 'I am as sorry as if the original fault had been my fault, because myself have seen his demeanour no less civil than he excellent in the quality [i.e. acting] he professes. Besides, divers of worship have reported his uprightness of dealing, which argues his honesty, and his facetious grace in writing, that approves his art.'

Who the divers of worship were that vouched for Shakespeare's good character is not recorded. We do know, however, that in the next year, 1593, he published *Venus and Adonis* with a dedication to Henry Wriothesley, third Earl of Southampton and Baron Titchfield. The respectfully formal terms with which the patron, then nineteen, is addressed do not argue close personal acquaintance on the poet's part, but a warmer note enters into the dedication, the next year, of *The Rape of Lucrece* to the same nobleman:

The love I dedicate to your Lordship is without end; whereof this pamphlet, without beginning, is but a superfluous moiety. The warrant I have of your honourable disposition, not the worth of my untutored lines, makes it assured of acceptance. What I have done is yours; what I have to do is yours; being part in all I have, devoted yours.

Both poems issued from the press of a former Stratford neighbour, Richard Field, whose father's goods John Shakespeare had appraised in 1592; Field, three years William's senior, had migrated to London in 1579. What dealings, if any, Shakespeare had with Southampton after the appearance of the two poems can only be conjectured, and of speculation there has been a sufficiency. No further document links the two men; the Earl is not one of the patrons to whom Shakespeare's old friends and colleagues, Heminges and Condell, dedicated the First Folio of his works in 1623. Many believe that Southampton is the Fair Youth celebrated in the Sonnets, and although this is possible, it cannot, in the nature of things, be demonstrated.

Shakespeare wrote *Venus and Adonis* and *The Rape of Lucrece* during the catastrophic plague season that halted London theatrical activity from the summer of 1592 until the spring of 1594. Non-dramatic writing cannot have diverted Shakespeare more than temporarily from his principal occupation. During the Christmas festivities of 1594 the Lord Chamberlain's men acted two plays before Queen Elizabeth at court, and the following March, Shakespeare along with William Kempe and Richard Burbage signed a receipt for the company's honorarium of £20. Kempe was then the outstanding comedian of the age; Burbage would soon gain equal pre-eminence as a tragedian. This first extant reference to Shakespeare as a member of a troupe thus shows him already fully established and representing his company in an official capacity. Burbage is again associated with the dramatist in a scurrilous anecdote that John Manningham, a young law student, jotted down in his commonplace book in 1602:

Upon a time when Burbage played Richard the Third there was a citizen grew so far in liking with him that before she went from the play she appointed him to come that night unto her by the name of Richard the Third. Shakespeare, overhearing their conclusion, went before, was entertained and at his game ere Burbage came. Then message being brought that Richard the Third was at the door, Shakespeare caused return to be made that William the Conqueror was before Richard the Third.

The story may or may not be true.

About another aspect of Shakespeare's career we have surer information: he acted in 1598 in Jonson's *Every Man in His Humour* and, in 1603, in the same author's *Sejanus*. From traditions of uncertain reliability we learn that Shakespeare played 'kingly parts', and that he took the roles of the faithful old servant Adam in *As You Like It* and the Ghost in *Hamlet*. He was not one of the celebrated actors of the period, although Aubrey reports that he 'did act exceedingly well'.

When in 1598 the Lord Chamberlain's men tore down their regular playhouse, the Theatre, and used the timber to build the Globe, they set up a species of proprietorship in which (as a later document shows) Shakespeare was entitled to ten per cent of the profits. These were considerable, although over the years the value of Shakespeare's share fluctuated, depending upon the number of shareholders. As part-owner he of course helped to direct company policy. Thus he served his troupe in a triple capacity: as playwright, actor, and business director.

In the royal patent by which the Lord Chamberlain's men became, in 1603, the King's men, Shakespeare's name appears near the head of the list. The next year he is the first mentioned of the nine players allowed cloth for new liveries in order to participate, as grooms of the King's chamber, in the coronation procession.

Shakespeare lived near where he worked. From tax assessments we know that before October 1596 he dwelt in St Helen's, Bishopsgate, a short distance from the Theatre, and that later (by October 1599) he had moved across the river to the Liberty of the Clink on the Bankside, where, in Southwark, the Globe stood. He may have been living on the Bankside as early as Michaelmas Term, 1596, when one William Wayte swore the peace against William Shakspere, Francis Langley, and two unknown women. This Langley owned the new Swan playhouse; Wayte was the stepson and instrument of William Gardiner, a litigious Surrey Justice of the Peace who sought to put the theatre out of business. The nature of Shakespeare's involvement in this feud remains a mystery; possibly he was a mere bystander.

Some time before 1604 he was lodging – for how long is not certain – with the family of a French Huguenot tiremaker (i.e. manufacturer of ladies' ornamental headdresses) in Silver Street, near St Olave's church in north-west London. So much we learn from a suit brought against Mountjoy in 1612 by his son-in-law and former apprentice, Stephen Belott. The documents in the action afford a rare personal glimpse of Shakespeare. The Mountjoys were eager to marry their daughter Mary, an only child, to Belott, who by 1604 had completed his apprenticeship and was working for a fixed salary in the groundfloor shop. But he held back, and Madame Mountjoy 'did send and persuade one Master Shakespeare that lay in the house to persuade the plaintiff to the same marriage'. The dramatist conveyed to Belott the father's promises with respect to the marriage portion, and also the information that, should he refuse the match, 'she should never cost him, the defendant her father, a groat. Whereupon, and in regard Master Shakespeare had told them that they should have a sum of money for a portion from the father, they were made sure by Master Shakespeare by giving their consent, and agreed to marry.' Thus deposed Daniel Nicholas, friend and neighbour of the Mountjoys. The wedding took place at St Olave's church on 19 March 1604. Later Belott quarrelled with his father-in-law over the dowry and a promised legacy; hence the suit. In his testimony Shakespeare, described as a gentleman of Stratford-upon-Avon, remembered the plaintiff as an apprentice who 'did well and honestly behave himself', and the defendant as one who showed 'great good will and affection towards the said complainant'. But the crucial points – the amount of the portion and when it was to be paid – Shakespeare could not recall, nor could he remember what Mountjoy had promised his daughter after his decease. The court referred the case to the elders of the French church in London for arbitration.

No records exist to connect the playwright's wife and family with any of his residences in the capital; presumably they awaited his visits to Stratford. According to Aubrey, 'Master William Shakespeare was wont to go into Warwickshire once a year.' Unlike Marlowe, he did not sever himself from his provincial roots, but instead carefully nurtured over the years his connection with the town of his birth. There he bought houses and land, and engaged in other dealings with the inhabitants: loans, sales, negotiations, and suits. These transactions testify to his prominence in the life of Stratford.

In 1597 he purchased the Great House of New Place. Three storeys high and with five gables (in the sketch made from memory by the eighteenth-century artist Vertue), it had a frontage of sixty feet on Chapel Street and a depth of seventy feet along Chapel Lane. The second largest dwelling in Stratford, New Place became Shakespeare's permanent residence until his death. In the seventeenth century the garden was noted for its grapevines, and there, tradition holds, Shakespeare planted with his own hands a mulberry tree; it eventually became the source of a ceaseless stream of curios and relics.

The family seems to have moved into the house in 1597, for early the next year a survey of the Chapel Street Ward showed Shakespeare as owning ten quarters (or eighty bushels) of corn and malt. In January 1599 he sold the Stratford Corporation a load of stone perhaps left over from the repair of the Great House.

No sooner had he bought the property than Shakespeare was open to other real-estate investments. 'It seemeth,' wrote Abraham Sturley on 24 January 1598 to Richard Quiney in London, '. . . that our countryman Master Shakspere is willing to disburse some money upon some odd yardland or other at Shottri or near about us.' This same Quiney, whose father had served together with John Shakespeare on Corporation business, wrote on 25 October the only extant letter to the poet. Addressed 'To my loving good friend and countryman Master William Shackespere', it requests a loan of £30 to help Quiney with his London debts. The fact that the letter was discovered among the Quiney papers suggests that it was never delivered.

On 1 May 1602 Shakespeare bought a large tract, 107 acres of arable land plus 20 acres of pasture, in Old Stratford, a farming area about a mile and a half north of the town. For this freehold estate he paid William and John Combe the substantial sum of £320 in cash. That month the poet also bought a cottage (perhaps to lodge a servant) and a quarter of an acre of land on the south side of Chapel Lane, facing the garden of New Place. Three years later, on 24 July 1605, Shakespeare invested £440 in the purchase of a half interest in the lease of tithes on 'corn, grain, blade, and hay' from Old Stratford, Welcombe, and Bishopton, and on 'wool, lambs, and other small and privy tithes' from Stratford parish; he also agreed to pay rents totalling £22 a year, and to collect - or have collected - the tithes himself. They brought him a net income of £60 per annum.

In 1608 Shakespeare sued John Addenbrooke, gentleman, for a debt of £6 in the Stratford court of record. The same bench had heard his complaint, a few years previously, against Shakespeare's neighbour, Philip Rogers, who had bought from him twenty bushels of malt and borrowed 2s but had repaid only 6s of the entire debt. Such litigation is commonplace in the period.

In the last two years of his life Shakespeare was involved (although not very deeply) in a fierce debate over enclosure in the Welcombe area, where lay some of his tithe holdings. Several landholders in the neighbourhood urged the enclosure, which would have combined the narrow strips of cultivated soil into larger units surrounded by fences. If more productive agriculture resulted, Shakespeare would have stood to gain; if, on the other hand, the scheme involved converting arable land into pasture, he would have been placed at a disadvantage. What his views on the question were, we do not know; possibly he favoured enclosure. Late in 1614 Thomas Greene, his cousin who was the town clerk of Stratford and a tithe holder opposing the plan, sounded out some of the leading citizens, among them Shakespeare, whose name appears in Greene's memoranda. On 23 December he noted: 'Letters written: one to Master Manneryng, another to Master Shakespeare, with almost all the Company's hands to either. I also writ of myself to my cousin Shakspeare the copies of all our oaths made; then also a note of the inconveniences would grow by the enclosure.'

Shakespeare's portfolio of real-estate investments included one made in London. On 10 November 1613 he sealed a deed for the purchase of the Blackfriars Gate-house from Henry Walker, 'citizen and minstrel of London', for £140. The next day Shakespeare mortgaged the property back to Walker for £60; apparently £80 was paid down in cash, with the mortgage a security for the remainder. So far as we can gather, the dramatist bought the house, which stood close by to the Blackfriars Theatre (from 1609 his company's principal playhouse), as a speculation rather than for use as a dwelling. He had by then retired to Stratford, and made only occasional visits to London.

Thus, during the middle years of his career, while he was becoming the most popular playwright of the London stage, Shakespeare maintained his ties with Stratford and built an estate that he would pass on to his heirs. Meanwhile, the cycle of birth and marriage and death went on. The parish register of Holy Trinity records, on 11 August 1596, the burial of Hamnet Shakespeare at the age of eleven. John Shakespeare died in September 1601; his widow survived him for seven years. The poet's favourite daughter Susanna married John Hall on 5 June 1607. A Stratford physician, he won (we are told) 'great fame for his skill, far and near'. Perhaps the pair lived for a time at the handsome house in Old Town, near the church, known today as Hall's Croft; after Shakespeare's death they took up residence at New Place. They had one child, Elizabeth, christened 21 February 1608. Shakespeare's younger daughter Judith did not marry until 1616, when she was thirty-one. She took for her husband Thomas Quiney, son of the Richard who had sought to borrow money from the poet in 1598. A vintner whose character was not exemplary, Thomas set up shop, shortly after the wedding, at The Cage, a house at the corner of High Street and Bridge Street in Stratford. They had three children, all born after Shakespeare's death.

One January, either in 1615 or 1616, when he was still 'in perfect health and memory', Shakespeare drew up his last will and testament. Later, after Judith's wedding, he called in his lawyer Francis Collins (who had previously represented him in some of his business transactions) to make revisions. This was on 25 March, and by then Shakespeare's health was failing: he signed in a quavering hand, and he could not recall the name of one of his three nephews – the solicitor had to leave a blank space.

In his will Shakespeare provided for his survivors. To the poor of Stratford he left £10. He remembered local friends: William Reynolds, Anthony Nash, and his brother John Nash. Thomas Combe, whose rich and usurious uncle had bequeathed the poet £5, received his sword; to his lifelong friend Hamnet

Sadler he gave money to buy a memorial ring. Nor did Shakespeare overlook his London colleagues of the days with the King's men, but left sums for rings to Richard Burbage, John Heminges, and Henry Condell; they would not forget him. His sole remaining sister, Mrs Joan Hart, was allowed to stay for the rest of her life in the Henley Street homestead, and was given £20 in cash and the testator's wearing apparel. Her three sons received £5 each. A godson, William Walker, aged eight, was left 20*s* in gold. To his daughter Judith, Shakespeare bequeathed his broad silver-gilt bowl, £100 as a dowry and another £50 for relinquishing her interest in the cottage on Chapel Lane; also an additional £150, provided 'she or any issue of her body be living at the end of three years next ensuing the day of this my will'.

The Halls, whom he designated as his executors, figure most prominently in the instrument. Their eight-year-old daughter Elizabeth received Shakespeare's plate. The bulk of the estate went to Susanna:

All that capital messuage or tenements with the appurtenances, in Stratford aforesaid, called the New Place, wherein I now dwell, and two messuages or tenements with the appurtenances situate, lying, and being in Henley Street within the borough of Stratford aforesaid; and all my barns, stables, orchards, gardens, lands, tenements, and hereditaments whatsoever, situate . . . within the towns, hamlets, villages, fields, and grounds of Stratford-upon-Avon, Old Stratford, Bishopton, and Welcombe, or in any of them in the said county of Warwick. And also all the messuage or tenement with the appurtenances wherein one John Robinson dwelleth, situate . . . in the Blackfriars in London near the Wardrobe; and all other my lands, tenements, and hereditaments whatsoever.

After her decease the entailed estate was to go to her eldest surviving son, and then to that son's male heirs, and (in default of such issue) to the male heirs of Shakespeare's younger daughter. Thus he sought to keep from dissolution the substantial estate that with toil and shrewd investment he had over the years assembled. But his intention was frustrated. Susanna bore no male children; Judith's three sons died young; Shakespeare's four grandchildren left no issue. Eventually the property passed to strangers.

Anne Shakespeare is mentioned once in an interlineation, apparently inserted in the will as an afterthought: 'Item, I give unto my wife my second best bed with the furniture', that is, with the hangings, bed linen, etc. This clause has given rise to endless and often heated controversy over the poet's domestic felicity or lack of it. 'His wife had not wholly escaped his memory,' wrote the great Edmond Malone in the eighteenth century: 'he had forgot her, – he had recollected her, – but so recollected her, as more strongly to mark how little he esteemed her; he had already (as is vulgarly expressed) cut her off, not indeed with a shilling, but with an old bed.' His comment influenced opinion for a long period, but eventually it was pointed out that a widow may have been entitled by custom to one-third of her husband's estate, and that there was therefore no need to mention this disposition in the will. The significance of the bequest can only be guessed, but possibly the bed carried sentimental associations, the best bed being reserved for guests at New Place.

On 23 April 1616 Shakespeare died. About his last illness we have no certain information, although half a century later the vicar of Holy Trinity, John Ward, noted in his diary a story that must then have had currency in Stratford: 'Shakespear, Drayton, and Ben Jhonson had a merry meeting, and it seems drank too hard, for Shakespear died of a fever there contracted.' This story has some plausibility – Jonson enjoyed his cup, and Drayton, who haled from Warwickshire, frequently visited the nearby village of Clifford Chambers. Judith Shakespeare's wedding may have provided the occasion for conviviality. But the anecdote is no more than that; medically it seems dubious, and as a gossip Ward is not entirely reliable.

On the twenty-fifth Shakespeare was laid to rest; so the parish register records. As a notable son of Stratford, he was buried within the chancel of Holy Trinity; more ordinary citizens, including his mother and father, were laid to rest in the churchyard. On the flagstone of the dramatist's grave appears this malediction:

> Good friend, for Jesus' sake forbear
> To dig the dust enclosed here!
> Bless'd be the man that spares these stones,
> And curs'd be he that moves my bones.

We do not know whether Shakespeare himself composed these lines, which are directed not to casual visitors to the church but to the sexton, who sometimes had to disturb the dead in order to make room for a new grave.

Within several years of the interment there was erected, to honour Shakespeare's memory, a monument in the north wall of the chancel, near the grave. A half-length bust of the poet is framed by a niched arch; a pen in his right hand, he is in the act of creation. Above the arch is emblazoned in basrelief the familiar coat of arms, as described in 1596 by the College of Heralds: 'Gold, on a bend sables, a spear of the first steeled argent; and for his crest or cognisance a falcon, his wings displayed argent, steeled as aforesaid, set upon a helmet with mantels and tassels.' (The words 'non sanz droict', appearing above the trick of coat and crest in two drafts of a Heralds' document, are taken to represent the family motto, but we have no evidence of their use as such by Shakespeare or his heirs.) Small nude figures representing Rest and Labour sit on either side of the arms; a skull forms the apex of the triangular design. The stonemason who carved the monument was Gheerart Janssen, of Dutch origin, whose shop stood in Southwark, a short distance from the Globe. The dramatist and his colleagues perhaps knew it.

In 1623 Heminges and Condell honoured Shakespeare with a monument of another kind by collecting and publishing his plays. They dedicated the volume to the Earls of Pembroke and Montgomery, who, we are told, showed

1 The Shakespeare monument in Holy Trinity Church, Stratford-upon-Avon. This
limestone bust was sculpted by Gheerart Janssen, before 1623

the author much favour while he lived; William Herbert, third Earl of Pembroke, would become a leading contender for the role of the Sweet Boy of the Sonnets, which had been published in 1609 with a dedication to 'Mr W. H.'. On the title-page of the Folio appears a clumsy portrait of Shakespeare engraved by Martin Droeshout; this likeness is commended by Jonson in a verse on the adjoining flyleaf. (The Droeshout portrait and the Stratford bust constitute the only authoritative representations of the poet, although claims have been made for many others, most notably the Chandos painting.) In their preface addressed 'To the Great Variety of Readers', the editors comment on the habits of composition of their colleague; 'His mind and hand went together, and what he thought, he uttered with that easiness that we have scarce received from him a blot in his papers.' To which Jonson rejoined, in his *Timber: or, Discoveries*, 'Would he had blotted a thousand!' But in the fifth preliminary leaf to the Folio he paid eloquent tribute to the memory of his beloved, the sweet swan of Avon who was not of an age but for all time. Another encomium came from the pen of Leonard Digges, a University College, Oxford, scholar, who was the stepson of Thomas Russell, a Warwickshire squire appointed by Shakespeare as one of the overseers of his will.

The claim of Heminges and Condell that Shakespeare never blotted a line invites scepticism (we know that he revised), but we do not doubt them when they describe their editorial task as a labour of love, designed 'without ambition either of self-profit or fame; only to keep the memory of so worthy a friend and fellow alive, as was our Shakespeare'. Apart from Greene, none of his contemporaries seems to have uttered a malicious word about Shakespeare. Chettle, as we have seen, praised his civil demeanour and uprightness of dealing. From others we hear of good Will, sweet Shakespeare, friendly Shakespeare, so dear loved a neighbour. The actor Augustine Phillips in 1605 remembered him in his will and bequeathed him a thirty shilling piece in gold. Praise did not come easily to Jonson, but in his *Discoveries*, when not under eulogistic obligations, he confessed that he loved the man and honoured his memory on this side idolatry: 'He was indeed honest, and of an open and free nature; had an excellent fancy, brave notions, and gentle expressions.' Aubrey wrote more than half a century after Shakespeare's death, and so his jottings belong to the mythos rather than to the factual record, but we are not inclined to distrust him when he notes 'He was a handsome well-shaped man, very good company, and of a very ready and pleasant smooth wit.'

Shakespeare's widow lived to see the installation of the monument in Holy Trinity, but not the publication of the First Folio. She died on 6 August 1623. A tradition holds that she 'did earnestly desire to be laid in the same tomb' with her husband, but the injunction against opening the grave prevailed, and she was instead placed alongside. John Hall died in 1635 and his wife in 1649.

2   Portrait of Shakespeare by Martin Droeshout from the title-page of the First Folio, 1623

They too lie in the chancel near the poet. Judith Quiney died in 1662, and Shakespeare's last surviving grandchild, Lady Elizabeth Bernard, in February 1670. New Place, bequeathed to the Bernards by her will, was rebuilt in 1702 and razed in 1759.

Note

1. Much confusion has arisen from the entry of licence, made the previous day in the Bishop of Worcester's *Register*, which names Anne Whateley of Temple Grafton as the bride. Presumably the entry clerk made a careless mistake. That Shakespeare's

wife was a Hathaway is confirmed by the independent tradition reported in Rowe's *Account* (1709).

Reading list

Baldwin, T. W., *William Shakspere's Small Latine & Lesse Greeke*, 2 vols. (Urbana, Illinois, 1944)

Bentley, G. E., *Shakespeare: A Biographical Handbook* (New Haven, 1961)

Chambers, E. K., *William Shakespeare: A Study of Facts and Problems*, 2 vols. (Oxford, 1930)

Eccles, Mark, *Shakespeare in Warwickshire* (Madison, Wisconsin, 1961)

Fripp, Edgar I., *Shakespeare, Man and Artist*, 2 vols. (1938)

Honigmann, E. A. J., *Shakespeare: the 'lost years'* (1985)

Hotson, Leslie, *I, William Shakespeare, Do Appoint Thomas Russell, Esq.* (1937); *Shakespeare versus Shallow* (1931)

Reese, M. M., *Shakespeare: His World and His Work* (1953)

Rowse, A. L., *William Shakespeare: A Biography* (1963)

Schoenbaum, S., *Shakespeare's Lives* (1970)
  William Shakespeare: A Documentary Life (1975); revised compact edition 1977
  William Shakespeare: Records and Images (1981)

Smart, J. S., *Shakespeare: Truth and Tradition* (1928)

2   Shakespeare and the thought of his age

SHAKESPEARE'S works, formed in the changing thought of his age, require a recognition of Renaissance intellectual conventions. These conventions, also, affected the attitude of Shakespeare's audience. This outline will identify some Renaissance conceptual modes which may usefully be recalled to the twentieth-century viewer and reader.

Despite an influential portrayal of '*the* Elizabethan world picture' as unaltered from the medieval, its notable features were complexity and variety, inconsistency and fluidity. Similarly, the recent reiterated 'frame of order' may be regarded, for our purposes, as, to a large extent, a background of Elizabethan commonplaces against which Shakespeare played complex and ironical variations. While his dramas assert the 'great chain of being', for instance, and the hierarchy of order, they also as frequently act out the opposite, the reality of disorder. Considering the rapidity of Renaissance change, moreover, generalizations about Shakespeare's age, or about such complex patterns as Renaissance Christianity, should ordinarily specify, with as much precision as possible, the time and place in question.

Transitional beyond many eras, mingling divided and distinguished worlds, the Shakespearian age witnessed numerous revaluations and reversals. Not unexpectedly, a favourite metaphor was the 'world upside down'; while a repeated mode of a central Renaissance work such as *Hamlet* is the interrogative. In view of Elizabethan complexities, the present condensed notes are thus subject to their own appropriate qualifications.

I Analogy

Most generally, for Shakespeare and his audience, a prevailing intellectual mode differing from our own was the analogical. Though an analogical world-view relating God and man, inherited from the Middle Ages, was in process of dissolution, the analogical habit of mind, with its correspondences, hierarchies, and microcosmic–macrocosmic relationships survived. Levels of existence, including human and cosmic, were habitually correlated, and correspondences and resemblances were perceived everywhere. Man as microcosmic model was thus a mediator between himself and the universe;

and knowledge of one element in the microcosm–macrocosm analogy was knowledge of the other. Blending faith with knowledge, actuality with metaphysics, analogy also joined symbol with concept, the internal with the external world. Analogy, indeed, provided the perceiver with the impression of aesthetically and philosophically comprehending experience.

While medieval analogical thought, including 'analogy of being' which likened man and God, had been largely regulated within the Church, Reformation and Renaissance currents tended to transform it. The Reformers' re-emphasis on man's fallen nature and darkened reason denied such human–divine likeness (at best, an analogy of faith). In the Renaissance revival of antiquity, including Stoic, Pythagorean, neo-Platonic, and hermetic influences, analogy became increasingly a syncretic and secularized instrument for unlocking what Paracelsus called the 'great secret wisdom'. Through this unified theory of the human imagination, poets sought with scientists to interpret the Book of Nature and to discover the harmonious, ordered, and interrelated universe.

In the Shakespearian theatre, analogy, in this sense a momentary leap between levels, correlated the disparate planes of earth (the stage), hell (the cellarage), and heaven (the 'heavens' projecting above part of the stage). Upon that stage, moreover, were spoken lines which might, through analogy, simultaneously allude to the universe, to the state or body politic, to the family, and to the microcosmic individual. Without awareness of analogical (rather than, e.g., allegorical) Christ-allusions, Shakespeare's auditors might have condemned as blasphemous Richard II's comments upon himself:

> Did they not sometime cry 'All hail!' to me?
> So Judas did to Christ; but he, in twelve,
> Found truth in all but one; I, in twelve thousand, none.   (4.1.169–71)

Or, among other instances, in *King Lear* they might have missed the relevant overtones of Cordelia's reference to her father's 'business' (4.4.24).

Shakespearian analogy connected a scale of creation which ordered the world's diversity. From Aquinas to Richard Hooker (d. 1600) that pattern, it has been held, comprised such principles as plenitude, or the view that the universe, created by God out of nothing, was, by the Creator's desire, to be populated through all possible kinds. A second principle was hierarchy or unilinear gradation; upon this scale, each of God's diverse creatures, in accordance with his distance from divine perfection, had an allotted position, observing 'degree, priority, and place' (*Troilus and Cressida* 1.3.86). The final principle, continuity, implied regular, rather than uneven or saltatory, progression in this universal chain of being. Thus, from God and the angels, through man, woman, the lower animals, vegetation, to the most inferior 'stones' or 'senseless things' (*Julius Caesar* 1.1.36), creation was unifiedly and uninterruptedly graded.

Because he possessed both soul and body, man occupied a pivotal place in the great chain of being. Externally, his individual actions found their implications echoed in macrocosmic nature. Macbeth's murder of Duncan reverberates through hell and heaven; Lear's madness embraces an inner and outer storm; and even contemplation of a crime, or the prospect of moral choice, might affect the outward world. Brutus observes, meditating on the cosmic correlatives preceding 'the acting of a dreadful thing', that

> The Genius and the mortal instruments
> Are then in council; and the state of man,
> Like to a little kingdom, suffers then
> The nature of an insurrection. (*Julius Caesar*, 2.1.66–9)

As moral choice brought into focus the cosmos, it simultaneously brought into question the identity of the chooser. Internally, man's mingled nature was expressed in a conflict between his divine soul or reason, and his baser appetites or passion. Precluded by the Fall from ascending in perfection to the angelic level, he might easily be tempted to descend to the bestial plane. In contrast to the more modern idea of human goodness, consciousness of Original Sin was uppermost. Shakespearian drama ponders the extremes of human possibilities, as in *The Tempest*'s magically learned Prospero and bestially ignorant Caliban. Recalling Pico della Mirandola's admiration, Hamlet's wonder at man's workmanship (2.2.304–5) is, however, contrasted by the murderous Captain's conception in *King Lear* of 'man's work' (5.3.40).

Inwardly, sinful predisposition, marked by pride, predominance of passion over reason, and neglect of degree, was outwardly analogous to political disorder, as well as to the decay of nature. The primitive Edenic 'golden age' was irrecoverable; and the predicted end of the world – 'The poor world,' notes Rosalind, 'is almost six thousand years old' (*As You Like It* 4.1.83–4) – was imminent. Natural degeneration, in contrast to our optimistic idea of progress, was everywhere evident: physically, man was a pygmy compared to his longer-lived progenitors; artistically, the ancients may have been superior; and even in suffering, as the closing lines of *King Lear* declare, the young 'Shall never see so much nor live so long' (5.3.325–6). While above the moon all had been considered permanent, below the moon ordinary matter, such as the body – 'this muddy vesture of decay' (*The Merchant of Venice*, 5.1.64) – was subject to mutability. Mutability itself was ruled with fearful, eroding effect by Time: life, the dying Hotspur observed, was 'time's fool' (*1 Henry IV*, 5.4.81) – man was also, like Romeo, the unpredictable 'fortune's fool' (*Romeo and Juliet*, 3.1.133). For many Elizabethans, despite their religious beliefs, 'injurious time' (*Troilus and Cressida*, 4.4.41) was obsessively a murderer. Except for such figures as Giordano Bruno (1548?–1600), on the other hand, it was left to the later seventeenth century, to John Milton and Blaise Pascal, to emphasize the fearful immensities of Space.

In addition to cosmic correspondences, analogical thinking implied hierarchy and order in the political realm. Proceeding from the idea of God as ruler of the macrocosm to the idea of monarch as ruler of the political world, argument by correspondence had evident royalist implications. That mode of argument led inevitably to the widespread Renaissance employment, derived partly from Aristotle's *Politics*, of the analogy of the body politic. The latter corresponded to the human body, whose heart or head corresponded to the king, and whose lower members resembled the lower members of the social organism. As the body obeyed the soul, and the world the Creator, so subjects were to obey the king. In *Coriolanus* a variation of the body analogy occurs in which the belly, compared by Menenius to the senators, is said to sustain the ungrateful and 'mutinous parts', including the 'great toe of this assembly' (1.1.94–153). That the body-politic correspondence was natural could be verified, in turn, by analogy with the family and its patriarchal head, as well as with the animal kingdom. Throughout the divine creation were primacies of various orders: like God in the macrocosm and the sun in the heavens were, for instance, the eagle among creatures of the air, and the lion among beasts of earth. Within all mankind, moreover, innately implanted by God, was an absolute 'law of nature', by which his rational creatures everywhere recognized right and wrong. In the scholastic tradition, the habitual knowledge of natural law, or the willingness to recognize right reason – synderesis – is the faculty of Macbeth's conscience implicitly dwelt upon in the tragedy after his murder of Duncan.

Hierarchically, the human soul, of which Malvolio professed to 'think nobly' (*Twelfth Night*, 4.2.53), was threefold: the highest, or rational soul, which man on earth possessed uniquely; the sensible, sensitive, or appetitive soul, which man shared with lower animals – its concupiscible impulse drove him towards, and its irascible away from objects; and the lowest, or vegetative (vegetable; nutritive) soul, distributed still more widely and concerned mainly with reproduction and growth. Further, the rational soul was itself divided into two kinds: the intuitive or angelic, whose knowledge was immediately infused, without any intervening process; and the discursive, involving rational effort and sense data. The soul was facilitated in its work by the body's three main organs, liver, heart, and brain: the liver served the soul's vegetal, the heart its vital, and the brain its animal faculties – the last contained motive, sensitive, and principal virtues (i.e. involving common sense, fantasy, and imagination, as well as reason, judgement, and memory).

Central to earth, lowest and heaviest planet in creation, man himself was formed by the natural combination within him of the four elements: in ascending hierarchical order, 'the dull elements of earth and water' (*Henry V*, 3.7.22–3), both tending to fall to the centre of the universe, and air and fire, both tending to rise. At point of death, Cleopatra exclaims:

> I am fire and air; my other elements
> I give to baser life.   (5.2.287–8)

While, if unmixed, the elements would separate into their proper spheres, in a mixed state they both abetted terrestrial instability and shaped man's temperament. Antony's eulogy of Brutus's qualities observes the exemplary mingling in him of the elements (*Julius Caesar*, 5.5.73–5). Each element possessed two of the four primary qualities which combined into a 'humour' or human temperament: earth (cold and dry: melancholy); water (cold and moist: phlegmatic); air (hot and moist: sanguine); fire (hot and dry: choleric).

Like his soul and his humours, man's body possessed cosmic affinities: e.g. the brain with the Moon; the liver with the planet Jupiter; the spleen with the planet Saturn. Assigned to each of the planets and the sphere of the fixed stars, and guiding them, was a hierarchy of incorporeal spirits, angels or daemons – intelligences which may be alluded to in Lear's proposal to Cordelia that they 'take upon' them 'the mystery of things' as if they were 'God's spies' (5.3.16–17). In parallel fashion, on earth, the fallen angels and Satan, along with such occult forces as witches, continued to tempt man and lead him on to sin. For a time, Martin Luther (1483–1546), for example, was afflicted by doubts as to whether his calling to reform the Church was, in inspiration, divine or diabolic. Hamlet expresses such fears of the Ghost, since 'the devil hath power / T'assume a pleasing shape' (2.2. 595–6). Macbeth finds himself all too susceptible to the weird sisters. And the disillusioned Othello suspects Satan's presence in Iago:

> I look down towards his feet – but that's a fable. (5.2. 289)

Although controversial, belief in the influence of the stars upon man's life was held by a majority of Shakespeare's audience. Indeed, distinguished astronomers, such as Tycho Brahe (1546–1601) and Johannes Kepler (1571–1630), were practising astrologers, and the eminent physicist, William Gilbert (*c.* 1540–1603), physician to Queen Elizabeth, maintained astrological views. Natural astrology (useful, e.g. for meteorological predictions governing such matters as the influence of planets on crops) was widely credited, but differentiated from judicial astrology (more suspect, as involving details of personal lives and political prognostications). While astrologers agreed that man's fate was determined by his planetary conjunctions, they continued to dispute whether the determining moment was that of conception or that of birth. Rejecting his father's supernatural determinism and astrological notions, the illegitimate and naturalistic-deterministic Edmund voices the attitudes of sceptical Renaissance spectators (*King Lear*, 1.2.98–127). Opposed to primogeniture and exclusion by accident of birth, Edmund's anti-legal and anti-social view holds that the heat of the conceptual moment itself determines the natural superiority of bastards (1.2.11–12).

Renaissance astrological views operated within a finite universe of spherical shape – the circle was regarded as perfection in form and motion – and the very small planet earth was at its centre and lowest point. Motionless itself, earth was at the centre of a series of moving concentric crystalline spheres, those of the Moon, Mercury, Venus, the Sun, Mars, Jupiter, and Saturn. Beyond Saturn were the fixed stars; beyond these was the *Primum Mobile* or First Mover; and beyond that was the void, containing neither time nor space. As the planets revolved, they produced, inaudible to mortal sense, the Pythagorean 'music of the spheres':

> There's not the smallest orb which thou behold'st
> But in his motion like an angel sings,
> Still quiring to the young-ey'd cherubins.

> (*The Merchant of Venice*, 5.1.60–2)

Recognizing Renaissance uses of analogy, the modern student should also note the radical differences between the philosophical preconceptions of our scientific age and those of the Shakespearian era. In addition to such influences as those of Francis Bacon (1561–1626) and Thomas Hobbes (1588–1679), as well as those of Kepler and Galileo Galilei (1564–1642), a major cleavage between a Shakespearian world-view and our own was effected by René Descartes (1596–1650). Towards the mid-seventeenth century, Cartesian dualism separated off mind from matter, and soul from body. While influential, this body–soul dichotomy was hardly new, and Descartes, as Professor Ryle reminds us, 'was reformulating already prevalent theological doctrines of the soul in the new syntax of Galileo. The theologian's privacy of conscience became the philosopher's privacy of consciousness, and what had been the bogy of Predestination reappeared as the bogy of Determinism.' For Descartes, all nature was to be explained as either thought or extension; hence, the mind became a purely thinking substance, the body a soulless mechanical system. Exalting philosophical rationalism and evicting mystery, casting doubt on the objective reality of the outside world, Cartesianism held that we can know only our own clear and distinct ideas. Putting aside, like Bacon, as unknowable or uncertain, final causes – the 'why' or purposefulness of things – Descartes considered objects as intelligible only as we bring our judgements to bear upon them. If only such knowledge alone were possible, it would follow that the analogical mode of knowing the universe was thenceforth outmoded. Further, from the Cartesian preference for clarity and its suspicion of our illusory and sensory judgements resulted in turn a misprizing of feeling and the affective life as no more than a confused idea. Such Cartesian scepticism and subjectivism led to a rejection as meaningless or obscure of previous centuries' Aristotelian perspectives.

For, in contrast to the Cartesian disjunction and its dissolution of the world of correspondences, the Elizabethan universe still held to Aristotelian premises of teleology, or purposefulness, and causal action. According to Aristotle, to know the cause of things was to know their nature. Familiar to Shakespeare's contemporaries were the Aristotelian four causes: the final cause, or purpose or end for which a change is made; the efficient cause, or that by which some change is made; the material cause, or that in which a change is made; and the formal cause, or that into which something is changed. Renaissance concern with causation may be heard in Polonius's labouring of the efficient 'cause' of Hamlet's madness, 'For this effect defective comes by cause' (2.2.101–3). Reflecting the controversy over final versus natural causes, Lear's pagan interrogation of the 'philosopher' concerns the 'cause of thunder?' (3.4.150–1), traditionally a divine manifestation, comparable to the 'cause in nature that makes these hard hearts' (3.6.77–8). Ironically, Othello's 'causeless' murder of Desdemona is prologued by a reiteration of 'cause':

> It is the cause, it is the cause, my soul –
> ... It is the cause   (5.2.1–3)

Further, in Shakespearian use of the language of formal logic may be found remains of Aristotelian and scholastic modes: e.g. 'syllogism' (*Twelfth Night*, 1.5.45); 'discourse of reason' (*Hamlet*, 1.2.150; *Troilus and Cressida*, 2.2.116); 'dilemma' (*The Merry Wives of Windsor*, 4.5.78; *All's Well that Ends Well*, 3.6.67); 'major', i.e. premise (*1 Henry IV*, 2.4.478); 'premises' themselves (*All's Well that Ends Well*, 2.1.200; *Henry VIII*, 2.1.63); 'fallacy' (*The Comedy of Errors*, 2.2.185); 'accident' (*Troilus and Cressida*, 3.3.83); etc. In Hamlet's 'Sense, sure, you have, / Else could you not have motion' (3.4.71–2) and in his 'forms, moods, shapes ... denote' (1.2.82–3), among other of his expressions, may be found further echoes of the Aristotelian tradition.

In the Aristotelian view, change involves a unity between potential matter and actualized form. Although matter in one of its potentialities is transformed by change, it endures through the altering process, as the wood endures in one of its actualizations, e.g. a table. Change is thus a process of becoming, effected by a cause which acts determinately towards a goal to produce a result. Implicit in the Elizabethan world-view was the Aristotelian idea of causation as encompassing both potentiality and act, matter and mind. Rejecting as self-contradictory the Aristotelian notion of 'changeful potency' (*Troilus and Cressida*, 4.4.96), Descartes, in contrast, considers process as a simple quality which things either have or do not have. Since it is merely extension, or passive geometrical space, he argues, the physical world cannot possess intrinsic possibilities for action. Implicit in a post-Cartesian world-view is thus the heritage presupposing a disjunction between mind and matter; a static and disparate, rather than interrelated idea of change; and a conception of motion as machine-like and activated by no final cause. In contrast, Elizabethan intellectual modes sustained the traditional notion of causation within a continuous and purposeful universe. Within that context, motion and action were engaged in a causal relationship extending throughout creation.

Shakespeare's pre-Cartesian universe, indeed, tended to retain a sense of the purposefulness of natural objects and their place in the divine scheme. While objects in the Aristotelian view of nature were distinguished by their own kind of movement – e.g. of fire, naturally upward; of earth, naturally downward – modern mechanics holds that laws of motion are the same for all material objects. For the Middle Ages and the Renaissance, objects, not as dead artifacts, influenced each other through mutual affinities and anti-pathies. Regarding nature ethically, for instance, Elizabethans could accept, medically, the correspondences of sympathies and antipathies in nature, including a homeopathic notion that 'like cures like'. Insufficiently evident to a post-Enlightenment spectator, moreover, the Elizabethan world was animistic and vitalistic, indeed, panpsychistic, magically oriented, and, from our view-point, credulous. Well into the seventeenth century, alchemical, hermetical, astrological, and other pre-scientific beliefs continued to exert, even on the minds of distinguished scientists, a discernible influence.

In contrast to our belief through experimental verification, Elizabethans tended to a greater degree to believe by authority, by imaginative appeal, as in myth, and by disposition to entertain the marvellous, as in Othello's

> ... Anthropophagi, and men whose heads
> Do grow beneath their shoulders.   (1.3.144–5)

Concerned with the need to believe, in an age of incipient doubt, Shakespeare's audiences witnessed in his central tragedies such struggles to sustain belief: Hamlet's need, in contrast to Horatio's, who at first 'will not let belief take hold of him' (1.1.24), to trust the Ghost; Lear's wracked concern regarding the heavenly powers; and Othello's desperate necessity to preserve his belief in Desdemona – 'and when I love thee not / Chaos is come again' (3.3.92–3). For Othello and Lear, belief is sanity: their agon involves the striving to retain both. Although within Elizabethan belief of various kinds might be found numerous shades between total credence and heretical doubt, over all there lingered a credulity, or a need for belief, that permeated their cosmos and penetrated the nascent sciences themselves.

II Transitions

While such inherited modes of thought provided some premises of Shakespeare's age, elements of his world as well as of his work often enough point towards the incipient disordering or breakdown of the analogical and pre-Cartesian tradition. In numerous spheres of Elizabethan thought occurred transitions and revaluations, if not actual crises and reversals.

Theologically, in the later sixteenth century, divine providence seemed increasingly to be questioned, or at least to be regarded as more bafflingly inscrutable. New orientations between man and the heavenly power, disin-tegrating the relative medieval sense of security, were in process of formation. Those changes coincided with such circumstances as a Renaissance revival of Epicureanism, which stressed the indifference of the powers above to man's concerns; a renewal of the ancient atomist and materialist traditions, along with other sceptical currents; and a reflection of the Reformation, especially of Calvinism, which argued, in effect, an incomprehensible and unappealable God, whose judgements of election and reprobation had already, beyond human intervention, been determined. In place of a special providence, capricious Fortune, with its counterpoise of *virtù*, or personal power, was re-emphasized in Machiavelli (1469–1527) and other Renaissance writers. Further, the Reformers, on the one hand, and such sceptics as Montaigne (1533–92), on the other, substituted for the earlier Deity a divine power who, beyond man's darkened reason, seemed inscrutably to hide himself. Like Calvin (1509–64), depreciating human reason and pride, Montaigne helped demolish man's own self-image which placed him above the animals, specially created and favoured by an analogical, anthropomorphic Deity. In sum, this new distancing of man from the now 'totally other' God had the effect of a Copernican revolution in man's pride in his privileged status. Despite his self-flattering conception, he might have discovered, like Lear, that he was not 'ague-proof' (4.6.105). In claiming special providence, as a speaker in one of Galileo's dialogues observes, 'We arrogate too much to ourselves.'

Such changes in the relations of man and his Deity inevitably provided an altered climate for tragedy, within which both divine justice (as in *King Lear*) and meaningful action (as in *Hamlet*) seemed equally unattainable. In a decreasingly geocentric universe, *King Lear* appears to question the forces above man's life, and *Hamlet* the powers beyond his death. For that northern European student, Hamlet, the quest for meaningful action, moreover, seems complicated by the irrelevance, from a Reformation viewpoint, of works towards salvation. The path of salvation – major concern of most Elizabethans – depended, according to that view, not on personal merit or action, but upon impenetrable divine election. For Hamlet, in relation to the Ghost, Reformation rejection of Purgatory appears further to complicate his task. Contrasting the Reformation and the Middle Ages, moreover, R. H. Tawney observes, 'Grace no longer completed nature: it was the antithesis of it.' The Reformers' radical split between the realm of grace and that of nature required, in a disorderly, brutal, and amoral world, a leap of faith. Alienated from the objective structure of the traditional Church, as well as from the release of the confessional, post-Reformation man, with burdened and isolated conscience, turned his guilt inward.

In contrast to *Hamlet* and *King Lear*, where evil appears more universally diffused, *Othello* and *Macbeth* evoke even more sharply a radical universe of evil, ever ready, seemingly, to work mankind harm. In Shakespearian tragedy generally, the extreme intensities of 'punishment' appear disproportionately incommensurate with 'guilt', or the instigating frailties of the human condition. Poetic justice and its twin, the 'tragic flaw', seem quantitatively as well as qualitatively less than adequate to account for the intense torments of

Shakespeare's tragic explorations. Rather than in the complacent satisfactions of poetic justice, many among Shakespearian tragic audiences may be said to have participated in a solemn celebration of the irreducible mystery of human suffering.

To turn from theological to philosophical contexts, the Renaissance epistemological crisis emphasized the notion of the relativity of perception, recalling the appearance-versus-reality motif recurrent through Renaissance drama. Present throughout dramatic history, it was a manifestation as well of theatrical illusion and the new theatre of the baroque. Confusion between appearance and reality, as well as the exploration of their validity, is a feature of such contemporary writing as Cervantes' *Don Quixote* (Pt. 1, published in 1605). The separation of reality from illusion, truth from mere hallucination, is, in part, the task set Hamlet by the Ghost. Recognizing the contradictoriness of all truth, as well as the conflicts in his intellectual heritage, Montaigne, doubting whether mankind would ever attain certainty, turned inward to explore his ambiguous and changing self. Perhaps, as Merleau-Ponty suggests, Montaigne ends with an awareness, related to the dialectic of drama, that contradiction is truth. As in Shakespearian drama, without dogmatic or reductive exclusions, he experiments, 'essays', and questions, in an open-ended and inconclusive manner, the world of experience. Of Shakespearian pertinence are numerous observations in Montaigne's essays: e.g. 'I engage myself with difficulty' (III, x); and 'In fine, we must live with the quick' (III, viii). In the plays of his dramatic English successor, Montaigne might have found that ideal creation he had imagined, which expressed not only ideas, but also the very life in which they appear that qualifies their significance.

Although, for some Renaissance philosophers, words retained the magic power or essence of the thing named, late medieval and Renaissance nominalism, such as Montaigne's, questioned the relation of language and reality. As do the speeches of some Shakespearian villains, Hamlet's 'Words, words, words' (2.2.191) may, in the light of his other expressions, reflect a nominalistic tendency. Concerning 'honour', for instance, Falstaff's celebrated casuistry (*1 Henry IV*, 5.1.131–40) suggests the tenuous state in that term's usage by 1598. Apropos, in the Elizabethan scramble for 'honour', upper-class social mobility had fostered a confusion in social hierarchy. Such lack of discrimination is indicated, more generally, in Hamlet's observation that 'the toe of the peasant comes so near the heel of the courtier, he galls his kibe' (5.1.136–8).

If the limits of language may be said to mark the limits of social life or civil existence, the abdication, for example, of Lear and his severance of the bonds of social duty help to isolate him from the orderly intercourse of dialogue. Reduced to communication outside the social order, he must resort to the discordant babble of madman, beggar, and Fool, sharing especially the Fool's disordered obliquity. Further, in *Coriolanus*, a profound exploration of the relation of language to civil life, of the word of the city itself, Coriolanus refuses the name, bestowed on him as an honour by the citizens, when he rejects the city that has rejected him. For Macbeth, like Lear, language crumbles when he loses his sense of purpose in life: time is creepingly measured out 'to the last syllable' (5.5.21); and life itself becomes an idiot's disordered and furious account (5.5.26–8), reduced, that is, to verbal nonsense.

Such questioning of language emerges in the relativism of Montaigne, to which, among other elements, Renaissance concern with the noble savage contributed. A man playing with a cat, the essayist had suggested, might, depending on perspective, be regarded as a cat playing with a man. Depending on perspective, too, how was man to evaluate his place in the chain of being in relation to the New World's recently discovered natives? Without European civilization, yet lacking the conflicts and corruption of their cultivated dis- coverers, such creatures as the Brazilian Indian, for instance, might, in manner of life, well be superior. Thus, Montaigne's cultural relativism sounded a note which was, partly owing to new geographical discoveries that literally reshaped man's world, and partly to influences set in motion by the Renaissance and Reformation, more widely echoed by the sixteenth century's close. Furthermore, the new cosmography and the cultural relativism of explorers and missionaries stimulated self-consciously critical questions regarding European institutions and values. When, at times, the Renaissance attempted to substitute Arcadia for Eden, displacing Adam by the noble savage, it set an earthly paradise in the New Isles of America. Like *The Tempest*'s, Montaigne's idyllic account of the primitive isles employs a negative form to catalogue utopian aspects. His description thus helps provide an intellectual context for Shakespeare's play, rather than a demonstrable source, since there were a number of such Renaissance accounts. In that New World romance, *The Tempest*'s old counsellor Gonzalo, in an inset speech reflecting the play's political-utopian preoccupations, unfolds a soft- primitivistic Golden Age reverie.

Relativism inhered, too, in the Renaissance's mingling of contradictory and disparate Christian and non-Christian currents. In its revival of Greek and Hebrew, and the introduction of radically different ways of regarding the cosmos, relativism as well as scepticism flourished. Moreover, a multiple and shifting hermeneutic, including revival of ancient emblematic, metaphorical, and symbolic traditions, furthered the questioning of absolute and authorita- tive readings. In such fundamental doctrines as the Creation, for example, a counter-orthodoxy existed in the Renaissance, involving the cosmogony of chaos. In addition to creation out of nothing by divine design, Renaissance thought, through Near Eastern and hermetic influences, also affirmed creation from pre-existing chaos. Such views and their attendant amphibious- monster imagery appear not only in Spenser and other Renaissance writers, but in Shakespeare also. In *Antony and Cleopatra*, for instance, contrasted with such orthodox order figures as Octavia and Octavius, is Cleopatra, 'serpent of old Nile' (1.5.25).

Philosophic value attitudes were also in process of relativistic transition. Shakespearian drama reflects conflict between traditional views, as in Aquinas, for whom value may be present and bound up in the object, and newer views of such figures as Bruno, with his aesthetic relativism, and Hobbes (b. 1588), with his notion of value as relative to a market-situation. Such later positions are implicit especially in Ulysses' exchanges in *Troilus and Cressida* 3.3, where the counsellor is manipulator both of men and of the market in honour. In Renaissance value theory, a turning point may also be reflected in Troilus' individualistic and wilful demand, 'What's aught but as 'tis valued?' (2.2.52). To this anarchic and subjective relativism, Hector's comprises a traditional restraining reply:

> But value dwells not in particular will:
> It holds his estimate and dignity
> As well wherein 'tis precious of itself
> As in the prizer.   (2.2.53–6)

In Edmund's libertine naturalism, similarly, is heard the dissolution of ethical absolutes and natural law, regarded as mere 'plague of custom' (*King Lear*, 1.2.1–4). Reaffirming the Sophists' distinction between 'natural right' and man-made law, and between nature (or *physis*) and convention (or *nomos*), Edmund's challenge shatters traditional absolutistic confidence in the universality of God's law. For Montaigne, as for Agrippa von Nettesheim a half century before him, what is in one place a virtue is elsewhere a vice; what was once a vice is regarded as a virtue. In the Shakespearian era, custom, previously linked with natural law, was regarded by some as a merely relative, or local rather than universal, hindrance to natural desire. Shakespeare's work, therefore, marks a transition between absolute natural *law* bestowed by God, and relativistic *natural* law, recognized by man. In this transformation, new explorations of previously unfamiliar lands and customs led to a more tolerant perspective.

Apropos of such explorations, if it is true, as Lord Keynes has suggested, that England was 'just in a financial position to afford Shakespeare at the moment when he presented himself', the following may also be true: Shakespeare reflected in his works the financial condition which could afford him. To the typical acquisitive enterprise, for example, of such English explorers as Richard Hakluyt (1552?–1616), England was indebted in large part for her possession of the American colonies. Significantly, Shakespeare's age participated in the transition between the older 'use value', by which price was conceived according to a form of intrinsic utility, and 'market value', price rising or falling according to scarcity or plenty of the commodity. Against the traditions of Aristotle and Aquinas, his age took part also in the conflict over forbidden usury, which, reflected in *The Merchant of Venice*, was being practically resolved in favour of a new Puritan class of lenders and investors. Often, though not always, handled negatively, mercantile imagery recurs in other Shakespearian plays, such as *Troilus and Cressida*, which, like Jonsonian comedy, is replete with buying and selling references. In *King Lear* notably, the Renaissance clash between love and quantity – *how much* love? – is most powerfully observed. Like *King Lear*, *Timon of Athens* condemningly explores, with more specific monetary allusion, a newer acquisitive impulse.

If analogical relationships had, in the theological sphere, been questioned, hierarchical correspondences supporting political order had also been challenged. While Shakespeare reflects a medieval image of the state as the body (e.g. in *Coriolanus*), the sense of unity sustaining the metaphor was, even in that play itself, in process of dissolution. Despite, moreover, a received notion of Shakespeare's subscription to the 'Tudor myth', the complexities both of his age and the plays should qualify that view. According to the 'Tudor myth', Shakespeare's histories were devoted to the glorification of Elizabeth's line, to propagandizing on behalf of the sanctity of the legitimate ruler, and to preaching against the sinfulness of rebellion. In short, Shakespeare's histories are held to be didactic dramatizations espousing the doctrines of the Establishment homilies (e.g. 'Against disobedience and wilful Rebellion'), directed to be read in the obligatorily attended Elizabethan church.

Against those who consider the plays orthodox 'mirrors of policy', however, it should be recalled that Elizabethan political views were themselves in process of change. For instance, the deposition scene of *Richard II*, which could be staged at one time, was omitted in the published quarto of 1597. Since the argument for divine right was bound up with Christian cosmology, alterations in the latter had begun to undermine the hierarchical argument by correspondence. If man and his specially created earth were no longer at the centre of the great scheme, human frailty at the Fall would seem to have had less occasion to corrupt the enormous or limitless universe. In addition, the monarchic analogy with God, or the First Cause, was also weakened by the tendency of Renaissance empiricists to distance the First Cause as unknowable, in favour of the study of God's visible second cause, nature. Further, such analogical principles as plenitude and the even scale of creation suggested, without evidence, a kind of rigid determinism and pre-arranged perfection. Reformation thought, moreover, had tended to uphold a God of will, rather than one of visible reason, and a world whose supposed rational order was imperceptible to man's darkened faculties. Such human weakness argued against mankind's alleged exemplary and unique state, a little lower than the angels. Against stable hierarchy, moreover, on the level of practical politics, the accelerated rise of the 'gentry' suggested less a fixed and immutable order than one that could be shaped by human will.

Furthermore, the premises themselves of Elizabethan political thought were paradoxical, being based, as derived from Henry VIII, at once on the divinity and mortality of the king's two bodies. Divinely enthroned, he is also 'elected', his power being drawn from Parliament or people, and his tenure dependent on his beneficent behaviour. In the contradictory Henrician propaganda to which Elizabeth was heir, the monarch could not be usurped. But if the latter were, the usurper himself should not be replaced, for the orderliness of the commonwealth had priority. These contradictions led, on the one hand, to Samuel Daniel's urging of total submission to authority, to prevent the disorders of war; and, on the other, to Michael Drayton's insistence on the ill effects of unfit rulers. Such paradoxical attitudes were part of the intellectual heritage of Shakespeare, and helped provide the foundations of his ironical, dialectical art. Those positions support the dramatic ambivalences, for instance, of *Richard II* and *Henry IV*. In the former, an inadequate ruler is usurped; in the latter, the son of a usurper plays out his ambivalent role as man and king-to-be, a contradiction underlying his duality of relationships. In *Richard II*, the pathos of Richard as suffering monarch is evoked at the same time that his unsuitability for kingship is affirmed; while Bolingbroke's usurpation is shown as simultaneously dubious and inevitable. Widely accepted is a related reductive view which affirms that the deposition and killing of Richard II recurs in *Henry IV* and *Richard III* as a central theme of England's guilt. The whole tetralogy is supposedly structured on sin and atonement for Bolingbroke's crime. Yet Richard II seems curiously absent from the plays his ghost is supposed to haunt, while the moralizing implications of God's vengeance upon England for usurpation and regicide appear textually unsustained. While he affirms the primacy of the common welfare, Shakespeare complexly transcends the accepted view's simple didacticism and poetically just formula of right and wrong and of the orderly sequence of sinfulness and atonement.

For Machiavelli and Machiavellianism, moreover, whose influence on Shakespeare's England has been demonstrated, worldly politics were shaped not by the City of God but by the will, desire, cunning, *virtù*, and energy of man. Machiavelli's anti-Aristotelian separation of politics from ethics proposes a behavioural study of 'policy', power, and reason of state. Among Elizabethan playwrights, it is Shakespeare who apparently provides the most numerous instances of 'policy' in the Machiavellian sense, e.g. in *Timon of Athens* where 'policy' is said to sit 'above conscience' (3.2.86). Machiavellian 'reason of state', the relativistic view that the interests of the state supersede principles of morality, was a recognized political notion of the later sixteenth century. In Ulysses's behaviour as well as in his celebration of the 'mystery of state' are discernible apologies for 'reason of state' and 'The providence that's in a watchful state' (*Troilus and Cressida* 3.3.196–204).

Among the strongest testimonies to the new Renaissance relativism, further, is the transformation of the traditional geocentric and well-enclosed Ptolemaic universe. While the Copernican revolution was only gradually accepted in England, its implications regarding man's conception of his status could not have been ignored in the Shakespearian climate. Indeed, Lear's shocked discovery of a universe apparently no longer specially concerned for his welfare, and ruled by apparently unbenevolent powers, suggests an analogue to the Renaissance questioning of scripturally based anthropo-centricity and geocentricity. In addition, implications of infinity and a plurality of worlds, proposed by the Copernican-influenced Bruno, were recognized, for instance, in Robert Burton's compendium of Renaissance thought, *The Anatomy of Melancholy* (1621). Suggesting discrepancies with religious orthodoxy, and Christ's unique incarnation in time, Burton asked, regarding a plurality of worlds and their possible inhabitants, 'are we or they lords of the world, and how are all things made for man?' Having broken the world's circle, how was man to reconstitute his own centuries-secured identity in the new vast and unfamiliar cosmos? In addition to Copernicus' innovations, and modifications in them by Tycho Brahe, other disturbing developments included the recognition that corruption and mutability affected not only the sublunar, but also the supralunar, universe. In 1572, a bright new star, or *nova* – followed by others in 1600 and 1604 – suddenly appeared, and gradually disappeared, an event interpreted as demonstrating the impermanence even of the translunary cosmos. For the Renaissance, the terrifying effect of such phenomena was traceable not merely to their novelty. They reinforced, in addition, a contemporary pessimism which tended to anticipate signs of decay as apocalyptic portents of the approaching universal dissolution. 'O ruin'd piece of nature!' exclaims Gloucester at sight of his king. 'This great world / Shall so wear out to nought' (*King Lear* 4.6.134–5).

Between an innovating Renaissance empiricism and an obsolescent schol-asticism, Shakespeare's plays move critically. From one point of view, it may be possible to approach *Othello* as a testing of that new empiricism. For, concerning Cassio and Desdemona, Iago has provided Othello with virtually all the evidence that a dehumanized and efficient empirical mind, devoid of the testimony of faith, love, and intuitive reason, might circumstantially collect. Indeed, the limitations of empiricism, albeit perversely distorted in the case of Iago, may suggest a critique of empirical data unmixed with human value. Yet, in its apparent scrutiny of empiricism, science, and what may be related to the inductive method, *Othello* seems to involve less an argument, as has been urged, on behalf of intuitive or angelic reason, than a negatively realistic, even Calvinist, commentary on the powers of human reason at all.

For Shakespeare's spectator, ultimately, this world no longer, as in the medieval metaphor, mirrored the reality of the next. As doubts and 'dread of something after death' increased concerning 'The undiscover'd country' (*Hamlet* 3.1.78), the beyond seemed more tantalizingly inaccessible. Instead of world-mirror, Shakespeare's era topically and repeatedly figured the world as stage, and man as actor in temporary and borrowed costume, strutting and fretting his meaningless hour. Continually, his theatrical self-reflexivity allows Shakespeare to resort to the temporary and illusory materials of the stage to depict man's worldly estate. Rather than acting out a meaningful role pointing towards the Last Judgement, Renaissance man might at times resemble a trivial plaything for the amusement of questionably benevolent higher powers. On such a stage he moved dialectically between the hopes and fears implicit in 'a special providence in the fall of a sparrow' (*Hamlet* 5.2.212–13) and 'As flies to wanton boys are we to th' gods' (*King Lear* 4.1.37).

III Dialectic

For the intellectual tensions of his analogical yet transitional age, Shakespeare's drama provided an appropriate conflict structure: a dialectic of ironies and ambivalences, avoiding in its complex movement and multi-voiced dialogue the simplifications of direct statement and reductive resolution. Further, the theatrical form itself permitted such internalizing of conflicts. For example, the questioning of identity inherent in drama, especially Renaissance drama, might be self-reflexively mirrored in the actor's assumed role as actor, as well as in his shifting of costumes; Renaissance ethical problems could be reflected in the necessity, within the dramatic action, of the actor's decision to take one direction rather than another, a movement tending to involve moral choice; and Renaissance epistemological crisis might be evoked through the emphasis on illusion and appearance-versus-reality of the theatrical setting itself, as well as through ambiguous juxtaposition of scenes, particularly in multiple plot structure. Embracing and juxtaposing the contradictions of his age, Shakespeare contrived an artistic virtue out of a contemporary necessity. Within his heterogeneous audience, playing off one antithetical preconception against another, he structured his works partly on numerous current issues of controversy. Manipulating such diverse attitudes, while engaging the attention of all, he achieved an integrated, yet complex and multifaceted, dramatic form.

Nothing if not critical, Shakespeare utilized such 'built-in' conceptual possibilities for his dramatic exploration of values. That exploring movement might be symbolized in a two-edged sword which, as it advances through the play, cuts with ironic sharpness in both directions. Recalling, for example, Augustine's view that, without justice, a kingdom is merely a band of robbers, Shakespeare shows us, in *1 Henry IV*, a kingdom as a band of robbers. In that piece the thieves of the tavern are measured ironically against the greater thieves of the court, the prize being literally in both cases, the 'King's exchequer' (2.2.53). Contrapuntally, the dialectic of 'robber robbing the robber' (travellers – Falstaff – Hal at Gadshill; Henry IV – the rebels – Hal) is played out on several social levels. As usual in Shakespeare, while judgements of value are orchestrated, commentary, depending on the spectator's theatrical perceptions, is tacit.

When T. S. Eliot, finally, in reply to Coleridge, questions Shakespeare's philosophical mind, denying that 'Shakespeare did any thinking on his own', it is apparent that the issues have been confused. Since drama operates dialectically, the main care must be not to decontextualize lines and interpret them apart from their fluid and dynamic ironies. The great thing is to grasp Shakespeare's unparalleled profundities within, as Dryden called it, 'the living labour of a play'.

Reading list

American Council of Learned Societies, Committee on Renaissance Studies, *Surveys of Recent Scholarship in the Period of the Renaissance*, first series (n.p., 1945)

Anderson, Ruth, L., *Elizabethan Psychology and Shakespeare's Plays* (New York, second edition, 1966)

Baker, Herschel, *The Wars of Truth* (Cambridge, Massachusetts, 1952)
  The Image of Man (New York, 1961)

Bamborough, J. B., *The Little World of Man* (1952)

Cassirer, Ernst, *The Individual and the Cosmos in Renaissance Philosophy* (New York, 1964)

Craig, Hardin, *The Enchanted Glass: The Elizabethan Mind in Literature* (New York, 1936)

Curry, Walter C., *Shakespeare's Philosophical Patterns* (Baton Rouge, Louisiana, second edition, 1959)

Elliott, J. H., *The Old World and the New, 1492–1650* (Cambridge, 1972)

Elton, W. R., ed., *Shakespeare's World: Renaissance Intellectual Contexts – a selective, annotated guide, 1966–1971* (New York, 1970)

Grant, Edward, *Much Ado About Nothing: Theories of space and vacuum from the Middle Ages to the Scientific Revolution* (Cambridge, 1981)

Greenleaf, W. H., *Order, Empiricism, and Politics: Two Traditions of English Political Thought, 1500–1700* (1964)

Hankins, John E., *Backgrounds of Shakespeare's Thought* (Hamden, Connecticut, 1978)

Haydn, Hiram, *The Counter-Renaissance* (New York, 1950)

Heller, Agnes, *Renaissance Man*, translation (1978)

Heninger, S. K., Jr, *Touches of Sweet Harmony: Pythagorean Cosmology and Renaissance Poetics* (San Marino, California, 1974)
  The Cosmographical Glass: Renaissance Diagrams of the Universe (San Marino, California, 1977)

Hodgen, Margaret, *Early Anthropology in the Sixteenth and Seventeenth Centuries* (Philadelphia, 1964)

James, Mervyn, 'English politics and the concept of honour, 1485–1642', *Past and Present Supplement* 3 (Past and Present Society, 1978)

Johnson, Francis R., *Astronomical Thought in Renaissance England: A Study of the English Scientific Writings from 1500 to 1645* (Baltimore, 1937)

Kantorowicz, Ernst H., *The King's Two Bodies* (Princeton, 1957)

Kocher, Paul H., *Science and Religion in Elizabethan England* (San Marino, California, 1953)

Koenigsberger, Dorothy, *Renaissance man and creative thinking: a history of concepts of harmony 1500–1700* (Hassocks, Sussex, 1979)

Koyré, Alexandre, *From the Closed World to the Infinite Universe* (New York, 1958)

Kristeller, P. O., *Renaissance Thought and its Sources*, ed. Michael Mooney (New York, 1979)

Levin, Harry, *The Myth of the Golden Age* (1969)

Lewis, C. S., *The Discarded Image* (1967)

Lovejoy, A. O., *The Great Chain of Being: A Study of the History of an Idea* (Cambridge, Massachusetts, 1936)

Macklem, Michael K., *The Anatomy of the World: relations between natural and moral law from Donne to Pope* (Minneapolis, 1958)

Nicoll, Allardyce, ed., 'Shakespeare in his own age', *Shakespeare Survey 17* (1964)

Ozment, Steven, ed., *Reformation Europe: A Guide to Research* (St Louis, 1982)

Popkin, Richard H., *The History of Scepticism from Erasmus to Spinoza* (Berkeley, California, 1979)

Skinner, Quentin, *The Foundations of Modern Political Thought*, vol. 1, *The Renaissance*; vol. 2, *The Age of the Reformation* (Cambridge, 1978)

Smith, Gordon Ross, 'A rabble of princes: considerations touching Shakespeare's political orthodoxy in the second tetralogy', *Journal of the History of Ideas*, 41 (1980), 29–48

'Shakespeare's *Henry V*: Another part of the critical forest', *Journal of the History of Ideas*, 37 (1976), 3–26

Stone, Lawrence, *The Crisis of the Aristocracy, 1558–1641* (Oxford, 1965)

Thomas, Keith V., *Religion and the Decline of Magic* (New York, 1971)

Tillyard, E. M. W., *The Elizabethan World Picture* (1943)

Walker, D. P., *Spiritual and Demonic Magic from Ficino to Campanella* (1958)

Wiener, Philip P., ed., *Dictionary of the History of Ideas*, 5 vols. (New York, 1973–4)

Winny, James, ed., *The Frame of Order: An Outline of Elizabethan Belief* (1957)

Yates, Frances A., *Giordano Bruno and the Hermetic Tradition* (1964)

Zeeveld, William G., *The Temper of Shakespeare's Thought* (New Haven, 1974)

3   Shakespeare the non-dramatic poet

SHAKESPEARE'S narrative poems, proudly published with dedications, are works of art. The unacknowledged (though perhaps not unauthorized) Sonnets are great poetry. The difference is more apparent when the higher achievement is considered first.

Wyatt and Surrey had 'Englished' the Petrarchan sonnet in the forties and fifties, yet struck a new note in their rebuke of the mistress or the king. The sonneteering vogue, however, only started with the publication of Sidney's *Astrophil and Stella* in 1591, followed in quick succession by Daniel's *Delia* (1592), Drayton's *Ideas Mirrour* (1594), Spenser's *Amoretti* (1595), not to mention a dozen minor sequences: Tofte's *Laura* closed the series in 1597. Shakespeare's sonnets may have been composed in this period; some of them at least were circulating in 1598, but only two had found their way into print by 1599 (in *The Passionate Pilgrim*) and the sonnet sequence was out of fashion when Thorpe's edition appeared in 1609.

Shakespeare wrote within a convention, but how much of the convention he left out deserves notice. With the justified exception of the narcissistic Adonis (53)[1] he banished the goodly train of gods and goddesses, so prominent in many minor sequences (Fletcher's *Licia*, Lynche's *Diella*, William Smith's *Chloris*, Tofte's *Laura*) and freely evoked by Sidney, Daniel, Drayton and Spenser. Cupid had played his pranks around Stella, Phillis, Licia, Diana, Idea, Diella, and Laura: he only appears in Shakespeare's coda, the last two sonnets, dissonant in the sequence unless we read into them unsavoury allusions to the sad end of the affair. 'Love', when addressed, is not personified as a god, and psychological or moral entities are not arrayed against each other. The military metaphors of the courtly love tradition, retained by Sidney and Spenser, have vanished. The unique moment of 'enamoration' is not recorded in the traditional way. The standard episode of the kiss, so aptly dramatized in *Astrophil*, is missing. The 'whining' tone Drayton himself thought fit to mock in the prefatory sonnet of *Idea* in 1599 – a clear instance of a change in literary fashion – is never heard, even in moods of distress, and the speaker's eye, 'unus'd to flow' (30), only sheds tears for 'friends hid in death's dateless night'. There is no pastoralism, no address to a river, no catalogue of delights and no cosmological, astrological, or heraldic sonnet. The usual blazon 'Of hand, of foot, of lip, of eye, of brow' ironically turns into a prophecy of the friend's undescribed beauty (106) or a semi-Bernesque portrait of the mistress (130). Shakespeare seems to follow Gascoigne's advice, little heeded by the Elizabethan sonneteers: 'If I should undertake to wryte in prayse of a gentlewoman, I would neither praise hir christal eye, nor hir cherrie lippe, etc. For these things are *trita et obvia*. But I would either finde some supernaturall cause wherby my penne might walke in the superlative degree, or els I would undertake to aunswere for any imperfection that shee hath' (*Certayne Notes of Instruction*, 1575). Hyperbolic praise without description and the framing of excuses for the youth's faults are indeed prominent characteristics in Shakespeare's sonnets.

Yet the main innovation is perhaps that they are not 'wooing' sonnets, though some of them are sonnets of adulation. The poems addressed to the fair youth are about love returned, or love betrayed, or love revived, and the favours of the 'woman colour'd ill' are at once enjoyed and despised. M. C. Bradbrook's claim that 'in addressing a friend and not a mistress, Shakespeare deprived himself at once of a good deal of the sonneteer's stock in trade' is often echoed. Yet many of the traditional themes and motifs might have been used to court a 'lovely boy'. Some of the conventions were rejected for other reasons. Others suffered a sea-change as three instances will show.

Complaints about the 'flinty heart' of the mistress, ultimately traceable to Dante's *donna pietra*, had filled the Elizabethan sonnet sequences. When the mistress had become the bay where all men ride, they were out of season. But when this cold indifference is ascribed to the aristocratic friend as one of those 'Who moving others are themselves as stone' (94), the conventional accusation becomes sharp insight into the ambiguities of character.

Daniel and other sonneteers ring the changes on the Ronsardian theme of the fair one bound to repent her cruelty 'When Winter snows upon her golden hairs' (*Delia*, 31–4). Shakespeare acknowledges that time 'will that unfair which fairly doth excel' (5) but he looks forward to the ageing of the lovely boy in subtler ways, not only in his persuasion to marry (a Renaissance topos, unusual however in a sonnet sequence) but in his later confident assertion: 'To me, fair friend, you never can be old' (104).

A third original development allowed by the patron–poet relationship is the introduction of a Rival Poet. An awareness of the reading public had been manifested by Sidney, but competition to win the favour of a patron is a Shakespearian theme and the rivalry becomes another means of expressing an intense yearning for the friend's love. The Rival Poet sonnets however are only an episode in a story the outlines of which we see darkly as in a glass – the mirror of the poet's mind reflecting events and reflecting upon experience.

A 'story' was not so common a feature in a Renaissance sonnet sequence. The clear pattern of Astrophil's courtship of Stella, culminating in Stella's admission of her love, yet rejection of the lover's 'desire' (66, 69, Eighth

Song), is almost unparalleled. Spenser's *Amoretti* imply a chronological progression (cf. 60, 62, 65, 68) toward the 'happy shore' (63), only reached, however, in the *Epithalamion*. The other sequences are usually a kaleidoscope of the lover's moods of comfort or despair without any narrative development between the falling in love and the final admission of failure in the attempt to prevail upon the lady's inflexible virtue.

The lineaments of the story told by Shakespeare are clear but the details are obscure. Sonnet 144 reads like a plot summary: the poet loves 'a man right fair' and 'a woman colour'd ill'; the latter 'Tempteth my better angel from my side / And would corrupt my saint to be a devil'. This seems almost too neat to be a reflection of experience: one thinks of a morality play or of the conflict between the two 'daemons' of the Platonists. But the web of relationships proves more intricate. The difference in social class between the speaker and the youth was not called for by the triangular scheme. The actual sharing of the mistress by the two men – a situation not unknown to the epigrammatists – was without precedent in sonnets. A fourth character in the sequence is the social world. Like Donne, Shakespeare isolates the true lovers in a hostile or mocking world (71, 72, 90, 112, 124, 125). Unlike Donne, however, he usually invites the youth not to neglect the world's opinions (71, 72) though he himself rejects the world's censure (121).

As W. H. Auden put it, 'every work of art is a self-disclosure, but the Sonnets disclose more than other Elizabethan poems because they reveal so much and so little'. Had Shakespeare invented a story to build poems on, Paul Ramsey claims, 'it would have been more dramatic and coherent'. Perhaps not, if earlier sequences were his model. But would a poet who had invented such a story be likely to indulge in enigmatic half-disclosures and allusions, irrelevant to his main theme, as in Sonnets 94, 107, 110 and 121 among others?

As Giles Fletcher granted in the dedication of *Licia*, 'a man may write of love and not be in love'. Northrop Frye rightly describes love as 'a kind of creative yoga' for the imagination of the courtly poet. And when Shakespeare claims he will 'truly write' (21), he is echoing Sidney's first sonnet: the claim was part of the convention. This does not mean that love poetry never expressed the poet's true feelings. Sidney had his sonnets in mind when he stated in *The Defence of Poesie*: 'Over-mastered by some thoughts, I yeelded an inky tribute to them'. We are often reminded that the speaker in Shakespeare's sonnets may be a *persona* like Spenser's Colin Clout. But Colin was supposed to speak the sentiments of Spenser, not the thoughts of other men as in Browning's *Dramatis Personae*. A Renaissance poet created *personae* when he wrote 'Heroicall Epistles' like Drayton's or like 'Sapho to Philaenis' (usually attributed to Donne); in lyric and elegiac poetry he could take a pose, feign or lie, but spoke in his own person (apart from a few love poems in which the woman is the speaker).

Sincerity in poetry does not mean autobiography but truth to oneself. The poet's awareness of self-delusion in his sonnets to the mistress (134, 137, 138, 141, 147, 148) is insistent, but it might be an artful variation on a theme harped upon in many comedies: the illusion of lovers. The tone, however, is utterly different. And the conscious attempt at self-deception in the relationship with the friend strongly suggests a personal involvement, as will later appear. The youth and the dark lady do not seem to be mere figments of the mind. Their identities, however, are unlikely to emerge with certainty out of the chronicles of wasted time.

Another debate will find no end: were the Sonnets printed in the right order? Yet one thing is certain: the order was not haphazard. Most obvious is the separation of the Young Man sonnets from the Dark Lady sonnets. The chronological order is broken if the triangular relationship set forth in Sonnet 144 is reflected in Sonnets 40–2. The parallels between the two main groups have been traced by C. F. Williamson (see Jones, *Shakespeare – The Sonnets*). Besides, the first seventeen sonnets have a common theme – the persuasion to marry – and in each group may be found pairs or triads with thematic links (e.g. sleeplessness, 27–8; guilt, 33–5; the stolen mistress, 40–2; eye and heart, 46–7; a journey, 50–1; expectation of death, 71–2; invocation to the Muse, 100–1; the *Will* sonnets, 135–6), sometimes reinforced by grammatical links (5–6, 73–4, 88–90, 133–4). Only the Young Man sonnets, however, disclose phases and openly allude to a succession of events and seasons. The quick alternation of moods appears at times improbable, but hardly more surprising than in many plays, where such an alternation is supposed to reflect the unpredictability of life. If the sequence is biographical, why should it be logical? The strongest objection to the Quarto order is Auden's: after the friend's trespasses (40–2) forgiveness was possible, love could even be more intense, but not with the 'innocent happiness' of Sonnet 53. A poet, however, may prove forgetful – or flattering – as well as forgiving.

Reading the Sonnets as a sequence has its dangers. Wordsworth complained of 'tediousness', Landor of 'weariness', Hazlitt of monotony. As Symonds observed in the age of Symbolism, 'the sonnet is not designed for a continuous narration but for the crystallization of thought around isolated points of emotion, passion, meditation, or remembrance'.[2] The influence of context, however, cannot be neglected in the interpretation of each poem.

Sonnets 1 to 19 constitute a prelude which subtly modulates from an invitation to marry and 'get a son', as 'beauty's legacy', to the twin promise of immortality through procreation and through poetry (17) and a declaration of the poet's love for the youth, incidental at first (10, l. 13; 13, l. 13), then open (19), giving thereafter pre-eminence to poetry. Sonnet 20 defines the nature of the poet's passion for the 'master-mistress': love, not sex. In Sonnet 21 Shakespeare outbids Sidney's opening professions of sincerity (*Astrophil*, 1,3): 'Oh, let me true in love but truly write'. The following sonnets to the friend may fall into the three cycles of Northrop Frye, moving each from confidence to melancholy, though the last phase of the third cycle 'replaces disillusionment with self-knowledge'. Sonnets 56 and 97, with their suggestion of revival, are, indeed, landmarks. But one can discern shorter groups of almost equal length: 22–32 (unclouded love), 33–42 (double betrayal), 43–52 (melancholy at night and in absence), 54–65 (immortality), 66–77 (death and corruption), 78–86 (the rival poets), 87–96 (estrangement), 97–108 (love revived and strengthened). From 109 to the 'envoy' (126) self-reproach and self-apology (110–13, 117, 120, 125) combine with the Miltonic conviction 'that better is by evil still made better' (119) and the assurance that 'Love is not Time's fool' (116, 123, 124). As Rosalie Colie noted, from Sonnet 97 onwards retrospection prevails.

Love for the youth is more than exalted friendship, a Renaissance ideal as Montaigne, Lyly, Sidney, and Spenser variously evidence. Such friendship was a privileged bond between individuals ('parce que c'estoit luy, parce que c'estoit moy', Montaigne, *Essais*, I.xxviii), a fellowship immune from the stresses and storms of heterosexual passion. But the love for the fair youth is at once chaste and streaked with a sense of guilt, at once a conscious straining to maintain a bond despite gross betrayal and a confident assertion that love alters not. Can it be explained?

Homosexuality was attacked as a fashionable vice in Marston's *Scourge*, in Guilpin's *Skialetheia*, in *Microcynicon*, in the epigrams of Kendall and Harrington. In *The Progresse of the Soule* Donne traced 'sinnes against kinde' to a passion for 'outward beauty', which can be found 'in boyes' (II, 468–70). The speaker's sensitiveness to the outward beauty of the 'lovely boy' (126) is extreme in Shakespeare's sonnets; though at times overshadowed by the claims of truth or constancy, it remains the main reason for his love. Yet there is no trace of the physical excitement roused by masculine beauty in Marlowe's *Hero and Leander*. When the poet disclaims 'love's use' (20), he is not sly or 'sportive' but sincere. The fair youth is throughout an object of aesthetic delight, to be spoken of with the kind of wonder later ascribed to Florizel before Perdita. Like Milton's Eve, he 'summs all Delight', all the loveliness and fertility of Nature, 'the spring and foison of the year' (53). Yet the poet soon discovers that 'Suns of the world may stain' (32) and his effort from then on is to preserve the glorious vision without losing his clear-sightedness. It leads him into casuistry (41–2, 134), and his self-abasement in willing slavery may leave us uneasy (57–8). If we keep in mind both the aristocratic and the religious aura of 'grace' the oxymoron 'lascivious grace' (40) best expresses the poet's response. He can condemn and praise or even bless, as 'the holy priests of Egypt bless' Cleopatra when she is wanton, 'for vilest things / Become themselves in her' (2.2.236–8).

Insensitiveness to the true complexity of this response has led many critics to over-emphasize the presence of irony. The poet, no doubt, admits ambivalence when he speaks of his love and hate (35), and the patron–poet, master–slave relationships complicate the traditional *odi et amo*, differently echoed in the Dark Lady sonnets. Resentment, veiled or flaring up, is present, but later diverted against the world's 'rank thoughts' (121), informers and slanderers, or 'dwellers on form and favour' (125). When the poet seems to praise those 'Who moving others are themselves as stone' (94), probable irony is confirmed by the couplet – though Shakespeare seems to have admired those who are not passion's slaves more than modern critics do. The tone is unmistakable in 'Farewell – thou art too dear for my possessing. . .' (87). But ironic readings can be unduly multiplied; for a Renaissance poet '*ironia* or the Drie Mock' (Puttenham) was a trope supposed to be clearly perceptible.

To mute the claims of irony is not to deny the contradictions: ecstatic assertions of constancy are constantly belied by other sonnets. Not the friend and the mistress alone, but the poet himself is the offender: the sonnets in which he confesses his inconstancy and 'unkindness' (117–20) are an obvious parallel to the sonnets on the young man's fault (32–6) and apparently irreconcilable with the fixity triumphantly claimed for love in the immediately preceding sonnet (116) and in the following ones (123, 124). To discover that 'ruin'd love' can be 'built anew' (119) does not justify the assertion that love is 'ever-fixed' and 'never shaken' (116). That the poet is speaking of his own love, which can endure the 'alteration' found in the friend, is clear: 'my dear love' in Sonnet 124 is the poet's love, not the youth addressed as 'dear my love' in Sonnet 13. But we have just seen that the poet's heart was not free from 'wretched errors' (119). Shall we read Sonnet 116 as an exhortation rather than a statement? Or shall we interpret the whole sequence as a search 'for a *style* that may attain a constancy beyond the material and moral vicissitudes of human existence', as in John D. Bernard's subtle essay?[3] That Shakespeare's faith in love is nourished by aesthetic ecstasy in poetic creation in the Sonnets as in the fifth act of *Antony and Cleopatra* may be granted, but Bernard's claim of an 'analogy with Dante' in the 'act of recording his final, ineffable vision' is questionable. Shakespeare is only recording the moments when the experience of human love is so intense that it is apprehended as immutable essence. But the vision is not mystic though the language is increasingly religious (106, 'prefiguring'; 108, 'hallowed'; 125, 'oblation'). In the envoy to the Young Man sequence the fair youth, who has 'grown' for three years at least and waded deep in the mire of human existence, is again addressed as 'my lovely boy'. Is not the poet trying to summon up the remembrance of an image of loveliness that first moved him to love, in a spirit of wonder not unlike the profane ecstasy felt by Joyce's Stephen Daedalus at the sight of the wading girl, 'touched with the wonder of *mortal* beauty' (my italics)? Only for a while will the youth be 'boy eternal' as in the dream of Polixenes: Nature's 'quietus is to render thee', to surrender beauty to 'death's dateless night'.

Had not the so-called 'procreation sonnets' sounded the note of mortality from the opening pages and announced the war with Time (15)? In their poignancy, their sombre magnificence, Shakespeare's 'mutability sonnets' are condensed 'Mutabilitie Cantos' where Time fails to rest on the pillars of Eternity. Sackville's Induction and Bellay's *Ruines of Rome* in Spenser's paraphrase are their background.[4] The world of the Sonnets is a world enclosed in time. Whether applied to poetry (18, 38) or love (108), 'eternal' seems to mean no more than lasting to the end of time, 'even to the edge of doom' (116), 'to the ending doom' (55). 'You live in this,' the poet tells the friend, 'till the judgment that yourself arise' (55). We hear of 'time's thievish progress to eternity' (77), but an Eternity all breathing human passion far above. Unlike Donne, Shakespeare never contemplates 'a love increased there above' ('The Anniversarie'); unlike Lord Herbert, he never hopes his love will be perfect 'where / All imperfection is refin'd' ('An Ode upon a Question mov'd'). Christian dogma – Judgement Day, the Resurrection – is accepted, yet the other world is excluded from the world of the Sonnets. Heaven and hell are in this life. In the great sonnet on Lust (129), 'heaven' is sensual bliss, as 'that kiss which is my heaven to have' (*Antony and Cleopatra*, 5.2.296–7). Hell is not what may come after death but 'the hell of time' experienced through a friend's unkindness (120). Sonnet 146 does not reflect 'an ironic humanism': C. A. Huttar's defence of the traditional Christian interpretation is convincing.[5] Yet even here the prospect of eternal life is only opened negatively.

Sin-consciousness, however, is present. Incidental in the Young Man sequence, it pervades the sonnets to the mistress, with the exception of playful and probably early variations on the already conventional theme of black beauty. With sarcastic wit and passionate unrest these sonnets convey the sad self-awareness of a lover who spurns himself for loving. Desire cries for food, not in Sidney's natural fashion, but with an 'uncertain sickly appetite' (147), foretasting the nausea that follows 'the expense of spirit in a waste of shame'.

Though self-consciousness and sex nausea were general phenomena among poets of the Donne generation they reflected personal experience. Occurrences of the word 'self' are not only more frequent in Shakespeare's sonnets (0.58 per sonnet) than in Daniel's (0.34), Drayton's (0.08 in *Ideas Mirrour*, 1594, against 0.41 in *Idea*, 1619), Sidney's (0.46) and Spenser's (0.48), but more significant as in 'Thou of thy selfe thy sweet selfe dost deceave' (4), a significance too often masked by modern printing. The poet seems to progress from a criticism of self-love in the narcissistic youth (1, 3, 4) and in himself (62) to self-analysis and self-reproach in the inward-turning later sonnets (109–12, 117–20) and defiant self-acceptance, 'I am that I am', in Sonnet 121. This is not, however, the self-centredness of Donne: the speaker has achieved self-realization first by making his 'love engrafted' to the friend (37), then by hitching it to the star of love itself as an absolute (116).

That the Sonnets 'record the intense immediacy' of an individual caught in a situation is true, but it is the immediacy of 'rumination', a term aptly used by the poet himself (64). The predominance of second person pronouns does not create drama: it can be found in verse letters, which some of the Sonnets seem to be. The interlocutor is removed in time and space and hardly ever supposed to speak. No temporal action is developing within the poem as in Donne's dramatic recreation of a scene, either present – 'Tis the yeares midnight, and it is the dayes' – or past: 'Comming and staying show'd thee, thee'. Sidney's sonnets had been more dramatic, though in a rhetorical way, when like the Roman poets he addressed characters standing by (92, 'Be your words made (good sir) of Indian ware'; cf. 14, 20, etc.) or focused attention on the moment of experience: 'Come let me write. . .' (34, cf. 40). Sonnet 50, written on horseback like Donne's 'Riding Westward', is hardly typical of Shakespeare's usual manner: a meditation in which time is suspended so that past, present, and future can be apprehended together as in the definition of lust 'had, having, and in quest to have' (129). Yet the Sonnets, though not dramatic in the stricter sense, come increasingly close to spoken language with remarkably Donne-like openings: 'That thou hast her, it is not all my grief' (42), 'When thou shalt be disposed to set me light' (88), 'So now I have confess'd that he is thine' (134).

Wit was expected in the sonnet. Shakespeare displays it in paradox and in wordplay, brilliantly discussed by M. M. Mahood. His wit transcends mere verbal ingenuity when he explores 'the paradox of words to convey the unsolvable paradox of life': he is 'not concerned with abstractions but personal relationships' and their ambiguities.[6] Verbal ambiguity, however, should not be exaggerated. The kind of equivocation the age delighted in, to be witty, had to be obtrusive: something to be understood, but not to be sought for as in *Finnegans Wake*. The 'dark conceit' of allegory was another matter. In his impressive edition of the Sonnets Stephen Booth ignored L. C. Knights's early warning to post-Empsonian commentators: his multiple meanings are too often obtained by focusing upon a part, almost forgetting the whole poem.[7]

Close reading is beneficial when it alerts the reader to the real complexities of the poet's art. This essay cannot show how structural modulations are introduced within the almost unchanging pattern of the Shakespearian sonnet, how delicately or forcefully alliterations, assonances, and cadence combine in beautiful or vehement utterance, how images are extended (as in the early plays), arrayed in stately and almost Spenserian procession, or how they come 'one on another's neck' (Sonnet 131) with dizzying speed, producing the mixed metaphors that characterize the dramatist's mature style. All this the reader well knows and may turn to Leishman and C. S. Lewis, Melchiori and Muir, Rosalie Colie and Winifred Nowottny, among other critics, for penetrating analysis. What may call for further comment is the evolution of the style within the sequence itself.

The contrast between the sterile imagery of the Dark Lady sonnets and the emphasis on fertility and increase in the Young Man sonnets has been noted. This contrast, however, is almost limited to the first half of the former group, where all living things are described as fighting against the destructive forces in Nature. Sonnet 65 acknowledges that beauty, 'whose action is no stronger than a flower', and 'summer's honey breath' cannot 'hold out / Against the wrackful siege of battering days'. As long as the poet holds a plea with this rage the poetry remains 'golden' in all senses of the word. The 'gold complexion' (18) and 'golden face' (33) of the orient sun, the 'sparkling stars' that gild 'the swart-complexion'd night' (28; cf. 14, 15, 26), 'earth and sea's rich gems' (21), a 'jewel' which 'Makes black night beauteous' (27), 'time's best jewel' (65) or 'captain jewels in the carcanet' (52), 'pearl which thy love sheds' (34) and images of nature evocative of the 'gaudy spring' (1) and 'summer's green' (12; cf. 5, 6, 18, 54, 56), 'April's first-born flowers' (21) and 'darling buds of May' (18) are so insistently presented to the imagination that the sense of their precariousness only enhances our aesthetic and natural delight. In their richness, their sensuous appeal and artful melodiousness such sonnets are, indeed, 'the very heart of the Golden Age', as C. S. Lewis claimed. The following sonnets are not 'drab', yet the poet departs from 'the Golden way of writing'. The poetry takes on the pale cast of thought; turning inward or to the world of 'policy' and corruption, it turns away from the world of natural beauty threatened only with natural decay. 'I would not dull you with my song' the poet seems to tell us as well as his friend and, *pace* C. S. Lewis, he now often *talks*, not *sings*. When the formal constraints of the sonnet and the rhyme scheme do not impose inversions, the verse becomes truly colloquial and in the absence of images may be prosy: 'Hearing you prais'd I say, "'Tis so, 'tis true"' (85). Proverbial phrases intrude: 'The hardest knife ill us'd doth lose his edge' (95, cf. 96.9–10). When the language is metaphorical it is often deprived of sensuousness and mainly suggestive through compression, violence, and the fusion of abstract and concrete: 'I will acquaintance strangle' (89), 'Come in the rearward of a conquered woe' (90). Praise is now declared 'rich' enough when saying only 'you alone are you' (84): the difference with Sonnets 18 and 21 is that the earlier poems, though rejecting 'proud compare', did evoke images of sensuous loveliness transcended by the friend's beauty while the later poem is utterly bare of such images. Hyperbole becomes abstract and 'beauty's rose' is no longer surrounded with fresh images of spring (1) but a superlative symbol: 'thy sum of good', 'my all' (109). Despite all abiding differences Shakespeare is moving nearer to Donne than to Spenser.

The date of the Sonnets is uncertain but the span of three years for their composition (implied by Sonnet 104 if it was not inspired by Horace's Epode XI) would have allowed this stylistic evolution, particularly if it extended from 1594–5 to 1597–8 or later. The 1592–5 period, favoured by the Southamptonians, seems less probable on stylistic grounds. As to parallels with the plays, Akrigg rightly observes that they are 'inconclusive when the sonnets are lumped together' but a predominance of parallels in a block of sonnets may prove significant. He finds no discernible pattern for Sonnets 53–126 and 142–54 while parallels for 1–52 and 127–41 are predominantly with works written in 1593–6. This is reconcilable with an assumption of chronological order in the Young Man sequence. The first block could be contemporary with *Love's Labour's Lost, Romeo and Juliet,* and *Richard II* (1594–6): the parallels in themes and imagery and the use of the sonnet form in the first two are striking. The sonnets of the second block (beginning with Sonnet 66) reflect a new trend, discernible in later plays and in the outburst of satires, epigrams, and verse letters at the end of the century. It becomes the dominant trend in the sonnets to the mistress, which is consistent with the feelings expressed. There is, though, a wide range of tone, from the playful Berowne-like witticisms on black beauty (127, 130, 132) to sarcastic or bitter acquiescence in the slavery of the senses and conscious self-deception (133–6, 138–40) and Hamlet-like disgust with sex (129, 141–2, 147, 152). No clear chronological pattern can be traced in these sonnets but the playful ones were probably the earliest and there is ample precedent for their anti-Petrarchanism within the sonnet convention itself. Though the friend's sweetness was still said to be 'ne'er cloying', the language shows the poet did frame his feeding 'to bitter sauces' (118). Along with the new generation of epigrammatists he may have found that 'sugared' sonnets without salt palled upon the taste.

Shakespeare, of course, could recapture the Golden style when he wished and there are splendid examples of it in the later sonnets to the Friend, yet with a difference: as in Samson's riddle the honey, the sweetness now came 'out of the strong', out of a firmer grasp, a maturer experience. The 'teeming autumn' succeeds the freshness of spring (97) and spring is more intense in retrospection: 'Three April perfumes in three hot Junes burn'd' (104). The rebirth of love (102) cannot efface the suffering endured: 'What freezings have I felt, what dark days seen!' (97) – words and cadence anticipatory of Hopkins's terrible sonnet: 'What hours, O what black hours we have spent'. The greater sonnets are those which enclose the whole world of experience within the well-wrought urn – 'the essence sucked out of life and held rounded here' as Virginia Woolf's Mrs Ramsay thought while reading Sonnet 98 in *To the Lighthouse,* a sonnet in which 'the lily's white' and 'the deep vermilion in the rose' are 'but sweet, but figures of delight', waived aside for 'the pattern of all those', the fair youth or rather the Beauty with whose 'shadow' poets have ever played.

The lily and the rose in *Venus and Adonis* belong to the world of the early sonnets and the reading of the narrative poems *after* the sonnet sequence leaves us convinced of their relative immaturity. When approached in the spirit of the literary historian their interest is undeniable. They are representative of two genres cultivated by Shakespeare's contemporaries and show once more his willingness to follow a convention. *Venus and Adonis* (1593) was suggested by Lodge's Ovidian epyllion, *Scillaes Metamorphosis* (1589) and delighted 'the younger sort', Gabriel Harvey *dixit*: only Marlowe's unfinished *Hero and Leander* can compete with it. The 'graver labour' promised in the dedication pleased 'the wiser sort'; like Daniel's earlier *Complaint of Rosamond*, *The Rape of Lucrece* (1594) is a historical narrative 'tragedie' whose ancestry can be traced to the *Myrroure for Magistrates* (1559). In both poems Shakespeare improves upon his models yet fails to transmute the convention successfully.

Parodying Keats on the Sonnets one could say that *Venus and Adonis* is 'full of fine things said unintentionally', though not arising here from 'the intensity of working out conceits', which are either precious ('A lily prison'd in a gaol of snow', l. 362) or semi-burlesque (the 'stillitorie' of ll. 443–4). The fine things are images from Nature – the 'dive-dapper peering through a wave' (l. 85) – vignettes of English country-life: the hare-hunting, 'moralized' by Venus as Jaques will moralize on deer-hunting (ll. 679–708), yet a digression; or the episode of the stallion and the jennet, intended as an inverted parallel to the wooing of Adonis by Venus, yet extended and enjoyed for its own sake (ll. 259–318). What the narrator's main 'intention' was remains uncertain. Contemporary opinion about the poem and Shakespeare's own admission that the next 'heir of his invention' should be 'graver' make it very unlikely that the intention was didactic. If the first part of the poem is meant to arouse the reader's own lust as Venus strives to inflame with desire the reluctant Adonis, it is less provocative and witty than Donne's Elegy 'To his Mistris Going to Bed'. The lusty goddess who plucks the youth from his horse, pushes him backward, lies on him as soon as he is down (ll. 41–4), or counterfeits fainting to clasp him to her breast (ll. 463–564), is a comic figure, grotesque at times, as when Adonis 'wrings her nose' to revive her (ll. 475). The situation could have been handled in a Cervantic manner but the contrast between the actions of the characters and the prevailing prettiness of the descriptive style creates in the reader an unresolved conflict of impressions. And if Venus's love's labours lost are comedy, the death of Adonis is tragedy. The two parts are linked by artful correspondences: the red-white imagery (ll. 901–2, 1053–4), the erotic wound of Adonis slain by the boar's kiss (ll. 1111–17), but the highly artificial style keeps us at a distance from the tragic scene and the emotions of Venus. Through the poem the artist seems at once hesitant about tone and too confident in the power of rhetoric. More favourable interpretations have been offered, notably by William Keach, describing the theme of the epyllion as 'the opposition between sexual love so intense and aggressive that it becomes self-frustrating and beauty so selfish and inaccessible that it becomes self-destructive'. Yet, even granting this, one may complain of prolixity and one would like to think the poet mocked the Elizabethan partiality to *copia* when he compared the 'tedious' lament of Venus to 'copious stories' that 'End without audience and are never done' (ll. 841–6). Vain wish, since wordiness grew worse in *Lucrece*!

The experience of the dramatist may be noted in the haste *in medias res*, the creation of atmosphere and the imagination of movement when Tarquin's ravishing strides lead him to the bed of Lucrece along corridors where the wind wars with his torch (ll. 302–15). The ravisher, alas, speaks too much and his 'disputation / 'Tween frozen conscience and hot burning will' (ll. 190–280, 348–57) is as otiose as Macbeth's soliloquies are dramatic. Lucrece in her turn pours out a flood of words which the rapist hears patiently. When he at last has done the deed, worse follows: a complaint of 338 lines. Anaphoric questions or injunctions, *exempla* and repetitions of all kinds succeed one another relentlessly. Narration is mercifully resumed when Lucrece calls her maid and the 'silly groom' whose blushes declare him an honest country servant, offering again a glimpse of real life in England. When, 'pausing for means to mourn a newer way', the heroine thinks of a painting made for Priam's Troy, this elaborate piece of *ut pictura poesis* lacks the sensuous vividness of Spenser's similar efforts and the tragic turns to the grotesque when she thinks of tearing with her nails the beauty of the strumpet Helen (ll. 1471–2; cf. ll. 1469–70, 1564). Throughout the poem symbolism is conventional: the 'silent war of lilies and of roses' (l. 71; cf. ll. 269, 386, 478–9) is as artificial as Swinburne's opposition of 'the raptures and roses of vice' to 'the lilies and languors of virtue'. Whether there is a graver theme than the moral conflict is not evident. The poet is hardly interested in the theological debate on Lucrece's suicide (only glanced at in ll. 1156–76) and ironic readings are baseless, as R. Levin has demonstrated.[8] The dramatist, one may add, was unlikely to blame a Roman heroine for dying in the high Roman fashion.

A Lover's Complaint, though published with the Sonnets, belongs in genre and style with the narrative poems. Its ascription to Shakespeare is now seldom denied and the lover has some resemblance with the narcissistic young man of the early sonnets.

If no sonnet was composed after 1600, which may be doubted (the eclipse of the 'mortal moon' in Sonnet 107 may allude to the death of Elizabeth), Shakespeare's last poem was 'The Phoenix and the Turtle'. It is unique and to some critics the greatest 'metaphysical' poem though utterly unlike Donne's *Songs and Sonnets*. It was included in a collection of apparently occasional poems, Chester's *Love's Martyr* (1601), but, whoever the dead birds were (speculation ranges from Sir John Salusbury and his wife to Essex and Elizabeth or Essex and Southampton), it transcends the occasion. When writing it Shakespeare, one feels, could not but think of some of the sonnets in which he had celebrated the love that made him one with the fair youth. His imagination carried the feeling to a new intensity by a play on abstractions in a liturgical setting. The play is as serious as Platonic dialectics or Christian speculations on the Trinity:

So they loved, as love in twain
Had the essence but in one:
Two distincts, division none;
Number there in love was slain.

The abstractions would not be so real if they were not steeped in strangeness from the opening words:

Let the bird of loudest lay
On the sole Arabian tree

This is the remoteness of the land Milton called 'Araby the blest'; the remoteness of a lost Eden in the wide world and the poet's heart. And to lovers of poetry, if not to the historian, this poem, though compact and difficult, can be allowed to speak for itself, the magic of sound and cadence making comment unnecessary.

Notes

1. Numbers in brackets refer to the Sonnet numbers, unless otherwise stated.
2. Quoted by A. Golden in 'Victorian renascence: the revival of the amatory sonnet sequence 1850–1900', *Genre* 7 (1974), 133–47.
3. '"To constancie confin'd": the poetics of Shakespeare's Sonnets', *PMLA* 94 (1979), 77–90.
4. See A. K. Hieatt, 'The genesis of Shakespeare's Sonnets; Spenser's *Ruines of Rome: by Bellay*', *PMLA*, 98 (1983), 800–14. The case, however, is overstated.
5. 'The Christian basis of Shakespeare's Sonnet 146', *Shakespeare Quarterly* 19 (1968), 355–65.
6. J. Bunselmeyer, 'Appearance and verbal paradox: Sonnets 129 and 138', *Shakespeare Quarterly* 25 (1974), 103–8.
7. Space does not allow demonstration. A gem of Lacanian ingenuity is the suggestion of a 'macaronic pun on *repair* – taken as if it were compounded of the Latin prefix *re-* and the French noun *père*' (Sonnet 3).
8. See R. Levin, 'The ironic reading of *The Rape of Lucrece*', *Shakespeare Survey 34* (1981), 85–92.

Reading list

Essays included in the collections of P. Jones, Landry and in *Shakespeare Survey 15* or mentioned in the notes are not listed.

ON THE POEMS AND SONNETS
*Bradbrook, M. C., *Shakespeare and Elizabethan Poetry* (1951)
Knight, G. Wilson, *The Mutual Flame: On Shakespeare's Sonnets and 'The Phoenix and the Turtle'* (1955)
*Nicoll, Allardyce, ed., *Shakespeare Survey 15* (1962)
Smith, Hallett, *Elizabethan Poetry* (Cambridge, Massachusetts, 1952)

ON THE SONNETS
Booth, Stephen, *An Essay on Shakespeare's Sonnets* (New Haven, Connecticut, 1969)

*Colie, Rosalie, *Shakespeare's Living Art* (Princeton, 1974)

Dubrow, Heather, 'Shakespeare's undramatic monologues', *Shakespeare Quarterly* 32 (1981), 55–68

Duncan-Jones, Katherine, 'Was the 1609 *Shake-speares Sonnets* really unauthorized?', *RES* 34 (1983), 151–71

Hammond, Gerald, *The Reader and Shakespeare's Young Man Sonnets* (1981)

Hubler, Edward, *The Sense of Shakespeare's Sonnets* (Princeton, 1952)

Hubler, E., *et al.*, eds., *The Riddle of Shakespeare's Sonnets* (New York, 1962)

*Jones, Peter, ed., *Shakespeare – The Sonnets*, Casebook Series (1977)

Krieger, Murray, *A Window to Criticism: Shakespeare's Sonnets and Modern Poetics* (Princeton, 1964)

Landry, Hilton, *Interpretation in Shakespeare's Sonnets* (Berkeley and Los Angeles, 1963)

*Landry, H., ed., *New Essays on Shakespeare's Sonnets* (New York, 1976)

*Leishman, J. B., *Themes and Variations in Shakespeare's Sonnets* (1961)

*Lever, J. W., *The Elizabethan Love Sonnet* (1956)

Mahood, M. M., *Shakespeare's Wordplay* (1957)

Martin, Philip, *Shakespeare's Sonnets: Self, Love and Art* (Cambridge, 1972)

Melchiori, Giorgio, *Shakespeare's Dramatic Meditations* (Oxford, 1976)

*Muir, Kenneth, *Shakespeare's Sonnets* (1979)

Ramsey, Paul, *The Fickle Glass: A Study of Shakespeare's Sonnets* (New York, 1979)

*Smith, Hallett, *The Tension of the Lyre: Poetry in Shakespeare's Sonnets* (San Marino, California, 1981)

ON THE POEMS

Hulse, Clark, *Metamorphic Verse: The Elizabethan Minor Epic* (Princeton, 1981)

Keach, William, *Elizabethan Erotic Narratives* (Hassocks, Sussex, 1977)

Underwood, R. A., *Shakespeare's 'The Phoenix and the Turtle': A Survey of Scholarship* (Salzburg, 1974)

4   Shakespeare and the arts of language

> My language? Heavens!
> I am the best of them that speak this speech,
> Were I but where 'tis spoken.   (*The Tempest*, 1.2.428–30)

Ferdinand's lines are a useful text for this chapter and not merely because, in this age of global travel, his surprised joy at hearing his own language spoken strikes a familiar chord. Transposed into the third person singular and the past tense, the lines could very well serve to record the received opinion of another kind of traveller: those who have explored the realms of Shakespeare's language, which is of course also the language of Ferdinand and many hundreds of other speaking characters. Shakespeare as an artist in language, it is generally agreed, is a natural genius nurtured by the state of his native speech, when and where it was spoken. Or, to use the language of one of the most experienced travellers in these particular realms of gold:

The extraordinary power, vitality and richness of Shakespeare's language are due in part to his genius, in part to the fact that the unsettled linguistic forms of his age promoted to an unusual degree the spirit of free creativeness, and in part to the theory of composition then prevailing.[1]

The aim of this chapter is not to argue that Shakespeare was (as one instinctively feels) the best of them that spoke that speech, but to travel, however briefly, over some ground which will show how Shakespeare the dramatist thought of the arts of language, how he used them, such as he found them, and how he developed those arts to suit his needs. But because this is much-travelled ground, mapped variously, and especially in recent years, by language historians and theorists and by literary critics of many 'schools', Ferdinand's lines have to be pressed into service yet once more: to yield a reminder of how easily, in the process of analysis, 'his language' will revert to 'my language'. Structures of critical belief are bound to structure what we hear or read, and the critic of Shakespeare's language is apt – like Ferdinand – to find his own identity and affirm his status in the language he uses.[2] As the danger more besets the more theoretical approaches, this chapter will attempt to explore 'his language' in terms that are practical-historical-dramatical.

The terms have, of course, to be practical in so far as Shakespeare left no

49

Directions for Speech and Style and no *Arte of English Poesie*, to tell us of his theories of language use, and dramatical in so far as the proof of his practice is in the impact of the language of his plays. But they also have to be, up to a point, historical for, even if Shakespeare was born with a unique verbal imagination, it matters that the medium it had to operate in was the English of the late sixteenth and early seventeenth centuries: a language which had no dictionary until 1604, and in which a fluid grammar and an almost obsessive interest in rhetorical structures gave both scope and spurs to experimentation with words and word-patterns. It matters, too, that this imagination could exercise itself in a climate of preoccupation with language. Language questions affected not only literature but practically every other sphere of cultural and social life as well: religion, philosophy, politics, law, etc. It was a particularly fruitful climate in that it could sustain – as was the case on so many other questions in the English Renaissance – apparently contradictory beliefs. On the origins, nature, or value of language Shakespeare would have been, to use a Keatsian phrase, 'capable of being in uncertainties, mysteries, doubts'. There were still those who held to the Biblical version of the origins and development of language: given by God to Adam, language fell with him, its perversion pointed by the tower of Babel and curable only by pentecostal grace.[3] Others would stress the aspect of human invention or, like Puttenham, credit nature with the origin and man with the art:

Utterance also and language is given by nature to man for perwasion of others, and aide of them selves, I meane the first abilitie to speake. For speech it selfe is artificiall and made by man, and the more pleasing it is, the more it prevaileth to such purpose as it is intended for.[4]

Again, some philosophers would assert the identity of name, or word, and thing, of language and meaning – a belief for which there were both Christian and neo-Platonic foundations – while others maintained a scepticism which had perhaps never been really suppressed since the English nominalists, and which surfaces in *The Advancement of Learning*, when Bacon writes that

words are but the images of matter; and except they have a life of reason and invention, to fall in love with them is all one as to fall in love with a picture.[5]

But against any theoretical scepticism stands the overwhelming practical belief in the efficacy of language held by those who wrote handbooks of rhetoric – Wilson, Peacham, Puttenham, and others. As they listed and analysed the tropes and figures of which the English language was capable, they also proclaimed, explicitly or implicitly, its power to express thought and feeling and to move others 'to such purpose as it is intended for'.

It is out of such fruitful ambivalences that Shakespeare's use of language springs: his apparently paradoxical combination of belief and doubt. If conceptually there is a gap between word and thing, rhetorically it is amazing what things a man or a woman can achieve. From beginning to end – from *Titus Andronicus* and the *Henry VI* plays to *The Tempest* – Shakespeare's plays testify to nothing so much as to his interest in what people can do to themselves and to each other by language – whether in the form of the comic wit of Rosalind (or Falstaff) or the tragic persuasiveness, unequalled among traditional Revenge ghosts and amounting to nothing less than emotional blackmail, of Hamlet's dead father, or the auto-suggestiveness of Leontes's speeches. And if language often constructs fictions rather than embodying truths, then again it is amazing what power – beneficial in an Edgar, malign in an Iago – those fictions can exercise. In this sense, Shakespeare's interest in the arts of language is as practical, as much directed towards *function*, as that of the rhetoricians. His ultimate interest, after all, is to persuade us, the audience, of the human realities of thought and feeling in his plays.

This is not to deny, but merely to put in a historical perspective, the amount of self-reflectiveness in Shakespeare's use of language – an aspect which has received much critical attention in recent years.[6] As language took such a prominent part in the life of the period, it is more natural than is sometimes recognized for Shakespeare's characters to discuss it, play with it, reflect on it. (Hamlet, for one, does all those things supremely.) Standing back from the details of the rhetorical manuals, or from a modern study like Sister Miriam Joseph's, one is left with the sense of how utterly self-conscious must have been the language use of the educated Elizabethan: even the most apparently spontaneous, mimetic phrase could be given a rhetorical analysis and a name. It is natural for Shakespeare's characters to be aware of registers and regional and class dialects, indeed virtually to identify language with a way of life, as in Warwick's reading of Prince Hal:

> The Prince but studies his companions
> Like a strange tongue, wherein, to gain the language,
> 'Tis needful that the most immodest word
> Be look'd upon and learnt.   (*2 Henry IV*, 4.4.68–71)

It is natural that they should note the absurdity of language reduced to formulas (such as Touchstone on lies, or Viola on wooing), or find language inadequate to extremes of emotion – love, grief, suffering – as does almost every character in *King Lear*. And it is natural that they should be conscious of the gap that can exist between language and truth, whether they are operative liars / actors like Richard III or less professional hypocrites, like Angelo. When characters laugh at excesses or deplore the possibility that 'words, words, words' may be merely false, Shakespeare's linguistic self-consciousness should not be confused with modernistic doubts about the veracity of language. Nor should Shakespeare as a language practitioner be confused with his own characters. Some of his most highly charged language is about the emptiness of words. When Angelo agonizes about a self-division perceived as a division between language and meaning –

When I would pray and think, I think and pray
To several subjects. Heaven hath my empty words,
Whilst my invention, hearing not my tongue,
Anchors on Isabel. Heaven in my mouth,
As if I did but only chew his name,
And in my heart the strong and swelling evil
Of my conception –
                                        (*Measure for Measure*, 2.4.1–7)

then of course the language behaves self-reflectively, and there is a formidable
gap between the rational logic of the rhetorical form and the illogic of the
passionate content. But all this co-exists with, and is in the theatre subsumed
into, the dramatic function and effect of the speech. Shakespeare enables the
actor playing Angelo to prove on the audience's pulses what it feels like being
thus divided, just as, a few moments later, he makes Isabella speak both in and
about language in order to express her reaction to that division: 'I have no
tongue but one; gentle my lord, / Let me entreat you speak the former
language' (2.4.139–40). Characters, even whole plays, may doubt the truth of
words; but the dramatist creating them does not doubt the efficacy of
language.

What is also remarkable about Angelo's speech is the very tangible sense of
language: it is through the 'chewing' of God's name, and through the
rendering of the 'invention' – the first of the five stages of composition in
traditional rhetoric – as a 'strong and swelling evil', that Angelo's mixture of
self-loathing and sexual urge is realized. As Molly Mahood points out in her
book *Shakespeare's Wordplay*, 'when Elizabethan rhetoricians spoke of the
power and force of words, their meaning may have been as much literal as
metaphorical'.[7] Shakespeare seems to have shared with many of his contemporaries a concrete, physical perception of language, both as it is spoken
and as it is received. We need only think of Cordelia who is 'sure my love's /
More ponderous than my tongue', and who explains her 'Nothing' by telling
Lear: 'I cannot heave / My heart into my mouth' (*King Lear*, 1.1.76–7 and 90–
1); of how Malcolm identifies Macbeth as 'This tyrant, whose sole name
blisters our tongues' (*Macbeth*, 4.3.12); and how Ulysses thinks that Nestor
should 'knit all the Greekish ears / To his experienc'd tongue' (*Troilus and
Cressida*, 1.3.67–8). Ears and tongues in the plays tend to be both literal and
metaphorical; and speech tends to be conceived of as both a physical and a
moral act. It is above all its relation to *life* that seems to fascinate Shakespeare:
a point, I think, not unrelated to Caroline Spurgeon's finding, after examining
all of Shakespeare's imagery and what it tells us, that 'it is the life of things
which appeals to him, stimulates and enchants him, rather than beauty of
colour and form or even significance'.[8] In the early *Titus Andronicus*, when
Marcus finds Lavinia raped and mutilated, he can still lament the loss of her
tongue, with Ovidian decorativeness, as 'that delightful engine of her

thoughts' (3.1.82); but in later plays it is obvious that the tongue is the 'engine' of much more, not to say a vital organ. It is vital to man as an individual and social being. Perhaps the most extensive articulation of this idea is to be found not (as one might imagine) in a death-speech, but in a speech where a character laments his sentence of exile as 'speechless death'. Mowbray, in the third scene of *Richard II*, is about to be deprived forever of the joy of speaking 'the language I have learnt these forty years, / My native English'; and his plangent piece of rhetoric, unprecedented in Shakespeare's historical sources, centres on the use of his 'tongue'. To be understood is as important as being able to speak; language is not speech unless it communicates; and so, as Mowbray anticipates his exile in a foreign country, he first imagines his tongue as 'an unstringed viol or a harp' –

> Or like a cunning instrument cas'd up
> Or, being open, put into his hands
> That knows no touch to tune the harmony –   (*Richard II*, 1.3.163–5)

and then the image changes to one of imprisonment:

> And dull, unfeeling, barren ignorance
> Is made my gaoler to attend on me.   (lines 168–9)

Finding directions by indirections, the adjectives and the noun of line 168 define language in its proper – expressive and communicative – function as that which makes life lively and creative, as the instrument both of feeling and of knowledge. It is essential to life, and yet it has to be 'learnt' as an art. In essence, one feels, Mowbray speaks for most Shakespearian characters, and for their creator.

Shakespeare learnt his language from men (and women) and books, from the Stratford grammar school and the London stage. *The Tempest* is the last unaided product of what must have been one of the most glorious learning processes in the history of language. For this reason – and not because it is typical; but then, in the uniquely varied range of plays, who dares to claim any one play as wholly typical? – I now wish to look at this play as a kind of model of Shakespeare's use of language, and particularly of those arts of language to which the rest of this chapter will be devoted.

Paradoxically (but only apparently so) the end product of Shakespeare's language-learning is sometimes silence: as Anne Barton and others have shown, *The Tempest* depends much on 'the suppressed and the unspoken'.[9] The reason why there is so much more silence in this play than in *Titus Andronicus*, where a tongue is literally lost, is of course that Shakespeare has learnt so much more about the theatre, the arts of which are often wordless. In the theatre language of *The Tempest* we hardly need Prospero's exhortations, 'No tongue! All eyes! Be silent' to realize how visions strike characters dumb, or how the plot itself has such symbolic dimensions that the simplest words –

such as Gonzalo's account of what each character has found 'in one voyage', including 'all of us ourselves / When no man was his own' (5.1.205–13) – reach further than the most elaborate metaphor could.

But even as the play reaches towards insights beyond language, it also comes straight out of the period's interest in language questions. The surprise in Ferdinand's lines which figure at the head of this essay rather assumes that he has read travellers' accounts of foreign tongues and strange eloquence. Shakespeare is not normally concerned about the fact that his characters speak English, whatever the fictive geography of his plays. Gower, in the greatest travelogue of them all, is exceptional in his self-conscious apologies for the use of 'one language in each several clime / Where our scenes seem to live' (*Pericles*, 4.4.5–6). In *The Tempest*, on the other hand, 'one language' is part of the fiction of the play. 'Where the devil', asks Stephano, when confronted with Caliban – in a cruder version of Ferdinand's surprise – 'should he learn our language?' (2.2.63). We already know the answer. In a version of the Biblical myth Caliban, like Adam in Paradise, was taught by Prospero 'how / To name the bigger light, and how the less, / That burn by day and night' (1.2.334–6). Miranda expands the epistemological aspect:

> When thou didst not, savage,
> Know thine own meaning, but wouldst gabble like
> A thing most brutish, I endow'd thy purposes
> With words that made them known.   (1.2.355–8)

As an extreme image of fallen man, Caliban corrupts language: 'You taught me language, and my profit on't / Is, I know how to curse'. He practises this 'profit' most imaginatively, turning his curses not least against the very language of Prospero and Miranda: 'The red plague rid you / For learning me your language!' (1.2.363–5). The corruption manifests itself, too, in the way he uses language to ingratiate himself with Stephano – who, in an unconscious parody of Prospero's language-teaching, offers 'celestial liquor' in order to 'give language to you' – and, like a Machiavellian politician, to start a plot against Prospero.

At other times, however, Caliban speaks what we can only call the language of the world of the play. In the following exchange, Shakespeare makes dramatic use of the contrast between levels of style, as Stephano's cynical and obtuse prose clashes with the verse in which Caliban describes the island.

Caliban.   Be not afeard. The isle is full of noises,
> Sounds, and sweet airs, that give delight, and hurt not.
> Sometimes a thousand twangling instruments
> Will hum about mine ears; and sometime voices,
> That, if I then had wak'd after long sleep,
> Will make me sleep again; and then, in dreaming,
> The clouds methought would open and show riches
> Ready to drop upon me, that when I wak'd,
> I cried to dream again.

Stephano. That will prove a brave kingdom to me, where I shall have my music for
    nothing.   (3.2.130–40)

Caliban's poetry, its sense of wonder carried by the rhythmic arrangement of
some of the most ordinary words in the language, seems aimed more at the
audience's response to Prospero's island than at 'characterizing' Caliban
himself. It shares the wonder of Prospero's great speeches, or of the lines in
which Ariel gives account of the tempest he brought about at Prospero's
bidding:

> Jove's lightning, the precursors
> O'th' dreadful thunder-claps, more momentary
> And sight-outrunning were not; the fire and cracks
> Of sulphurous roaring the most mighty Neptune
> Seem to besiege, and make his bold waves tremble,
> Yea, his dread trident shake.   (1.2.201–6)

    Like Caliban's speech, Ariel's evokes a strange, magical world. They work
to similar ends at very different levels of verbal artifice. Caliban's lines have
the limpid simplicity of *some* of Prospero's: 'We are such stuff / As dreams are
made on; and our little life / Is rounded with a sleep', for example; though in
Prospero's case the speaker and the context weight the simple vocabulary with
significance. Ariel's lines are as rotund as others by Prospero ('I have
bedimm'd / The noontide sun, call'd forth the mutinous winds . . .': 5.1.41–
57, for example), and, as against the artful naturalness of Caliban's lines,
they are blatantly and purposefully artful. The compound epithet, 'sight-
outrunning', which the rhetoricians would have classified as the figure of
epitheton, functions to evoke the unfathomable quality of the storm, and of the
play. It combines with the unusual word order of the lines (an *anastrophe*) to
suggest an arcane world. Delaying the verbs both foregrounds the tremendous
nouns and adjectives and, at the same time, throws the verbs themselves, when
they finally appear, into relief. The rhythm moves breathlessly across the verse
lines, to pause only on the verbs, which in themselves add up to a crescendo
('were not' . . . 'besiege' . . . 'tremble' . . . 'shake').

    To sum up, if *The Tempest* depends on silence and the unspoken – on visual
effects, on music, and on that which lies under or beyond the words – it also
depends on language: verse and prose, plain or figured. The arts of language
are used by characters who in themselves embody both the uses and the
abuses of language, and who function both as characters and as parts of the
play as a whole. Language, in the end, defines the nature and the structure of
that whole. If the author of *Titus Andronicus* could be described, in the phrase
Coleridge used for his own early verse, as 'putting of thoughts into verse', then
we might adduce *The Tempest* as an example of thoughts, verse (and prose),
and dramatic form having become inseparable.

    That this is so, Coleridge would ascribe to Shakespeare's imagination 'or
esemplastic power';[10] and, whatever we think of Coleridge's coinage, 'esem-

plastic' or 'having the function of moulding into unity', it would seem that *moulding* is exactly what Shakespeare does with the arts of language as he finds them. We see this nowhere more clearly than in his handling of vocabulary, the raw material of language, which he regards as peculiarly malleable. If a word to fit his purpose did not exist, he would remould an existing one, or create an altogether new one. Here, of course, he could avail himself of the fluidity and freedom of language in a period when vocabulary was rapidly expanding and no norm or standard of meaning existed for particular words. Obviously Shakespeare's audience did not sit – or stand – spotting neologisms: the absence of dictionary definitions must have meant that they were not always able to tell whether a word was new, or used in a new sense. Retrospectively, we can tell, thanks to the *Oxford English Dictionary* and to scholars such as Alfred Hart and, more recently, Marvin Spevack, who have provided statistical proof of Shakespeare's ever-expanding vocabulary and its inventiveness.[11] Such statistics – of the number of words in any one play which were new to Shakespeare, or new to the English language, or never to be used again by him – indicate both how each of Shakespeare's plays demanded its own vocabulary and how he developed the potentials of the English language even as he developed the potentials of the stage.

We know from the plays and the Sonnets that Shakespeare despised the affectation of newfangledness or pedantry: Holofernes and Sir Nathaniel are guilty of both, having been 'at a great feast of languages and stolen the scraps', the latter consisting mainly of Latinisms (*Love's Labour's Lost*, 5.1.33–4). Shakespeare's word-making, when not parodic in intent (as with the famous 'mobled queen' in *Hamlet*, 2.2.496–8), is a matter of moulding language to the shape of the experience to be expressed. Thus he turns verbs into nouns, or vice versa – as in Edgar's compassion for Lear: 'He childed as I father'd' (*King Lear*, 3.6.110) – or directs the energy of a verb by adding a prefix. Again, it is worth remembering that such manipulation was a recognized literary technique. Puttenham in his 'Booke of Ornament', the third book of *The Arte of English Poesie*, writes of the alteration made 'sometimes by *adding* sometimes by *rabbating* of a sillable or letter to or from a word', for which he sees a very practical function: 'sometimes it is done for pleasure to give a better sound, sometimes upon necessitie, and to make up the rime'.[12] When Shakespeare made up the word 'enskied' in Lucio's line to Isabella, 'I hold you as a thing enskied and sainted' (*Measure for Measure*, 1.4.34), then he may have done so for all the reasons given by Puttenham, but he also clearly had a reason of his own. Lucio approaches Isabella on this, their first, encounter in a cavalier fashion: 'Hail, virgin, if you be, as those cheek-roses / Proclaim you are no less' (1.4.16–17). But Isabella's style of speaking and being makes him realize his mistake; and he apologizes for his 'familiar sin / With maids to seem the lapwing, and to jest, / Tongue far from heart' (lines 31–3). And so he brings his heart and tongue together raptly to define the 'thing enskied and sainted', in a manner both evocative and precise. The word marks the shift in tone and serves, by this almost literal elevation, also to mark the gulf which separates Isabella from other girls, and which is crucial to the play.

Examples of Shakespeare's functional inventions are legion; here it need only be said that the 'new pride' and 'variation or quick change' which Shakespeare disclaims for his verse in Sonnet 76 are all put to use in the plays. Although, for example, he may have suspected the 'compounds strange' of rival poets, his early works show that he was impressed by what Spenser and Marlowe could achieve by compounding words; and in his later works he finds in this technique a way of activating the language: creating out of the combination of two words something which is more than the sum of both, and which therefore economically defines a quality or evokes an experience. The use can vary from the solemn, as in Cleopatra's 'Now from head to foot / I am marble-constant' (*Antony and Cleopatra*, 5.2.237–8), to the abusive, as when Thersites calls Ajax 'thou mongrel beef-witted lord' (*Troilus and Cressida*, 2.1.13); and it can establish the physical and moral quality of a scene, like the night of Lear's suffering:

> This night, wherein the cub-drawn bear would couch,
> The lion and the belly-pinched wolf
> Keep their fur dry, unbonneted he runs.   (*King Lear*, 3.1.12–14)

It would seem, from such examples, that Shakespeare's verbal imagination was also his dramatic imagination. Perhaps the best category of 'variation' to demonstrate this is his use of words beginning with *un-*. G. L. Brook has found that Shakespeare has more than 600 words with that prefix, half of them occurring only once. According to Alfred Hart, such words amount to nearly four per cent of Shakespeare's vocabulary, and about a fourth of them are new to literature, of Shakespeare's own coinage.[13] Behind these dry statistics lies Shakespeare's extraordinary fondness for expressing negatives as contradictories of the corresponding positive terms; or, to put it differently, his sense of vocabulary as something not only malleable but also almost inherently dramatic. Richard II is 'unking'd', Lady Macbeth asks spirits to 'unsex' her, Antony comes 'smiling from / The world's great snare uncaught', and all these verbs catch up the tension between the negative and the positive, set up a sense, within what is, of what could have been. The potentials of the language are activated by the dramatic situation and vice versa.

Increasingly, as one pursues Shakespeare's relationship with the arts of language, one is reminded of Henry James's delight at having found 'a key that, working in the same *general* way, fits the complicated chambers of *both* the dramatic and the narrative lock'.[14] If for 'narrative' we substitute 'linguistic' we have, I think, a working description of Shakespeare's 'key'. This becomes even more obvious when we move from the raw material of vocabulary to the way in which this material is structured into larger units of speech by grammar and syntax: that is, to rhetoric. Elizabethan manuals distinguished two main categories of deviation from 'plain' language: *tropes* – devices like metaphor, allegory, hyperbole, metonymy (substituting the attribute for the thing) and synecdoche (substituting the part for the whole) – which change the meaning of a word or sentence, and *figures*, which – under names far too many and varied in their terminology to list here – give physical shape and structure to the language.[15] If we are to trust Theseus's analysis, Shakespeare saw both these activities as essential to the poetic process:

> as imagination bodies forth
> The forms of things unknown, the poet's pen
> Turns them to shapes, and gives to airy nothing
> A local habitation and a name.   (*A Midsummer Night's Dream*, 5.1.14–17)

Changing and enrichment of meaning by tropes, verbal and visual, remains a basic Shakespearian technique, much explored by students of his poetic and theatrical imagery. Concentrating for the moment on 'shapes' rather than on 'a local habitation and a name', we find that the shaping of Shakespeare's language seems to issue from the same imaginative centre as his shaping of dramatic action and structure. Perhaps, if we remember that Shakespeare was not formally trained in play-writing whereas he was grammar-school trained in the arts of language, this is not so surprising. Rhetoric teaches the control of structures and of an audience. In one sense the whole art of the theatre, and of drama, is one of synecdoche: the part for the whole. It is not simply that battles have to be represented by two men fighting, with alarums off, but that the whole structural principle is one of choosing and arranging such parts as will best stand for the whole action and most move the audience. Comparing any Shakespeare play with its main source narrative or play will bring out his sense of synecdoche.

The principles behind the most popular rhetorical figures were those of alerting a listener's mind by various forms of repetition, parallelism, and contrast or antithesis. The same principles underlie much of Elizabethan and Jacobean dramatic form; and they never cease, however transmuted and flexibly applied, to underlie Shakespearian dramatic structure, from *Titus Andronicus* to *The Tempest*. What is unique in Shakespeare is the progressive marriage of verbal and structural rhetoric. In the earlier plays – during the composition of which he may have been writing his two narrative poems and many of the Sonnets – he seems at times to have narrowly conceived of the structural units of drama as verbal units in a poem: the limitations of this are apparent in the last scene of *The Two Gentlemen of Verona* where, neglecting the realities of human experience embodied by the actors on stage, he tries to do in terms of drama what the closing surprise couplet does in a sonnet:

> And, that my love may appear plain and free,
> All that was mine in Silvia I give thee.
>   (*The Two Gentlemen of Verona*, 5.4.82–3)[16]

But very early – perhaps even in the *Henry VI* plays, with their range of voices and events, and certainly in *Love's Labour's Lost*, where the 'wooing doth not end like an old play' – he could also overcome such limitations. By the time he wrote *Romeo and Juliet* he was able to structure the first meeting of the lovers, visually and verbally, by using the basic characteristics of the English sonnet: the argument by conceit and pun, the drive towards an ending. The kiss is as inevitable an outcome of the human situation, and of the co-presence of the two bodies on stage, as it is a logical outcome of the sonnet structure. The self-reflectiveness of Juliet's 'You kiss by th' book' (*Romeo and Juliet*, 1.5.108) measures both her loving wit and the fact that 'books' *can* be true.

By the time Shakespeare began to write for the stage, the dramatic potential and audience appeal of highly patterned language had been proven. It is well known that Shakespeare learned from Lyly's prose symmetries, from Kyd's poetic structuring of passion and his ironic use of *stichomythia*, and from Marlowe's 'high-astounding' words and rhythms. It is well understood, too, thanks to scholars such as Brian Vickers, how Shakespeare's own development in his use of figures went 'from stiffness to flexibility' and to an increasingly wide range of dramatic functions. Clearly this is not a steady evolution towards naturalism and 'honest plain words' (*Love's Labour's Lost*, 5.2.741). False rhetoric is as much a mark of duplicity in *Hamlet* or *King Lear* as it was in *Titus Andronicus*, but not all rhetoric is false; and sometimes it is what a character feels, and not what he ought to say, that is expressed through elaborate rhetoric, as with Hamlet or Othello. Nor should levels of rhetorical artifice be equated with the difference between verse and prose. As Brian Vickers has shown in *The Artistry of Shakespeare's Prose*, Shakespeare largely conformed to the stylistic conventions of the drama of the period by giving prose to speakers of an inferior class – servants, or clowns – and verse to their betters, and by marking in prose letters and proclamations entering into the play from the outside world.[17] But he also moulded the convention to his own needs by using shifts from one mode to the other in order to realize a change in mood in a character, such as Hamlet, or a breakdown of control, such as Lady Macbeth sleep-walking or Othello degenerating into nearly-inarticulate frenzy: 'noses, ears, and lips. Is't possible? Confess! Handkerchief! O devil!' (*Othello*, 4.1.42–3). Besides, Shakespeare's prose often utilizes and adapts highly artificial rhetorical patterns, notably in a play written so largely in prose as *As You Like It*, or in a character whose verbal inventiveness is of such structured spontaneity as Falstaff's. In Shakespeare's theatre, where the visual language is mainly made up of the groupings, exits and entrances of people, the language spoken by those people is as much a part of the action as what they do; and rhetoric is the 'esemplastic' force which unites language and action.

It is easy enough to see this in an early play like *Richard III*. The repetitive verbal patterns define and confirm the thematic structure of the action: all those figures which relentlessly create symmetrical structures are part of the

overall pattern of curse / fulfilment, deed / consequences, crime / punishment. As the ghosts of those whom Richard has murdered return to curse him,
so they are translated into the 'thousand several tongues' of his conscience and
the *anaphora* and *parison* of his own speech:

> And every tongue brings in a several tale,
> And every tale condemns me for a villain.   (*Richard III*, 5.3.194–5)

In individual scenes, figures of rhetoric become physical and moral tools, most
strikingly when Richard woos Anne over the dead body of her father-in-law,
King Henry VI. By the time Richard grasps the visual aid of a sword to drive
home his verbal power – a sword directed not at his victim but at himself:

> Lo here I lend thee this sharp-pointed sword;
> Which if thou please to hide in this true breast
> And let the soul forth that adoreth thee,
> I lay it naked to the deadly stroke,
> And humbly beg the death upon my knee –   (*Richard III*, 1.2.174–8)

the demonstrative pronouns demonstrate, above all, how at this stage in the
scene verbal and visual figures have merged. Richard's wit here lies in making
the sword, as it were, the subject of a climax, or *gradatio*, of pleading:

> Nay, do not pause; for I did kill King Henry –
> But 'twas thy beauty that provoked me.
> Nay, now dispatch; 'twas I that stabb'd young Edward –
> But 'twas thy heavenly face that set me on.   (lines 179–82)

At this point – and in the circumstances even this phrase becomes a pun – the
pressure of words and gestures on each other is such that he can clinch Anne's
unspeakable position by a figure of repetition (*antanaclasis*) in which, within a
line, 'take up' changes meaning and effect: 'Take up the sword again, or take
up me' (line 183). A rapid fire of *stichomythia* completes the surrender.

   Perfect of its kind as this scene is, the kind is limiting and the relationships
which can be dramatized by this technique are limited. In his later tragedies
Shakespeare relies less on extended patterns of formal rhetoric and more on
figures which condense experience. A quick exchange of stichomythic lines
between Hamlet and his mother carries the entire crux of Hamlet's situation,
as a combination of *parison* and *epistrophe* compresses the family relationships:

> *Queen.* Hamlet, thou hast thy father much offended.
> *Hamlet.* Mother, you have my father much offended.   (*Hamlet*, 3.4.9–10)

The contrast between the artificiality of this exchange and the naturalism with
which Hamlet leads into it – 'Now, mother, what's the matter?' – is as
markedly ironic as is the clash between the pronouns (including Hamlet's
'you' to counter the Queen's 'thou') in the couplet. Similarly, the ironic use of
anaphora to point Othello's obsession –

Desdemona. Heaven doth truly know it.
Othello.   Heaven truly knows that thou art false as hell –   (*Othello*, 4.2.39–40)

shows the hopelessness of Desdemona's position, as Othello's response wraps itself round her statement, lengthening the line and breaking the rhythm into chaos.

In their unobtrusiveness, these figures are as much part of the structure of the play in which they are used as are the elaborate symmetries of *Richard III*. It needs no rhetorical analysis to point out that Brabantio's parting shot at Othello,

> Look to her, Moor, if thou hast eyes to see:
> She has deceiv'd her father, and may thee,   (*Othello*, 1.3.292–3)

is pregnant with irony in terms of what is to follow. At the time Othello responds imperturbably 'My life upon her faith'; but when Iago echoes the line – 'She did deceive her father, marrying you' (3.3.210) – his reaction is a rapid 'And so she did'. The echo gives Brabantio's words, in retrospect, some of the power of a curse. He was, in fact, however naturalistic the line may sound, employing the figure of *syllepsis*, in which a verb, expressed only once, lacks grammatical congruence with at least one of its subjects. The point is that the syllepsis is not just a handy way of compressing Brabantio's farewell into a stinging couplet by leaving out the infinitive of 'deceive'. The lack of congruence here is not only of grammar but of logic – the very same illogic which two Acts later will undo Othello. The language gap is also a fatal gap in reasoning.

In a related fashion the figure of *hypallage*, or transferred epithet, can be seen to reflect something basic to the play of *Macbeth*. The hero envisages 'wither'd murder' moving 'With Tarquin's ravishing strides' (2.1.55) and at that moment, when he is moving towards the murder of Duncan, the figure seems entirely adapted to the imagination of the speaker: always one step ahead. But Banquo, not a very imaginative man, muses on whether the witches were real or not: 'have we eaten on the insane root / That takes the reason prisoner?' (1.3.84–5); and later he uses the same figure to describe how 'the temple-haunting martlet' has settled under the eaves of Macbeth's castle and there 'made her pendent bed and procreant cradle' (1.6.8). Part of the generally elliptic and ambiguous language of the play, this particular figure is also part of a world where people and things exchange qualities and where past, present, and future interpenetrate. In that sort of world, cradles may be procreant, roots insane, and strides ravishing. As in the example from *Othello*, there is an action taking place in the language itself, imaging the play's action. And these are of course only two instances of a general truth: that the mature plays each have their own significant language structures and speech-modes. The stripping down of King Lear is also a stripping down of language, from eloquence, through simple, basic questions – 'Is man no more than this?' – to a single word, 'never', five times repeated. The world of *Antony and Cleopatra* is structured by hyperboles, to ensure that Cleopatra dies 'a lass unparallel'd'; that of *Hamlet* by a continual asking of questions, until 'the rest is silence'.

I have saved the subject of Shakespeare's use of tropes, especially metaphors, till the end, partly because it has been so much written on already and partly because most of what I have said about Shakespeare's dramatic use of figures applies to tropes as well. Ever since the publication of Caroline Spurgeon's book, *Shakespeare's Imagery and What It Tells Us*, scholars, critics and even directors have been alert to the part played by iterative imagery in the dominant tone and the structure of the plays. Similarly, the evolution of Shakespeare's imagery, from more decorative uses in the very early plays to the functional metaphors of the mature plays, where characters seem, as it were, to think in images, has been much commented on ever since Wolfgang Clemen's pioneering study of *The Development of Shakespeare's Imagery*. To see that evolution in a nutshell one might note how self-consciously and elaborately Titus Andronicus justifies his imagery:

> I am the sea; hark how her sighs do blow.
> She is the weeping welkin, I the earth;
> Then must the sea be moved with her sighs;
> Then must my earth with her continual tears
> Become a deluge, overflow'd and drown'd   (*Titus Andronicus*, 3.1.226–230)

and compare this with the unobtrusive way in which the sea enters the language of *The Tempest*, or the naturalness with which Antony and Cleopatra identify each other with celestial bodies. In the last two, imagery is not only more intrinsic, it also changes the whole meaning of the play.

The Elizabethan manuals of rhetoric were emphatic about the 'force' of metaphor:

Lastly, our speech doth not consist only of wordes, but in a sorte even of deedes, as when we expresse a matter by Metaphors, wherein the English is very frutefull and forcible.[18]

Shakespeare's own peculiar force came to be his ability to release, in his metaphors, the energy of the English language and at the same time to render the proper quality, the unique being, of thoughts, feelings, or dramatic situations. A single example must suffice. When Hamlet knows that he is dying, his one reference to his own condition is:

> O, I die, Horatio!
> The potent poison quite o'ercrows my spirit.

> (*Hamlet*, 5.2.344–5)

The verb 'o'ercrows' – triumphs over, as in a cockfight – captures, from within the tragic situation, an extraordinary mixture of jest and deadly earnest, pathos and courage, which is surely Hamlet's quintessential spirit. The 'bad' Quarto's version of this moment shows the reporter trying to remember what Hamlet had said, but failing and falling back on the expected. So he produces the traditional evocation of pathos through a row of symptoms:

> O my heart sinks, Horatio,
> Mine eyes have lost their sight, my tongue his use.

In the difference between these two passages we have, I think, an epitome of the way Shakespeare, in his use of metaphor, passed through and beyond convention.

He passed beyond the rhetoricians, too, in his perception of metaphor as what Richard Carew, in the passage just quoted, called 'a sorte even of deedes'. On the stage his metaphors can become deeds, as when Othello takes up Iago's animal imagery, or even characters in the imaginative world of a play, as when Macbeth sees 'pity, like a naked new-born babe, / Striding the blast'. They can truly change the meaning not only of words but of the visible reality in front of us, as when Cleopatra turns her death scene into a triumphant reunion with Antony and a re-creation of their first meeting at Cydnus. Imagery which interprets, changes, and expands the meanings of the deeds we witness is of course central to Shakespeare's art. At this point we are brought back to some of the questions considered at the beginning of this essay, for, even while glorying in the sheer verbal creativeness of a Falstaff or a Cleopatra, Shakespeare may well also have remembered the undertow of suspicion of metaphors which Puttenham, for one, articulated when he wrote of their purpose 'to deceive the eare and also the minde, drawing it from plainnesse and simplicitie to a certaine doubleness'. For, he concludes, 'what else is your *Metaphor* but an inversion of sence by transport?'[19] The answer lies in the fact that in the end Shakespeare was neither a rhetorician nor a philosopher of language but a practising dramatist. The problem of the relationship between language and truth is one that he *uses*, rather than solves. Yet, in his use of the full – visual and verbal – language of the theatre, he sometimes closes for us the gap between word and thing, name and person, language and reality.

There is such a moment near the end of *All's Well That Ends Well*. 'Is it real that I see?' asks the King as Helena enters, and she seizes on the gap –

> No, my good lord,
> 'Tis but the shadow of a wife you see,
> The name, and not the thing –

thus giving Bertram the chance of a line which closes it;

> Both, both. O, pardon!   (*All's Well*, 5.3.306–8)

Diana's riddle, pivoted on the double meaning of 'quick' – 'one that's dead is quick' – had introduced Helena's appearance, and for an interpretation Diana needs simply a stage direction to Helena's entry: 'And now behold the meaning'. The 'meaning' lies in the marriage (hardly a metaphor here) of word and vision, as the moment holds within it all that Helena has worked and suffered throughout the play to achieve – wifehood (and incipient mother-hood), both as a name and a thing. Bertram, as his deception by Parolles has shown, has too easily taken the wrong word for the thing. He refused to accept Helena as a wife because she lacked a noble name. What brings wife and name together, and all the implications of this consummation of an action, is such a moment of revelation and discovery as only the theatre can create – a moment like that from which post-classical theatre began, with the three Marys realizing that Christ is not in the tomb. It is also like moments of reunion in Shakespeare's last plays. In lines like Leontes's 'O, she's warm!', or Marina's 'My name is Marina', or Pericles's 'Thou that beget'st him that did thee beget', the gap is closed, not only between name and thing, word and vision, but also between the arts of language and the arts of the theatre.

But *All's Well That Ends Well* does not end there. Bertram retreats from the absoluteness of 'Both, both' to the potential scepticism of an 'if', and the King can conclude only that 'All yet *seems* well'. Wonder is a momentary experience, not something you can live in for ever after. Ferdinand, after the joy of recognizing 'my language', had to turn to log-carrying. In the end, perhaps the reason why Shakespeare's language is 'the best' is that it can express the most ordinary as well as the most exalted moments, and that his use of the arts of language has room for the most casual speech as well as the most elaborate rhetoric.

Notes

1. Sister Miriam Joseph, *Shakespeare's Use of the Arts of Language* (New York, 1947), p. 3.
2. See Marion Trousdale, *Shakespeare and the Rhetoricians* (Chapel Hill, North Carolina, 1982).
3. See Margreta de Grazia, 'Shakespeare's view of language: an historical perspective', *Shakespeare Quarterly* 29 (1978), 374–88.
4. George Puttenham, *The Arte of English Poesie* (1589), book I, chapter 3 (Menston, 1968).
5. Francis Bacon, *The Advancement of Learning* (1605), p. 25.
6. See, e.g., Keir Elam, *Shakespeare's Universe of Discourse: Language Games in the Comedies* (Cambridge, 1984).
7. Molly Mahood, *Shakespeare's Wordplay* (1957), p. 171.
8. Caroline Spurgeon, *Shakespeare's Imagery and What It Tells Us* (Cambridge, 1935), p. 50.
9. Introduction to New Penguin edition of *The Tempest* (Harmondsworth 1968), p. 16.
10. Samuel Taylor Coleridge, *Biographia Literaria*, chapter 13.

11. Alfred Hart, 'Vocabularies of Shakespeare's plays', *Review of English Studies* 19 (1943), 128–40, and 'The growth of Shakespeare's vocabulary', *ibid.*, 242–3. Marvin Spevack, 'New words between *Henry IV* and *Hamlet*' (pamphlet produced by Englisches Seminar, Westfälische Wilhelms-Universität, 1976).

12. *The Arte of English Poesie*, book III, chapter 10, p. 134.

13. G. L. Brook, *The Language of Shakespeare* (1976); Alfred Hart, *Shakespeare and the Homilies* (Melbourne, 1934), p. 253.

14. See Leon Edel, *The Life of Henry James*, 3 vols. (1953, 1962, 1963); reprinted in 2 vols. (Harmondsworth, 1977), II, 179.

15. See Brian Vickers, 'Shakespeare's use of rhetoric', in Kenneth Muir and S. Schoenbaum, eds., *A New Companion to Shakespeare Studies* (Cambridge, 1971), pp. 83–98, and also the same author's *Classical Rhetoric in English Poetry* (1970).

16. See my essay on *The Two Gentlemen of Verona* in Malcolm Bradbury and David Palmer, eds., *Shakespearian Comedy: Stratford-upon-Avon Studies* 14 (1972), pp. 31–57.

17. See Brian Vickers, *The Artistry of Shakespeare's Prose* (1968).

18. Richard Carew, *The Excellency of the English Tongue*, in Gregory Smith ed., *Elizabethan Critical Essays*, 2 vols. (1904), II, 288.

19. *The Arte of English Poesie*, book III, chapter 7, p. 128.

Reading list

Baldwin, T. W., *William Shakespeare's Small Latine & Lesse Greeke*, 2 vols. (Urbana, Illinois, 1944)

Blake, N. F., *Shakespeare's Language: An Introduction* (1983)

Brook, G. L., *The Language of Shakespeare* (1976)

Burton, D. M., *Shakespeare's Grammatical Style* (Austin, Texas, 1968)

Carew, Richard, *The Excellency of the English Tongue* (?1595–6), ed. G. G. Smith, in *Elizabethan Critical Essays*, 2 vols. (1904), II.

Clemen, W. H., *The Development of Shakespeare's Imagery* (1951)

Doran, M., *Shakespeare's Dramatic Language* (Madison, Wisconsin, 1976)

Edwards, P., Ewbank, I.-S., and Hunter, G. K., eds., *Shakespeare's Styles* (1980)

Elam, K., *Shakespeare's Universe of Discourse: Language-Games in the Comedies* (Cambridge, 1984)

Faas, E., *Shakespeare's Poetics* (Cambridge, 1986)

Hawkes, T., *Shakespeare's Talking Animals* (1973)

Hibbard, G. R., *The Making of Shakespeare's Dramatic Poetry* (Toronto, 1981)

Hoskins, John, *Directions for Speech and Style* (1599), ed. H. H. Hudson (Princeton, New Jersey, 1935)

Howell, W., *Logic and Rhetoric in England, 1500–1700* (Princeton, New Jersey, 1956)

Hulme, H. M., *Explorations in Shakespeare's Language* (1962)

Hussey, S. S., *The Literary Language of Shakespeare* (1982)

Jones, R. F., *The Triumph of the English Language* (Stanford, California, 1953)

Joseph, Sister Miriam, *Shakespeare's Use of the Arts of Language* (New York, 1947)

Lanham, R. A., *The Motives of Eloquence* (New Haven, Connecticut., 1976)

Mahood, M. M., *Shakespeare's Wordplay* (1957)

Nowottny, W. M. T., *The Language Poets Use* (1962)

Peacham, Henry, *The Garden of Eloquence* (1577, enlarged edition 1593); introduction by W. G. Crane (Gainesville: Scholars' Facsimiles, 1954)

Puttenham, George, *The Arte of English Poesie* (1589), ed. G. D. Willcock and A. Walker (Cambridge, 1936)

Rainolde, Richard, *A Booke Called the Foundacion of Rhetorike* (1563), ed. F. R. Johnson (New York, 1945)
Sonnino, L. A., *A Handbook to Sixteenth-Century Rhetoric* (1968)
Spurgeon, C. F. E., *Shakespeare's Imagery and What It Tells Us* (Cambridge, 1935)
Trousdale, M., *Shakespeare and the Rhetoricians* (Chapel Hill, North Carolina, 1982)
Vickers, B., *The Artistry of Shakespeare's Prose* (1968)
  Classical Rhetoric in English Poetry (1970)
Wilson, Thomas, *The Arte of Rhetorike* (1567), ed. G. H. Mair (Oxford, 1909)

5   Playhouses and players in the time of Shakespeare

F ROM the variety of evidence at our disposal, we can reasonably conclude that the life of a professional actor in Shakespeare's England was always precarious and sometimes profitable. One unpredictable hazard was the terrible and mysterious bubonic plague, which had been intermittently dormant and virulent in England since 1348. Major outbreaks in London caused the banning of public assemblies in 1563, 1574, 1577, 1578, 1581, 1593, 1603, 1625, and 1636, and subsidiary outbreaks led to a restraint on plays in 1580, 1583, 1586, 1587, 1594, 1604, and 1605. It became an established custom to order the closing of the London theatres when registered deaths reached forty in any one week. It was particularly galling for the actors that the spread of plague coincided with the hotter summer months, the very best period for performance in the outdoor playhouses. Provincial tours became a familiar part of the annual routine, but even then there was the risk of plague to add to the uncertainties of travel, hospitality, and makeshift performance spaces. To take a single curious example, in 1564, the year of Shakespeare's birth in Stratford-upon-Avon, that small market town lost over a quarter of its population to the plague. There were legal hazards, too. Companies of actors and the audiences they attracted constituted a potential threat to the good order of Tudor England, and a 1572 'Act for the punishment of Vagabonds' made it illegal for strolling players to perform without authorization. The safest protection was the nominal patronage of a noble lord, and the great Elizabethan companies came to be distinguished by the name of their patron, whose livery they could wear on appropriate occasions.

The companies

Philip Henslowe's *Diary* provides the best evidence we have of the day-to-day organization of an Elizabethan acting company. Henslowe was a shrewd commercial speculator whose decision to involve himself in theatre is in itself evidence of the profitability of drama in Elizabethan London. Having begun his business life as apprentice to a dyer, he enriched himself by marrying the dyer's widow and continued to accumulate money and property by dealing in

67

the manufacture of starch as well as by involving himself in pawnbroking, real estate, money-lending, and the building and management of theatres. The gathering of papers loosely called a *Diary* is an eccentric document, less a systematic account-book than the record of a wealthy man's determination to keep his affairs in order, but it offers, however irregularly, priceless information about repertoire, income from entrance fees, the payment of actors and of playwrights, and the expenditure on production of plays. Henslowe was associated with one of the two great companies of the last decade of Queen Elizabeth I's reign, the Admiral's Men. Their patron was Lord Howard, and their leading actor, Edward Alleyn, was Henslowe's son-in-law. Lord Howard is known to have authorized a company of players as early as 1576, but the pre-eminence of the Admiral's Men was prepared for by Alleyn's triumph in the great succession of Marlowe's plays between 1587 and 1593. During that period they established themselves at Henslowe's Rose theatre on the south bank of the Thames.

It may be that Henslowe's decision, supported by Alleyn, to build a new theatre, the Fortune, north of the river, near Cripplegate, in 1600, and to make it the headquarters of the Admiral's Men, was precipitated by the uncomfortable proximity, on the south bank, of the leading rival company, the Lord Chamberlain's Men, at the Globe. Most of the members of this famous company, formed in 1594, are well known. Its leading tragic actor, Richard Burbage, was the son of the builder and proprietor of the first important purpose-built playhouse in England, the Theatre, and it was probably there that they settled on a management structure distinct from that of the Admiral's Men. By 1597, six of the Chamberlain's Men seem to have held shares in the company. They were Richard Burbage, the famous comedian Will Kemp (or Kempe), the eventual co-editor of the first Folio edition of Shakespeare's plays, John Heminges, Thomas Pope, Augustine Phillips, and William Shakespeare. The sharers financed each production and divided the takings proportionately. There were presumably company meetings to determine how the profits would be used; but the owner of the theatre would have to be paid his rent (it may be that James Burbage, like Henslowe, asked for half or the whole of the money taken for admission to the gallery) and the hired men – actors, musicians, stage-hands etc. – would need their wages. Some or all of the boys who played the female roles were apprenticed to the sharers and may have had to settle for board, lodging, and pocket-money.

At the end of 1596, the superiority of the Chamberlain's Men over all their rivals was confirmed by the invitation to provide all six of the command performances during the Christmas festivities at court, but 1597 was to be a troubled year for the professional theatre at large. Under pressure from the officers of the city of London, the Privy Council issued an order to the effect that:

Her Majestie being informed that there are verie great disorders committed in the common playhouses both by lewd matters that are handled on the stages and by resorte and confluence of bad people, hathe given direction that not onlie no plaies shalbe used within London or about the citty or in any publique place during this tyme of sommer, but that also those playhouses that are erected and built only for suche purposes shalbe plucked downe.

The trouble may have arisen out of a performance, by the Earl of Pembroke's Men at the Swan, of a lost play called *The Isle of Dogs*, the provocative outcome of a collaboration between Ben Jonson and Thomas Nashe. Whatever its particular offence, it provided a pretext for the officers of the Guildhall to force home their long-standing dislike of the unruly theatre. The Privy Council, of which both the Lord Admiral and the Lord Chamberlain were members, was by inclination protective of players, but it could not be seen to sanction so manifest an overstepping of the mark. In the event, nothing happened – no theatres were 'plucked downe' and plays continued to be performed in the immediate vicinity of the walled city of London – but there seems no reason to doubt that the theatre companies experienced intimations of mortality. There is a strong likelihood that the Privy Council, even as it issued its ominous order, was planning to preserve the two favoured companies, the Admiral's and the Chamberlain's, but whilst the former was well settled in the Rose, the latter was threatened with homelessness. James Burbage's lease on the Theatre expired in April 1597. He himself had expired two months earlier, bequeathing his claim on the vexed property to his elder son Cuthbert. Richard's inheritance was the Parliament Chamber of the dissolved Blackfriars priory, which his father had purchased the year before, converted into a practical indoor theatre and been prevented from exploiting by a ban on its use as a public playhouse. The resourcefulness of the Chamberlain's Men was severely tested throughout 1597 and 1598. Eventually, with an opportunism that may have been perilously close to desperation, they decided to take advantage of a clause in James Burbage's lease authorizing the tenant to dismantle and remove the building. Some or all of the timbers of the Theatre were transported, probably on the night of 28 December 1598, down Bishopsgate Street and across the Thames to a site not much more than a hundred yards from Henslowe's Rose. At their new theatre, the Globe, the Chamberlain's Men entered on a decade of dramatic achievement scarcely rivalled by any other company in the whole history of the English theatre.

The broad outline of the theatrical year was by then established. A company's performances in the outdoor theatres would begin in London as early as possible in September, or even in late August if plague deaths were low enough. The period between September and Christmas was the longest uninterrupted playing spell and a crucial indicator of the company's popularity and consequent prosperity. It was during this period also that the Office of the

Revels would select pieces for performance at court, which would bring the bonus of a generous separate payment and the comparative comfort of indoor performance in the depths of winter. That it was the custom literally to drum up audiences is evident from a letter sent by the Lord Chamberlain to the Lord Mayor of London, asking that his Men be permitted to perform in the Cross Keys tavern in Gracechurch Street:

the which I praie you the rather to doe for that they have undertaken to me that where heretofore they began not their plaies till towards fower a clock, they will now begin at two and have done betwene fower and five, and will nott use anie drumes or trumpettes att all for the callinge of peopell together, and shall be contributories to the poor of the parishe.

The letter is the best evidence we have on the timing of performances. A two o'clock start was certainly sensible, since the main meal of the day was taken between ten o'clock and noon and the audience would wish to be home before dark. The request was made in October 1594, but it is fair to assume that the change of practice to which it refers held good throughout the year. Audiences as well as actors were evidently willing to defy the frosts of winter, and performances continued through January and into February, to be officially, though inconsistently, suspended during the forty days of Lent. The rise in plague deaths was so regular, as was the associated exodus from London of all its most prosperous citizens, that provincial tours were a necessary part of the summer routine. Their capacity to tour and to play at court indicates the adaptability of the theatre companies and the fluidity of their staging methods. If, as seems likely, the city tragedians who arrive unannounced in Elsinore are based on the Chamberlain's Men, their versatility is exemplary. They can revive an old play on demand, as Shakespeare's colleagues revived *Richard II* at the dangerous request of the Earl of Essex's friends in 1601,[1] they can master a new speech in an afternoon or improvise a dumb show, and they can adapt their performance for a small indoor stage. That Shakespeare himself was unenthusiastic about touring is implied by Hamlet's question, 'How chances it they travel? their residence, both in reputation and profit, was better both ways' (2.2.352–4).

One answer, more pithily given in the probably pirated 'bad' Quarto of 1603 than in the elaborated Folio text, is provided by 'Gilderstone':

I' faith my Lord, novelty carries it away,
For the principal public audience that
Came to them, are turned to private plays,
And to the humour of children.   (lines 978–81)

The reference is to one of the curiosities of the Elizabethan and early Jacobean stage, the vogue for the companies of boy players performing in their private theatres. The major companies were those composed of choristers from St Paul's and from the Chapel Royal. Their occasional involvement in the performance of plays can be dated from at least the fourteenth century, but the mid sixteenth saw a marked increase, and in the 1570s the Children of Paul's and the Children of the Chapel Royal were ahead of the adult companies in establishing themselves in theatres of their own. John Lyly was the first of many accomplished Elizabethan dramatists to provide specially written material for the choristers, whose performances the Queen enjoyed, but it was Lyly's vigorous engagement on behalf of the established church in the Marprelate controversy[2] that led to the dissolution of the boys' companies in about 1590. They were revived, after a discreet interval, nearly ten years later, when the Children of the Chapel Royal were permitted to perform in the Blackfriars theatre, from which the adult Chamberlain's Men were barred, and the Children of Paul's returned to their refurbished playhouse. From 1600 to 1608 their popularity was a genuine threat to the adult companies and ✗ they were able to attract plays from all the leading dramatists of the period, with the exception of Shakespeare. But James I preferred the lavish spectacle of the masque to the precocious display of pubescent talent, and in 1608 the Children of Paul's abandoned the performance of plays. The Children of the Chapel Royal, displaced at last by Richard Burbage and his colleagues, struggled on for a few more years in the less salubrious precinct of the Whitefriars, and were eventually absorbed by an adult company, probably in 1613.

It is not easy to understand, let alone recover, the relish felt by fashionable Elizabethan audiences for boy actors. What we can say is that the plays written for them were plays about adults, and that much pleasure was taken in the portrayal of adult vice by boys who could be presumed not fully to understand the words they had committed to memory. There was also the embellishment of music. Songs and instrumental pieces were a regular and prominent part of performances at the private theatres of the children's companies, and their comparative insignificance at the adult theatres was often a source of regret. It was, however, the mature flexibility of the adults that enabled them to survive the difficult transition from the Tudors to the Stuarts. James I, always concerned about the power of the English barons, was quick to restrict patronage of theatre companies to members of the royal family. He adopted the Chamberlain's Men himself, and it was as the King's Men that, in 1608, they added the indoor stage of the Blackfriars to their established outdoor ✗ stage at the Globe. The Admiral's Men were awarded the patronage of Prince Henry, and on his untimely death in 1612 became known as the Palsgrave's Men, servants of the Elector Palatine who had married James I's daughter.

The theatres

When James Burbage, master carpenter and leading member of the first great Elizabethan acting company, the Earl of Leicester's Men, decided to build a theatre, he was speculating boldly on the basis of a discernible trend in popular entertainment. To be sure, plays had been performed in public places for centuries – in market-places, on village greens, wherever there was room to set up a stage and accommodate spectators – and in private places too – in the great halls of noble houses, in several schools, in the echoing refectories of Oxford and Cambridge colleges or London's Inns of Court. The problem for a businessman was how to extract money from the spectators. There were architectural precedents to serve as a builder's guide in the enclosed space of inn-yards with their surrounding galleries as well as in the tiered auditoria of cockpits and bear-baiting arenas, but no one before Burbage had worked out a wholly reliable way of making profitable the public performance of plays. His project might well have failed – for one thing, the national repertoire of plays was very small in 1576 – but its success can be measured by the rapid spread of theatre building in the vicinity of London.

The Theatre. England's first purpose-built playhouse was prudently sited, as all Elizabethan theatres came to be, outside the city walls, in this case north of the Bishopsgate along Shoreditch, and therefore outside the direct jurisdiction of the Guildhall. There is virtually no documentary evidence about it, but it is assumed, by inference, to have been a polygonal structure, with three galleries and, probably, a removable stage. James Burbage would have provided it with some backstage facilities, perhaps no more than dressing-rooms and storage space. During its twenty years of active use, it housed many acting companies, and was the likely headquarters of the Chamberlain's Men from 1594 to 1597. When its lease expired, its timbers were dismantled to provide building material for the first Globe.

The Curtain. Built in 1577 on a site off Shoreditch and close to the Theatre, the Curtain survived until about 1627. Never a prominent playhouse, it was probably made available by its proprietors (Henry Lanman or Laneman is the only one known by name) to any companies that felt the need of it. There is a strong possibility that the Chamberlain's Men staged *Henry V* here in 1599 – the play's apologetic Chorus is only too well aware of the playhouse's shortcomings – and it is known to have been used by Queen Anne's Men and Prince Charles's Men during the reign of James I. We can reasonably assume that it was modelled on the Theatre.

Newington Butts. Almost nothing is known about the theatre in the village of Newington, south of Southwark. The earliest reference to it dates from 1580, and the latest from 1594. It was used by Lord Strange's Men in 1591–2 and by the combined companies of the Lord Admiral and the Lord Chamberlain in 1594, when Henslowe had an interest in it. The possibility that it was a converted inn-yard cannot be rejected.

3 A section from Henslowe's *Diary* recording receipts from the theatre in Newington Butts between 18 July and 7 August 1594. 421 plague-deaths were registered in London, and it may have been to avoid a restraint on playing that the Admiral's Men and Chamberlain's Men teamed up to perform at this outlying theatre. Henslowe's list mentions 18 performances of 9 different plays during this 21-day period

The Rose. The building of this theatre on the south bank of the Thames was financed by Philip Henslowe and a certain John Cholmley in about 1587. Between then and its demolition in about 1605 it underwent minor conversions to update it, but retained its thatched roof and its timber frame on a brick foundation. Until the building of the Fortune, it was the home of the Admiral's Men, who were briefly replaced, after their move, by the Earl of Worcester's Men.

The Swan. Given a permanent place in theatre history by the chance survival of a drawing by the Dutch visitor Johannes de Witt, the Swan was, in fact, an ill-starred theatre. Built in 1595–6, it was the property of a financial speculator called Francis Langley. De Witt considered it 'the largest and most distinguished' of London's theatres when he visited the city in 1596. All modern attempts to reconstruct a 'typical' Elizabethan outdoor theatre are reliant on de Witt's drawing of the interior of the Swan, with its three galleries, its large stage and heavy stage doors and its stage canopy supported by substantial pillars. The curious fact is that only one surviving play can be said with any certainty to have been performed at the Swan, Thomas Middleton's *A Chaste Maid in Cheapside*, staged at some time between 1611 and 1614. Situated not far from the Rose, it was the home of the Earl of Pembroke's Men until 1597, when that company broke up in some disorder after their contentious production of *The Isle of Dogs*. Its subsequent history is scrappy.

4   Arend van Buchell's copy of a drawing of the Swan Theatre. The original was
sketched by Johannes de Witt, probably in 1596

The Globe. The lack of information about the theatre that housed Shakespeare's company when his writing career was at its height has licensed a vast amount of speculative reconstruction. We must assume that, when the Chamberlain's Men instructed their builder, Peter Streete, they would not have wished their new home to be in any way inferior to the Swan. Recent research by John Orrell has persuasively proposed that the Globe was 'a polygon inscribed within a circle, about 100 feet or so across',[3] and that other Elizabethan playhouses had similar measurements. This is significantly larger than had been previously supposed, and helps to justify his further surprising calculation that its audience capacity was 3350. There is, however, no reason to assume that the maximum was often reached, nor that Orrell's conclusions will remain unchallenged by later researchers. His findings are dependent on the logical possibility that the first Globe, destroyed by fire in 1613, provided the foundations for the more elaborate second Globe, erected in 1614 and demolished in 1644.

The Fortune. The building contract for this theatre, built in 1600 to the orders of Philip Henslowe just outside the Cripplegate in the Liberty of Finsbury, has survived. The document is open to interpretation, but it is clear that the Fortune was square rather than polygonal, and that its stage was to be similar in dimensions to that of the Globe. We can assume that Henslowe consulted with the leading members of the Admiral's Men, and that the decision to site the new playhouse north of the river was taken partly as a conscious counter to the greater hold of the Chamberlain's Men on the south bank. Edward Alleyn was a partner in the enterprise, and his presence, together with a repertoire of plays unrivalled by any company other than Shakespeare's, guaranteed for the Fortune a popularity which became increasingly flecked with notoriety in the decade before its burning in 1621. The second Fortune, despite the expensive innovation of brick construction, had a dismal history. It was opened in 1623 as the home of the Palsgrave's (formerly Admiral's) Men, but the company did not survive the devastation of the 1625 plague, and the Fortune fell into lesser hands. During the reign of Charles I it was a well-known trouble-spot. Having been partly demolished in 1649, it was finally torn down in 1662, the year in which building was begun on the first Restoration playhouse in Drury Lane.

The Hope. Opened in 1614, the Hope was intended by its owners, Philip Henslowe and Edward Alleyn, to serve as both playhouse and animal-baiting arena. It was situated close to the Swan, on which it was modelled, and the surviving contract stipulates that it should have 'a stage to be carryed or taken awaie'. A notable innovation was the cantilevered canopy over the stage, which obviated the need for the stage pillars, thereby allowing a total clearance of the arena for the better display of animal-baiting. Ben Jonson's *Bartholomew Fair* was performed at the Hope during its first year of operation, but it seems

5   The size and splendour of the second Globe is perhaps exaggerated in Wenceslaus Hollar's drawing of the west part of Southwark. The cantilevered roof of the Hope can be seen to the right and the courts of Winchester House in the foreground

rarely to have been a serious rival to the second Globe and became increasingly reliant on blood sports. It was demolished in 1656.

These are the known outdoor or 'public' theatres of Shakespeare's London. The list could properly be supplemented by reference to the inn-yard theatres, of which the best documented are the Boar's Head in Whitechapel (active from *c.* 1599–*c.* 1609) and the Red Bull in Clerkenwell (active from *c.* 1605–*c.* 1630), which became the popular home of blood-and-thunder drama during the tenancy of Queen Anne's Men. But London had also its indoor or private theatres. Shakespeare must have seen plays performed by the Children of Paul's in the house within the cathedral precinct converted for their use, and he might also have visited the first Blackfriars theatre, converted for the use of the Children of the Chapel Royal by Richard Farrant in 1576. He came to know the second Blackfriars theatre well, after its occupation by the King's Men in 1608. As the company's leading dramatist, he would also have been expected to adapt plays for presentation at court, whether in the Great Hall of Hampton Court, the second Banqueting Hall at Whitehall or its neo-Palladian successor, built to the taste of James I and much more suited to the staging of masques than of plays. The audience at court was, of course, a privileged one, but the private theatres were open to any of the public who could afford the greater entrance-fee. The staging techniques of the King's Men at the second Blackfriars were almost certainly more elaborate than at the first Globe. Some account had to be taken of the scenic innovations of the court masques under the first great designer of the English theatre, Inigo Jones. But it must be remembered that the Blackfriars was run in tandem with the Globe, so that what was done at one theatre had to be adaptable to the other. It is pertinent, then, to ask what were the minimum facilities that enabled a company like the King's Men to present the great plays of the Elizabethan age, leaving it to stage directions and the internal evidence of the texts themselves to provide examples of dramatic episodes (or even particular theatres) in which more than the minimum was available as required. To answer the question, we have no better guide than the de Witt drawing of the Swan, a theatre built only a few years before Shakespeare's Globe.

The outstanding features of the Swan stage, as de Witt drew it, are the surprisingly bulky Corinthian columns and the two wooden double-doors, with heavy hinges that clearly indicate that the doors opened outwards on to the stage. There is no sign of a trap, though it seems unlikely that the Swan was without one, nor are there any drapes, but that is of uncertain significance since they could easily be set if required. The absence of an inner stage is less equivocal. Although a discovery space of some kind may have been built in to later theatres, it is not essential. Elizabethan actors walked out on to the platform to present a story. By retreating behind it, they would not only have ignored the common sense of audibility and visibility but also have carried that story off with them. The doors of the Swan, set square in the tiring-house facade, provided the actors with a strong upstage entrance, and it is important to remember that, on the open stage, every play as well as each episode within every play begins with an entrance. Three doors, or as many as five, may have been provided in later theatres, but two would suffice for almost all surviving Elizabethan and Jacobean plays. The move downstage to a commanding speaking position is not made easier by the pillars. They are there to support the hut with its suspension-gear for 'flyings' and storage space for the throne, the most important piece of furniture on the Elizabethan stage. Although the resourceful actors habitually incorporated the pillars in the action, they would have preferred to be without them. We have already noted that Henslowe had the Hope built 'without any postes or supporters to be fixed or settvpon the saide stage', and it is likely that the builders of the second Globe adopted the same structural principle.

Elizabethan stage directions refer frequently to an area 'above', less frequently to one 'below'. There is sufficient room beneath de Witt's platform to permit the effective use of a trap, and the Globe too could evidently accommodate actors there, even Shakespeare himself if the tradition that allots him the part of the Ghost in *Hamlet* is to be trusted. The natural place for the 'above' is the gallery over the stage doors, which may also have housed the musical consorts, after the fashion of the musicians' galleries in the halls of the great houses. On the other hand, the people de Witt has drawn look more like spectators than musicians. We have to recognize the possibility that the gallery was a multi-purpose space. Such hesitancy is typical of attempts to reconstruct the conditions of Elizabethan performance: we must be prepared, whilst reaching for certainty, to settle for probability. The on-stage figures sketched by de Witt can provide us with a final ground for speculation. If they are actors, as we must presume they are, they offer us a sense of varied styles of performance. Downstage centre is a plain bench, a solid piece of stage furniture and one scarcely suitable for the richly gowned actor seated on it. Behind and just far enough to the right of the seated actor to be easily visible by most of the audience is a 'lady'. Her gesture is balanced and formal. The third figure, extravagantly bearded and very close to the groundlings, could be in bizarre motion. The scene, however impressionistically de Witt has recorded it, serves to remind us of the Elizabethan readiness to mingle the stately and the grotesque within a single sequence. Behind the actors, the closed stage doors may be a conventional indication that an indoor scene is in progress. When either of them opens, the next episode will begin.

The actors

There is ample evidence of the upward social mobility of Elizabethan actors. Edward Alleyn's rise from simple membership of the Earl of Worcester's Men in 1583 to the joint-Mastership of the Royal Game in 1604, and the subsequent founding of Dulwich College, is the most spectacular, but Shakespeare and several of his colleagues in the Chamberlain's Men acquired their share of wealth and respect in a profession never wholly distinct from vagabondage. The idea that a man might follow the trade of playwright was in its infancy, and it was the actor who commanded the stage.

We do not know how Shakespeare's plays were originally acted. The

6 C. Walter Hodges's drawing (1965) of an Elizabethan playhouse. The gallery seating is speculative: recent research by John Orrell suggests that there were more degrees and much less leg-room

schedule of the Chamberlain's Men cannot have ~~varied significantly from that~~ of the Admiral's Men, whom we know to have performed sometimes as many as ten different plays in a two-week period. Polished performance of the kind familiar to twentieth-century audiences of the long run is impossible in such circumstances. Even if we grant to Elizabethan actors a remarkable memory for lines, there must have been a frequent call for the prompter's aid, and it is absurd to suppose that the playwright's text never suffered. We can only guess at rehearsal practice, but it seems reasonable to contain speculation within two assumptions – that leading actors would work hard in private preparation, and that conventional stage groupings, not only of attendant lords and servants but also of characters in dialogue, removed any need for 'blocking' the disposition of actors on the platform. Only 'unconventional' scenes would demand rehearsal; the rest could be played according to familiar routines. There are widely divergent views about the style of acting. At one extreme are the formalists, who believe that Burbage conducted himself with the gestural and verbal precision of a trained rhetorician, and at the other the naturalists, for whom on-stage Burbage is not readily distinguishable from off-stage Burbage. Both schools of thought neglect a feature of all popular theatre forms – their impurity. If Shakespeare and his contemporaries had intended their plays to be acted in a single style, they would have written them in a single style. It was not the unity of a work of art but the variety of a story that the actor served. We should be prepared to recognize in the alternation of prose and verse, of rhetoric and of simple narrative, signals to the actor to vary his style. The notion of a play's 'consistency' would have been foreign to the Chamberlain's Men. Their discipline was that of the scene or episode, not of so large a unit as an act and certainly not of a whole play.

Successful actors may well have benefited from a formal training in rhetoric, and appropriateness of gesture was more likely to gain applause than eccentricity. It was, presumably, Alleyn's ability to suit the action to the word and the word to the action that Ben Jonson had in mind when he wrote that 'others speak, but only thou dost act'. It was not enough that an actor could speak well. Physical grace and precision were equally important. An actor would need to fence, to dance, and sometimes to perform the 'feats of activity and tumbling' that were favoured by audiences at court as well as in the theatres. 'Ability of body' was his pride, and a valuable resource for the busy playwrights who knew their audience's preferences. Elizabethan actors went out on to the platform to deliver the next episode in a story. To help them get the order right the book-keeper wrote out a 'plot' and hung it in the tiring house. One or two of these 'plots' have survived, though none from Shakespeare's company. Written on foolscap, divided into two columns, with marginal notes on properties and sound effects, they listed the names of the actors as well as the characters they were to impersonate in each episode. Given the opportunity to excel, the actor would have jumped at it – the theatre was not yet respectable enough to smother its showmen and entertainers – but he knew, from the moment he opened the stage door, that his task was to present, not simply himself, but also a necessary part of the story. What brought audiences to the outdoor theatres in winter was not the indulgence of exhibitionism nor the greed for great literature so much as the love of a good story.

Of the various kinds of scene with which Elizabethan playwrights charged their actors, three are easily distinguishable: the great set-pieces (regal assemblies, trials, duels, battles), dialogues, often in the heightened poetry of lovers and sometimes rounded off with a soliloquy, and the almost improvisatory interludes, usually involving comic or low-life characters. The last of these would have required little or no rehearsal, since the extemporary mood of such scenes must have depended on the relationship between the actors and their audience, and their language could survive paraphrase in performance. It seems likely that clowns, fools, and jokers would have been happy at the front of the stage in intimate contact with the spectators. The dialogues, particularly those involving a boy / woman, were probably practised in order to correct or adjust emphasis, though there would have been no need to occupy the stage for such rehearsals since the disposition of the characters on the platform would have been dictated by convention. The same would certainly be true of the 'blocking' of the set-pieces. Every actor, from king to attendant lord, would know the formal etiquette of the occasion and position himself according to the laws of hierarchy. It is the passages in which the good order of the set-piece is fractured that would have needed the most careful rehearsal. Battle scenes are a particularly interesting example of Elizabethan staging. Despite the apology he offers through the Chorus to Act 4 of *Henry V*, Shakespeare obviously had confidence in the ability of the Chamberlain's Men to turn 'four or five most ragged foils' into a battlefield, another example of the attractiveness of 'feats of activity'.

Although we know from an inventory among Henslowe's papers that the Admiral's Men were tolerably stocked with stage properties, we must assume that the platform on to which the Elizabethan actor walked was fairly empty. It was he who had to fill it. Timidity or half-heartedness is fatal in such a setting. Plays were performed with a minimum of scenic and mechanical aids, but in lavish costumes. Disguise flourishes in the drama, partly because it is conspicuous on a bare stage, and partly because the audience took an exaggerated interest in clothes. It was the fashion to distort the natural lines of the body, to pinch, to pad, to stiffen, and the actors would have been ill advised to dress carelessly in front of a critical audience. The wardrobe-master (tireman), a craftsman as well as an administrator, was an important member of every acting company. Leading actors would be expected to provide their own costumes, whatever the cost. We learn from Henslowe, for example, that Richard Jones of the Admiral's Men paid £3 for 'a man's gown of Peachcolour in grain', a sizeable proportion of an annual income that can scarcely have exceeded £30. Boys and hired men, on the other hand, were probably →costumed out of stock. Edward Alleyn's inventory of costumes belonging to the Admiral's Men in about 1602 lists 14 'Clokes', 17 'Gownes', 17 'Antik sutes', 17 'Jerkings and dublets', 11 'frenchose' (French hose) and 8 'venetians' (Venetian hose or, perhaps, breeches). The importance of gowns and cloaks in particular is evident from payments recorded in Henslowe's *Diary*. The Admiral's Men, after the deduction of costs, could rarely hope to take more than £3 from a performance, and yet they paid £9 to make two women's gowns for *The Two Angry Women of Abington* and £12 10s to get two cloaks out of Henslowe's pawn in 1598. A surviving drawing, dating from about 1594, of a scene from *Titus Andronicus* shows a bizarre mixture of Roman and Elizabethan costumes, and we must assume that attempts at historical accuracy were sporadic and inconsistent. It was more important to look good than to look right, and it is a fair guess that many of the original audience spent more time discussing the clothes than the performance of the actors. The London apprentices who, according to John Stow, 'did affect to go in costly apparel and wear weapons and frequent schools of dancing, fencing and music'[4] might well have found their models on the stage.

Notes

1. On 5 or 6 February 1601, Sir Gelly Meyrick, an associate of the Earl of Essex, offered to pay the Chamberlain's Men to perform *Richard II*, a contentious play because of its deposition scene. The performance took place on 7 February, the eve of Essex's abortive insurrection. To the surprise of many, the Queen chose to pardon the Chamberlain's Men and execute the Earl of Essex.
2. The Marprelate controversy was sparked off in 1588 by the publication of a pamphlet attacking some of the practices of the established church, and continued to rage until the end of 1589. In all, the unknown puritan who wrote under the name 'Martin Marprelate' completed seven pamphlets, whose wit and effectiveness called out responses from anglican leaders, and Thomas Nashe and John Lyly were the most famous of the anti-Martinist pamphleteers. It was the eagerness of the authorities to bring the controversy to an immediate end after the capture of the Martinist printing press that turned them against their own supporters, including John Lyly and the children's companies.
3. John Orrell, *The Quest for Shakespeare's Globe* (Cambridge, 1983), p. 107.
4. John Stow, *A Survey of London*, ed. John Strype, 2 vols. (1720), II, pp. 328–9.

Reading list

THE COMPANIES

Baldwin, T. W., *The Organization and Personnel of the Shakespearean Company* (Princeton, New Jersey, 1927)
Beckerman, Bernard, *Shakespeare at the Globe* (New York, 1962)

Bentley, G. E., *The Profession of Player in Shakespeare's Time, 1590–1642* (Princeton, New Jersey, 1984)
Bradbrook, M. C., *The Rise of the Common Player* (1962)
Gurr, Andrew, *The Shakespearean Stage* (Cambridge, 1970)
Nungezer, Edwin, *A Dictionary of Actors* (Yale, 1929)
Thomson, Peter, *Shakespeare's Theatre* (1983)

THE CHILDREN'S COMPANIES
Gair, Reavley, *The Children of Paul's* (Cambridge, 1982)
Hillebrand, H. M., *The Child Actors* (Urbana, Illinois, 1926)
Shapiro, Michael, *Children of the Revels* (New York, 1977)

THE THEATRES
Bentley, G. E., *The Jacobean and Caroline Stage*, 7 vols. (Oxford, 1966), VI
Chambers, E. K., *The Elizabethan Stage*, 4 vols. (Oxford, 1923), II
Edwards, Christopher, ed., *The London Theatre Guide, 1576–1642* (The Bear Gardens Museum, London, 1979)
Foakes, R. A., *Illustrations of the English Stage 1580–1642* (1985)
Hodges, C. Walter, *The Globe Restored* (1953)
  Shakespeare's Second Globe (1973)
Linnell, Rosemary, *The Curtain Playhouse* (Curtain Theatre, London, 1977)
Orrell, John, *The Quest for Shakespeare's Globe* (Cambridge, 1983)
Reynolds, G. F., *The Staging of Elizabethan Plays at the Red Bull Theatre, 1605–1625* (New York, 1940)
Rhodes, Ernest L., *Henslowe's Rose: The Stage and Staging* (Kentucky, 1976)
Smith, Irwin, *Shakespeare's Blackfriars Playhouse* (1966)
Wickham, Glynne, *Early English Stages*, 3 vols., II, parts 1 and 2 (1963 and 1972)

THE STAGECRAFT OF ELIZABETHAN ACTORS
Dessen, Alan C., *Elizabethan Stage Conventions and Modern Interpreters* (Cambridge, 1984)
Linthicum, M. C., *Costume in the Drama of Shakespeare and His Contemporaries* (Oxford, 1936)
Seltzer, Daniel, 'The actors and staging', in *A New Companion to Shakespeare Studies*, ed. K. Muir and S. Schoenbaum (Cambridge, 1971)
Styan, J. L., *Shakespeare's Stagecraft* (Cambridge, 1967)

6 Shakespeare and the theatrical conventions of his time

Many problems bedevil the modern interpreter of Shakespeare's plays, but especially puzzling, whether for critic, editor, or director, is the gap that exists between us and the original stage conventions, those 'terms upon which author, performers and audience agree to meet, so that the performance may be carried on'.[1] Some of Shakespeare's contemporaries (Ben Jonson is the most notable example) did take pains to edit their dramatic works for the benefit of a reader, but, as R. B. McKerrow has noted, the original manuscript delivered to the players by the playwright was 'merely the substance, or rather the bare bones, of a performance on the stage, intended to be interpreted by actors skilled in their craft, who would have no difficulty in reading it as it was meant to be read'.[2] Such a manuscript, then, was a theatrical script, written to be performed by Elizabethan theatrical professionals, not a literary text, written to be read by modern editors and critics. To treat such playscripts today as poems in dialogue form or as modern novels is then to flirt with the danger of screening out part of the original theatrical language or logic of presentation shared by Shakespeare, his actors, and his spectators.

The elements of that theatrical language vary widely. Thus, few readers or playgoers today have difficulty with such theatrical conventions as the soliloquy or the aside or impenetrable disguise (although each continues to generate difficulties in 'realistic' terms – witness the widespread use in cinema and television productions of 'voice over' soliloquies and the concomitant cutting of many asides). Other facets of playgoing taken for granted at the Globe, however, are less compatible with our expectations. In the most general terms, 'going to the theatre' today usually means sitting in a darkened auditorium and watching actors perform in a lighted space, a sense of theatre alien to Shakespeare and his audience. Similarly, playgoers today take for granted a two- to three-hour performance with one fifteen-minute interval, but for most of his career Shakespeare would have seen his plays performed from start to finish with no breaks (and the alternative, in the private theatres or in the public theatres after about 1610, would have been brief pauses, with music, between each of the five acts).

The sense of theatre or theatrical convention that a modern reader brings to Elizabethan and Jacobean playscripts can have an immediate effect, therefore, upon interpretation. As a point of departure, let us consider two scenes from Jacobean drama, one obscure, one very familiar. First, at a climactic point in *The Two Noble Ladies* (one of the few extant playhouse manuscripts) two soldiers drag Justina on-stage with the intention of drowning her in the Euphrates:

> *1. Soldier.* Come, now w' are allmost at our journeys end;
>   This is swift Euphrates, here cast her in . . .
> *2. Soldier.* Come this way, this way, heare the streame is deepest.
> *1. Soldier.* I am enforc'd I know not by what pow'r
>   To hale her this way.
> *2. Soldier.* what strange noise is this?
> *1. Soldier.* dispatch, the tide swells high.
> *2. Soldier.* what feind is this?
> *1. Soldier.* what furie ceazes mee?
> *2. Soldier.* Alas, I'm hurried headlong to the streame.
> *1. Soldier.* And so am I, wee both must drowne and die.[3]

The modern reader seeking to reconstruct the staging of this moment will note the repeated gestic phrases ('This is swift Euphrates, here cast her in'; 'heare the streame is deepest') that, according to our logic of presentation, could indicate the presence on-stage of a river or body of water. Granted such an inference, directors or theatre historians might then debate what is 'necessary' to stage this scene (on-stage water? a 'wave machine'?) and move on to extrapolate what is necessary or appropriate for other related moments (so that one on-stage river can beget others).

But in this instance the manuscript provides specific (and revealing) stage directions. Thus, at line 1166 ('what strange noise is this?') the marginal signal reads: '*Enter 2. Tritons with silver trumpets*'; next to the subsequent lines we find: '*The tritons ceaz the souldiers*' and '*The Tritons dragge them in sounding their trumpets.*' Regardless of our expectations today, the original effect was keyed not to an on-stage river but to Tritons and trumpets. The sense of headlong, precipitate action, of drowning in a swelling tide, was conveyed not by the direct representation of water or immersion but by signals in the dialogue and violent stage business in conjunction with the imaginative participation of the audience. In this scheme, ironically, 'what feind is this?' does refer to a visible on-stage figure, but 'This is swift Euphrates, here cast her in' requires no more than a gesture from the actor towards the stage floor or the edge of the stage. But without the unusually informative playhouse stage directions, the modern interpreter could easily have reversed the process and postulated a 'real' Euphrates and 'imaginary' fiends.

For a second example, one might consider the moment just before Macbeth's 'Tomorrow, and tomorrow, and tomorrow.' Shortly after the entrance of Macbeth, Seyton, and soldiers, a stage direction calls for '*a cry within of women*' (5.5.7.s.d.),[4] at which point Macbeth asks 'what is that noise?'

and Seyton responds: 'It is the cry of women, my good lord.' After a powerful short speech ('I have supped full with horrors . . .'), Macbeth asks again: 'wherefore was that cry?' to which Seyton responds: 'The Queen, my lord, is dead' (lines 15–16), a revelation that elicits the famous speech. The Folio, however, provides no exit and re-entry for Seyton between his two lines, so the only authoritative text gives us no indication of how he finds out that the queen is dead. Since few modern interpreters can abide such an untidy situation, most editors include an exit for Seyton after his first line and an entrance before his second (with the insert usually, but not always, enclosed in square brackets), while directors do likewise, or have Seyton send off a lesser functionary who returns, or have Seyton walk to a stage door, confer with someone off-stage, and return to Macbeth. If we are to understand that Lady Macbeth has died at the moment of the cry (which would rule out Seyton knowing of her death at the outset of the scene), the announcer of the news, according to our logic of interpretation, must have some means of learning the news. Therefore, our sense of theatre calls for an exit or some other visible means of getting the news on-stage.

Since such exits and entrances often *are* omitted in the original printed texts, such an interpretation may well be correct. But imagine the scene as presented in the Folio. Macbeth would ask his first question ('what is that noise?') and get the answer ('it is the cry of women'). No one leaves the stage; Seyton remains by his side. After his ruminations about fears and horrors, Macbeth asks again:'Wherefore was that cry?' and Seyton responds: 'The Queen, my lord, is dead.' In this rendition, the audience cannot help seeing that Seyton (to be pronounced *Satan*?) has no normal (earthly?) way of knowing what he knows. But he *does* know. Macbeth may be too preoccupied to notice the anomaly, but, if staged this way, the spectator cannot help being jarred, to the extent that the anomaly would become a significant part of the context for the nihilistic comments that follow. A focus upon *how* Seyton knows of the death almost inevitably leads to the addition of stage business that provides a practical explanation for that 'how' and satisfies our sense of theatre or theatrical convention, but such insertions may mask a distinctive Jacobean effect linked to a contemporary sense of theatre, an effect that emphasizes the mystery behind that 'how' and strikes one as eerie, powerful, perhaps quite unnerving. After all, how do the witches know what *they* know?

To consider such examples is to take an important first step: the recognition that our sense of theatre (or 'horizon of expectations') represents but one set of possibilities. As a test case, one should bear in mind the many cinematic conventions to which we give unthinking consent. Although to a modern sensibility cinema may embody the epitome of realism, what is 'real' about sitting in a darkened auditorium, watching figures larger than life (especially in close-ups) projected on to a flat screen and seen through camera angles that often do not correspond to our normal viewing range, while listening to voices, not from the lips of the speakers, that boom around us in stereophonic sound accompanied by music from a full orchestra (and how many of us have thought through the implications for 'realism' of background music in cinema or television)? Similarly, a modern reader of Elizabethan plays often chuckles at the narrative shorthand provided by a choric figure like Time in *The Winter's Tale* or a stage direction like *Exit at one door and enter at another* (to indicate a quick change in time or locale), but at the cinema that same individual will have no difficulty in recognizing moving calendar pages as the passage of time, accepting necessary exposition from the headlines of newspapers, or inferring the whole of a journey from seeing a figure get on a plane in one airport and get off in another. Although the camera can provide more detail for the viewer of cinema or television than could be presented on the Elizabethan stage, nonetheless complex events (a long journey, the flight of an arrow) require a selectivity in presentation that enlists our conventional responses, for, in any medium, the exposition of essential information without some form of narrative shorthand can be very cumbersome.

Clearly, the stage conventions taken for granted by Shakespeare and his spectators were linked to the physical characteristics of the Elizabethan theatres, for (as suggested by references above to the assets of the camera) any set of presentational conventions is a function of what the medium can and cannot provide. Although the limited evidence precludes firm conclusions about theatrical architecture and configurations, some essential facts about the original theatres and playing conditions are clear. Thus, whether at the Theatre or the Globe or the Blackfriars, Shakespeare's plays were presented on a sizeable platform stage to an audience on three (perhaps four) sides. Unlike modern actors, Elizabethan players could not resort to variable lighting or elaborate sets; rather, whether a theatre was daylit or candlelit, the company had little or no control over the light for any individual scene, while the absence of any equivalent to the modern curtain meant that large properties like beds, scaffolds (for executions), and bars (for courtroom scenes) had to be carried or thrust on to the stage and then removed when no longer appropriate. A small percentage of the extant scenes may require a trap-door or a discovery space or an area above for Juliet's balcony or Antony's pulpit, but most plays throughout the period require only actors in costume delivering their lines on a large platform (roughly a thousand square feet at the Globe) without the support of variable lighting, large properties, sets, or any imaginary fourth wall.

As a result, many effects to which we have grown accustomed in cinema, television, and naturalistic theatre were impossible or impractical in the age of Shakespeare (as with the immersion in the Euphrates presented in *The Two Noble Ladies*). Yet few would disagree that some of the finest plays ever written were conceived for and originally performed in the Globe and Blackfriars. Clearly, Shakespeare and his fellow dramatists knew how to use their stage for maximum effect and shared with actors and spectators a sense of theatre suitable to that stage. A major key to that shared sense of theatre lies in the active role demanded from the audience. Thus, in the Prologue to *Henry V* Shakespeare's spokesman apologizes for the limits of 'this unworthy scaffold' in conveying 'so great an object' as Agincourt; still, the players can 'on your imaginary forces work' if the viewers are willing to 'suppose', to 'make imaginary puissance' by dividing one man into a thousand parts, to 'think, when we talk of horses, that you see them / Printing their proud hoofs i' th' receiving earth', in short, to 'piece out our imperfections with your thoughts'. Again, the Chorus to Act 3 pleads with the audience to 'suppose', 'behold', 'do but think', 'grapple your minds', 'work, work your thoughts, and therein see a siege', and, finally, 'still be kind, / And eke out our performance with your mind.' Before Agincourt, the Chorus to Act 4 apologizes in advance for disgracing this great event 'with four or five most vile and ragged foils, / Right ill-disposed in brawl ridiculous', but asks the audience: 'Yet sit and see, / Minding true things by what their mock'ries be.' Repeatedly Shakespeare asks his audience to accept a part for the whole, to supply imaginatively what cannot be introduced physically on to the open stage.

This expectation of the spectator's imaginative participation is an essential ingredient in the staging and stage conventions of the age of Shakespeare. Typical are the stage directions that call for figures to enter '*as from dinner*' (*A New Way to Pay Old Debts*), or '*as from Torments*' (*A Shoemaker, A Gentleman*), or '*as out of a cave's mouth*' (*Sophonisba*), or '*from tilting*' (*Pericles*), or '*from hunting*' (*Titus Andronicus, The Taming of the Shrew*). Sometimes, the dramatist provides additional details: Frankford enters '*as it were brushing the Crumbs from his clothes with a Napkin*' (*A Woman Killed With Kindness*); King Arthur appears '*with a spear in his rest, as from the tilt*' (*Tom a Lincoln*); hunting scenes are often keyed to the winding of horns, green costumes, and appropriate weapons. With or without such details, the '*as from*' stage direction represents an essential part of the strategy for using the Elizabethan open stage, a strategy that builds upon a few clear signals and the actor's skill to convey, deftly and economically, a recently completed or continuing action. What results is a theatrical shorthand for the spectator, an alternative to a full scene or more extensive narrative detail. Thus, although the opening scene of *The Tempest* is a notable exception, most of the many shipwrecks necessary to romance plots follow Heywood's practice in *The Captives* where a figure enters '*all wet as newly shipwrecked and escaped the fury of the seas*'. When necessary or appropriate, the dramatist could present a banquet or other elaborate event, but, more often, Shakespeare and his fellow dramatists sidestepped on-stage hunts, fires, shipwrecks, and public executions and instead, using the *as from* or *as to* technique, provided the spectator with a sense of the rich, busy, very 'real' world just off-stage.

As a corollary, absence of sets and fluidity of staging meant that the few details actually visible to an Elizabethan playgoer could carry considerable weight, so that a theatrical shorthand emerged linked to costume and portable properties. Such shorthand need not be impenetrable to the modern eye or even limited solely to productions in the age of Shakespeare (I have seen a modern dress production of *Timon of Athens* in which two of the false friends entered *as from tennis* and *as from swimming*). But some details commonplace then are not immediately meaningful today. For example, in Elizabethan playscripts female figures regularly appear with their hair dishevelled to indicate madness, rape, or extreme grief (as in *Richard III*, *Troilus and Cressida*, and *Hamlet*, Q1), so that disorder of the coiffure indicates a more significant disorder or violation. Similarly, to indicate a journey recently completed or about to be undertaken (or to connote haste) the dramatist would have a figure enter booted (see Falstaff's comments just before his rejection by Henry V). Particularly widespread is the appearance of male or female figures in nightgowns or other unready dress, whether to denote the time of day (night or early morning) or unreadiness (as with Brabantio in the opening scene of *Othello*) or a troubled state of mind (as with Henry IV for his famous speech in *2 Henry IV*, 3.1).

Without such shorthand, battle scenes (surely among the most difficult to realize effectively on any stage) would have been impossible at the Globe. As already noted, Shakespeare himself was conscious of the danger of lapsing into the 'brawl ridiculous' when presenting Agincourt through only 'four or five most vile and ragged foils'. Nonetheless, rather than avoiding battle scenes, Elizabethan theatrical professionals found practical solutions, with particular emphasis upon the part standing for the whole. Thus, in place of the sweep of battle possible in the cinema, the Elizabethan playwright provided small groups of combatants (in twos and fours) in 'excursions' on- and off-stage, with all this activity accompanied by elaborate sound effects ('alarums') that included trumpet calls, the clash of steel, and the firing of weapons. A stage direction, for example, from *Captain Thomas Stukeley* reads: '*Alarum is sounded, divers excurtions, Stukly persues, shane Oneale, and Neale Mackener, And after a good pretty fight his Lieftenannt and Auntient rescue Stuklie, and chace the Ireshe out. Then an excurtion berwixt Herbert and O Hanlon, and so a retreat sounded.*'[5] Through such theatrical synecdoche, the whole of a battle is to be imagined or inferred through the parts displayed, an approach to mass combat well suited to a large platform stage and limited personnel.

This principle, whereby a dramatist relies upon the spectator's imagination to transform a part into a whole, is basic to theatre of all ages but is particularly important for many Elizabethan scenes. An especially revealing example is provided by Heywood's presentation of the death of Nessus the centaur in Act 1 of *The Brazen Age*. Hercules, alone on stage, describes for the audience the centaur's progress across the river with Dejanira upon his back ('Well plunged bold Centaure') but then must rage impotently as he witnesses the attempted rape and hears his bride cry for help (four times). Finally, Hercules announces: 'I'le send till I can come, this poisonous shaft / Shall speake my fury and extract thy bloud, / Till I my selfe can crosse this raging floud.' The stage direction then reads: '*Hercules shoots, and goes in: Enter Nessus with an arrow through him, and Dejaneira.*' Moments later, 'after long strugling with *Euenus* streames', Hercules reappears 'to make an end of what my shaft begunne'.[6] To depict a figure on one side of a river shooting a figure on the other side, Heywood has resorted to alternating scenes, reported action, off-stage sounds, and, most important (in his version of what has become a stock cinematic effect), a presentation of the initiation and resolution of the central event ('*Hercules shoots . . . Enter Nessus with an arrow through him*') rather than the full sequence (the flight of the arrow and the striking of its target). Like the spectators awaiting the battle of Agincourt in *Henry V*, Heywood's audience is then expected to use its 'imaginary forces' to 'eke out our performance with your mind' – in this case, to supply the off-stage river and, most important, the link between the shooting of the arrow and the entrance of a figure with an arrow through him.

Of the many scenes that build upon this combination of the spectator's imagination and available stage conventions, some of the most provocative for the modern reader are linked to night and locale. Scenes that take place in the dark demonstrate the gap which exists between presentation then and now. Again, 'going to the theatre' today (with the exception of outdoor matinees) means sitting in a darkened auditorium watching actors perform in a lighted space. In striking contrast, Shakespeare and his fellow dramatists wrote their plays for an auditorium in which (presumably) viewers could see each other as clearly as they could see the events on-stage. The Elizabethan actors then presented their plays in light (whether natural, as at the Globe, or artificial, as at the Blackfriars) that essentially remained constant during the course of a performance, changing only when the sun moved behind a cloud or descended lower in the sky or when torches were carried on-stage. Indeed, given the presence of such torches, night scenes (from the point of view of the spectator) may actually have been brighter than day scenes.

Although Shakespeare could not draw upon variable lighting as a tool, nonetheless night and darkness play an important part in many of his plays – for plot, imagery, and general atmosphere. How then did the players distinguish between stage 'light' and stage 'darkness'? The first and most obvious tool is dialogue, for characters often tell us or each other about night or darkness (as in Hamlet's ' 'Tis now the very witching time of night' – 3.2.373); as with many other kinds of relevant information (e.g., about locale and time), the words spoken by the actors serve as the primary vehicles for signalling stage light and darkness. To enhance the spoken words, however, dramatists could also call upon various stage conventions. Most familiar is the introduction of torches or other lights to establish the existence of on-stage darkness (as in the final scene of *Romeo and Juliet* where both Paris and Romeo enter with torches). Less familiar but also quite common is the use of costume, especially the nightgown, to denote night or interrupted sleep. Throughout the period both *Enter with torches* (or candles or lanterns) and *Enter in a nightgown* are widespread; for example, *Alphonsus Emperor of Germany* begins: '*Enter Alphonsus the Emperor in his night-gown, and his shirt, and a torch in his hand.*'

In addition to torches and nightgowns, the actors could draw upon the imagination of the audience and 'play' night. In 2 *The Iron Age*, for example, Heywood directs the Greeks inside the Trojan horse to '*leap from out the Horse. And as if groping in the dark, meet with Agamemnon and the rest.*' Like the *as from* stage directions, such *as if* behaviour is basic to this and other conventions on the open stage. Similarly, if a torch or candle was cited as the only source of light in a given scene, to extinguish that light was to indicate stage darkness, an effect readily enforced through dialogue and 'as if' acting (and especially appropriate for comic confusion and mistaken identity, as in Fletcher's *The Maid in the Mill*). Often the spectator knows it is night because he or she sees something not visible to on-stage figures, as in Haughton's *An Englishman for My Money* where, throughout a long comic night sequence, a figure is suspended in a basket hanging between the stage floor and the 'above', a striking stage picture that remains in full view of the audience for some time but is not noted by a host of characters who come and go during the scene. In both Fletcher's *Women Pleased* and Massinger's *The Guardian* a jealous husband in the dark wounds what he thinks is his wife but is actually her servant, only to be confounded when he returns with a light to find his wife untouched.

We might sum up as follows the significant differences between the presentation of night and darkness now and then. To convey 'night' today, a director uses lighting to establish stage darkness and then has the actors enter carrying torches or groping in the dark or unable to see something of importance; we therefore *start* with a verisimilar stage night as a justification for confusion in the dark. But an Elizabethan dramatic company would have used dialogue, torches, nightgowns, groping in the dark, and failures in 'seeing' – all presented in full light – to establish the illusion of darkness for a spectator who, presumably, would infer night from such signals and stage behaviour. For us, the lighting technician supplies night and the actors perform accordingly; for them, the actors provided the signals and the audience cooperated in supplying the darkness. For us, one figure fails to see another *because* the stage is dark; for them, one figure failed to see another *therefore* the stage was *assumed* to be dark. Our theatrical sense of cause-and-effect (the stage is dark, therefore a given action took place) may then be misleading. Rather, at the Globe or Blackfriars a greater burden lay upon the dramatist, the actor, *and* the spectator to sustain the illusion of night and darkness through imaginative participation. Again, it is worth remembering the injunctions from *Henry V*: 'let us . . . / On your imaginary forces work'; 'piece out our imperfections with your thoughts'; 'eke out our performance with your mind'.

Another revealing difference between then and now can be seen in the presentation of 'place' or locale. Thanks to a tradition of editing and typography that dates back to the eighteenth century, readers of Shakespeare's plays have come to expect a 'place' to be attached to most scenes ('a wood near Athens', 'a room in the castle'). But what exactly does 'another part of the forest' (to cite a notorious example) mean when linked to a production designed for a large open platform where the 'forest' is largely if not totally the product of the 'imaginary forces' of the spectator? As Bernard Beckerman has demonstrated, scenes at the Globe could be localized (in a specific place) or unlocalized (with no indication whatsoever) or generally localized (about sixty per cent) wherein the stage represents 'a place at large' (e.g., Rome or Troy) 'but not a particular section of it'. According to Beckerman, Shakespeare's stage 'was constructed and employed to tell a story as vigorously and excitingly and as intensely as possible', with the spectators informed about the locale 'by the words they heard, not the sights they saw', so that 'place was given specific emphasis only when and to the degree the narrative required'.[7] To the original audience, 'place' was an adjunct of the narrative, not an end in itself.

At times, Shakespeare's handling of locale may seem cavalier to the precise modern reader. Perhaps most perplexing is the final scene of *Coriolanus* which, at the outset, appears to be set in Antium (the native town of Aufidius and the locale cited by Plutarch) but at the climax clearly shifts to Corioli (so as to set up a parallel to the triumph in Act 1 in that city that won Caius Marcius his name). Apparently, in this instance such links or analogues mattered more to Shakespeare than any rigid consistency. Elsewhere, the locale could shift without figures even leaving the stage, most notably in *Romeo and Juliet* where Romeo and the masquers '*march about the stage*' rather than exiting (thereby signalling a change in locale), while '*Servingmen come forth with napkins*' (thereby establishing the new locale as the Capulet house); then, after some dialogue among the servants, '*Enter all the Guests and Gentlewomen to the Maskers*' (1.5.15.s.d.). Our expectation of a 'change in scene' or an exeunt–re-entry to denote a change in locale is here superseded by another principle, perhaps best described as dramatic economy. Similarly, in the final movement of *Henry VIII*, after Cranmer has been forced to wait 'at the door', an elaborate stage direction calls for the entrance of six figures along with a council table, chairs, and stools; when Cranmer receives permission to enter, he then '*approaches the council table*' (5.3.7.s.d.). As with Romeo and the masquers, a new 'place' comes to a figure already on-stage, or, in different terms, the door that separates Cranmer from the council has changed from a stage door (for an off-stage council) to the stage space between the waiting figure and the seated lords at the table. Again, a Jacobean sense of continuity or dramatic economy or theatrical 'space' has superseded later strictures about outside–inside or the cleared stage.

At times, however, Shakespeare and his contemporaries *were* concerned with placing their action, for stage directions do call for figures to enter '*in prison*', or '*in a tavern*', or '*in the woods*', or '*in his study*', or '*a-shipboard*' (*Pericles*). How such signals were translated into actions and properties, however, is often not clear. Thus, at least some of these stage directions should be understood to be *as in* or *as if in*. For example, in *Greene's Tu Quoque* a figure enters '*as in his study reading*'; in *Coriolanus* two officers '*lay cushions, as it were in the Capitol*' (2.2.o.s.d.). Here the 'study' or 'the Capitol' is conveyed not by furniture or our sense of a set but by a figure reading a book or officers laying down cushions, just as a beach could be conveyed by figures with digging tools (*The Two Maids of More-Clacke*) and a shop or interior by women sewing (*The Shoemaker's Holiday, Coriolanus*). Elsewhere, the actors may have introduced portable properties to convey deftly a sense of locale: a grate for a prison; a tree for a forest; a sign or bush for a tavern; ropes thrown down for a ship. However, except for the bar to set up a courtroom, surprisingly little evidence survives to document such shorthand through emblematic properties. Again, what may seem quite logical to us (to use bars or a grate to denote a prison) need not have been part of the shared assumptions in the age of Shakespeare.

In contrast, considerable evidence points to the keying of locale to the presence of representative figures whose costumes or accessories provided the major signals for the spectator. Thus, sea scenes regularly call for a captain or some other recognizable nautical figure; pastoral or forest scenes provide shepherds, foresters, or huntsmen (with *As You Like It* an excellent example); courtroom scenes are linked to judges and other legal personnel in their distinctive costumes; the famous garden scene in *Richard II* is keyed to the presence of the gardeners, not to any discernible stage properties. Some tavern scenes do require stage furniture (such as the tables and chairs needed for *1 Henry IV*, 2.4), but most need no more than the presence of a host, vintner, or drawer in a recognizable costume along with hand-held bottles and glasses, just as the occasional inn scene needs only a host or innkeeper. The most widely invoked locale, the prison, could be presented in a variety of ways, including a trap-door for a dungeon below (as in *Believe as You List* and *The Island Princess*) or fetters on the incarcerated figure (as in *Cymbeline* and *A Woman Killed With Kindness*), but the one common denominator for a substantial number of scenes is the presence (along with one or more prisoners) of a jailer, keeper, or Lieutenant of the Tower who is often identified by a distinctive set of keys.[8]

For many readers, the presence of a jailer, captain, shepherds, or drawer will not satisfy a modern sense of locale, any more than torches, nightgowns, and 'as if' behaviour will convey forcefully a sense of darkness. Yet an audience attuned to the open stage, where objects not portable or part of the costumes could pose awkward problems, would have been especially alert to any distinctive detail or item of dress and would have made certain inferences (perhaps unconsciously) not always evident to us. The fetters, sheephooks, nightgowns, and boots presented to that audience could serve merely as narrative shorthand for the exposition of locale, time, or atmosphere or, when used by a dramatist like Shakespeare, could generate complex and meaningful moments. For example, if the 'convent' associated with the order of St Clare in *Measure for Measure* is conveyed solely through the costumes of the novice Isabella and '*Francisca, a nun*' (1.4.0.s.d.), then as Isabella moves through the play she metaphorically carries that convent (and its particular strictness) with her. Her costume (and any significant alterations in it) can therefore become quite meaningful, whether to demonstrate her continuing rigidity or to act out some important change (e.g., in the final scene when she kneels at Mariana's request or when she responds to the Duke's offer of marriage). The convent as a 'place' (quickly left behind) is far less important to the play as a whole than the habit of mind of the central figure who had chosen it. If both 'place' and choice are epitomized by the same costume, metaphorically the convent has been projected into the streets of Vienna, the halls of justice, and the prison, in a fashion easily obscured when we ask the wrong questions about verisimilitude or locale in the original scene.

To screen out the original stage conventions is to run the risk then of eliminating or blurring some distinctive Shakespearian metaphors and effects. Again, scenes involving on-stage darkness provide the most instructive examples. Thus, in *Macbeth* the murder of Banquo (3.3) is often presented today in such a deep theatrical darkness that a spectator cannot make out what is happening, but in a Jacobean production the audience would have 'imagined' the darkness yet seen the action quite clearly. The scene, moreover, enacts both a murder and an escape, both of which are associated with the putting out of a light: 'who did strike out the light?' asks the Third Murderer; 'was't not the way?' replies the First. The original spectator would therefore have recognized that the three Murderers end the scene with the body of Banquo in a conventional darkness (as signalled by the putting out of an on-stage light), but that spectator would also have seen clearly their frustration and failure ('We have lost best half of our affair') represented by their inability to extinguish the light that is Fleance. The killing of Banquo and the putting out of the light help to epitomize what the Macbeths, the creatures of night and darkness, are doing to Scotland (and to themselves), but a modern director's imposition of a verisimilar stage night upon the scene may over-simplify the situation by calling attention away from a significant failure on the part of the forces of darkness. Modern productions often realize the rich darkness of the murder at the expense of the glimpse of light in a visible escape.

Modern stage darkness can blur other metaphoric effects. For example, playgoers familiar with modern productions of *A Midsummer Night's Dream* expect to see the comic confusion of Acts 2 and 3 acted out in 'moonlit' woods, but, in the original production, all of the play's scenes, whether in Athens or the woods, night or morning, were played in the same light. One result of invoking the original conventions is a greater emphasis upon failures in 'seeing' linked not only to poor visibility (or even to the love-juice itself) but to the transforming power of love or the imagination, a motif orchestrated throughout the play (as in Helena's speech in 1.1.232–5 or Bottom's shrewd observation that 'reason and love keep little company together nowadays' – 3.1.130–1). With no verisimilar stage darkness, many of the comic events may seem more clearly linked to such speeches. In particular, the climactic confusion involving Demetrius and Lysander, in which each takes Puck for his intended opponent and is therefore led astray, becomes less a consequence of dim light (this scene is often played in a stage mist or gloom) or even of Puck's magical control than an acting out in one highly theatrical moment of the brand of myopia or blindness ever present in this part of the comedy. The implicit suggestion in many modern productions that physical darkness causes these and other errors may blur some shrewd comic insights into the nature of love and lovers.

Even more revealing is Shakespeare's presentation of such metaphoric not-seeing 'in the dark' in the observation scene of *Troilus and Cressida* (5.2). At the outset, Ulysses and Troilus 'stand where the torch may not discover us' in order to watch Cressida and Diomedes and in turn be watched by Thersites. Here the modern reader or spectator takes for granted an on-stage darkness that helps us to believe that the figures being observed (especially Cressida and Troilus) remain unaware of the observers; so, according to our conventions, Cressida and Diomedes would be in the light and Ulysses, Troilus, and Thersites in shadow or darkness. But if the scene is played in full stage light and 'imaginary darkness', greater emphasis falls upon the inability or unwillingness of the key figures to see or understand each other. Thus, in her farewell to a Troilus she imagines far away, Cressida comments: 'One eye yet looks on thee, / But with my heart the other eye doth see', and adds: 'Ah, poor our sex! This fault in us I find, / The error of our eye directs our mind.' These lines could be especially telling if she were looking at or in the direction of a Troilus she cannot (or can no longer) 'see'. Moments later, after Troilus has tried to convince Ulysses and himself that 'this is not Cressid', Thersites asks: 'Will 'a swagger himself out on's own eyes?' thus emphasizing the disillusioned lover's attempt to block out what has actually been seen. A staging of this scene in full light would not only make more visible the actors' expressions and gestures but would also heighten various lapses in 'seeing' in both psychological and metaphoric terms.

To sum up the interpretative potential in the original conventions, let us focus upon two anomalous moments. First, at the end of *King Lear*, 2.2, Kent is left alone in the stocks, Edgar enters for a speech of twenty-one lines, and, after his departure, Lear and his group arrive to find Kent. Few modern interpreters have been comfortable with this sequence. As a result, critics have mused about 'where' Edgar is to be 'placed'; until quite recently, editors have provided a heading such as 'the open country' or 'a wood' for Edgar's speech (traditionally designated as 2.3 even though no scene divisions are indicated in Q1 or the Folio); directors usually use lighting to black out Kent and highlight Edgar during his speech. To the modern reader or spectator, the presence of the stocks and the recently completed action involving Oswald, Edmund, Cornwall, and others implies one 'place' (e.g., the courtyard of a castle) that proves incompatible with a fleeing Edgar (especially given a lapse of time and the pursuit through open country implied in an escape by means of 'the happy hollow of a tree'). Obviously, most critics, editors, and directors would prefer not to have Kent and Edgar visible at the same time.

But what about the original production at the Globe where the King's Men had no way to black out Kent? On the unencumbered Globe stage with few distractions for the eye, such a juxtaposition of these two distinctive figures would produce a highly emphatic effect that would strongly enforce any interpretation based upon links between Kent and Edgar, a form of theatrical *italics* that could not be missed by an attentive viewer. The original audience would not have been troubled by the imaginary darkness in which Edgar failed to see Kent; indeed, Edgar's stage behaviour in itself could have been a major signal for stage night. Given their conditioning, that audience would not have been concerned with 'place' unless the question had been called to their attention. The stocks would then signal not a courtyard or other specific locale but rather a general sense of imprisonment or bondage (or the perversion of an instrument of justice, as developed more fully, again with Cornwall and Regan, when Gloucester is bound to a chair in 3.7), just as Edgar would be assumed to be in flight, anywhere. The chameleon-like flexibility of the open stage here makes possible a juxtaposition rich with potential meanings, an effect much diminished, however, in modern editions and productions.

Duke Senior's banquet in *As You Like It* poses similar problems for the modern interpreter. According to the dialogue, the banquet is set up on-stage in 2.5 (see lines 26–7, 55–6) and then enjoyed in 2.7 with no indication that it is removed for the brief 2.6 (the first appearance of Orlando and Adam in Arden). In his New Variorum edition, Richard Knowles finds the introduction of the banquet in 2.5 'totally unnecessary, for the banquet could have been carried on, as banquets usually were, at the beginning of scene 7' (p. 109). Directors too must wrestle with this apparent anomaly. Thus, in his 1977–8 production at Stratford Festival Canada, Robin Phillips rearranged the scenes into the sequence 2.6–2.5–2.7, while, in his 1980–1 production for the Royal Shakespeare Company, Terry Hands cut the relevant lines in 2.5 so that the banquet first appeared in 2.7.

As most editors and critics would agree, Shakespeare did not *have* to introduce a banquet into 2.5. Yet he *did*. Despite the prevailing post-Elizabethan assumptions about locale, scene divisions, and the cleared stage, can we not consider the *advantages* of having a 'banquet' in full view of the audience during the speeches that constitute 2.6? In particular, we should bear in mind how the presence of such food would affect our reaction to Adam's 'O, I die for food' and Orlando's subsequent 'if' clauses: 'If this uncouth forest yield anything savage, I will either be food for it or bring it for food to thee . . . I will here be with thee presently, and if I bring thee not something to eat, I will give thee leave to die; but if thou diest before I come, thou art a mocker of my labour . . . thou shalt not die for lack of a dinner if there live anything in this desert.' If the food Orlando will find in 2.7 is seen by the audience during 2.6 (present but symbolically just out of reach), these 'if' clauses carry a different weight (e.g., compared to analogous speeches during the storm scenes in *King Lear*). To clear the stage in order to satisfy our sense of 'place' or scenic division is to simplify the original scene and to run the risk of eliminating a rich and potentially meaningful effect, a good insight into the nature of Arden (or perhaps romantic comedy), especially since the 'if' clauses of 2.6 are recapitulated and intensified in 2.7 (see lines 113–26) and then developed at length by Rosalind in 5.2 and 5.4. Much virtue in if. And much virtue in the flexible Elizabethan stage and stage conventions.

Throughout this chapter, I have chosen to emphasize those stage conventions that, at least initially, may perplex the modern reader as opposed to those more readily accessible such as the soliloquy and the aside. By introducing various problems and anomalies, I have sought to call attention to the terms upon which the original dramatists, actors, and spectators agreed to meet, especially when those terms differ in some significant way from our own often unstated (and vaguely formulated) sense of theatre. To recognize the original conventions is often to recover distinctive Shakespearian metaphors and meanings and to expand our awareness of the full range of his best plays. In contrast, to impose our conventions or sense of theatre upon Elizabethan drama is to transform the scenes, to delete Shakespeare's italics, to deny the choric pleas of *Henry V*, and, like the hempen homespuns in *A Midsummer Night's Dream*, to supply our version of Moonshine and Wall.

Notes

1. Raymond Williams, *Drama from Ibsen to Brecht* (1968), p. 13.
2. 'The Elizabethan printer and dramatic manuscripts', *The Library*, 4th series, 12 (1931), 253–75, p. 266.

3. Ed. Rebecca G. Rhoads for the Malone Society (Oxford, 1930), lines 1150–71.
4. Citations from Shakespeare are from *The Complete Pelican Shakespeare*, gen. ed. Alfred Harbage (Baltimore, 1969), one of the modern editions I have found most reliable in its handling of the original theatrical signals.
5. Ed. Judith C. Levinson for the Malone Society (Oxford, 1975), lines 1170–5.
6. *The Dramatic Works of Thomas Heywood*, 6 vols. (1874), III, 180–2.
7. *Shakespeare at the Globe 1599–1609* (New York, 1962), pp. 66, 108.
8. For more detailed discussion and full documentation of this and other points set forth in this chapter, see Alan C. Dessen, *Elizabethan Stage Conventions and Modern Interpreters* (Cambridge, 1984).

Reading list

Beckerman, Bernard, *Shakespeare at the Globe 1599–1609* (New York, 1962)
Bentley, Gerald Eades, *Shakespeare and His Theatre* (Lincoln, Nebraska, 1964)
Bethell, S. L., *Shakespeare and the Popular Dramatic Tradition* (1944)
Bradbrook, M. C., *Themes and Conventions of Elizabethan Tragedy* (Cambridge, 1935)
Coghill, Nevill, *Shakespeare's Professional Skills* (Cambridge, 1964)
Dessen, Alan C., *Elizabethan Stage Conventions and Modern Interpreters* (Cambridge, 1984)
Doran, Madeleine, *Endeavors of Art* (Madison, 1954)
Graves, R. B., 'Elizabethan lighting effects and the conventions of indoor and outdoor theatrical illumination', *Renaissance Drama*, new series 12 (1981), 51–69
Gurr, Andrew, *The Shakespearean Stage 1574–1642* (Cambridge, 1970)
Harbage, Alfred, *Theatre for Shakespeare* (Toronto, 1955)
Hattaway, Michael, *Elizabethan Popular Theatre* (1982)
Hellenga, Robert R., 'Elizabethan dramatic conventions and Elizabethan reality', *Renaissance Drama*, new series 12 (1981), 27–49
Hunter, G. K., 'Flatcaps and Bluecoats: visual signals on the Elizabethan stage', *Essays and Studies* 33 (1980), 16–47
Reynolds, G. F., *The Staging of Elizabethan Plays at the Red Bull Theater 1604–1625* (New York, 1940)
Slater, Ann Pasternak, *Shakespeare the Director* (Brighton, 1982)
Styan, J. L., *Shakespeare's Stagecraft* (Cambridge, 1967)

7   Shakespeare and the traditions of comedy

SHAKESPEARE took the traditions of comedy and transformed them. Not all of them: the more urban comedy of manners from classical New Comedy, which Ben Jonson used so strikingly and which emerged again after the Restoration, he never made his chief interest. But the tradition of English romantic comedy coming to him from Lyly and Peele and others, with its roots in medieval literature and even older folklore, this he grasped and transmuted. Shakespeare's voice is as distinctive as Mozart's. He was in the current of Italian traditions, and could make brilliant adaptation of New Comedy in Plautus; but the result is always an unmistakably Shakespearian harmony.

His forebears made a distinction between laughter and comedy. Comedy in the Middle Ages meant what Aristotle meant: that is, what is not tragedy, anything which ends happily. Thus Dante's most uncomic poem of Hell, Purgatory, and Heaven is called *La Divina Commedia*; the religious play-cycles from York and elsewhere were comedies in that they told of Christ's victory, and so were the morality plays like *Everyman* which showed the triumph of spiritual salvation. Mrs Noah refusing to go into the ark, however, and Mak caught sheep-stealing, were comic: they caused laughter, and were something different, belonging to the tradition of Chaucer's *Miller's Tale* rather than *The Clerk's Tale*.

Surviving fragments suggest other traditions of dramatic comedy in England in the late Middle Ages, even closer to folk experience, though connected with the morality figures of the Vice, or the Seven Deadly Sins, and curiously ignoring the European farces of sexual intrigue. The broad English tradition, it seems, was content with splashes of comic effect.

The early Tudor interludes of Heywood, though closer to the French, suffer from weakness of form. Tautness of construction, and much else, came into English comedy from the classical world, in the Tudor enthusiasm for New Comedy. This term is used properly to differentiate the Greek playwright Menander, who used stock figures to make social points, from Aristophanes's more ritual Old Comedy: but it more commonly refers to the two Roman imitators of Menander, Plautus and Terence, of the second century B.C. Revolutionary sixteenth-century schoolmasters in England, ultimately following Erasmus, saw that study of such comedies in the

schoolroom not only gave the chance to learn Latin as spoken on the streets of
Rome, and elements of shape and form, but were also something health-
giving. Comedies like this could show ordinary people their follies and vices
and influence good behaviour, and were thus a moral force.

The history of literary criticism is also the history of attempts to make an
honest creature, as it were, of comedy. Even in its courtliest forms it is
apparently out of all scale with the great heights tragedy can reach. The
fourth-century grammarian Donatus worked from Terence to produce a
formula for comic plots, and though he was much rehandled in the Renaissance, theory of comedy remained thin until after Shakespeare's day. What
little Elizabethan theorizing there is works over the same ground: comedy
teaches good behaviour. Even Sidney hardly gets further than Plato in saying
that we must attend to 'the odd as well as the even'. (That the 'odd' might be
seductive was seized by theatre's enemies, of course.) Comedy was, however,
understood to move to a harmony – 'At last, though long, our jarring notes
agree' – and improve the body – 'mirth and merriment, / Which bars a
thousand harms and lengthens life' – and at the end even more satisfaction
should follow – 'Nothing but sit and sit, and eat and eat!' (*The Taming of the
Shrew* 5.2.1, Induction 2. 132–3, 5.2.12.) Some of that satisfaction came from
the very words themselves, and such critical theorizing as there is in the 1590s
expresses pride that the English poets had purified the language, and new
confidence in the value of a national language.

Shakespeare's immediate influences were learned. He knew well enough
the vernacular comic traditions. But *Ralph Roister Doister* (1552), sometimes
called the first English comedy, with its rocking metre, heavy rhyming and
broad comic effects, was written by the headmaster of Eton; and the low-life
Gammer Gurton's Needle (1553) for Christ's College Cambridge by a Fellow,
and possibly revised by a Bishop of Oxford – facts that might prevent us
getting too taken up with theories about the emergence of unstoppable forces
of popular culture. The biggest influence on Shakespeare's time comes from
university men. John Lyly, grandson of the colleague of Erasmus and More,
an Oxford man in two senses whose courtly games in *Euphues: The Anatomy of
Wit* (1578) were hungrily copied, wrote for the Earl of Oxford's boys, who
played at court and for coterie audiences: learned plays for knowledgeable
hearers, performed by schoolboys: emotion in them is distanced, cool,
described rather than experienced. Lyly and his contemporary George Peele
(author of *The Old Wife's Tale*) avoid strong feeling. They are adept at
patterning subtly different and exquisitely suggested possibilities of love –
usually – in courtly terms. Lyly aimed at 'soft smiling, not loud laughing', even
with his lower characters. All the university wits – and with Lyly and Peele we
include Thomas Nashe, Robert Greene, Thomas Lodge and Christopher
Marlowe – gave to the drama a multifaceted artefact, full of shifting modes

and plots, references and illusions and spectacle, and a language for the stage that was a shower of gold indeed. The flowering of these playwrights was all over some few years after the Armada in 1588; their importance for the tradition of English comedy was great. They transmitted the wide band of comedy from the most hoary folk rituals like the maypole dances to the most courtly masquing, to audiences equally mixed. Elsewhere in Europe, court and commons kept apart. The Italian court comedy, and the vulgar *commedia dell'arte*, never combined. *Commedia* figures, as we shall see, appear in the King of Navarre's court in Shakespeare's *Love's Labour's Lost*, and in that confluence Shakespeare was true to his Englishness. The university wits could not have done this without the new formation of professional companies and permanent theatres: without these, the line from *Gammer Gurton's Needle* would have petered out. In the thirty years before Shakespeare began, about thirty-five comedies are known to have been written (half are lost); tragedy was the more solid form. As Shakespeare reached his finest form, so the stream of theatre in London, flowing for many decades, swelled. Private performances and half a dozen big public playhouses meant a large ready audience. Over the two decades of his writing life from 1590, more than two hundred comedies were written (a quarter are lost), and comedy took over largely from tragedy.

But though London was unusual for its mixed theatre, and properly famous, the growth was European. Early Tudor plays were often translations (*Everyman* from Dutch, comic interludes from French). Shakespeare in London could not help but have interests as wide as Europe, and Italian exuberance in particular spills all over his plays. He was infected by the high Italian spirits which cheerfully mixed the genres themselves. His two Italian tragedies, *Romeo and Juliet* and *Othello*, can both be seen as domestic comedies gone horribly wrong. Such mixing we have already seen in the comedies of the university wits, and it is visible in English poets like Spenser and Marvell. But Italy gave drama greater licence still, and at the same time allowed Shakespeare to connect to an exotic landscape of places, people, and fresh manners. He set comedies in Verona, Padua, Venice, Messina, Illyria, Florence, Rome, and Sicily – and if I can get away with Illyria and Sicily as Italian, then I add that Prospero's island is said to be between Naples and Carthage. Two comedies have Italian towns in the title. Sixteenth-century Italian comedy is rich in social and sexual intrigue, and is firmly city-based. Young men fall in love, with more than one eye on inherited wealth – 'Hath Leonato any son, my lord?' is Claudio's opening shot in his serious wooing of Hero, Leonato's daughter (*Much Ado About Nothing* 1.1.256). Rank helps greatly – Claudio at first gets the grandee, Don Pedro, Prince of Arragon, to woo for him. Silvia, the object of two gentlemen of Verona, is daughter of the Duke of Milan, as is Miranda in *The Tempest*. Business skills and possessions are important. There is often talk of merchant venturing which can shade in ethical terms into deceit, and malice from a self-seeking villain.

'Shakespeare's tragedy', wrote Samuel Johnson, 'seems to be skill, his comedy to be instinct'. His particular genius can be as much seen in what he did not do, as in what he did. He left to Ben Jonson and others the extension of New Comedy into a London comedy of corrupt manners and the relentless pressure of commodities, whether money or sex. Though critics since the Victorians have been quick to see satire, Shakespeare's interests are less centripetal, as it were, than will make the sharpest satire. His reach is always outward, to the larger dimension, to what Johnson called 'the genuine progeny of common humanity'. Shakespeare can bring London to life with the vividness of Dickens when he wants to: in the *Henry IV* plays it is present in full colour. But his only true citizen comedy is set in a small country town, Windsor, with the climax in the Great Park. His only true city plays are about other things (*Measure for Measure, Coriolanus*).

Comedy, or the comic, is everywhere in Shakespeare; even, momentarily, in *Macbeth*, and *King Lear* has its fool. The history plays, those without Falstaff, have passages in the traditions of comedy: a production of *King John* which goes for humour does not distort the text overmuch; and *Richard III* is famously played to laughter. In the world of comedy, where instincts and social imperatives come together, Shakespeare has a place, with his fools and juxtapositions, in the humanist alternative tradition of Folly itself, running from Erasmus and More to Gulliver and *The Dunciad* and *Tristram Shandy*. But in his riches of music and dance and song, in the calling up of enchanted places, in his catching of a person to the life in half a line, in the steady forward movement to an ending which, like 'the whole tract of a comedy', as Sidney had hoped, 'should be full of delight', he is outstanding in an English tradition of comedy which runs from Chaucer, through Restoration comedy, Fielding and Jane Austen and Dickens, to Wilde and Shaw.

The special Shakespearian music sings of two things especially: a remarkable widening of the understanding of humanity, and an even more extraordinary deepening of the understanding of love, and how that leads to, and matures in, marriage.

Three comedies have reasonable claims to be Shakespeare's first: *The Two Gentlemen of Verona*, *The Taming of the Shrew*, and *The Comedy of Errors*, written just before or just after 1590. All have suffered from a curious circularity of thought which says that such plays are bad because they are early, and we know that they are early because they are bad. Yet two of the three have recently come forward strongly. Only *The Two Gentlemen of Verona* still keeps audiences away. It has quite jagged problems, such as uncertainty about where it is set, a mass of internal contradictions, plot-ends so loose as to be alarming, and above all the absurdity of the last 118 lines, containing a succession of emotional nonsenses from the two heroes. One hero suddenly threatens to rape his friend's girl: his friend, after acknowledging a perfunctory apology, then apparently gives the girl to the would-be rapist. 'One's impulse,' Quiller-Couch wrote, 'is to remark that there are, by this time, *no* gentlemen in Verona.'[1] The further perfunctory tying-up feels something of a mockery. Even so, if this play were anonymous it would be an acceptable Elizabethan comedy on the Lylian model: courtly, amorous, verbally self-conscious, its subject the difficult clash of love and friendship, with journeys and forests and outlaws, letters and disguises and angry aristocratic fathers, all the full convention of Renaissance romance. Shakespeare has learned well from Lyly. He works on the small emotional scale of four very young people, freshly in love, and avoids the intensity of presented relationships. The play is famous for tending to avoid anything more complex than a duologue, but frequently the courtship is not even that, being a statement of feeling, rather than the feeling demonstrated. With its separable units it seems designed for performance in the corner of a room, possibly by children, with adults for the Duke and the clowns (the outlaws as juveniles, a schoolboy gang, make a lot of sense). Such separation marks off Launce, the first of Shakespeare's commentating clowns whose monologues are in thematic and structural relation to the main plot, and even take some of the feeling. The Shakespearian integration of low-life and high-life characters, indeed, is far beyond Lyly, as is the striking sense of a complex world of activity just behind the stage, as it were, conveyed through imagery. Most Shakespearian is the interest in the girls: Julia is well drawn; and the heart of the play, rather than a debate about love or friendship, is a living 'she'. Her disguise becomes something more than convention derived from Lyly and the boys' companies, as one finely built scene (4.2) shows in its gamut of feeling lightly touched – Julia's responses are especially wide-ranging. This play is richer in true feeling, indeed, than is sometimes noticed. Not only is the courtesy literature brought to life, but vistas open which change the whole sense of the landscape, like Proteus'

> For Orpheus' lute was strung with poets' sinews,
> Whose golden touch could soften steel and stones,
> Make tigers tame, and huge leviathans
> Forsake unsounded deeps to dance on sands.   (3.2.78–81)

The Taming of the Shrew is like *The Two Gentlemen of Verona* inside-out. Julia, single-minded, is faithful and resourceful in loving her Proteus, however off-putting his behaviour; so the adventurer Petruchio is determined to woo the 'shrewd ill-favour'd wife' however peculiarly she carries on. Moreover, the couple marry halfway through the play, and that central relationship has great intensity to the end. Again in contrast to *The Two Gentlemen of Verona*, *The Taming of the Shrew* has been almost too popular. A two-hundred-year-old

tradition, begun with gross re-writings, has seemed to make the play an
invitation to male brutality. That is not as visible in Shakespeare's text as many
suppose. Conflict in a marriage, with a termagant wife, has a long ancestry in
folk, medieval, and classical comedy. Shakespeare as usual does something
else. A necessarily unhappy glance at the supposed analogues is enough to
show that Katharina doesn't belong in the 'shrew' tradition at all. She is
softened and given identity. Moreover, she obviously 'wins', though in a much
more fulfilled sense than any of her predecessors would ken. In another world
from such wifely submission as is wanted in the Christopher Sly scenes, the
play shows a possibility of marriage as a rich, shared, sanity. Achieving that
involves achieving a harmony of selfhood, and Petruchio, an actor himself,
recognizes Katharina's capacity to find herself in acting – the whole play is
alive with interest in theatre. The end of *The Taming of the Shrew*, with its
revelation of everyone's true nature and a fine bravura piece, is as satisfying
as that of *The Two Gentlemen of Verona* is not. Though some critics have
found difficulty with Katharina's big speech to the company, it is not hard
to see it also as her private demonstration to her husband that she under-
stands, and delights in, their future together in a highly energized world of
acting.

Her story, with Petruchio's – and they are always together after their first
meeting – is set, with some brilliance, into another story, one of theatrical
dressing-up and obvious pretences by the suitors of her sweet sister, who
attracts Ovidian richness of language. And that is illusion: at the end Bianca
shows herself petty, even shrewish. In a cunningly spun double plot (itself
introduced by another, in the Sly scenes) Shakespeare's very searching eye on
all these people, and their true natures, should remove from the play such
labels as 'farce' or 'prentice-work', and instead announce a new kind of
Elizabethan comedy, called Shakespearian.

Already visible is Shakespeare's strong comic drive. Change comes through
great energy. Kate's loss of her false identity, and recovery of a true self,
changes her and everyone around her: at her last entry, her father is
astonished. What has happened to her has been more than a temporary
holiday: the final harmony is a new balance of released forces.

Such passions and bewilderments are very much the material of *The Comedy
of Errors*. Here Shakespeare's solution of technical problems, and the skill of
the construction, surpass even *The Taming of the Shrew*. At 1800 lines
Shakespeare's shortest play, it had an early performance as part of the revels at
Gray's Inn in December 1594, and it still has the feel of having been written to
catch the alert minds of a specialist young audience. *The Comedy of Errors*
maintains a classical unity of place – in a harbour town economically
sketched in – and of time, like that other sea play, *The Tempest*, with
which it has affinities: the events are the climax of a long history.
Shakespeare developed here two popular plays by Plautus, particularly

a brisk and lively play called *Menaechmi*. He made many changes: he gave the wife a name and some clarity of outline, and added a significant sister and a splendidly unexpected Abbess, who probably arrived from Shakespeare's reading of the story of Apollonius of Tyre, a romance retold in Gower's *Confessio Amantis*. Thus at the start of his career he used a tale in which the sea divides and then unites a family, adding more wonder to a classical play full of astonishments: and he did the same at the end of his career, in both *The Tempest* and *Pericles* – in the latter again dependent on Gower and Apollonius, particularly for wonders concerning women. Shakespeare makes the women in *The Comedy of Errors* a central concern, held together by his concentration on the newcomer to the town, who is soon doubting his senses and his identity. For Shakespeare took Plautus's pair of separated twins, identically dressed, and doubled them, adding identical servants. At a stroke he generated vastly greater pace and complexity and capacity for significant confusion, all taking place now not in Epidamnum but in magic Ephesus, where St Paul fought with beasts.

Such progression of possibilities could have produced an endless hall of mirrors, but the frame of a tragic father facing execution at sunset makes all the illusions judged in the shadow of a confrontation with death, and makes, too, the well-constructed, complicated, profound conclusion very satisfying. Quiller-Couch, in his introduction to his New Cambridge Shakespeare edition in 1922, said that it was seldom staged. One might have reason to envy him. The play has now arrived, but usually with wild trappings not always in control, and in American productions stage mayhem seems the norm at the moment. This is a pity. Played cool and clear, it can enchant, and reveal unexpected sophistication of imagery as well as vigour.

Love's Labour's Lost opens the door to a new greatness. It deals with attempts to defeat time and death as a lyric play, a copious outpouring of verbal delight:

> For valour, is not Love a Hercules,
> Still climbing trees in the Hesperides? (4.3.336–7)

It almost certainly belongs to the same mid-decade years as three other intensely lyrical plays, *A Midsummer Night's Dream*, *Romeo and Juliet*, and *Richard II*. *Love's Labour's Lost* has no known source, and almost no action. Some ladies arrive, and at the end a messenger arrives. It brings with it puzzles, not the least being the number of apostrophes in the title. The two good texts, Quarto and Folio, exhibit teasing mismatches. There is silence about why the famous nine worthies are altered, and how two principals, Armado and Moth, arrive (perhaps they wander in from Lyly's *Endimion* of ten years before). As yet unexplained games are played with numbers, particularly three and nine. But these are more profitable conundrums than earlier excitements about 'real' French history, or clues to suspiciously mysterious Elizabethan secrets. Four major productions in England since the Second

World War, and a parallel critical revolution, have now begun to give back to us what was at one time a popular aristocratic play. Once more, the Shakespearian quality includes mastery of construction. There are nine scenic units. The last marshals a score of named characters in a dramatic sweep of nearly a thousand lines which moves through a marvellous succession of comic moods to a great *coup de théâtre*, the entry of Marcade, and that entry is capped again by Shakespeare taking the key word of his message from him, and giving it to the Princess – 'Dead, for my life!' (5.2.708). This exhilarating last scene brings to a new setting, as Berowne points out, the stock Italian *commedia* characters, 'The pedant, the braggart, the hedge-priest, the fool and the boy' (5.2.539), such types being more characteristic of Jonson.

All the sonneteering of the King and his lords, all the formal courtly patterns of wooing (no-one woos alone), all the delicacy of the swiftly shifting moods of the women, even the fully worked-out character of Berowne, all this arrives not at courtly wedding-feasts and dancing, but at a chasm of human reality, mapped by the Princess. Berowne protests:

> Our wooing doth not end like an old play:
> Jack hath not Jill. These ladies' courtesy
> Might well have made our sport a comedy   (5.2.862–4)

and the twelve-month gap before the happy ending, if there is one, is, as Berowne adds, 'too long for a play'. Yet that is not even yet the end. Armado, the fantastical Spaniard, the *miles gloriosus* of New Comedy now touched into sensitive, feeling life, and given an emergent part so that he comes naturally to control the ending, has arranged two paradoxical songs, of Spring and Winter. These final words express nothing more than ordinary human realities surviving.

Penelope Gilliatt wrote of the Royal Shakespeare Company production of *Love's Labour's Lost* in 1965: 'The play . . . has the grasp of a genius who has suddenly found his life's work under his hands.'[2] The six plays written between 1595 and 1600 are rightly taken as the crown of Shakespeare's achievement in romantic comedy, though each has detractors, and one has been the target of misdirected abuse. At first sight we start on safe ground with *A Midsummer Night's Dream* – but only at first sight. Even if we discount Jan Kott's blinkered, though strangely influential glimpses of Eastern bloc *angst*,[3] and even if we acknowledge that Peter Brook's 1970 production was possibly not revelatory for everyone, we must still admit that understanding of this play is now a long way from gossamer-with-Mendelssohn.

Another aristocratic lyric comedy, again with nine scenic units and a last act dominated by a play-within-a-play, *A Midsummer Night's Dream* challenges the very working of imagination, perception-mechanisms, and the human propensity to dote. Not for nothing does Oberon make Puck anoint eyes. Not for nothing does Puck's comment, 'Lord, what fools these mortals be'

(3.2.115), apply as well to the attempts by men who have probably never seen a play to put one on as to obsessed young people. The fairy world, verbally ablaze with warfare and mischief, is anything but sweet. It compounds the terrors of the wood in the blackness of night, and the disturbing humiliation of Titania, and yet claims at the end to be the force capable of holding deformity away from human generation. Bottom is the only human allowed a glimpse of this world. (Theseus, the paragon of order – Top rather than Bottom – dismisses it.) Bottom reaches for words to describe his 'dream', and can only find, and muddle, the high biblical phrases in which St Paul touched on his vision of God. His sense of scale, at least, is right. The play brushes the numinous and, in the same scale, both inexplicable hatred and the terrible power of sudden desire,

> Swift as a shadow, short as any dream,
> Brief as the lightning in the collied night . . .
> So quick bright things come to confusion. (1.1.144–5, 149)

A Midsummer Night's Dream is once again sourceless, though Harold Brooks's excellent Arden edition of 1979 shows many influences. But its technical achievements are awesome. It creates constellations, in many modes, and kaleidoscopic patterns. The ducal and the fairy courts complement each other, and the clash of love and authority is cross-related in half-a-dozen situations with the tension of a sonnet. Unity comes from the constantly felt drive towards the final celebration. And even the mother of the little changeling boy has identity. From the infants who, perhaps, played the first fairies at a wedding, with their seven words clearly cued ('And I'), to their high-fashionably intellectual elders, the play has always reserved a special appeal, and an understanding that, as Quince says, 'That you should here repent you, / The actors are at hand' (5.1.113–14).

Range is of a different order in *The Merchant of Venice*, where two interwoven stories from folklore come to us so minimally signalled as to knock judgement quite off balance. The Venetian blades, Bassanio and his friends, can be played as admirable adventurers or self-seeking brutes; Antonio, the merchant of the title, as a benign 'father' or a sick *isolé*; Shylock, the moneylender, as a touchingly drawn victim or as a villainous stage 'Jew' – or all on points between. We are seeing clearly, now, one of the principles of mature Shakespeare, that of indeterminacy. The plays are more open, more patient of interpretation, than is comfortable. Comedy, by the oldest tradition of all, is subversive – even of fixed meaning.

Portia, for example, is many things. She lives under the open skies of Belmont, and has wealth, as the first scene tells us, of different kinds. She is a heroine of romance, open to classical and legendary comparison, giving amorous promise, living with colour, space, and money. The second scene shows her a faithful daughter with character, sophistication, and wit. She contrasts with the enclosed busy male world of Venice and its projects, and comes to modify it, though only after she has been released from a fixed restriction even tighter than those in Venice: and the wooings are all successful by Act 3 scene 2. As the play goes on, she carries symbolic medieval values of the Four Daughters of God – Mercy, Justice, Peace, and Truth. Act 4 shows these at work. But they are soon forgotten. Portia shows little mercy to Shylock and forgets him wholly after he has left. The final Act, as in *A Midsummer Night's Dream*, is taken up with quite new material. What now occupies Portia is the scale of the clash between the demands of male friendship and married love; and Antonio, who loved Bassanio, has finally, like Shylock, to creep off alone. Portia, like a finely cut diamond, shows many lights.

Antonio declared early in the play that he wanted to be considered Shylock's enemy. This fierce conflict, almost fatal to one and probably fatal to the other, resonates so strongly because of Shakespeare's development of Shylock. Jews were rare, and alien, in England, and the Lopez trial made them objects of fear. Marlowe's Barabas in *The Jew of Malta* (1589) shows what satanic-comic grotesques that tradition could mould. Further, taking interest on money-loans was an important issue tied closely to Jewish concerns.

Shakespeare again paints altogether more finely. Shakespeare's concern is Shylock's otherness. The Christians in the play are extravagant, wasteful, over-generous – but their money does produce value, even if momentary:

> Enrobe the roaring waters with my silks,
> And, in a word, but even now worth this,
> And now worth nothing.   (1.1.34–6)

The value extends to the word. Shylock's horror at this, and at much else, is because he is from a system so different, and so well drawn, that he comes from another world altogether. His immediate predecessor is not Barabas but Oberon. Yet he is given more solid humanity than anyone else in the play, with his spat-on gaberdine, his suspicion of supper-parties, and his grief transposed into a wilderness of monkeys.

Such subversion of tradition becomes the vital sign of Shakespeare's most mature mind. And subversion takes massive flesh in Falstaff. Shylock transcends traditional stereotypes by being made of human clay. Falstaff carries that burden of clay to limits of both clay and burden ('My womb, my womb, my womb undoes me', *2 Henry IV* 4.3.22) and subverts, as a full-time occupation, any attempt at a stance for judgement. A mocker of illusions, he yet lives himself by illusion. Like Antonio, he has to fight for the love of his friend against a richer destiny, but he cannot grasp that he is losing. The trial scene in *The Merchant of Venice* (4.1) fails to establish a judicial norm at all, in part because it is a play-within-a-play. Falstaff in *1 Henry IV* takes the central fact of Hal's life, his relation with his father and his inevitable life as king, and with Hal play-acts it. Like Mistress Quickly, we do not know where to have these characters in the Falstaff plays. Indeterminacy now grows apace. Falstaff is the medieval Vice, and Gluttony, and the *miles gloriosus*, and the Fat Man of the comic duo – and also the speaker of a prose the like of which had not been heard before. He creates and tries desperately to sustain for Hal a fictional world of the madcap Prince (though far from the cap being mad, as Shakespeare transformed his material, it is not even mildly dotty: the 'wild Prince' does little except play wide games in the dark at Gadshill and later pick Falstaff's pocket). Yet Falstaff does this in a play also remarkable for the sudden widening of the spectrum of English people and occasions realistically presented. The detail in the architecture over ten acts touches uncomfortable reality at all points – both 'I never thought to hear you speak again' and 'How a good yoke of bullocks at Stamford Fair?' (2 *Henry IV*, 4.5.92, 3.2.37) – and the scenic forms, and metaphoric tensions and stresses, which hold the construction in place, all point to 'real' and 'alternative' worlds.

In the underrated comedy *The Merry Wives of Windsor* all values have taken ten paces sideways. The 'other' place and its set of controls has become the home base. The alien worlds are now those of London tavern and national history, a 'reality' glimpsed only in hints of a Garter ceremony at the Castle and a tiny reference to Fenton's court life. The local-borough domestic world of this play is the proper reality, set largely in one house in an autumn countryside, in a rich world of close marriage. Even Falstaff, though much talked about, has a trick of not being there. Sterne, in that very English comic masterpiece, *Tristram Shandy*, totally ignores boy-girl-and-adventures romance and brings centre stage the unheroic people and events which make up almost anyone's local life, and his central romance is between two middle-aged brothers. The heart of *The Merry Wives of Windsor*, as its title shows, is two long-married women and their friendship. Ford's citizen jealousy, traditional in age-old streams of *fabliau* from all over Europe, is milked for raw comedy but not central. Falstaff's casting of himself in the tradition of irresistible lover is a splendidly funny failure, and he is shooed away with laughter. The comedy's best tricks come in the last scene, with an interior play again (and again it is amateur theatricals: only the visiting players in *The Taming of the Shrew* and *Hamlet* are Equity members). These local actors, who could earlier 'make fritters of English' and speak incomprehensibly inside the play, suddenly shed their parts and all speak 'proper' verse – and then find that they too have been tricked, as the two young lovers have used the dramatics for their own success.

Even liberated, permissive Falstaff, who held within his compass – just – a weighty comic ancestry of temptation, was in Windsor quite unable to damage the local bonds between men and women who, apart from Ford's obsession and Anne Page's mild passion, remained uninfected and simply amused – and in the fine final stroke, forgave and included him:

> Good husband, let us every one go home
> And laugh this sport o'er by a country fire;
> Sir John and all.   (5.5.228–30)

Marriage in that rooted world was far too strong to break up, or even to lose a single bolt from its structure.

The play merits more attention, for Shakespeare's interest in the long-married, and the mothers so absent from other plays. The Quarto (and Folio) text of *Much Ado About Nothing* announces at the beginning '*Enter Leonato . . . Innogen his wife . . .*' and that is virtually all we ever hear of her. Perhaps Shakespeare felt that a mother for Hero would tilt the play away from Beatrice: her place is taken by another middle-aged man, a brother for Leonato, who comes into his own later in an all-male four-hander where he emerges from the side to confront the aristocratic guests with strong and basic truths. Like *The Merry Wives of Windsor*, *Much Ado About Nothing* is set almost entirely in a house, but now in a golden Mediterranean town enjoying victory celebrations. The house is warmly, even lovingly, described. At the Governor's, life is comfortable, gracious, and witty. The wit is of recent, and English, ancestry, in the fashion of Lylian word-games, Euphues modified to exchanges between clever characters in comedy. Verbal sport of a less knowing kind comes from Dogberry, Verges, and the Watch, who wander in as it might be from Sheep Street, Stratford-upon-Avon. Theirs is an English kind of bumbling which is nothing so grand as Folly, but gets hold of, and holds on to, the truth. The central plot, of the abused fiancée, is an old story which appears all over Europe, and might have reached Shakespeare through Italian versions or through Spenser. It rehearses yet again that conflict between friendship and love which has haunted in some form most of the plays we have considered. Now we have the version where the best friend slanders the girl in order to detach her and win her for himself, except that Shakespeare has moved the slanderer right away from the girl herself, and given him no motive except dark mischief. The result is complex, contributing to that multiplicity of theme and tone which is so much a mark of Shakespeare, and allowing a range of lights to play on the central interest: Beatrice with, or without, Benedick. Inside the Governor's house and the occasion of its grand visitors, inside the formal and public wooings of his daughter, inside the multiple mischief caused by Don John, is the electric awareness of each other of two people who are at the climax of a long friendship. By one of the oldest traditions of Shakespearian comedy, the title of this play is really, as Charles I wrote in his Second Folio, 'Benedik and Betrice'. And as Leonard Digges wrote in 1640,

> let but Beatrice
> And Benedicke be sene, loe in a trice
> The Cockpit Galleries, Boxes, all are full.

Audiences are enchanted by a process of continual discovery, from which no-one in the play is exempt. The Prince of Arragon himself, the Duke Theseus figure, whose stand-easy, holiday demeanour should not hide the fact that he has the chief part after Benedick and is formidable in his nobility – even he has to discover, like Theseus, what it is to be a ruler and in serious error from lack of 'noting', a word which some see hinted in the play's title. The audience is in the secret of Don John, and enjoys the process of discovery of his villainy, which depends as much on Beatrice's sense that there is mischief abroad as on Dogberry's garbled reporting; the centre of both characters is a vulnerable innocence, and both are proved right. And for Beatrice, the sudden knowledge 'O, on my soul, my cousin is belied!' (4.1.146), brings other insights as suddenly. The counterpointing of elements in the plot allows Shakespeare to suggest in Beatrice and Benedick a long-paced awareness of each other, even probably a former love-affair, and such long reach is psychologically necessary for their private discoveries. Presented with Hero's tragedy, Beatrice sees at once her own: that because she had been wounded she had become fixed in her defences against men, and Benedick in particular. Moreover, she also sees that if Benedick and she are to move forward in the new acknowledgement of love, Benedick has to break, like Berowne and Bassanio before him, with his defensive male camaraderie, and she challenges him to 'Kill Claudio' (4.1.287). Dogberry, Verges, and the Watch hold a key to the villainy: just as this is assurance that nothing will go badly wrong, so there is assurance that Beatrice and Benedick will achieve the richest of harmonies in the Shakespearian exuberance of their exchanges. Their discovery of love is a discovery of parts of themselves hidden away, and revealed through dramatic sketches set up for them to hear. Their playlets are different. Ursula and Margaret simply play back to Beatrice her usual responses when confronted with a man, and show how fossilized she has made herself, as a defence. Benedick, in his sketch, is offered something with less detail. He could be wounding in his wit ('What, my dear Lady Disdain! Are you yet living?' 1.1.101) and it is Beatrice's wounding wit he tries to escape. ('I cannot endure my Lady Tongue. *Exit.*' 2.1.245.) Yet he has only to overhear the fact of Beatrice's love, and he crumbles instantly. The three lordly men he overhears have really no notion of how a woman might behave, and desperately pass cues to each other in a long, silly game of consequences (2.3.83–200); but Benedick from the first hint has been listening to a different music.

What follows transcends any tradition. We watch two people discover their love before our eyes, two who are compelling in their love because they are already such complete people, and finding greater completeness still in being together. It is unthinkable that marriage would reduce them; and it is in another country from the rigidities of Petrarch: Benedict absolutely 'cannot show it in rhyme' (5.2.23–37). The new strong and supple prose, and the mechanism of the play, are so organized that long magical discovery can be watched as it happens.

Both *As You Like It* and *Twelfth Night* are unusual. This is the more surprising in that *As You Like It* sits squarely in several conventions. The pastoral dream, whereby sophisticates return to an urban life changed by brief country living, goes back through Renaissance and earlier Europe to Theocritus in third-century B.C. Greece. The story of dispossessed younger brothers wandering in dangerous forests, of fantastic conversions from evil ways, of love in the greenwood, are part of European romance tradition. Rival Dukes, a melancholic, a fool, a lover, a girl in boy's clothes, are taken from the Elizabethan stock-cupboard, as are the touches of satire. Shakespeare follows – closely – a popular prose romance published ten years before, Thomas Lodge's *Rosalynde. Euphues Golden Legacie*, which itself told an old story.

Yet *As You Like It* is quite new. There are important changes to Lodge's tale, which knows nothing of Jaques, for example, and his unpleasant detachment and boring self-advertisement, or of Touchstone and his parodic, chameleon-like folly. More strikingly, the busy plot of the first two acts comes to full closing cadences at the end of the second act. At that point everything stops. What follows, instead of plot, is a succession of encounters. The focus is on Rosalind, who explores the experience of falling in love, with increasing wit, often at her own expense. She is voluble and articulate: she speaks twice as much as Viola, for example. But her move from 'crush' to profound love is, as Beatrice knew herself, engaged in mutuality. She and Orlando transcend their form. The largely aristocratic experience of falling in love, with its courtly antecedents, is changed here into a new, more vulnerable mode, less fixed to one 'fatal' occasion. Rosalind is anti-Petrarchan, healthily removing illusions from Phebe. She undercuts conventions even more than Touchstone (or than Jaques thinks he does). Touchstone, knowing that love leads to marriage, puts marriage first. Rosalind, knowing herself 'many fathoms deep' in love – 'it cannot be sounded' – is engaged in cutting away even the conventions of gender. Her sexuality is firm: early on she sighs for her child's father. But her understanding of gender expands as the play goes on, meeting Orlando with new possibilities of married mutuality. There is nothing among the Lylian boys to compare with this. The mechanism for this liberation starts with the long stasis of the last three acts, giving room, until chiming 'tomorrows' start hastening the end, for Rosalind's unfolding of aspects of love, unpressed by plot, and this indeed in the most accessible of the major comedies, in prose that cries out to be spoken. It works through Ganymede becoming something called 'Orlando's Rosalind': by exploring wit and love with Orlando as a 'boy' Rosalind discovers when it is more than a game. The structure is supported by Celia, a sharer in the discoveries and a commentator. It comes to a climax with an 'if', in which, as Touchstone said, there is much virtue. Rosalind, it seems clear, keeps some subtler resonance in the ceremony with Hymen:

she doesn't come out of her boy's clothes; she suddenly hasn't time. Beatrice, in her new insight, cries three times 'O that I were a man!' Rosalind spends much of the play as a 'man'. Viola in *Twelfth Night* does the same, but in the more extreme position of having a male twin for her to be. Gender here is more volatile than ever. Volatility is, indeed, a characteristic of this strange, sad play, which contains the funniest scene Shakespeare wrote, the box-tree scene (2.5). The play's ingredients are the very stuff of European comedy: two fairyland courts made of fantasies of love, a singing melancholy fool, below-stairs frolics with a dim-witted gull and a drunken knight making a comic pair, a pert maid, a repressive steward, and above all the parted identical twins.

The play teases with upsetting perspectives. Viola and Olivia, similar in name and much else, cause each other suddenly to unfreeze into sexual love of a most indirect, if not impossible, aim. Toby, a thief and a drunkard, 'exposes' Malvolio, who then does not change at all – and Maria marries Toby as a reward. An alarming number of people in the play are close to a borderline of insanity. Much of the verse is love poetry as exquisite in delicacy, tact, and a sense of evanescence as any to be found anywhere, but shot through with unhappiness. The subtext is unusually dark. Malvolio is cruelly, and unnecessarily, punished, for no crime except that of preferring an orderly house.[4] Toby turns on his gull with a vicious rejection. Sebastian, wary in a strange place, marries on the instant an importunate girl he has never met before: it does not help to recognize that both are probably about seventeen, and that Olivia has unwittingly married into the aristocracy. Every device seems overcharged. In spite of the sudden, and very absorbing, rush of plot in Act 5 whereby Sebastian's entry turns everything around, causing everyone to run about, it is not at all clear how things will end. Viola is given as a wife to Orsino who minutes before was using 'him' as his page. The future seems bleak for many. For Maria, Andrew, Malvolio, certainly: Feste seems to tell us so about himself in his final song. The principal lovers have swung too violently for comfort. Supernatural intervention is conspicuously absent. Conventions seem to have gone sour, and the mutuality achieved in *Much Ado* and *As You Like It* is simply not there. The best one can say is that the play, in the tonal range of its poetry, is hauntingly beautiful like an impressionist painting. The lovers' urgency, and volatility, allow into that picture otherwise unrecordable feelings. 'Thy mind is a very opal' says Feste to Orsino: so is the play. Viola looks to time for resolution, and does not investigate the future.

Reaching this point in the canon in an essay on the comedies, it is traditional to change the colour of the ink and write about the Problem Comedies or Problem Plays. Those are however nineteenth-century tags, put on because of supposed parallels with Ibsen and social problems. Rather than label *All's Well That Ends Well* and *Measure for Measure* problem plays, I would see a movement from Touchstone's 'if' in which plays settle into much greater indeterminacy of genre, making the idea of comedy darker, its texture thicker. The movement is quite clear in *Twelfth Night*. Pontifications about the rebirth of a new society are inappropriate at that ending. Doubts about the possibility of clear judgement which emerge from an investigation of the contemporary plays *Henry V, Julius Caesar, Troilus and Cressida* and, most immediately, *Hamlet*, haunt Shakespeare's last work in the comedy genre.

The immediate source of *All's Well That Ends Well* is the story of Giletta of Narbonne in Boccaccio's *Decameron*, which Shakespeare probably took from the translation by William Painter in *The Palace of Pleasure*. The story had several other written versions in Europe, but flowing into it are older folk traditions, and these are often rather desperately invoked to rescue the play.[5] But to do that is to distort. Shakespeare has complicated even Boccaccio by adjusting the story, by adding major characters – the Countess, Lafeu, Parolles, Lavache – by making Helena more radiant and more problematic, and Bertram without any redeeming feature at all. In *All's Well That Ends Well*, to be young is to be uncaring, selfish and rigid, with the exception of Helena. But she uses an old-fashioned remedy to cure the king, and though her inexplicable love for Bertram is fresh, she belongs with the older values, so elegiacally and calmly contained in the Countess and her household. What verse there is tends to Shakespeare's coming, dense, manner, making sometimes few concessions to the hearer. In this it matches the comedy, where expectations tend not to be met. The heroine, who is likeable, achieves her man, with determination and resource, but by means of a dubious bed trick, which has no ancestry in Elizabethan comedy, though a longer history in myth. Moreover, the hero works hard at being unworthy of her. His journeys, to the court in Paris, to war in Florence, do nothing to change him. Transformation is displaced to the weak hanger-on Parolles who learns, by being humiliated in a barrack-room jape, to stop lying and live by 'simply the thing I am'.

For its first recorded stage life the play, much cut, was a Parolles play. It then became an angelic Helena's vehicle, and in our century a Problem Play, and then paired with *Measure for Measure* to become, improbably, a Christian allegory. Some speculation proposes this play as the mysterious *Love labours wonne* paired with *Love's Labour's Lost* in Francis Meres's *Palladis Tamia* in 1598. Arguments of dating make it unlikely. More weighty is the sense that such a title would be even more inappropriate for the play than the one we have. Even the King, who is determined to be bland, ends the play with the doubtful 'All yet seems well, and if . . . '. *All's Well That Ends Well* suggests doubts about the genre itself. There is in Bertram a cussed determination not to play the romantic game as the traditions would make him. He awkwardly refuses to be transformed from a frog.

Such cussedness is the main characteristic of Shakespeare's final comedy, *Measure for Measure*. The prisoner Barnardine refuses to be executed just to suit Vincentio's plans. Claudio too fights for his life. The plot itself rebels, and Vincentio's confident assertions are often betrayed. Narrative, like Pompey's explanation before Escalus, becomes impossible. This active play moves between three dark places – palace, brothel, prison – only further taking in a garden-house where blackness is so thick that another bed trick can take place. The unfreezing of absolute fixity which we noticed in, for example, Olivia, leads here only to more bafflement. If Angelo's brittle evil is exposed, and the laws are being tightened, how can he escape on the very grounds that led to Claudio's death-sentence? If Isabella can come to understand a little of her own terror of her sexuality, why is she denied courtship, never mind love, by Vincentio, whose 'What's mine is yours, and what is yours is mine' reads to modern ears more like sexual harassment? Vincentio is disreputable: a man of authority, like Theseus or Don Pedro, who has slid out of his responsibility for the chaos in Vienna to become a meddling false friar.[6] The baffling, entertaining figure of Lucio does not help modern understanding of a play where matters generally seem to be running counter to traditions to produce a particularly hollow 'happy ending'. Shakespeare is transforming the traditions of comedy into something, still called comedy, which challenges all those many traditions. Now with a change even more rapid and close to the end than Viola's in *Twelfth Night*, with a stunned and silent Isabella, Shakespeare leaves comedy.

The Folio lists *The Winter's Tale* and *The Tempest* with the comedies – indeed, opens the book with the latter. *Cymbeline* closes the volume, tacked on to the last of the tragedies. *Pericles* it omits altogether. We think of these four plays as theatrical romances, and something must be said of them here, and of *Two Noble Kinsmen* which followed. Shakespeare's retelling, with Fletcher, of the tale of love versus friendship best known from Chaucer's *Knight's Tale*, consists probably of Act 1, some of Act 3, and most of Act 5. The main plot remains firmly in the realm of fiction, and the stitching is not always perfect; but the play has at least resisted any allegorizing, and deserves fuller modern attention.

   Shakespeare and his company, now the King's Men, were able to move into the small indoor private Blackfriars theatre in 1608, when they took over a house style which favoured tragicomedy and romances in the manner of Beaumont and Fletcher. For this theatre, as well as for the Globe, the plays at the end of Shakespeare's working life were written. His interest, between *Measure for Measure* of 1604, and *Pericles* of 1608, had gone much further down the dark road into tragedy.

   Pericles, performed while work on *King Lear* was probably still going on, seems a mish-mash. Once we have understood that it is, as it were, five scenes from the life of St Pericles, we are still only part way to appreciation, hindered by the unhappy state of the only text, the Quarto of 1609. But it will usefully introduce the elements these four romances have in common, starting with the cavalier treatment of dramatic method. *Pericles* takes place over the whole Mediterranean, and, like *The Winter's Tale*, over many years: *The Tempest* on one island on one afternoon. *Cymbeline* produces, as if a conjurer were showing off, a dozen distinct dénouements at the end (some count two dozen). *The Winter's Tale* keeps off stage the scene we have been waiting for, the reunion of father and daughter. That is the more striking when recovered daughters are so significant in all four plays: four virtuous and beautiful lost princesses who become the instruments of restoration. The gods, or magic, intervene: time does not wholly destroy; the sea can bring together; nature is creator and healer. Stage effects are more elaborate. The sentimental Blackfriars romances are made by Shakespeare to touch more areas of human experience, and toughened. Even his romances have a strong realistic streak.

Pericles is a morality play and takes up recognizable elements from fairy-tale and romance from Shakespeare's earlier comedies (riddling; the sea). It is in the modest control of Gower, who uses his 'song that was old' to forestall over-sophisticated mockery and open up more childlike responses, as to a parable. Marina, who uses a special art to restore her father, is innocently human. To see her mixture of naïvety and sophistication as also the play itself is to open up suggestions of the power of theatre to make miracles happen, to release human feeling and penetrate to truth, something we have been aware of in this essay since *The Taming of the Shrew*. It is now more important. The romances give a new quality to the transition from theatre to street.

Cymbeline (1609) does this rather with tongue in cheek. Johnson referred to the 'unresisting imbecility' of the plot, and the language, though capable of great beauty, is sometimes so circuitous that we may feel that some of the characters have been taught to speak by Henry James. There are moments of scalp-tingling oddness, like the heroine waking outside a cave from a drugged sleep on a headless corpse dressed in her husband's clothes. We note the cool way Shakespeare mixes ancient and Roman Britain, Renaissance Italian sexual intrigue, Stuart court propaganda, and Jupiter descending on wires '*in thunder and lightning, sitting upon an eagle. He throws a thunderbolt. The Ghosts fall on their knees.*' But the faithfulness of Imogen ('Fidele') carries the play's principal charge. Shakespeare's romances can bear the freight of abstractions like time, art, and nature. Imogen is not an abstraction, but a living and brave girl, who does find her family and cause the final peal of truths to ring out.

The Winter's Tale (1610) continues from *Pericles* in using the idea of miracle, and develops the concern with time and death, and how to defeat them, from *Love's Labour's Lost*. Though, like all the four romances, it provoked neo-classical purist hostility from Ben Jonson, like them this play was popular at all levels. It is a tale, the stuff of fireside stories, with a morality play deep inside it, and it is at the same time heavily dependent on Greene's prose romance of twenty-two years before, *Pandosto*, with certain crucial changes, such as removing the explicit grounds for Leontes's jealousy, not allowing Hermione to die, and reversing Sicily and Bohemia. The play creates its own imaginative world, self-contained and strongly communicated, with a tough realism that is quite unromantic in understanding, for example, responsibility for suffering, and in the interrelation between king, court and country. Hermione is breathingly real before the final miracle. She is pregnant and bears a child, something that we could not imagine of Viola. She defends herself with a full firm declaration of exactly how she is wronged. Yet she is also the personified virtues:

> . . . innocence shall make
> False accusation blush, and tyranny
> Tremble at patience.   (3.2.28–30)

Inside those phrases are ideas of acting, and this play is altogether alert to the theatrical, that radioactive area between illusion and truth. Leontes knows his accusation to be true. Autolycus swears his ballads are true. Perdita is only playing at shepherdesses; everyone in Bohemia acts, and the long episode in that country is another play-within-a-play. As the play progresses the artifice comes to be more realistic, until in the famous *coup* it is impossible to tell whether art or nature has made Hermione. The characters, and the audience, are told, 'It is requir'd / You do awake your faith' (5.3.94–5), to trust imaginative work to recreate life. It is Leontes, of course, who has experienced the miracle.

A very great artist in his last works is usually seen to be taking extraordinary risks: Beethoven springs to mind. It is best not to see *The Tempest* (1611–12) as Shakespeare's farewell to his art – after all, parts of *Two Noble Kinsmen* and *Henry VIII* were to come – but as a marvellously advanced, and fresh, experiment with the neo-classical unities of time, place, and action, and an adventure with art and illusion, nature and nurture, reason and magic, created out of a tempestuous release from which characters emerge as even more theatrically vivid. As in the sort of big dream only given three or four times in a lifetime, significances in an apparently endless progression continually appear in *The Tempest*, and it has attracted metaphysical speculation of many kinds. Shakespeare writes at the height of his genius about his art of theatre and its creation, rightly relating sleep and imagination as means through which truths reach our deepest minds, transforming even the means of perception: 'Those are pearls that were his eyes' (1.2.398).

He has come a huge distance from Lyly and *The Two Gentlemen of Verona*. In *The Tempest*, romance, court masques, stage devices, voyagers' narratives, neo-Platonic theories, hermetic magic, high pastoral and more, all on a haunted island where one is never more than a few paces from the sea, go to the making of action, characters, and poetry which inhabit a realm beyond any tradition except that of the weight of glory.

> ... in dreaming,
> The clouds methought would open and show riches
> Ready to drop upon me, that, when I wak'd,
> I cried to dream again.   (3.2.135–8)

Notes

1. *The Two Gentlemen of Verona* ed. Sir Arthur Quiller-Couch and John Dover Wilson (Cambridge, 1921), p. xiv.
2. *The Observer*, 11 April 1965.
3. Jan Kott, *Shakespeare Our Contemporary* (1964).
4. The title of this play has led to much solemn pronouncement about Saturnalia and Misrule, though without any agreement about what that means. Confident assertions concerning life in Elizabethan England, never mind Illyria, do not always carry conviction. C. L. Barber's service in showing how close comedy could be to the spirit of ancient English festivals, in *Shakespeare's Festive Comedy* (1959), has given rise to exaggeration. This play is clearly not *set* at Twelfth Night, the last day of Christmas, the Feast of Epiphany. It is best to say that we don't know what the title is supposed to mean.
5. See Howard C. Cole, *The 'All's Well' Story from Boccaccio to Shakespeare* (1982).
6. It is one of the curiosities of modern criticism that the merest whiff of religion in Shakespeare can produce edifices of allegory. A peppering of religious phrases in this play has set certain critics busily fixing stained glass images in the windows of an illusory chapel. One of these depicts Vincentio, transformed, ridiculously, into 'a Christ-figure'. Flat burglary as ever was committed. The play's title is not Christian. It echoes a phrase from Matthew 7 which itself echoes an Old Testament idea: it can mean just retribution, or moderation as a virtue, or both.
Note: I am grateful for conversations with Helen Sprott and Sarah Wintle while writing this essay.

Reading list

Bradbrook, M. C., *The Growth and Structure of Elizabethan Comedy* (1955)
Bradbury, Malcolm and Palmer, David, eds., *Shakespearean Comedy* (1972)
Brown, John Russell, *Shakespeare and his Comedies* (1957)
Bullough, Geoffrey, *Narrative and Dramatic Sources of Shakespeare*, 8 vols.: I *Early Comedies, Poems, Romeo and Juliet* (1957); II *The Comedies 1597–1603* (1958); VIII *Romances: Cymbeline, The Winter's Tale, The Tempest* (1975)
Cody, Richard, *The Landscape of the Mind* (Oxford, 1969)
Coghill, Nevill, 'The basis of Shakespearian comedy' in *Shakespeare Criticism 1935–60*, ed. Anne Ridler (Oxford, 1963)
Felperin, Howard, *Shakespearean Romance* (Princeton, 1972)
Frye, Northrop, *A Natural Perspective* (New York, 1965)
Hattaway, Michael, *Elizabethan Popular Theatre* (1982)
Jones, Emrys, *The Origins of Shakespeare* (Oxford, 1977)
Kermode, Frank, 'The mature comedies', in *Early Shakespeare*, ed. John Russell Brown and Bernard Harris (1961)

Leggatt, Alexander, *Shakespeare's Comedy of Love* (1974)
McFarland, Thomas, *Shakespeare's Pastoral Comedy* (Chapel Hill, North Carolina, 1972)
Nevo, Ruth, *Comic Transformations in Shakespeare* (1980)
Pettet, E. C., *Shakespeare and the Romance Tradition* (1949)
Rabkin, Norman, *Shakespeare and the Problem of Meaning* (Chicago, 1981)
Salingar, Leo, *Shakespeare and the Traditions of Comedy* (Cambridge, 1974)
Smith, Hallett, *Shakespeare's Romances* ((San Marino, California, 1972)
Snyder, Susan, *The Comic Matrix of Shakespeare's Tragedies* (Princeton, 1979)
Stevenson, David Lloyd, *The Love-Game Comedy* (New York, 1946)
Weimann, Robert, *Shakespeare and the Popular Tradition in the Theatre* (Baltimore, 1978)
Welsford, Enid, *The Fool* (1935)
Wilson, F. P., *Shakespearian and other Studies* (Oxford, 1969)
Young, David, *The Heart's Forest* (New Haven, 1972)

8   Shakespeare and the traditions of tragedy

THOUGH he began (as one must) with the list of plays that Shakespeare's workmates had set out as 'tragedies' on the contents page of the First Folio, A. C. Bradley soon decided that only four plays really fulfilled the requirements for 'pure tragedy' (*Hamlet, Othello, King Lear, Macbeth*). Bradley begins *Shakespearean Tragedy* with an empirical investigation of the 'tragic facts' present in the plays of the full list (excluding *Cymbeline*, as all modern writers do). He establishes effectively that these plays can be described as stories of exceptional suffering and calamity, leading to the death of a dominant figure of high social standing – a figure intensely committed to his chosen course of action, who is given primary responsibility for what happens in the plot, and whose responsibility for the choices made is most powerfully projected by the rhetoric of his struggle with his own nature. Given the philosophic and aesthetic assumptions laboriously built up in the course of the nineteenth century, it is hardly surprising that Bradley eventually rests his conception of pure tragedy on 'character', on the quality of the agent. It is even less surprising that, having established his paradigm, he proceeds to concentrate on the plays which embody it most completely, discarding the others.

What Bradley says about his four plays is by no means distorting: none of his successors as Shakespearian critics has given us a system at once so transparent in the assumptions used and so comprehensive in the instances brought into play. Yet the whole project of 'Shakespearean Tragedy' would certainly have puzzled Shakespeare and his fellows, for whom a tragic quintessence must have appeared as much the product of charlatanism as an alchemical quintessence. There is no evidence that Shakespeare or anyone else in his period thought these four 'pure' examples to be different in kind from other tragedies being written on every side. Two of them (*Hamlet* and *Othello*) were indeed quite popular throughout the seventeenth century, but the esteem for them that was often expressed is esteem that links them to other plays instead of differentiating them. Such popular characteristics as clever intrigue, exciting conflicts of values, unexpected transformations, sharply pointed dialogue, serious poetic moralizing, mark mainly the variousness demanded of a successful theatrical repertory and take us far from notions of a fixed literary hierarchy, from the hushed reverence of a *Festspielhaus*, from the philosophic vision of a tragic world 'travailing for perfection, but bringing to birth, together with glorious good, an evil which it is able to overcome only by self-torture and self-waste' (to return to Bradley's famous definition of tragedy).

To spend much time arguing that Shakespeare's tragedies *then* evoked reactions different from those that are commonplace *now* is, of course, to commit oneself to cliché. The difficulty of applying modern modes of thought to Shakespeare is tediously obvious. Yet a purely historical justification of Renaissance dramaturgy is no less simple-minded. A 'comprehensive view-point' is, it would seem, a contradiction in terms; and if particular points of view are to be defended it can only be in relation to the general outlooks they imply. An essay on 'Shakespeare and the Traditions of Tragedy' commits one to modes that allow fruitful discussion of the elements of tradition and to an assumption that comparative study of dramatic techniques can give central information about the plays themselves.

The traditions and techniques of tragedy that Shakespeare inherited from his professional predecessors and from the most esteemed literary figures of his own age differed from those formulated by Bradley mainly in their vagueness and their general applicability. Bradley dismissed the 'Roman tragedies' (*Julius Caesar, Antony and Cleopatra, Coriolanus*) from his considera-tion, on the grounds that they are 'tragic histories or historical tragedies' and therefore impure. But the historical (or, more properly, political) aspect of these plays is an inescapable part of their Elizabethan inheritance. The subject-matter of the early touring companies' morality plays was recurrently political.[1] The elite drama of the mid-century – the self-consciously classical tragedies of the Inns of Court – turned its shapely back on such hybrid or 'mongrel' forms and 'climbed to the height of Seneca his style', but failed to follow up a rejection of popular style by a rejection of popular political content. *Gorboduc* (1562),[2] written in part by the Queen's cousin, and *The Misfortunes of Arthur* (1588), 'presented to her Majesty by the gentlemen of Gray's Inn', are both concerned with tragic situations which arise not from the facts of character but from matter more important to a governor – faulty political judgement. Marlowe's *Tamburlaine* (1587), which may be thought of as the breakthrough event of the Elizabethan popular stage, combining the lively variousness of popular entertainment with the dignity and coherence of elite drama, looks like an anti-political play, showing how good political advice, care in government, dynastic dignity, are all helpless when faced by the destiny embodied in individual heroic *virtù*. But the anti-political is only a sub-set of the political. *Tamburlaine* cannot be considered, any more than any other non-Shakespearian tragedy, a 'pure' play of character. Bradley's remark that the fall of a Hamlet or an Othello makes us 'vividly conscious of the possibilities of human nature' represents a powerful modern response to Hamlet or Othello.

But it deprives of background ('decontextualizes' in the current jargon) the plays that have the most obvious appeal to the modern reader's mind and isolates valuation from the full range of dramaturgy the plays contain. In what follows I aim to deal with tragic dramaturgy rather than the tragic vision, to look at Shakespeare's tragedies, implicitly if not always explicitly, in relation to the concerns and techniques that were widely shared among his sources, his rivals and his collaborators in a tightly-knit theatrical community. The loss, in terms of deep identification with single heroes, may be thought to be compensated for by an increased sense of the variousness of tragic experience. Shakespeare should emerge as a dramatist continuously making real choices among real alternatives.

The thunderclap opening of the prologue to *Tamburlaine* is an obvious document in any treatment of Elizabethan ideas of tragedy. The claim to have re-achieved what Marlowe's room-mate Kyd calls

> . . . stately-written tragedy,
> *Tragedia cothurnata*, fitting kings,
> Containing matter, and not common things,

emerges, of course, only implicitly from the dismissal of all recent drama:

> From jigging veins of rhyming mother wits,
> And such conceits as clownage keeps in pay,
> We'll lead you to the stately tent of war,
> Where you shall hear the Scythian Tamburlaine
> Threatening the world with high astounding terms
> And scourging kingdoms with his conquering sword.
> View but his picture in this tragic glass
> And then applaud his fortunes as you please.

'I will lead you,' says Marlowe, 'into a drama which is (like Kyd's *tragedia cothurnata*) "stately", concerned with lofty characters and terrifying action, powerfully projected by a language of superhuman energy. The story will show you the hero as the victim of fortune (as in so-called "tragedies" heretofore), but this protagonist will not be one who is simply the victim of fortune. Though he must fall, Tamburlaine will challenge the limits of destiny. It may be that, seeing his fortunes in "this tragic glass", you will applaud his challenge instead of feeling dismay at the mere fact of challenge.' The word *tragedy* is not used in this prologue, it will be noticed. The title-page, however, tells us that the matter is 'divided into two tragical discourses', and there can be little doubt that the generic claim is present throughout. The whole pressure of the prologue is towards an assertion that here (at last) true tragedy has reached the English popular stage, with height of style or sublimity in the poetry used, with characters of the greatest dignity and power that can be imagined, with *pathos* or pain and *phobos* or terror prominent in the story, and with an ending which does not simply justify the ways of God but indicates that the tragic power of great men lies in their capacity to defy necessity.

Marlowe's claim to be introducing something new on to a commercial stage paid for by 'clownage' cannot be contradicted, if only because we know too little about the 'rhyming mother wits' to argue against him. This does not mean, however, that there are no English plays before *Tamburlaine* that can be called 'tragic' or even 'tragedy'. Pickering's *Horestes* (1567) and Preston's *Cambyses* (1561) have obvious connections with tragic form and with the tradition of tragedy, the former being a version of the Orestes story, telling how he took revenge against his mother, Clytemnestra, the latter dealing with a Tamburlaine-like Persian tyrant, determined to exert his will against any who oppose him. Both these plays, however, allow the search for variety to confuse their tragic potential. On the title-page *Cambyses* calls itself 'A Lamentable Tragedy', but then adds (accurately enough) 'Mixed Full of Pleasant Mirth'. The decline and fall of Cambyses himself is tragic in outline, but the presentation of his 'odious death by God's justice appointed' is careless of more immediate causes and so loses tragedy in didacticism. Morality characters like Commons Complaint, Cruelty, and Murder diffuse the connection between choice and responsibility that effective tragedy maintains. Both plays were presented at court, but that does not seem to have affected much their rough-and-tumble manner of proceeding. Indeed the court notice of *Cambyses* refers to it as 'Ruff, Huff and Snuff' – these being the three clown characters who interrupt the serious action with their haphazard jokes and pratfalls. We may take it, apparently, that the court performance of these plays (as of later plays) was only a replication of their commercial performance. The conditions of that performance have been described lucidly by David Bevington[3] and are spelled out in detail on the title-page of *Cambyses* – thirty-eight characters so set out as to be playable as six men and two boys. The commercial life of the play, that is, derives from performances by small and presumably peripatetic troupes, capable of packing 'em into draughty halls in provincial towns, evoking strong and various emotions of wonder, horror, laughter, moral self-satisfaction, in audiences with little experience or literary sophistication. Even *Tamburlaine*, we are told by the publisher, was originally acted with 'some fond and frivolous gestures' which 'haply . . . have been of some vain-conceited groundlings greatly gaped at', but it is presented, at least in the published version, for readers of a different class, who would find such digressions 'far unfit for . . . so honourable and stately a history' and merely 'tedious unto the wise'. Between the published *Cambyses* (c. 1569) and the published *Tamburlaine* (1590) the relationship of play to audience has thus changed radically. At the end of the process we are no longer dealing with the humility of theatrical wares hawked in a back-street market. In *Tamburlaine* 'the right honourable the Lord Admiral his servants', a celebrated company of professional actors, playing in the metropolis, headed by Edward Alleyn, the most famous tragedian of his age, offer us the privilege of joining 'the wise' in an enactment of 'stately history' by a cast composed of emperors, kings and soldans and projected by a verse which 'the wise' will recognize as possessing the resonance, the range, the flexibility of the most admired poetry of ancient culture – the poetry of 'the stately tent of war' in Homer, Virgil, Lucan, Statius. Marlowe, I am suggesting, sets out before his audience a claim that he has written in *Tamburlaine* the first English tragedy (truly understood), not for a closet audience of lawyers or statesmen, like *Gorboduc* or *Gismond of Salerne* (1566; 1591), not as mere translation, like *Jocasta* (1566), but as a public play among public plays, written for professional performers in properly equipped theatres, yet demanding of its paying audience that they bring taste and discrimination equivalent to that demanded by narrative poetry.

To say that Marlowe broke the ice that Shakespeare sailed his ship through is not, of course, to say that Marlowe's plays supply the principal models for Shakespeare's. I have argued elsewhere[4] that Kyd's *The Spanish Tragedy* (1587) with its complex, ironic, multi-layered structure, its subtle mixture of divergent tonalities, offered Shakespeare his prime tragic model. But Marlowe must be allowed to have formulated the claim for tragedy and generated the expectations and the excitement that theatre needs.

The word 'tragedy' carries always a strong classical flavour. Consequently it has always seemed natural, when searching for sources or models of English tragedy, to look first of all at the plays of Greece and Rome. Yet in spite of the lengthy effort made, very little connective tissue has been found. The Greek connection has indeed been little heard of in recent years. Emrys Jones has argued[5] for the influence of Euripides's *Hecuba* (easily available to Shakespeare in a Latin translation), but I must confess that even this limited claim seems quite unconvincing. Nor do I suppose that there is a strong dramatic link with the closet drama of Seneca, whose frozen horrors are designed for static declamation and can have offered little or nothing to professional actors or to the audiences who went along for the excitement of quick-fire action and surprise. It is one of the achievements of twentieth-century criticism to have freed the idea of tragedy from its classical exemplars, reminding us of the importance of 'narrative tragedy'[6] in the period and of *The Mirror for Magistrates* in particular, which Shakespeare certainly knew, and allowing also (what seems to follow) that Ovid's *Metamorphoses* can be read as an anthology of such 'tragedies'. Shakespeare's own narrative tragedy, *Lucrece* (1594), shows clearly enough his connection with this tradition. It also shows – what the Ovidian background no doubt encouraged – the strong tendency in Shakespeare's art to flamboyant display, to self-conscious and baroque elaboration of classical materials. *Titus Andronicus* (1594) is the play that gives the clearest indication of this flamboyant art; but in a play – even this one – the impulse to amplification must be held in check by the need to channel an audience's attention. Shakespeare's professional life imposed essentially conservative limits on his art; in the main his tragedies belong, as one might expect, inside the received conventions of tragedy that audience and actors both required, the latter more especially, since without agreed conventions they could not survive in conditions of repertory virtually without rehearsal.[7] Yet Shakespeare's art is also, as anyone who reads him alongside his contemporaries will know, an art of perpetual surprise. He keeps a calculated indeterminacy in the relationship between elements in his plays so that the audience is always being betrayed into new adjustments. If we look at the plays in relation to their sources we will see that the changes made are hardly ever designed to clarify motive or interpretation. Rather the opposite: when a source offers a clear indication why things go one way rather than another, Shakespeare is likely to make the issue more obscure. He multiplies the range of instances, sets opposites and complementarities together, and amid competing possibilities refuses to let us know who is right and who is wrong, Hal or Falstaff, Caesar or Brutus, Kate or Bianca, Old Hamlet or young Hamlet.[8] His plays accept, as is inevitable, the standard expectations an audience brings to the theatre; but such expectations are never treated passively, never left unquestioned or untransformed. Genre is an important part of expectation, and Shakespeare's plays tend to live along the edge of generic boundaries – comedy liable to be clouded by tragic potential, history wavering between tragedy and comedy, tragedy slipping into comic routines – so that cross-lights dazzle our assumptions and unsettle the focus of any fixed viewpoint.

As early in his career as *Romeo and Juliet* (1595) we can see Shakespeare taking over a story with a clear moral bias and seeming both to affirm and deny the moral he inherited. Arthur Brooke's *Romeus and Juliet* (1562) is a poem whose moralism is often exaggerated, the tone of the preface being read as representative of the whole. The attitude to the lovers found in the narrative section is, in fact, more sympathetic than is usually supposed. But Brooke's 'drab' poetic vocabulary is not really capable of conveying anything like spontaneous pleasure. The narrator's representation of love is in terms of 'wounds', 'pain', 'thraldom', 'poison', 'woeful breast', 'smarting whip', etc., so that the immediacy of youthful emotion is always mediated by a middle-aged moralist who looks before and after along the line of the narrative and notices that 'frail unconstant Fortune' is certain to destroy the pleasures of love. Shakespeare preserves much of this. He never denies that the lovers are rash and foolhardy, desperate and careless. Indeed the nature of the tragic story still requires that we allow them to be so. But the rashness of the lovers is also rephrased, in the medium of theatrical direct address, as spontaneity, as perpetual optimism, as charm. The old folk, Capulets and Montagues, know the world, but they are not allowed to know the hearts of the young lovers as we are made to know and share them. The Nurse and Friar Lawrence retain some of the qualities of the 'drunken gossips and superstitious friars' that

Brooke's preface refers to, but the Nurse's self-dramatization has a comic immediacy that disables such a view; and yet this view is affirmed as soon as we re-establish the tragic perspective of the whole story. We are not told that this love is worthwhile; we are not told that it was a tragic error. The power of the play depends indeed on such contradictory elements being simultaneously presented.

Love, as an emotion uniquely variable in the judgements it evokes, seems particularly appropriate to the art of variation that Shakespeare practises. We can see the range of its effects in the four tragedies which use it as a central interrelating emotion – *Romeo and Juliet*, *Troilus and Cressida* (1602), *Othello* (1604), *Antony and Cleopatra* (1607), in each case with a strongly comic viewpoint as part of the tragic totality. Love is also a natural trigger for tragic conflict, making the repudiation of social and external norms appear an inevitable prerequisite for the intense realization of self. The social worlds of the plays and the realities of political coexistence that underwrite them – these are bound to reject the claim of love and poetry to have experienced a superior reality. The rhetoric of society steadily undercuts this radiant poetry and offers a series of darkenings – satiric, realistic, philosophic, parodic – to dim its brightness and deny its independence. It is worth noticing that the four tragedies I have mentioned, when arranged (as here) in the usual chronological order, show the rhetoric of society as working with steadily increasing effect as the lovers themselves grow older. Romeo and Juliet are passionate and powerless children; Troilus and Cressida are young lovers oppressed by the important social roles their world imposes on them; Othello and Desdemona are maturely married and socially dominant; Antony and Cleopatra are at the end of lifetimes of infinite power and infinitely indulged eroticism. It seems probable that Shakespeare aligned himself with different age groups as he himself grew older. What is significant in a study of tragedy is not, however, what he saw but what he did with what he saw, the nature of the tragic limitation to love that is raised up to confront each generation of lovers. In *Romeo and Juliet* the tragic impediments (equivalent to Northrop Frye's famous 'blocking figures' in comedy)[9] are the parents, and, beyond them, the bifurcated community, representative of tradition and the past. We understand the pathos and helplessness of these innocents by seeing their position in a world they did not ask for, which they do not endorse and which they cannot affect (in life, at any rate). Romeo's attempt to express a revalued relation to Tybalt is a typically ironic example of this helplessness. He seeks to embody in a social form the new individual perception that love has given him, but the gesture is neither understandable nor effective; indeed it merely brings the essential conflict to the social surface and so precipitates the tragedy.

Troilus and Cressida might appear equally helpless, but the blocking agency here (the Trojan war) has a crushing inevitability about it very different from the haphazard quarrels of the Montagues and Capulets, and powerlessness seems to be more like the natural condition of man. The power of this war to undermine and devalue life is, moreover, not simply presented as an external force distorting action; it eats also into the minds of those who act and love, compromising their thinking no less than their doing. 'Innocence' is harder to accept as a natural quality in *Troilus and Cressida* than in *Romeo and Juliet*. It seems to be touched by self-consciousness and calculation when found in the world of Menelaus or Helen, not to mention Pandarus, a 'goer-between' with motives quite remote from the idealistic benevolence of Friar Lawrence. The ease with which idealism here turns into jealous rage, weakness into deviousness, cannot be blamed entirely on the external events; the lovers themselves must share the blame. We are bound to imagine that Cressida (in particular) could, if she chose, be more like Juliet and not allow a change of circumstances to become a change of mind. The collapse of strong idealistic assertion into compromised action brings the tragic emotions of *Troilus and Cressida* very close to bitter comedy. Shakespeare's generic brinkmanship is carried here to an extreme: heroism and incompetence alternate so rapidly that puzzlement finally takes over from perception.

When we come to *Othello* we find ourselves dealing with characters whose tragic fate derives clearly enough from their own deliberate choices, not from any pressure in their environment. Othello and Desdemona, whatever their difference in age, are alike in their calm and clear-eyed acceptance of themselves as responsible moral agents. Desdemona tells the senate:

> That I did love the Moor to live with him,
> My downright violence and storm of fortunes
> May trumpet to the world.   (1.3.248–50)

She is aware of the extraordinary figure she must be cutting in this scene and of the misinterpretation that will naturally attach to what she has done, but she is neither strident in self-justification nor hesitant and tentative. If her choice proves tragic (as it does) this is not because of any weakness in the capacity to choose. Othello is indeed a tragic choice, but he is not a wrong choice, for he totally fulfils the deepest impulses in her entirely admirable nature. Desdemona chooses the best of men, but even the best of men, the play insists, is subject to corruption. Cassius's words to Brutus in *Julius Caesar*:

> The fault, dear Brutus, is not in our stars,
> But in ourselves, that we are underlings   (1.2.141–2)

have a resonance for Shakespearian tragedy larger than the particular case of Brutus would indicate. Cassius seeks to 'whet' Brutus to political action against the dominance of Caesar. But *Othello* is probably Shakespeare's least political tragedy. Othello is an underling not because he fails to be a 'master of his fate' but because he is human. Faced by the intensity of total commitment, absolute love, men must be underlings because they are not gods, because they are vulnerable, they mistake, rage, fall down, become comic grotesques, as Othello does when he tries to listen in on Cassio and Iago talking about Bianca. Under such circumstances love for the best of men can be no more than a commitment to the fallible. However heroic the commitment, however true the perception of an ineffaceable goodness, the rot cannot be stopped nor the wrong step redirected. For the quality of faith in another, which is the highest expression of love, is necessarily tragic when the faith is fastened to a frail and changeable object, alias a human being. Othello is simultaneously the most glamorous of Shakespeare's heroes and the most vulnerable; and the simultaneous presence of these two opposed qualities is not used to mark a division in Othello's nature (though some critics would argue that it is so)[10] but rather a necessary condition of the heroic presence. The blocking agency in this play cannot be construed as either an external force, nor yet as a so-called 'tragic flaw'[11] in the particular nature of the hero – unless, that is, such 'flaws' are merely symptomatic of being human. The presence of an Iago, of an embodied spirit of negation, an equal and opposite force of separation and de-idealizing, is another aspect of this same spirit of paradox. In these dramatic worlds the balance of attitudes operates between characters as much as it does between aspects of a single mind, permitting that indeterminacy and perpetual reformation of judgement which is a mark of all good drama and of Shakespeare's authorship in particular. The source in the *Hecatommithi* of Giraldi Cinthio gave Shakespeare a down-to-earth tale of well-planned murder and an ethos dominated by ruthless self-interest. But Shakespeare chose to present the story in terms of an ethos of exotic romance and golden eloquence. Yet he still allows practicality its say. For if Iago is mean-spirited and Othello is heroic, can we not also say that Iago is a realist and Othello a poseur, that Iago knows the world and that Othello does not even know himself? Each of these judgements is capable of endless modification and much of our fascination in reading and rereading, seeing and re-seeing *Othello* comes from the interplay between them.

In *Othello* Shakespeare takes a traditional military hero with all the glamour that attaches to that role, places him in an inappropriate domestic setting, and gets him to play a traditional comic role as the despised *cocu imaginaire*, so that the openness of love and the meanness of possessiveness sound against one another. Something of the same paradox appears in the presentation of another glamorous military hero, Mark Antony, shadowed by another traditional comic role, that of the infatuated rich old man, held in thraldom by a calculating harlot. The shadow is, of course, only a minor effect of the substance. Much more central to Shakespeare's treatment of love in *Antony and Cleopatra* is the blocking force created by their public prominence and by the pressure of the public roles on supposedly private emotions. In *Antony and Cleopatra* the rhetoric of idealizing faith always hovers on the edge of mere rhetoric; even the lovers' kisses (as in 1.1.37) have something of the quality of lip-service to the images of public greatness which both of them want and need. The movement of the love-tragedies from *Romeo and Juliet* to *Antony and Cleopatra* has carried Shakespeare's tragic lovers from political nonentity to political dominance. It is a first natural assumption that this enlargement of power must also be an enlargement of love. Certainly the great can exercise the greatest freedom in their choices; they are the least liable to become the victims of other persons' wills. But this escape into one freedom is achieved only by accepting another servitude. The emotions that such characters are free to display publicly are pressed to assume the form that will give them the best publicity. And so the route that carries the forbidden love of Romeo and Juliet through the well-known secret of Troilus and Cressida, the public love of Othello and Desdemona, to the world-renowned love of Antony and Cleopatra, is not a pattern of increments but one of compensating gains and losses. Balancing of this kind rules out irony, we should notice, as a principal effect. Shakespeare does not say, in *Antony and Cleopatra*, that love between great persons is necessarily great love, nor does he allege that the change from innocence to sophistication changes faith into falsehood. He allows truth in both these positions, and keeps the comic potential of the deceived lover story as one of the play's recurrent features; Cleopatra's is, in fact, one of the great comic roles in Shakespeare – all the greater because the comedy is only part of her story. Yet the comedy of love which shows the innocent self-betrayal of the lover and the limitation in his grasp of reality is not, in *Antony and Cleopatra*, shown in any simple alternation with the tragic potential in love's fiction of privacy and invulnerability (as in *Romeo and Juliet*). In this play the two aspects are found inside the same moments and at many points seem to be the same thing, love being shown as simultaneously innocent and sophisticated, heartfelt and calculating, true and deceptive, worldly and other-worldly. In the other love-tragedies love is discovered as a new and transforming emotion that renders unimportant all other aspects of life. Love is not a new emotion for Antony or (more especially) Cleopatra, nor does it render unimportant the rest of their experience. It is, in fact, an integrated part of lives lived through many other spheres, so that questions about identity – 'Who is this *I* who is in love?' and 'Who is this *you* I am in love with?' – are not given a sufficient answer by the simple fact of being in love, but have to be treated also as questions about history and politics and power and publicity. Even when Antony imagines the Elysium of love after death it is characteristic that he imagines it in terms of rivalry for reputation:

> Dido and her Aeneas shall want troops,
> And all the haunt be ours.   (4.14.53–4)

Cleopatra too, even in the final scene when there is nothing left to lie for, sets up a scenario of love which is both splendid and suspect: 'I am again for

Cydnus / To meet Mark Antony', she tells Charmian. Her death will re-enact her greatest triumph, her ensnaring of Antony. She kills herself, certainly, to establish against Caesar's hegemony the supremacy of his rival as a great lover; but she is also self-pleasing in the sense of power it gives her to be able to call Caesar 'ass unpolicied'. Shakespeare does not allow us to separate the desire for love from the desire for power but shows that it is the tragedy of mature love that these two desires (held together) must destroy one another.

Antony and Cleopatra presents public responsibility as the opposite if not the enemy of love, and here as elsewhere in his work Shakespeare identifies public responsibility with Rome. He is not alone, of course, in making this connection; it was the standard assumption of his sources and his age (and of many other ages also). 'Roman Tragedy' is thus likely to be the story of a public duty that is tragic because it frustrates the hunger of the heart for private satisfaction. Here as elsewhere Shakespeare was able to outdo his contemporaries chiefly in the range of ambiguities and bi-focalities which he imposed on traditional themes. *Titus Andronicus* (1594), his first 'Roman' tragedy, is a prime example of this power of ambiguity, often seen only as evidence of incompetence at this point in his career. Titus himself is presented as a characteristic republican Roman: as father, as warrior, as magistrate, as citizen, he shows an inflexible and incorruptible devotion to law and precedent and an unhesitating suppression of personal life and all the softer emotions – mercy, pity, love. In these terms he belongs in the gallery of early Roman heroes: Horatius Cocles, Mutius Scaevola, Lucius Junius Brutus, Regulus, Cincinnatus, whose fame pervaded the whole of Europe. But *Titus Andronicus* is not simply a celebration of these iron virtues; it tells us a story that is designed to show that the exercise of such social virtue must be paid for at the highest individual cost. Titus enters the play having given, it would seem, more than enough: of twenty-five sons he has lost twenty-one in the wars he has won for Rome. But he is about to give even more: he declines to take the reward of the state's highest office; he refuses to permit the late Emperor's younger son to inherit, even though the latter is, we learn, a better man than his brother. As a result of these dutiful actions Titus loses three more sons, his daughter is raped and mutilated, his own right hand is stolen from him (as it were) by a trick, and he is mocked for being foolish enough to fall for such tricks. In all this he does not once let go of the moral system which has, we understand, sustained him and his culture throughout preceding time; he refuses to ransom his prisoner, the prince of the Goths, insisting that his compact with his dead sons will not allow mercy in the present. He kills his own son, Mutius, for being disobedient and rebellious. Shakespeare is obviously anxious to create the most violent opposition possible between a morality based on unquestioning obedience and respect for the past, militaristic honour and strict hierarchy, and (set against that) a morality based on feelings, on the fulfilment of desires, with a fair tolerance for anarchy and discontinuity. The characters are ranged on either side of this divide, with no suggestion of possible compromise between them, so that all that can be achieved is a blood-bath followed by a new start for the few survivors – a not unusual Elizabethan model for tragedy. What the unremitting violence aimed at Titus gives us is, however, more than a justification for the final bout of counter-violence. It is not so much the threat of death as the insistence that Titus's whole life has been a failure and that his beliefs are a tedious irrelevance that takes us to the centre of the action. For beyond the limit of what is tolerable lies a world in which the divide between right and wrong no longer divides. Titus's madness allows him to move close to his enemies while still judging them, act like them and yet be appalled by their wickedness. His distraught poetry projects a range of experience more mysterious, more terrifying, more subjective and unstable than 'Roman' assumptions can allow for. This victim of politicking has to face politics as they appear not in a notional Roman world but in a real world controlled by greed and passion and irrationality. The dénouement seems to show Shakespeare remembering the degeneracy of the Empire more clearly than the origins of the Republic.[12] Rome is 'saved' and the nightmare of Gothic rule is ended when Titus's last son, Lucius, reconquers the city with an army of Goths. The question whether this is really a salvation or only another step towards decay is bound to be part of our response to such a conclusion. The tormented heart of the play certainly seems to insist that there is no way back to Roman normality. The appalled poetic vision at the centre of *Titus Andronicus* is one in which the individual's belief that he has rights is confronted by the discovery that he has none and that only change is permanent (a moral Shakespeare may well have learned from Ovid's *Metamorphoses*).

When set against the Dostoevskian hysteria of *Titus Andronicus*, the later Roman plays, with structures incorporating the calm political perspective of their source in Plutarch's *Lives*, may appear to have bought coherent historical interpretation at the cost of a certain theatrical flatness. *Julius Caesar* (1599) is sometimes judged a play entirely worthy of the end it has achieved – recommendation as a schoolboy classic. Looking beyond the extreme difference of treatment we can see, however, that *Julius Caesar* and *Titus Andronicus* are based on the same contrast between political duty and private emotion. Brutus is no Titus, Caesar is no Saturninus, yet the tension between integrity and success links the later as surely as the earlier pair. Naturally, it seems, Shakespeare's tragic gaze is fastened, once again, on the example of integrity. High principled suffering and failure allow him to present what poetry can best convey – the sense of self not as an entity that can be made instrumental but as a condition that registers the mysterious correspondences between inner and outer experience. The superb competence of Caesar and (in more limited spheres) of Antony and Octavian appears to be closely connected with their incuriosity about their 'real' selves or about the meaning of what they are doing. It would be simple-minded to suppose, however, that

Brutus's tendency to poetic contemplation makes him a more poetic figure. In the famous scene of Caesar's funeral Brutus's speech has only *ethos* to recommend it; he more or less tells the assembled populace that, being himself, he cannot make a speech. Antony, however, has no such inhibitions. The *personae* he manipulates – Caesar's friend, your friend, humble suitor, grieving follower, outraged victim, angry vindicator – each of these is calculated to have a precise effect in a calculated sequence of effects. The brilliant political orator and the tongue-tied visionary – such contrasts show the complexity with which Shakespeare has developed his basic contrast. Clearly Brutus is the 'hero' of the play; but what do we mean by 'hero'? Shakespeare does not conceal the fact that Brutus is something of a prig, and also a military and political incompetent. His vision of a revitalized Roman republic is allowed no real substance; 'Let him be Caesar' is the strongest public support he ever achieves in the play. The movement he leads exists, as he knows, mainly as a vehicle for the malcontented and the envious. He has a touch of the martyr complex, and this offers us, once again, an ambiguity in judgement. Is the search for martyrdom model behaviour? Should we say, adapting T. S. Eliot on Thomas à Becket, that Brutus's murder of Caesar was 'the right deed for the wrong reason'[13] or only the wrong deed for the right reason? Between these ambiguous possibilities the play seems designed to puzzle us. Ernest Schanzer thought that this characteristic of *Julius Caesar* put it into the special category of 'problem plays'.[14] This teasing relationship with reader or spectator is, however, so recurrent a feature of the plays that it may not mark any category more specialized than 'Shakespearian'.

It is a notable mark of Shakespeare's ability to turn round and around the value-systems he works with that in *Coriolanus* (1608) he can show us Roman integrity, the central claim to virtue in both Brutus and Titus, as much less a virtue than a limitation. The contrast between the solitary man of integrity and the wheeling-dealing tribunes, with their manipulated voters, might seem set to repeat the pattern of these previous Roman plays, where admirable private qualities are contrasted with suspect public ones. But the priggishness which Coriolanus shares with Brutus is now less a consequence of his fixed principles and more an unthinking quality of self-regard. Brutus and Titus are idealists by temperament, whatever we think of their actions and what follows from them. *Timon of Athens*, often dated 1607, but whose chronological relationship to the other tragedies is really impossible to fix, shows us the process by which idealism turns into an obsession with the superiority of the self. In *Coriolanus*, however, idealism is no longer an issue. The fulfilment of self in the capacity to condemn and despise and banish others is achieved in this play without any understood process of self-discovery or self-knowledge. George Bernard Shaw called *Coriolanus* 'Shakespeare's greatest comedy',[15] and we may note that such a comedy of self-ignorance takes the cycle of tragedies back full circle (*Coriolanus* often being regarded as the last-written of the tragedies) to the endorsement of social rather than individual values. Romeo and Juliet saw themselves as natural inhabitants of a comedy world in which good intentions can expect to receive community support and so fulfil themselves in happy endings. They are betrayed into tragedy almost without noticing what is happening. In *Coriolanus* the relationship between the two genres is worked in an opposite direction. Though a figure of power, responsibility, representativeness, Coriolanus is betrayed by his own crassness into the condition of what Shaw, with typically paradoxical exaggeration, calls 'comedy'. With immense labour and the deployment of transcendent talent Coriolanus engineers his own irrelevance. Endings are, of course, the elements that separate comedies from tragedies most obviously, and the formal ending of *Coriolanus* marks the genre quite decisively. But the implication of that ending remains more ambiguous. We may choose to regard Coriolanus's discovery that he cannot reject his mother as a genuine anagnorisis; what he discovers, however, is that his life has been meaningless and that he has no values left to live by. The final scene takes us through the generic motions of violent death and final encomium, but the effects are undercut here by our knowledge that the hero's capacity for self-projection is already drained away in a world where heroic gestures are measured as political entities and found to be lacking in dimension.

The Roman tragedies keep a strong presence of history and politics, with their de-idealizing practicalities, as perpetual check on the tendency of the tragic hero to reshape the world around him in the image of his own desires – hence, no doubt, Bradley's distaste for them. The group of plays I am calling 'chronicle tragedies' (*King Lear*, *Macbeth*, *Hamlet*) is much more to Bradley's taste; they do not escape from history and politics, but the history they deal with is so archaic that politics tends to be replaced by ritual and history by anthropology. *King Lear* (1605) is the most obvious example of these substitutions. The division of the kingdom, the exiling of the good counsellor and loyal heir, the banishment of the old king, the recovery of legitimacy by an invasion from across the sea – these potentially political events are handled with so powerful a sense of their universal significance that merely political interpretation comes to seem reductive. *Macbeth* (1606) is closer to history as that is generally understood. But the hallucinatory vision that play gives, of a world polarized between Good and Evil, where kings (Duncan of Scotland, Edward the Confessor of England) have power principally as vessels of Grace, and where castles and trees and darkness and light exist more strongly in a metaphorical than a literal order – all this makes merely historical focus inadequate.

Every father of grown-up children recognizes the general truth of Lear's situation, yet the play shows no eagerness to explore the facts of any such realistically conceived case or to document its detail, in the manner of *Othello* for example. The individuals in *King Lear* move always across landscapes of the widest extent, criss-crossed by innumerable simultaneous purposes. *King Lear* enacts the meaning of fatherhood rather than its experience, aided in this by the presence of the duplicate father, Gloucester, and his antithetical sons, one virtuous, one vicious, who by the symmetry they provide reinforce our sense that we have here an abstracted pattern rather than a particular history. Indeed when we come to compare *King Lear* with its source in the old play of *King Leir* (1590) we find good evidence of Shakespeare using the radically different quality of story he found in Sidney's *Arcadia* (his source for the Gloucester plot) to counteract the pious providentialism that the old play provided, making a deliberate effort to render history as mystery. The love-auction in Shakespeare's first scene is handled as if it were a ritual from a religion whose other traces have entirely disappeared. As soon as we try to describe this action in personal terms we lose our bearings. What is going on here, we ask. Why do Lear and Cordelia pile one folly on top of another? There is no other sign that Cordelia is particularly foolish. It is possible, of course, to assume that Shakespeare was just being incompetent. Nahum Tate congratulated himself that his 1681 version of the play had rescued *King Lear* from its author's inconsequence and provided the characters with acceptable motives. He does not seem to have noticed that Shakespeare had already been offered acceptable motives in his source play, and had rejected them. Evidently it was Shakespeare's intention to present human actions stripped of their conventional explanatory surface and rendered not less but more mysterious by every effort the characters make to connect causes with results or generalize events into examples. In such an unanchored world of prehistory the mixture of the familiar with the strange, the known and the unknowable, is strongly biased towards the strange and the unknowable. Even the humour here belongs in the company of the anarchic, the wild, the desperate. Lear's fool is a jester by profession, but the effect he creates is not one of professional control and expertise but of jokes pulled out of agony and frustration, of crazy interconnections offered as the last efforts to signal towards meaning. Lear's madness makes a similar effect ('Thou wouldst make a good fool', he is told). Hamlet's madness is attached, initially at least, to a specific purpose, but Lear's madness represents only the fragmentation of all significance in a world where the differentiation of human identity from animal nature is no longer embodied in the conduct of the exemplary leaders of society but can only be picked up, piece by piece, from accident and hallucination.

The power of individual imagination to uncover beneath the social surface (made suitably vague by its remoteness in time) only the solitary intensities of appetite – this is given an even purer and clearer expression in *Macbeth*, where, in spite of its 'historical' source in Holinshed's chronicles, all the weight of the play's interest lies precisely on that mysterious point where imagination and what we call reality turn out to be interchangeable, where

                                        present fears
          Are less than horrible imaginings,

and where

          My thought, whose murder yet is but fantastical,
          Shakes so my single state of man
          That function is smother'd in surmise,
          And nothing is but what is not.   (1.3.137–42)

G. Wilson Knight and others have argued[16] that the imagery of *Hamlet* shows us how the language of the Ghost opens up in that play a world of evil and disease that eventually pervades the whole action. Statements of this kind are logically suspect, since the significance of the images is not integral to them but depends on the interconnections that the interpreter provides. But in *Macbeth* the poetic language of the hero is certainly being used by Shakespeare to project a vision of shapeless and unarticulable evil lodged far inside the practical world of wars and titles and inheritance, at a point where the constraints of custom and culture can hardly penetrate and may be quite irrelevant. In the social present of Macbeth's history such evil is conventionally thought of as belonging to the past:

          Blood hath been shed ere now, i' th' olden time,
          Ere humane statute purg'd the gentle weal;
                . . . The time has been
          That when the brains were out, the man would die,
          And there an end.   (3.4.75–80)

But the uncivilized past, like the primitive mind, is never in fact 'purged' by social enactment; like the Weird Sisters, it lurks in the empty spaces only awaiting recall. And in *Macbeth* it is recalled into a present and a culture where it finds itself, not as in *Hamlet* a bizarre intruder into a modern scene, but fully aligned and at home, as if it were a cancer colonizing its helplessly cooperative host. Macbeth and his lady 'cancel and tear in pieces' the great bond of civilization with its recurrent demand that men should live inside the understood restrictions of custom and accept the limitation on what is possible for the individual to achieve legitimately. The promise of the witches and of the imagination is a promise of liberation from the petty present, but the fulfilment achievable is only liberation into a more archaic and inflexible system of gain and loss. The killing of Macbeth completes the play, as is formally required, but we cannot see the death as a disaster for one who is already marked (like his wife) as the victim of a far more terrible system of justice, from which death offers the only possible escape:

          Better be with the dead,
          Whom we, to gain our peace, have sent to peace,
          Than on the torture of the mind to lie
          In restless ecstasy.   (3.2.19–22)

The political enactments of the present time in *Macbeth*, and the final promise of more (English) civilization to come, cannot seem other than a superficial response to the dark world ruled over by revenging Furies. This does not mean that we should not recognize the pallid Malcolm and his good intentions as the best response available. Without its political dimension *Macbeth* could not hold together as a play. The overwhelming poetic vision of an alien world that is also, and irresistibly, part of our inmost being – this has somehow to be contained inside the drab and patient mediocrity of small men trying to be good.

I have kept *Hamlet* (1601), the third of these 'chronicle tragedies', to the last, but not because it was the last to be written. It was, in fact, the first. I have broken chronology here because *Hamlet* is of the three plays the most ambiguously connected to the idea of 'chronicle tragedy' as I have spoken about it, and it needs the examples of *Lear* and *Macbeth* to make clear the games it is playing with the notion of a chronicle past. Hamlet is placed unambiguously in a modern age: he was educated at a new university (Wittenberg), lives in a specific extant castle (Elsinore), and is a connoisseur of modern plays and modern fencing. In this intellectual milieu ghosts are hard to believe in, and Hamlet's fellow-student Horatio speaks for both when he says

> I might not this believe
> Without the sensible and true avouch
> Of mine own eyes. (1.i.56–8)

Yet not only is the original source story in Saxo Grammaticus's *History of the Danes* as mysteriously antique as that of *King Lear* and as barbarously northern as that of *Macbeth*, but Shakespeare's play itself embodies that alien archaism as its central motivating cause. The ghost of Hamlet's father, clanking in medieval armour, fresh from a world in which national destinies were settled by personal combat, demands not only that the play embody his cry for revenge but that the ethic of his revenge take over the thinking of his modernist son. As the great exemplar of *The Spanish Tragedy* makes clear (not to mention the *Oresteia*) 'Revenge Tragedy' is particularly well suited to inhabit this borderline between the demand of an archaic religion and its fulfilment in a secular and politically self-conscious present. What the play of *Hamlet* seems to show us is how one may use the shadowy indefiniteness of the first of these to counteract the reductive practicality of the second. Awareness that the play, like the spectator, lives in the compromising present gives its audience a sense of immediate connection with the world depicted, but the looming power of the play comes rather from the shadows cast on to the sharply defined present from the mysterious past – power which Freudian ideologues wish to express in a Freudian vocabulary, but which is equally well expressed in any vocabulary that sets the esoteric against the exoteric, the hidden against the explicit, the difficult against the easy, seeing the latter as an inadequate or distorting representation of the former. The immediacy of Hamlet as our representative, a modern reflector of ancient pieties, gives him a hold on modern responses which is not shared by either King Lear or Macbeth, who are seen more usually in the middle distance of their archaic cultures. No one would dream of extending Coleridge's 'I have a smack of Hamlet myself, if I may say so'[17] to include the other chronicle heroes. Yet the world of Hamlet's poetic imagination and the vocabulary (if not the purpose) of his madness oppress us with the same powerful alienness as we find in these other explicitly strange and barbaric heroes. Hamlet appears to be both familiar and remote, friendly and hostile, welcoming and dismissive, gregarious and solitary, humble and imperious. The paradoxes in his character correspond to the paradoxes that pervade tragedy. On the one hand these Shakespeare plays reassure us that our individual experience is of representative significance and show us that the words of power are our own words. On the other hand tragedy tells us that our lives are lived in self-protective ignorance, in an alien world where the most meaning that can be hoped for is a concatenation

> Of carnal, bloody, and unnatural acts;
> Of accidental judgments, casual slaughters;
> Of deaths put on by cunning and forc'd cause,
> And, in the upshot, purposes mistook
> Fall'n on the inventors' heads.   (5.2.373–7)

Notes

1. See David Bevington, *Tudor Drama and Politics* (Cambridge, Mass., 1968).
2. Dates of plays, unless otherwise specified, are taken from *Annals of English Drama* by Alfred Harbage, revised by S. Schoenbaum (1964).
3. See David Bevington, *From Mankind to Marlowe* (Cambridge, Mass., 1962).
4. George K. Hunter, 'Tyrant and martyr: religious heroisms in Elizabethan tragedy', in *Poetic Traditions of the English Renaissance*, ed. Maynard Mack and George de F. Lord (New Haven, 1982).
5. Emrys Jones, *The Origins of Shakespeare* (1977).
6. See Willard Farnham, *The Medieval Heritage of Elizabethan Tragedy* (Berkeley, 1936).
7. See Michael Hattaway, *Elizabethan Popular Theatre: Plays in Performance* (1982).
8. Compare Stephen Booth, *'King Lear', 'Macbeth', Indefinition and Tragedy* (New Haven, 1983).
9. Northrop Frye, 'The argument of comedy', in *English Stage Comedy* (English Institute Essays 1948), ed. W. K. Wimsatt, (New York, 1949).
10. F. R. Leavis, 'Diabolic intellect and the noble hero', in *The Common Pursuit* (1952).
11. See Peter Alexander, *Hamlet, Father and Son* (1955) for a useful discussion of this concept.
12. See George K. Hunter, 'Sources and meanings in *Titus Andronicus*', in *The Mirror up to Shakespeare*, ed. Jack C. Gray (Toronto, 1984).
13. T. S. Eliot, *Murder in the Cathedral* (1936), p. 44.
14. Ernest Schanzer, *The Problem Plays of Shakespeare* (1963).

15. G. B. Shaw, Preface to *Man and Superman* (1903).
16. G. Wilson Knight, 'The embassy of death', in *The Wheel of Fire* (1930).
17. S. T. Coleridge, 'Table Talk, 1827' reprinted in Raysor, *Coleridge's Shakespeare Criticism*, 2 vols. (1930), II, p. 352.

Reading list

Barker, Harley Granville, *Prefaces to Shakespeare*, 1927, etc.; reprinted in 2 vols (1946–47)
Bayley, John, *Shakespeare and Tragedy* (1981)
Booth, Stephen, *'King Lear', 'Macbeth', Indefinition and Tragedy* (1983)
Bradley, A. C., *Shakespearean Tragedy* (1904; second edition, 1906)
Brooke, Nicholas, *Shakespeare's Early Tragedies* (1968)
Brower, Reuben, *Hero and Saint: Shakespeare and the Greco-Roman Heroic Tradition* (1972)
Clemen, Wolfgang, *Tragedy Before Shakespeare* (1961)
Edwards, Philip, *Shakespeare and the Confines of Art* (1968)
Farnham, Willard, *The Medieval Heritage of Elizabethan Tragedy* (1936)
Frye, Northrop, *Fools of Time: Studies in Shakespearean Tragedy* (1967)
Heilman, Robert B., *This Great Stage: Image and Structure in 'King Lear'* (1948)
  Magic in the Web: Action and Language in 'Othello' (1956)
Holloway, John, *The Story of the Night: Studies in Shakespeare's Major Tragedies* (1961)
Knight, G. Wilson, *The Wheel of Fire* (1930)
  The Imperial Theme (1931)
Knights, L. C., *'Hamlet' and Other Shakespearean Essays* (1979)
  Some Shakespearean Themes (1959)
McCallum, M. W., *Shakespeare's Roman Plays and their Background* (1910)
Mack, Maynard, *'King Lear' in our Time* (1965)
Margeson, J. M. R., *The Origins of English Tragedy* (1967)
Moulton, R. G., *Shakespeare as a Dramatic Artist* (1885)
Rabkin, Norman, *Shakespeare and the Common Understanding* (1967)
Rossiter, A. P., *Angel with Horns* (1961)
Spivack, Bernard, *Shakespeare and the Allegory of Evil* (1958)
Waith, Eugene M., *The Herculean Hero* (1962)

9   Shakespeare's use of history

A T the end of *Henry V* the Chorus reappears to deliver the Epilogue. For the first time he speaks to us in the past tense, relaxing from the urgent immediacy with which he has hitherto been demanding that we '*now* behold, / In the quick forge and working-house of thought' (Chorus 5, 22–3) the story he has to tell us. As the Epilogue develops, the events in which we have been participating resume their place in distant history:

> Small time, but, in that small, most greatly lived
> This star of England. Fortune made his sword;
> By which the world's best garden he achieved,
> And of it left his son imperial lord.   (Epilogue, 5–8)

There is no sense that the events with which the dramatist has excited and moved us are being devalued; on the contrary, they remain poignantly impressive – 'in that small, most greatly lived'. All at once, however, the events of Henry's reign seem to have become distant and beyond our grasp, 'like far off mountains, turnèd into clouds'. As the Chorus reaches his conclusion our gaze is directed even more firmly towards the past. Shakespeare's chronicle sources divide themselves into chapters by the reigns of kings: not only are we here invited to contemplate such a transition; we are reminded also that the next phase of the past has itself already supplied the needs of a dramatist eager for plot material:

> Henry the Sixth, in infant bands crown'd king
> Of France and England, did this king succeed;
> Whose state so many had the managing
> That they lost France and made his England bleed;
> Which oft our stage hath shown.   (Epilogue, 9–13)

In an interview given in 1956 Thornton Wilder contrasted the narrative with the theatrical mode. 'A novel is what *took place*', he says – the same is even more obviously true of a history book – and he contrasts this with theatre: 'A dramatist is one who believes that the pure event, an action involving human beings, is more arresting than any comment that can be made upon it. On the stage it is always *now*; the personages are standing on that razor-edge, between the past and the future, which is the essential character of conscious being.'

And he adds, a little later: 'The theatre is supremely fitted to say: "Behold! These things are."'[1] It is precisely our sense of that razor-edge that the Epilogue to *Henry V* is exploiting. As it concludes, the dramatic experience becomes historical; *now* becomes *then* and theatre yields place to the chronicle from which it was drawn.

To begin a discussion of Shakespeare's use of history with the final Chorus of *Henry V* is to begin at the end, or almost so. With the exception of *Henry VIII*, a later and probably collaborative play, *Henry V*, written in the summer of 1599, is the last of Shakespeare's history plays.[2] It provides, however, a convenient starting place for this essay, for it shows Shakespeare at a point of self-consciousness in both technique and achievement. 'Which oft our stage hath shown', remarks the Chorus, and the dramatist can look back on a decade or so in which his use of history as theatrical source material had produced nine plays. The grouping of these into two tetralogies (with *King John* as an isolated excursion into a much earlier reign) reflects an obvious aspect of their conception: the first tetralogy plunges into the disintegration of political stability following the death of Henry V, the inexorable movement towards civil war, and emergence of Richard III's destructive power; the second tetralogy examines the period of history leading up to this cataclysmic half-century, establishing the conditions from which it grew, perhaps also seeking its causes. Because Shakespeare turned first to the later period of history, the completion of *Henry V* was also the completion of a long-cherished project, and one has a sense, in that last chorus, of the central span of a great arch having finally and triumphantly been placed in position. It is an arch that links, in the divisions of history we have since become accustomed to, the medieval with the modern period. It reaches from the son of the Black Prince to the grandfather of the queen in whose reign the plays were written, from the last years of the fourteenth century to 1485 and to that battle at Bosworth which must have seemed at the time merely the most recent in a long and bloody series of civil war skirmishes, but which – with the benefit of historical hindsight, aided, perhaps, by the myth-making power of the national dramatist – has since been regarded as a turning point in English history.

Writing apparently in response to what may have been the earliest of Shakespeare's history plays, the first part of *Henry VI*,[3] Thomas Nashe describes the effect which the death of the play's principal character, Lord Talbot, produced on its audiences:

How would it have joyed brave Talbot, the terror of the French, to think that after he had lien two hundred years in his tomb he should triumph again on the stage, and have his bones new-embalmed with the tears of ten thousand spectators at least, at several times, who in the tragedian that represents his person imagine they behold him fresh bleeding.[4]

The episode is (thanks no doubt to the vividness of recent theatrical memory) the one example he chooses to cite of the theatre's capacity to excite us with plays 'wherein our forefathers' valiant acts, that have lien long buried in rusty brass and wormeaten books, are revived' and their virtues and vices 'most lively anatomized'. It is a nice coincidence that so early an enterprise in this work of revivification should have been so enthusiastically greeted.

The gulf which Nashe perceived between the reading of history and the theatrical reliving of it, between the 'wormeaten books' of the chronicles and the 'lively anatomized' immediacy of the stage, is something that Shakespeare must have pondered frequently as he mined the historians for theatrical material. At one point in *Richard III* he introduces a discussion of it rather in the terms used by Nashe a year or two earlier. It has just been decided that the young King Edward V should take up his residence in the Tower of London, soon to provide the setting for the most notorious (and last) event of his short reign. Our imaginations thus alerted to the historical resonances of the Tower, the boy suddenly invites our consideration of the nature of history: 'Did Julius Caesar build that place?' he asks, and Buckingham provides a meticulously historical response:

> He did, my gracious lord, begin that place,
> Which, since, succeeding ages have re-edified.

Still Edward is not satisfied:

> Is it upon record, or else reported
> Successively from age to age, he built it?

Assured that it is 'upon record', he responds:

> But say, my lord, it were not register'd,
> Methinks the truth should live from age to age,
> As 'twere retail'd to all posterity,
> Even to the general all-ending day.   (3.1.69–78)

The contrast between a 'register'd' past, a past 'upon record', and a past with the capacity to 'live from age to age' is precisely the contrast that Nashe draws between books and brass on the one hand and the 'lively' anatomy of theatre on the other.

As Shakespeare, at the end of the 1580s, began to contemplate his plays on the Wars of the Roses, the volumes to which he turned in his search for what was 'upon record' and 'register'd' about the past of England had hardly yet had the opportunity to become wormeaten. The two enormous tomes into which were bound the three volumes of Raphael Holinshed's *Chronicles of England, Scotland, and Ireland* had been published in their much augmented second edition, ten years after the first, in 1587. They were thus the most up-to-date and authoritative source book of English history to which Shakespeare could have referred, offering, in closely printed, black-letter, folio pages an account of the history of Britain, in something over three and a half million words, from the sons of Noah to the year, and even the month, of printing. Twenty and more years later Shakespeare was still using them when he came to write *Henry VIII*, and in the meantime they had supplied him with material for all the English history plays and for *King Lear*, *Macbeth*, and *Cymbeline*. In nearly all the plays he supplemented his reading of Holinshed, turning most often to one of Holinshed's own sources, Edward Hall's account of the English Civil Wars published in 1548 under the title *The Union of the Two Noble and Illustre Families of Lancaster and York*. Hall's influence is particularly strong in the *Henry VI* plays, though pervasive throughout both tetralogies, but since Holinshed's dependence on Hall's account is often close, it is not always easy to separate the primary from the secondary source. Other chronicles and histories, earlier history plays, historical poetry, even manuscript materials, were variously used by Shakespeare in creating his history plays.[5] In spite of the range and depth of reading and selection behind all the plays, however, it is clear that the principal enterprise upon which Shakespeare embarked was turning the overwhelmingly informative *then*-narrative, which those great volumes of Holinshed offered, into the liveliness of *now*-theatricality.

Before considering Shakespeare's use of history in individual plays, it may be worth asking why he used it at all. The editors of the 1623 Folio confidently divided their volume into 'Master William Shakespeare's Comedies, Histories, and Tragedies', but that intermediate genre between the classically recognized forms of comedy and tragedy is not altogether self-defining or self-explanatory. The history play had emerged in the earlier sixteenth century from the morality form, and depended upon the replacement of 'Everyman', the *humanum genus* representative, by the nation, or *respublica*, as the figure at the centre of the moral struggle.[6] From the list of plays based on English history before *1 Henry VI*, however, both extant and lost, it is clear that the genre was really little more than emergent before Shakespeare seized upon it and gave it life.[7]

The history plays and their immediate sources are rooted, at a deeper level, in the Tudor Englishman's persistent interest in matters historical. Throughout the reign of Elizabeth history books poured from the presses, both original works on English and foreign history and translations of modern European and classical historians.[8] They constantly reiterate the inescapable educative potential of history. John Stow, whose diligence in the compilation of chronicles earned him in his day the affectionate, if not altogether enviable, epithet of 'Laborious', must stand as the sole example of a phenomenon which could be multiplied a hundredfold. In the preface to his *Chronicles of England* of 1580 he remarks that

it is as hard a matter for the Readers of Chronicles, in my fansie, to passe without some colours of wisedom, invitements to vertue, and loathing of naughtie factes, as it is for a welfavoured man to walke up and downe in the hot parching Sunne, and not to be therewith sunburned.[9]

It is precisely this attitude which Thomas Nashe takes up in his defence of plays in *Pierce Penniless*. Plays are, he writes, 'for the most part . . . borrowed out of our English Chronicles', and like them they 'show the ill success of treason, the fall of hasty climbers, the wretched end of usurpers, the misery of civil dissension' (p. 65). Here are the well-worn arguments in favour of history being used to defend the theatre, a situation which must have seemed immensely reassuring to a profession by no means free from attack at the beginning of the 1590s.

There were other pressures, however, inducing dramatists to interest themselves in history as the last decade of the century was beginning. One was certainly commercial. The huge increase in theatrical activity in these years, discernible especially in the establishment of more permanent playing places in London, created a need for plays in numbers hitherto undreamt of. The rapidity with which plays were written, put on, and exhausted emerges clearly from the theatrical account-book of Philip Henslowe.[10] Henslowe's records also make clear the alacrity with which dramatists turned to English history as a ready source of plots, so that, by the end of the century, there was scarcely a reign, from the Conquest to the coming of the Tudors, that had not been dramatized. The great upsurge in national self-awareness in the last years of the sixteenth century also had its inevitable effect on the eagerness of audiences to be informed of their nation's past, and the willingness of dramatists to provide the information. To suppose that the passion for history plays stemmed exclusively from national euphoria following defeat of the Spanish Armada in 1588 would be absurd, for the emergence of the genre clearly precedes that date; but to suppose that it was unaffected by it, and by the intense anxiety concerning national security before and after it, would be equally unwise.

Above all, however, one must seek one's answer to the question of why Shakespeare wrote history plays in the man's fascination with politics. If comedy is that form of drama which concerns itself with social man, and tragedy with moral or ethical man, then history is above all an exploration of human political behaviour, of the desire for power, of men's response to gaining it and to being deprived of it. Power in English history meant kingship, and the relationship between the theoretical amplitude of the office and the human limitation of the man who holds it. Shakespeare's 'use of history' consists, then, in selecting, shaping, amplifying, and frequently in adding to, chronicle material in order to intensify concentration on political issues and on their human consequences.

One example must serve as the only detailed illustration of this. In the third scene of Act 2 of *Richard II*, Bolingbroke, illegally returned from exile, confronts his uncle the Duke of York, Lord Protector of the realm in the King's absence. Figure 7 reproduces the page from Holinshed's chronicle which is the source for this episode, the middle paragraph of the second

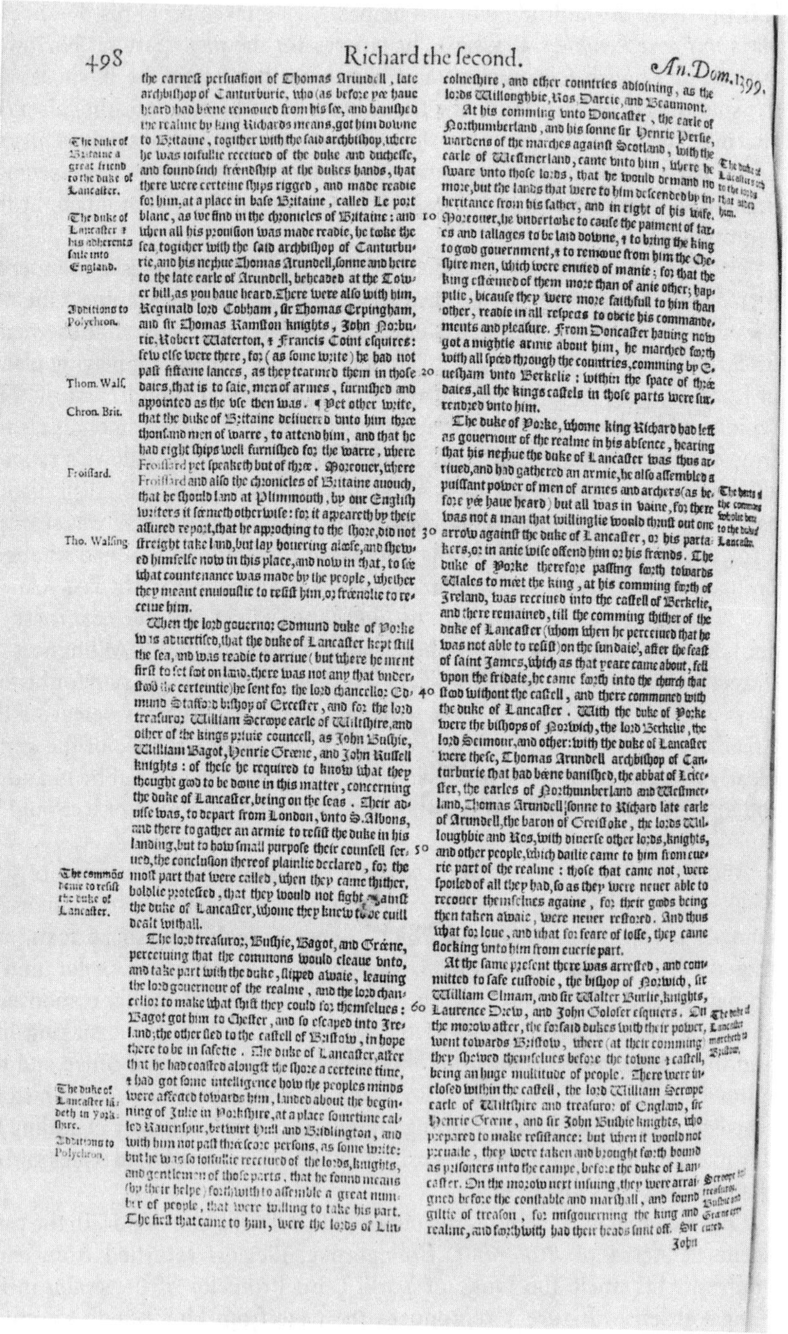

498 Richard the second. An. Dom. 1399.

the earnest persuasion of Thomas Arundell, late archbishop of Canturburie, who (as before ye haue heard) had béene remoued from his sée, and banished the realme by king Richards means, got him downe to Britaine, togither with the said archbishop, where he was ioifullie receiued of the duke and duchesse, and found such fréendship at the dukes hands, that there were certeine ships rigged, and made readie for him, at a place in base Britaine, called Le port blanc, as we find in the chronicles of Britaine: and when all his prouision was made readie, he tooke the sea, togither with the said archbishop of Canturburie, and his nephue Thomas Arundell, sonne and heire to the late earle of Arundell, beheaded at the Tower hill, as you haue heard. There were also with him, Reginald lord Cobham, sir Thomas Erpingham, and sir Thomas Ramston knights, Iohn Norburie, Robert Waterton, & Francis Coint esquires: few else were there, for (as some write) he had not past fiftéene lances, as they tearmed them in those daies, that is to saie, men of armes, furnished and appointed as the vse then was. ¶ Yet other write, that the duke of Britaine deliuered vnto him thrée thousand men of warre, to attend him, and that he had eight ships well furnished for the warre, where Froissard yet speaketh but of thrée. Moreouer, where Froissard and also the chronicles of Britaine auouch, that he should land at Plimmouth, by our English writers it séemeth otherwise: for it appeareth by their assured report, that he approching to the shore, did not streight take land, but lay houering aloofe, and shewed himselfe now in this place, and now in that, to sée what countenance was made by the people, whether they meant enuiouslie to resist him, or fréendlie to receiue him.

The duke of Britaine a great friend to the duke of Lancaster.

The duke of Lancaster & his adherents saile into England.

Additions to Polychron.

Thom. Wals.

Chron. Brit.

Froissard.

Tho. Walsing.

When the lord gouernor Edmund duke of Yorke was aduertised, that the duke of Lancaster kept still the sea, and was readie to arriue (but where he ment first to set foot on land, there was not any that vnderstood the certeintie) he sent for the lord chancellor Edmund Stafford bishop of Excester, and for the lord treasuror William Scrope earle of Wiltshire, and other of the kings priuie councell, as Iohn Bushie, William Bagot, Henrie Gréene, and Iohn Russell knights: of these he required to know what they thought good to be doone in this matter, concerning the duke of Lancaster, being on the seas. Their aduise was, to depart from London, vnto S. Albons, and there to gather an armie to resist the duke in his landing, but to how small purpose their counsell serued, the conclusion thereof plainlie declared, for the most part that were called, when they came thither, boldlie protested, that they would not fight against the duke of Lancaster, whome they knew to be euill dealt withall.

The commons leaue to resist the duke of Lancaster.

The lord treasuror, Bushie, Bagot, and Gréene, perceiuing that the commons would cleaue vnto, and take part with the duke, slipped awaie, leauing the lord gouernour of the realme, and the lord chancellor to make what shift they could for themselues: Bagot got him to Chester, and so escaped into Ireland; the other fled to the castell of Bristow, in hope there to be in safetie. The duke of Lancaster, after that he had coasted alongst the shore a certeine time, & had got some intelligence how the peoples minds were affected towards him, landed about the beginning of Iulie in Yorkshire, at a place sometime called Rauenspur, betwixt Hull and Bridlington, and with him not past thréescore persons, as some write: but he was so ioifullie receiued of the lords, knights, and gentlemen of those parts, that he found means (by their helpe) forthwith to assemble a great number of people, that were willing to take his part. The first that came to him, were the lords of Lincolneshire, and other countries adioining, as the lords Willoughbie, Ros, Darcie, and Beaumont.

The duke of Lancaster landeth in Yorkshire.

Additions to Polychron.

At his comming vnto Doncaster, the earle of Northumberland, and his sonne sir Henrie Persie, wardens of the marches against Scotland, with the earle of Westmerland, came vnto him, where he sware vnto those lords, that he would demand no more, but the lands that were to him descended by inheritance from his father, and in right of his wife. Moreouer, he vndertooke to cause the paiment of taxes and tallages to be laid downe, & to bring the king to good gouernment, & to remooue from him the Cheshire men, which were enuied of manie; for that the king estéemed of them more than of anie other; happilie, bicause they were more faithfull to him than other, readie in all respects to obeie his commandements and pleasure. From Doncaster hauing now got a mightie armie about him, he marched foorth with all spéed through the countries, comming by Euesham vnto Berkelie: within the space of thrée daies, all the kings castels in those parts were surrendred vnto him.

The duke of Lancaster sweareth to the lords that aided him.

The duke of Yorke, whome king Richard had left as gouernour of the realme in his absence, hearing that his nephue the duke of Lancaster was thus arriued, and had gathered an armie, he also assembled a puissant power of men of armes and archers (as before yée haue heard) but all was in vaine, for there was not a man that willinglie would thrust out one arrow against the duke of Lancaster, or his partakers, or in anie wise offend him or his fréends. The duke of Yorke therefore passing foorth towards Wales to méet the king, at his comming foorth of Ireland, was receiued into the castell of Berkelie, and there remained, till the comming thither of the duke of Lancaster (whom when he perceiued that he was not able to resist) on the sundaie, after the feast of saint Iames, which as that yeare came about, fell vpon the fridaie, he came foorth into the church that stood without the castell, and there communed with the duke of Lancaster. With the duke of Yorke were the bishops of Norwich, the lord Berkelie, the lord Seimour, and other: with the duke of Lancaster were these, Thomas Arundell archbishop of Canturburie that had béene banished, the abbat of Leicester, the earles of Northumberland and Westmerland, Thomas Arundell sonne to Richard late earle of Arundell, the baron of Greistoke, the lords Willoughbie and Ros, with diuerse other lords, knights, and other people, which dailie came to him from euerie part of the realme: those that came not, were spoiled of all they had, so as they were neuer able to recouer themselues againe, for their goods being then taken awaie, were neuer restored. And thus what for loue, and what for feare of losse, they came flocking vnto him from euerie part.

The hearts of the commons wholie bent to the duke of Lancaster.

At the same present there was arrested, and committed to safe custodie, the bishop of Norwich, sir William Elmam, and sir Walter Burlie, knights, Laurence Drew, and Iohn Golofer esquires. On the morow after, the foresaid dukes with their power, went towards Bristow, where (at their comming) they shewed themselues before the towne & castell, being an huge multitude of people. There were inclosed within the castell, the lord William Scrope earle of Wiltshire and treasuror of England, sir Henrie Gréene, and sir Iohn Bushie knights, who prepared to make resistance: but when it would not preuaile, they were taken and brought foorth bound as prisoners into the campe, before the duke of Lancaster. On the morow next insuing, they were arraigned before the constable and marshall, and found giltie of treason, for misgouerning the king and realme, and foorthwith had their heads smit off. Sir

Iohn

The duke of Lancaster marcheth to Bristow.

Scroope lord treasuror, Bushie and Greene executed.

7 A page from Holinshed's *Chronicles* (1587) describing the meeting of Bolingbroke and the Duke of York at Berkeley Castle

column describing the meeting at Berkeley Castle which Shakespeare turns into a pivotal scene of his play and the surrounding material offering further illustration of Shakespeare's processes of selection and adaptation. The busy diligence with which the historian gathers quantities of detailed fact to place indiscriminately before his reader – the precise day of the week upon which the feast of Saint James fell in the year 1399, the careful lists of persons present, the exact location of the meeting – are typical of the hundreds of pages of Holinshed that Shakespeare worked from to produce his history plays. But when it comes to the constitutional and personal confrontation of Lord Protector and illegally returned exile, of uncle and nephew, the chronicler offers only the bland statement that York 'communed with the duke of Lancaster'. Shakespeare seizes on the moment, sorting through the chaff of detail to create a scene which exploits the personal and familial relationship of the chief participants and directly confronts the legal, political, and constitutional issues left dormant in Holinshed's account, and so makes theatre from them.

As soon as York appears he makes his own position clear, both constitutionally as head of state in the King's absence, and historically and mythically as the last survivor of those seven sons of Edward III whose untroubled and glorious reign has been regarded earlier in the play as a lost golden age:

> Com'st thou because the anointed king is hence?
> Why, foolish boy, the king is left behind,
> And in my loyal bosom lies his power.
> Were I but now lord of such hot youth
> As when brave Gaunt, thy father, and myself
> Rescued the Black Prince, that young Mars of men,
> From forth the ranks of many thousand French,
> O, then how quickly should this arm of mine,
> Now prisoner to the palsy, chastise thee
> And minister correction to thy fault! (2.3.96–105)

Bolingbroke's presence in England is classified, similarly uncompromisingly, as 'gross rebellion and detested treason' (109). The heart of the issue is the extent of the King's power in a system of government by monarchy, the nature of the relationship between the King and the Law. It is an issue about which Englishmen were to argue with increasing urgency for the half-century after the play was written and which led, with an inexorability which this episode seems almost to predict, to a scene played before the Banqueting House in Whitehall in 1649, when the execution of Charles I settled the question with awesome finality. The basis of Bolingbroke's argument is that the King has deprived him of inalienable rights, fundamental to the legal system of primogeniture by which the country is governed:

> Wherefore was I born?
> If that my cousin king be King in England,
> It must be granted I am Duke of Lancaster. (2.3.122–4)

York is in no position to offer an answer based on royal prerogative, for he has already committed himself to Bolingbroke's position – almost, indeed, in the same terms. When Richard seized Gaunt's properties two scenes earlier, York had protested at the violation of succession, which deprived Bolingbroke (Hereford) of his birthright:

> Take Hereford's rights away, and take from Time
> His charters and his customary rights;
> Let not tomorrow then ensue today;
> Be not thyself – for how art thou a king
> But by fair sequence and succession?   (2.1.195–9)

In the theatrical immediacy of confrontation between the old man and the young, their followers alert to the sharpness of the argument, stirring menacingly perhaps, in anticipation of the military solution which seems inevitable, one sees Shakespeare's relationship with historical source material in its essence. The pressure of the past – of the historical past and of the past of these dramatic characters – bears down on this moment, as York, confronted, unanswerably, with the power of his own arguments, allows theatrical control of the scene, and with it political control of the nation, to ebb away from him. The theoretical basis of the confrontation remains legal, as Bolingbroke again appeals to him:

> What would you have me do? I am a subject,
> And I challenge law – attorneys are denied me;
> And therefore personally I lay my claim
> To my inheritance of free descent.   (2.3.133–6)

But beyond that legal theorizing there lies, in York's admission, the ultimate political truth of military power:

> Well, well, I see the issue of these arms.
> I cannot mend it, I must needs confess,
> Because my power is weak and all ill left.   (2.3.152–4)

The last struggles of the representative of the old traditions, son of Edward III and companion in victory to the Black Prince, have a kind of elegiac pathos. He asserts what we can indeed vouch for: 'I have had feeling of my cousin's wrongs, / And labour'd all I could to do him right'; he repeats once more the truth as seen from a position of constitutional orthodoxy: 'you that do abet him in this kind / Cherish rebellion, and are rebels all'; and he admits the simple fact that legal theory and political conservatism, when confronted with an argument supported by a larger army, are emasculated: 'I do remain as neuter' (141–59). The government has fallen:

> So fare you well;
> Unless you please to enter in the castle,
> And there repose you for this night.   (2.3.159–61)

The implications of York's capitulation are revealed as the scene ends. Northumberland insists that

> The noble Duke hath sworn his coming is
> But for his own; and for the right of that
> We all have strongly sworn to give him aid. (2.3.148–50)

A few lines later, however, a third chime of that potent syllable *sworn* offers to us, and perhaps to Bolingbroke too, a first glimpse of the frightening vista which military overthrow of the theory that King and Law are inseparable has opened up. Bolingbroke accepts his uncle's offer of hospitality and in tones of coaxing blandishment or veiled threat (the actor has a range of choice) leaves him no option but to join the next phase of the operation:

> An offer, uncle, that we will accept.
> But we must win your Grace to go with us
> To Bristow Castle, which they say is held
> By Bushy, Bagot, and their complices,
> The caterpillars of the commonwealth,
> Which I have *sworn* to weed and pluck away. (2.3.162–7)

Between swearing that he comes 'but for his own' and swearing to take over the administration of justice and cut off the heads of the King's subjects there is no apparent connection. Bolingbroke has breached the whole system that binds subject to king. 'I am loath to break our country's laws' murmurs York in a last feeble attempt to resist the sweeping tide that has engulfed him (169). But we next see him, the puppet governor, standing by powerless while his nephew executes a surprisingly dignified pair of the King's favourites for a catalogue of alleged crimes which seem curiously to have been directed more against Bolingbroke than against the state. The revolution has begun.

A little space has been devoted to this fulcrum scene of *Richard II* because its methods offer a conveniently compact example of Shakespeare's work in detail on the adaptation of history to theatre. If we turn from detail to the broader strategies of manipulation of chronicle material in the history plays *Richard II* again provides a convenient starting point. Shakespeare's politicization of his source is apparent in the scene of York's confrontation with Bolingbroke. Other, non-political, motives, however, are at work in the play, exploring areas of personal grief and loss. The play is rare among the histories in containing little non-historical material and few fictional characters. The most significant of these is the Queen, a figure so different from Richard's historical queen (a child-wife who figures hardly at all in Holinshed's account of the period) as to be virtually an invention of the dramatist. She acts as a minor but clear example of a phenomenon discernible throughout the history plays: the use of a non-historical character to interpret political events or modify our response to them. She appears on three significant occasions. The first is to lament the absence as a loving husband of the man we have hitherto perceived only as an incompetent and unprincipled monarch. The second is to reinterpret, at the level of personal loss, news of Richard's fall from power which we have first heard as political gossip. The last occasion parallels, in the separation between husband and wife, the rift which Bolingbroke has created between Richard and the crown he was born to, a rift which Richard ritualizes in his final meeting with the Queen:

> Doubly divorc'd! Bad men, you violate
> A twofold marriage – 'twixt my crown and me,
> And then betwixt me and my married wife . . .
> Part us, Northumberland; I towards the north,
> Where shivering cold and sickness pines the clime;
> My wife to France, from whence set forth in pomp,
> She came adorned hither like sweet May
> Sent back like Hollowmas or short'st of day.   (5.2.71–80)

There is nothing like this in Shakespeare's history books. The theatrical image it produces – armed men physically pulling apart a man and his wife – relates directly to what has been done to the relationship between Richard and his birthright, presenting it at a poignant level of emotional loss and personal grief. The historical issues in the story of an English monarch of two hundred years ago are thus widened and generalized into an experience that becomes, for its audience, both universal and immediate. The pain and suffering of this king, and this husband, come – quite literally in Richard's vision – to every fireside:

> In winter's tedious nights sit by the fire
> With good old folks, and let them tell thee tales
> Of woeful ages long ago betid;
> And ere thou bid goodnight, to quit their griefs
> Tell thou the lamentable tale of me,
> And send the hearers weeping to their beds.   (5.1.40–5)

In that image of Richard as both a 'tale' from 'ages long ago', and as a continuingly relevant example for the making of human story in the present and the future, both the 'then-ness' and the 'now-ness' of the history play are subsumed.

In the first tetralogy of historical plays Shakespeare had confronted and, through a massive feat of historical imagination, converted into dramatic form, a phase of English history perhaps unrivalled in the chronicles for its complexity and violence of incident. 'They lost France, and made his England bleed', is what he remembered as he looked back, a few years later, on his dramatization of this period, and in spite of the complications of the material, Shakespeare's line throughout, and the dramatic pattern he imposes on it, are never in doubt. The idea of progression from order to chaos is realized in the *Henry VI* trilogy for the most part in directly theatrical terms, demonstrable most obviously in the ordered ritual with which *Part 1* begins – a king dead and laid to rest in the full panoply of ceremony – and the end of *Part 3*, which presents another scene of the death of a king, but one now slaughtered bestially, without ceremony, dignity, or remorse. The dissension which intrudes into that first funeral ceremony, a ritual which should have celebrated the glory of the past and declared the stability of the present, grows into a force that will destroy the basis of English power in France, undermine the legal bonds that hold society together, and finally tear apart even the primitive links within the family. The latter is epitomized, with potent simplicity, in Shakespeare's dramatic image of Towton, most terrible of Civil War battles, in which a father has died at the hands of his son and a son at the hands of his father. Once every kind of social and human bond – ceremonial, chivalric, legal, and familial – has thus been whittled away, the figure of the lone destroyer who acknowledges no ties emerges to a world now available for him to bustle in. 'I am but shadow of myself . . . My substance is not here' Talbot riddles in *Part 1* (2.3.49–50) when captured by the Countess of Auvergne, his apparent admission of personal weakness in fact asserting the more than personal strength he feels in solidarity with the hidden soldiers who will shortly arrive to support him: 'These are his substance, sinews, arms, and strength' (62). 'I have no brother, I am like no brother . . . I am myself alone' (5.6.80–83) is the cry of solitary self-assertion by Richard of Gloucester as he stabs the pathetic and defenceless Henry VI at the end of *Part 3*. 'I am but shadow of myself . . . I am myself alone': the movement from the one to the other is the journey charted by the trilogy.[11]

In Talbot's death in *1 Henry VI* something of the tension between the methods of the historian and the methods of the historical dramatist is distilled. Sir William Lucy offers an epitaph for Talbot which might have been taken directly from a chronicle or a tomb – the very 'wormeaten books' and 'rusty brass' of Nashe's description:[12]

> But where's the great Alcides of the field,
> Valiant Lord Talbot, Earl of Shrewsbury,
> Created for his rare success in arms
> Great Earl of Washford, Waterford, and Valence,
> Lord Talbot of Goodrig and Urchinfield,
> Lord Strange of Blackmere, Lord Verdun of Alton,
> Lord Cromwell of Wingfield, Lord Furnival of Sheffield,
> The thrice victorious Lord of Falconbridge,
> Knight of the noble order of Saint George,
> Worthy Saint Michael, and the Golden Fleece,
> Great Marshal to Henry the Sixth
> Of all his wars within the realm of France.

Joan of Arc cuts into the comfortably distancing effect of that kind of memorial historiography with a trenchant reminder of immediate theatrical reality:

Him that thou magnifi'st with all these titles,
Stinking and fly-blown lies here at our feet.   (4.7.60–76)

The figure who emerges so decisively in the later stages of *3 Henry VI* to ride the chaos that follows the social and constitutional disintegration we have been observing, takes control theatrically as well as politically. The role in which actors have boosted, and sometimes made, their Shakespearian reputations, from Burbage to Olivier and beyond, is one of flamboyant histrionic self-consciousness:

Why, I can smile, and murder whiles I smile,
And cry 'Content!' to that which grieves my heart,
And wet my cheeks with artificial tears,
And frame my face to all occasions.   (3.2.182–5)

Ingenuity and resourcefulness of that order in the arts of performance are seen to dwarf political aptitude:

Can I do this, and cannot get a crown?
Tut, were it farther off, I'll pluck it down.   (3.2.194–5)

What we shall see in *Richard III* is no less than a contest between the dynamism and energy of the performer, confident in his act and in his ability to control the audience, and the inexorable patterns of historical progression – a conflict for control of the history play itself.

Richard's control of his own play is remarkable. He has nearly a third of its text and all its significant soliloquies, and most of the latter are grouped near the beginning, so that we may be early conditioned into accepting his view of events. Shakespeare allows himself some unusually drastic rearrangements of historical material to assert Richard the more effectively in these early stages. Into the opening episodes come the funeral of Henry VI from 1471, Richard's marriage with Anne Neville from 1472, the imprisonment of Clarence from 1478, and the last illness of Edward from 1483. The drawing together of these events, and their presentation to us through the perspective of Richard's commentary upon them, gives the impression that Richard himself is controlling the making of history, just as he seems to be controlling the shaping of the play. The theatrical immediacy of the man dominates from his first syllable 'Now', and our sharing of plans with him, and of his pleasure in seeing them fulfilled with a patness guaranteed by the foolishness of his victims, creates an alliance between protagonist and auditorium that gives the illusion of total freedom from the irritable factuality of history. In the process of dramatization the omniscient voice of the chronicle narrator has been filtered out and Richard the actor and Richard the doer become theatrically as well as verbally synonymous:

And therefore, since I cannot prove a lover
To entertain these fair well-spoken days,
I am determined to prove a villain
And hate the idle pleasure of these days.   (1.1.28–31)

The language is (obviously enough) of theatre – 'plots have I laid, inductions dangerous' (32) – and the tense inexorably present. Not for nearly five hundred lines does the past make itself felt. Shakespeare's counterweight to the mesmerizing theatricality of Richard is Queen Margaret, the character with the longest and most bitter memories, the only one to appear in all four plays of the tetralogy. As one by one the victims of her curses succumb to the fate ordained by history, they look to the past imposition of those curses, to the present of their fulfilment, and to the future realization of their implications, thus spinning a web of inevitability that ultimately enmeshes even the bustle of Richard. The past catches up with him, one might say, and this is precisely the idea that Shakespeare has dramatized in the scene just before the final battle in which Richard is haunted by the ghosts of his victims, eleven in number – a specific rendering of the historian's vague allusion to 'divers images like terrible devils' troubling Richard in his sleep. The tension, at the heart of the play's dramatic mechanism, between, on the one hand, Richard's illusory freedom and capacity to entertain and, on the other, the preordained patterns of history which have cast him simply as the last phenomenon of the Civil War, engrossing to himself the crimes of the past so that when he is gone Richmond may herald a new era, is retrospectively discovered in that utterance which at first seemed to declare his independence most flamboyantly. 'I am determined to prove a villain' is offered, and at first taken, as an assertion of individual will; but in that passive voice and the sense of *determined* as 'preordained' or 'foredoomed' the play's tension is reflected in miniature. The theatrical creativity of the historical dramatist, and of his creations, is ultimately controlled by the patterns decreed by history.

In *King John*, and in the last three plays of the second tetralogy, Shakespeare's use of history achieves its fullest complexity through the intermixture of fictional characters and material adapted from chronicle sources. The role of the Bastard in *King John*, altogether unhistorical, acts rather as the audience's window on the events of history. At first detached and irresponsible, the Bastard shares with us in soliloquy his amusement and contempt for the hypocrisy of those in power – and thus, by the simple means of making us laugh, achieves our alliance. But as the seriousness of events undermines even his detachment, he finds himself more and more deeply involved, so that, by the end of the play, what political and military leadership exist in England are provided by the Bastard himself. It is one of the curious tricks in Shakespeare's use of history here that he keeps from his audience until the penultimate scene the fact that King John has an heir. Our theatrical imaginations, freed from chronicle fact, are thus lured into foreseeing an ending quite different from the one which becomes inevitable the moment we learn that

> The lords are all come back,
> And brought Prince Henry in their company.   (5.6.33–4)

In the end the Bastard is altogether freed from the historical context and brought forward to speak the final lines:

> Come the three corners of the world in arms,
> And we shall shock them. Nought shall make us rue,
> If England to itself do rest but true.   (5.7.116–18)

The Bastard's position in the early part of *King John* as fictional fringe commentator on political and historical episodes is one that Shakespeare developed much more fully in the two parts of *Henry IV*. There is nothing particularly promising to a dramatist in the chroniclers' accounts of the reign of Henry IV. It seems a rather messy episode, the usurper of Richard's throne defending his position against a motley assortment of rebellions, with the focus occasionally shifting to events in France and Scotland. Shakespeare confines the action to England, concentrates the focus on Prince Hal and his development through rebellion and unquiet to kingship (halving, in the process, the historical age of Hotspur to act as a foil for him), invents the character of Sir John Falstaff and creates around him a comic world which provides a constant alternative to the events of history. A tension is thus developed which runs through both parts of the play between a comic, timeless, sensual world and a world that is time-dominated, political, and harsh. 'Now, Hal, what time of day is it, lad?', asks Falstaff at his first appearance (*Part 1*, 1.2.1), and the reply, demonstrating the superfluity of his concern with time, stresses those aspects of human experience – cups of sack, capons, wenches in flame-coloured taffeta – that do impinge upon and measure Falstaff's existence. The conflict which pervades the plays is thus set up at once: a battle between Falstaff and comedy on one side, and Prince Hal and time, with history as one of its manifestations, on the other. And since we are in a history play, and not a comedy, the outcome of that battle is inevitable. Even in the soliloquy that closes this scene Hal foresees himself 'redeeming time' (1.2.210); what we watch, with constantly renewed delight, is Falstaff's valiant endeavour to defend himself against the intrusions of time, history, and reality. He does it with consistently inventive verbal ingenuity, always managing to discover some 'trick . . . device . . . starting-hole' to hide himself from 'open and apparent' exposure (*Part 1*, 2.4.253–6). In a play that examines the career of a prince destined to be the victor of Agincourt, Falstaff represents the irresponsible, amoral alternative. But in this mixture of comedy and history, crimes that would be forgivable in comedy turn out to be politically and historically unpardonable: 'Let us take any man's horses: the laws of England are at my commandment' (*Part 2*, 5.3.133–5). The expulsion of Falstaff as the play narrows its sights to the political future is inevitable, foreseen, and necessary:

> I will lay odds that, ere this year expire,
> We bear our civil swords and native fire
> As far as France. (*Part 2*, 5.5.106–8)

In the rejection scene Falstaff is silenced, deprived of the means of verbal self-defence which is his life-line: 'Reply not to me' (*Part 2*, 5.5.56). And time carries the play forward to the future and to Agincourt.

The search for a golden world, where time and history can be kept at bay, is almost fulfilled at Justice Shallow's establishment in Gloucestershire. Here, by playing with the time-scales so that distant memory is set with vivid clarity alongside the immediate facts of the price of ewes and bullocks at the local fair, a sense of timelessness is achieved. Rebels may be defeated, kings may die at Westminster, but the well-chain still needs a new link and the appropriate variety of wheat must still be sown on the headland. Shallow, one of His Majesty's Justices of the Peace, is even unaware of which king he serves under, and one has the feeling that he might never find out, and that it would scarcely alter the principles of his jurisprudence if he did, but for the arrival of Pistol with 'happy news of price' (*Part 2*, 5.3.95) that one king has succeeded another. And there, in the simplest form of historical progression, we are reminded that we are in a history play. 'Take any man's horses' leads directly to the pain of rejection, and that pain (for Hal as for us) leads in turn to the triumph of Agincourt.

In *Henry IV* Shakespeare exploits to the uttermost the formal possibilities of the history play. The juxtaposition of the fictional and the factual, of the apparently infinite comedy of Falstaff and the restrictive framework of the historical pattern to which Hal is doomed to yield, create a depth and poignancy of relationship and interaction richer than anything elsewhere in the history plays. Shakespeare's dramatic use of history is, perhaps not surprisingly, at its most profound when he uses it most freely.

In *Henry V* Shakespeare inherited from every source he could have consulted an uncompromisingly enthusiastic account of a legendary hero–king. 'A majestie was he that both lived and died a paterne in princehood, a lode-starre in honour, and mirrour of magnificence: the more highlie exalted in his life, the more deepelie lamented at his death, and famous to the world alwaie', concludes Holinshed, in by-no-means unrepresentative phrases.[13] Shakespeare adopts the tone, and some of the language, of these eulogies in a solution to the problem of putting such a paragon on stage which is unique among the history plays (and all but so in the canon): a chorus before each act. In the contributions of the chorus we hear again the voice of the omniscient historian, interpreting events, guiding our reactions, demanding our approval, and (curiously when such a voice becomes part of a play), suggesting the inadequacy of theatre for the realization of history – and this in Shakespeare's ninth history play:

> Can this cockpit hold
> The vasty fields of France? Or may we cram
> Within this wooden O the very casques
> That did affright the air at Agincourt?   (Chorus 1,11–14)

Set against the chorus's uncomplicated enthusiasm for Henry, however, is the complexity of the play's exploration of government by a hero–king whose reputation is based on prowess in war, the destructive horror of which is constantly made apparent. Not that Shakespeare eschews the heroic image; rather he asks us to examine it more intelligently than the historians on whom he depends for source material and whom he reflects in his chorus. This is partly effected, as in the *Henry IV* plays, by the use of a comic subplot which insists, in the early stages of the play, on a different perspective on the main action. Each of the first three choruses, indeed, is followed by a scene which undercuts its heroic tone. The first chorus, from the appeal for a 'muse of fire', leads into the conspicuously unheroic conversation of the two clerics, scheming to avoid taxation and planning a war as a means of diverting Henry's attention; the second, with its image of the 'youth of England' 'on fire', is followed by those remarkable representatives of the youth of England, Bardolph, Nym, and Pistol, planning their marauding expedition to France as a ghastly parody of the King's; the third chorus introduces, appropriately enough, Henry's exhortation to his troops before Harfleur, but the mood is immediately overturned by the arrival of the noticeably untigerlike Bardolph and his fellows, finding the attractions of an alehouse in London more powerful than those of the breach in Harfleur walls.

We arrive at Agincourt, then, with an awareness of war as the tool of scheming politicians, an opportunity for petty crooks to make money, the inspiration for cowardice as well as for valour. In the Agincourt scenes themselves we are allowed at last our glimpse of the heroic Henry. In Act 4 the mood of the chorus and the scenes that follow finally coincide and the King for the first time, through soliloquy, confronts the audience and his own responsibility for the situation his policies have created. Shakespeare even takes the risk of setting forth casualty figures of ten thousand French dead to twenty-five English, which Hall had dismissed as 'fables' and Holinshed contrasted with the more realistic reports of 'other writers of greater credit'. 'O God, thy arm was here' says the King (4.8.104), and for a moment we wonder whether perhaps it was. This shift in the tone of the play's attitude to its source material, made plausible and convincing through the breadth of its earlier exploration, is reinforced in the handling of the non-historical subplot.

Paralleling the political struggle in *Henry V* for control of France is a comic struggle for control of the play's fictional scenes between Pistol, who constantly undermines heroics through parody, and Fluellen, whose quaint enthusiasm for Henry has a certain infectiousness. The struggle is won by Fluellen, who finally drives a humiliated Pistol from the play.

The death of Bardolph epitomizes Shakespeare's control, through fictions he has himself invented, of our attitude to the genuinely historical events of the play. Holinshed and Hall report the execution of an unnamed soldier, at the King's command, for stealing from a church. Shakespeare has Fluellen report the execution of Bardolph, a focus of our comic affection through three plays, by the Duke of Exeter. The price of military success is sharply brought home to us; the heroics of Agincourt are vulnerable to red-nosed irreverence so the latter must be silenced. But to keep the episode off-stage, to remove responsibility from the King, and to report it with the approval of an entertaining Welshman, preserves the possibility of presenting those heroics persuasively when the time comes. Through such intermixture of history and fiction, a drama is created with a variety of perceptions that one would hardly have dared hope for from the monolithic material provided by the historians.

As he ends the play, and looks back on it and on the great cycle that is now finished, one senses Shakespeare at a turning point in his career. A major achievement in the dramatization of English history is complete; there must be satisfaction in that, and also, perhaps, relief, for the next phase of English history no longer demands attention – 'which oft our stage hath shown'. Within a few weeks of *Henry V*, in September 1599, Thomas Platter, a Swiss visitor to London, went to see 'in the straw-thatched house . . . the tragedy of the first Emperor Julius Caesar, very pleasingly performed'.[14] Turning aside from English history, Shakespeare is free to consider other systems of government besides monarchy (and it may be no coincidence that this is the very topic of *Julius Caesar*). With source material drawn from an historian concerned with the 'Lives of Noble Grecians and Romans' rather than with the history of a nation, a more intense exploration of individual human response to political situations becomes inevitable. Within a year or so of creating Brutus, Shakespeare was working on *Hamlet*.

He returned to English history only at the end of his career, with *Henry VIII*. The peculiar qualities of the work – its authorship problem, its extraordinary addiction to pomp and ceremony, its desire to project itself into the present through Cranmer's final eulogy of Elizabeth and James, so that, alone among the history plays, *Henry VIII* neither shows nor reports the death of its titular hero – are beyond the scope of this essay. What is relevant here is the urgency of its concern with the way history should be used in drama. *All is True* is its alternative title, and its prologue reassures those who come to plays 'out of hope they may believe' that they 'may here find truth' (8–9). The aim is to show 'The very persons of our noble story / As they were living' (26–7).

Towards the end of the play we have, in the reactions to Wolsey's death, a precise example of theatrical historiography attempting to represent the past truthfully. Queen Katherine offers a ruthless assessment of Wolsey's shortcomings:

> He was never
> But where he meant to ruin, pitiful,
> His promises were, as he then was, mighty;
> But his performance, as he is now, nothing.   (4.2.39–42)

And then comes from her servant, Griffith, a gentle, measured view from another perspective:

> He was a scholar, and a ripe and good one;
> Exceeding wise, fair-spoken, and persuading;
> Lofty and sour to them that loved him not,
> But to those men that sought him sweet as summer.
> And though he were unsatisfied in getting –
> Which was a sin – yet in bestowing, madam,
> He was most princely . . .
> And, to add greater honours to his age
> Than man could give him, he died fearing God.   (4.2.51–68)

This exchange offers a close rendering of Holinshed's somewhat ambiguous verdict on Wolsey and its departure from the power and acuteness of the verse of history plays earlier in the Folio is perhaps a reflection of quality as well as of kind. But in its dramatic confrontation of points of view, its clothing of contradictions within the record of the past in personalities that explain those contradictions, and its concern adequately to represent the complexities of historical truth in theatrical form, it provides a consistent, if modest, conclusion to all the energy with which history had been delved in the earlier plays. If the opinion of the majority of scholars is right, and John Fletcher is in control at this point, he now gives to Queen Katherine – whose trial scene a little earlier in the play was probably Shakespeare's last great achievement in the dramatization of the past,[15] and who is now facing her own death – a reply which recalls that sense of the theatre's ability to reanimate history, that ability for which Thomas Nashe had enthusiastically commended the first of Shakespeare's history plays. Queen Katherine's lines (4.2.69–72) may thus, perhaps, take on something of the quality of a tribute, from his heir apparent as principal dramatist of the King's Men, to Shakespeare's achievement, spanning more than two decades of endeavour, in the creation of theatre from history:

> After my death I wish no other herald,
> No other speaker of my living actions,
> To keep mine honour from corruption,
> But such an honest chronicler . . .

Notes

1. Thornton Wilder, interviewed by Richard H. Goldstone, *Paris Review* 15 (1957), 37–52; reprinted in *Writers at Work: The 'Paris Review' Interviews*, with an introduction by Malcolm Cowley (1958), pp. 91–107 (quotations from pp. 99, 100). I am indebted to my colleague Dr T. P. Matheson for drawing my attention to this passage.
2. The Chorus to Act 5 of *Henry V*, with its reference to Essex's expedition to Ireland – 'the General of our gracious Empress / . . . from Ireland coming, / Bringing rebellion broached on his sword' – dates the play between Essex's departure in March 1599 and his return, in failure, in September. For a discussion of the more precise dating, see *Henry V*, edited by Gary Taylor (Oxford, 1982), pp. 4ff.
3. To take *1 Henry VI* as wholly Shakespearian, and as the first-written play of the *Henry VI* trilogy, is to accept the arguments of A. S. Cairncross in the new Arden edition of the play (1962), endorsed by (among most subsequent critics) the latest editor, Norman Sanders, in the New Penguin edition (Harmondsworth, 1981). The doubts of earlier scholars, however, have not entirely disappeared from commentary on the play and the question cannot be regarded as finally settled.
4. Thomas Nashe, *Pierce Penniless his Supplication to the Devil* (1592), in *Selected Works*, edited by Stanley Wells, Stratford-upon-Avon Library 1 (1964), pp. 64–5.
5. The most thorough treatment of the source material of the history plays is in volumes III and IV of Geoffrey Bullough's *Narrative and Dramatic Sources of Shakespeare* (1960, 1962). See also Kenneth Muir, *The Sources of Shakespeare's Plays* (1977).
6. The origins and early development of the history play are discussed by Irving Ribner, *The English History Play in the Age of Shakespeare*, revised edition (1965), pp. 30ff.
7. See the lists of plays, extant and lost, designated as 'History' in *Annals of English Drama*, edited by Alfred Harbage, revised by S. Schoenbaum (1964).
8. H. S. Bennett, *English Books and Readers, 1558–1603* (Cambridge, 1965), pp. 214–20, makes clear the importance of history in the Elizabethan book trade; so too does Louis B. Wright, *Middle-Class Culture in Elizabethan England* (Chapel Hill, North Carolina, 1935), pp. 297–338.
9. *Chronicles of England* (1580), sig. *4[r] (p. [vii]).
10. *Henslowe's Diary*, edited by R. A. Foakes and R. T. Rickert (Cambridge, 1961). See also *Documents of the Rose Theatre*, edited by Carol Chillington Rutter, Revels Plays Companion Library (Manchester, 1984).
11. This point is made by Edward I. Berry, *Patterns of Decay: Shakespeare's Early Histories* (Charlottesville, Virginia, 1965), p. 73.
12. That the lines are indeed derived from a funeral monument is suggested by G. Lambin, 'Here lyeth John Talbot', *Etudes Anglaises* 24 (1971), 361–76.
13. *The Third Volume of Chronicles* (1587), sig. Kkk2[r] (p. 583).
14. Quoted from Ernest Schanzer's translation in his article 'Thomas Platter's observations on the Elizabethan stage', *Notes and Queries* 201 (1956), 465–7.
15. The assignment of Act 2, Scene 4 to Shakespeare and Act 4, Scene 2 to Fletcher follows the distribution of the text accepted by most scholars since Spedding first suggested it in 1850. There have, however, been some notable dissenters from this orthodoxy.

Reading list

Berry, Edward I., *Patterns of Decay: Shakespeare's Early Histories* (Charlottesville, Virginia, 1965)

Blanpied, John W., *Time and the Artist in Shakespeare's English Histories* (Newark, Delaware, 1983)

Bullough, Geoffrey, ed., *Narrative and Dramatic Sources of Shakespeare*, 8 vols.: III *Earlier English History Plays*; IV *Later English History Plays* (1960, 1962)

Driver, T. F., *The Sense of History in Greek and Shakespearian Drama* (New York, 1960)

Jones, Emrys, *The Origins of Shakespeare* (Oxford, 1977)

Kaiser, Walter, *Praisers of Folly: Erasmus, Rabelais, Shakespeare* (1964) [section on Falstaff]

Kantorowicz, Ernst, *The King's Two Bodies: A Study in Medieval Political Theology* (Princeton, New Jersey, 1957) [section on *Richard II*]

Kelly, Henry Ansgar, *Divine Providence in the England of Shakespeare's Histories* (Cambridge, Massachusetts, 1970)

Levy, F. J., *Tudor Historical Thought* (San Marino, California, 1967)

McKisack, May, *Medieval History in the Tudor Age* (Oxford, 1971)

Ornstein, Robert, *A Kingdom for a Stage: The Achievement of Shakespeare's History Plays* (Cambridge, Massachusetts, 1972)

Prior, Moody, E., *The Drama of Power: Studies in Shakespeare's History Plays* (Evanston, Illinois, 1973)

Quinones, Ricardo J., *The Renaissance Discovery of Time*, Harvard Studies in Comparative Literature 31 (Cambridge, Massachusetts, 1972)

Reese, M. M., *The Cease of Majesty: A Study of Shakespeare's History Plays* (1961)

Ribner, Irving, *The English History Play in the Age of Shakespeare*, revised edition (1965)

Rossiter, A. P., 'Ambivalence: The dialectic of the histories', in *Angel with Horns* (1961)

Saccio, Peter, *Shakespeare's English Kings: History, Chronicle, and Drama* (Oxford, 1977)

Sanders, Wilbur, *The Dramatist and the Received Idea: Studies in the Plays of Marlowe and Shakespeare* (1968)

Sprague, Arthur Colby, *Shakespeare's Histories: Plays for the Stage* (1964)

Tillyard, E. M. W., *Shakespeare's History Plays* (1944), revised edition (Harmondsworth, 1969)

Vickers, Brian, *The Artistry of Shakespeare's Prose* (1968) [section on Falstaff]

Weiss, Theodore, *The Breath of Clowns and Kings: Shakespeare's Early Comedies and Histories* (New York and London, 1971)

Wilders, John, *The Lost Garden: A View of Shakespeare's English and Roman History Plays* (1978)

Wilson, John Dover, *The Fortunes of Falstaff* (Cambridge, 1944)

10   The transmission of Shakespeare's text

'To determine what Shakespeare wrote' – that crude formulation of the editorial task is ambiguous, pointing to two areas of inquiry, canonical and textual. Was Shakespeare the author, in whole or in part, of *Edward III*, first published in an anonymous Quarto of 1596? Many scholars have believed so, but the poet Swinburne was not among them. In the course of a long diatribe against the play and those who considered it Shakespeare's, he quoted for special contempt the lines in which King Edward tells the Countess of Salisbury that for the sake of her love he will even murder his Queen:

> Fairer thou art by far than Hero was;
> Beardless Leander not so strong as I:
> He swum an easy current for his love;
> But I will through a helly spout of blood
> To arrive at Sestos where my Hero lies.

Singling out the King's declaration that he will swim 'through a helly spout of blood', Swinburne exploded: 'I should . . . have thought it impossible that any mortal ear could endure the shock of this unspeakable . . . verse, and find in the passage which contains it an echo or trace of the "music, wit, and oracle" of Shakespeare.'[1] The expression 'a helly spout' is certainly grotesque, but a less bigoted Swinburne would have discounted it at once as the Quarto compositor's misreading of 'Hellespont': emended, the King's rhetoric remains extravagant, but is no longer inept. Swinburne has based a critical point, and an argument about authorship, upon a blatant error. He is by no means unique in being so misled, for the early printed texts of many English Renaissance plays are pestered with corruption. Some of Shakespeare's most memorable lines owe their familiar form to the inspired restoration-work of editors. And notions about the way that certain 'bad Quartos', in particular, are related to the Shakespeare canon have changed as textual analysis has revealed more about their nature. This chapter offers a brief guide to knowledge and speculation about 'what Shakespeare wrote' – about which works, or parts of them, are his, and which words constitute their authentic texts.

'You don't expect me to know what to say about a play when I don't know

who the author is, do you?', protests Bernard Shaw's Flawner Bannal in
Fanny's First Play, going on to explain that 'If it's by a good author, it's a good
play, naturally.' Few drama critics have been quite so frank about their
assumptions, but the reputations of such plays as *Titus Andronicus*, *Pericles*, and
the three Parts of *Henry VI* have been intimately bound up with shifting
opinion about their authorship.

The basis of the canon was laid in 1623, seven years after Shakespeare's
death, when his fellow actor–sharers in the King's Company, John Heminges
and Henry Condell, collected thirty-six of his plays in the First Folio. The two
actors were well placed to know which plays their friend had written, but
collaboration between dramatists and the refurbishing of old plays were
common in the Elizabethan–Jacobean theatre, and inclusion of a play in the
First Folio is no guarantee that it is *solely* Shakespeare's. On the other hand,
dramatic writing by Shakespeare might have been excluded from the Folio
because Heminges and Condell regarded the play in which it appeared as
predominantly not his, because they were confronted by problems of
copyright or censorship or were unable to provide satisfactory texts, or
because there were gaps in their knowledge about the earliest stages of
Shakespeare's career, before the Chamberlain's Company – later the King's –
was formed in 1594. Indeed, this last factor might conceivably have led them
to include plays that they would otherwise have rejected.

In fact early plays do raise some of the major questions of the Shakespeare
canon. Before two anonymously published texts known as *The First Part of the
Contention betwixt the two famous houses of York and Lancaster* (1594) and *The
True Tragedy of Richard Duke of York* (1595) were shown in the 1920s to be
memorially reconstructed versions of 2 and 3 *Henry VI* as preserved in the
Folio, they were generally held to be collaborate works by Marlowe, Greene,
Nashe, Peele, and others, which Shakespeare, probably with some assistance,
revised and expanded into the Folio histories. *1 Henry VI*, *Titus Andronicus*,
and *The Taming of the Shrew* were also apportioned among Shakespeare and
his contemporaries. But once the belief that Shakespeare began writing for
the theatre as botcher of other men's plays had been undermined by
recognition of the derivative nature of *The Contention* and *Richard Duke of York*,
the three Parts of *Henry VI* were increasingly seen as forming, with *Richard III*,
a coherent tetralogy conceived and executed by Shakespeare alone, while
confidence in the complete authenticity of *The Taming of the Shrew* and *Titus
Andronicus* rose as they, along with *Henry VI*, were vindicated in performance.
The earliest-composed Folio plays reveal, it is argued, a protean young poet-
actor searching among the reputable writers of his day for appropriate stylistic
models, and only intermittently finding his own distinctive voice. Present
opinion ought not, however, to harden into immutable orthodoxy: extreme
variations in the style of *1 Henry VI* remain puzzling, and the mechanical
repetition of words, phrases, and grammatical mannerisms in act one of *Titus
Andronicus* is not easily paralleled in Shakespeare's undoubted work.

Though denying Shakespeare *Edward III*, Swinburne was a zealous advocate of his claim to another anonymous Elizabethan play, *Arden of Faversham* (1592). Both *Edward III* and *Arden of Faversham* were assigned to Shakespeare in untrustworthy printers' catalogues of 1656, and these ascriptions were independently revived, on purely aesthetic grounds, in the eighteenth century, and vigorously debated in the nineteenth. The current verdict is that Shakespeare may well have contributed to *Edward III*, probably being responsible at least for the Countess scenes, but that – contrary to the majority opinion of Victorian critics – he had nothing to do with *Arden of Faversham*, whose affinities with Shakespeare's earliest plays nevertheless continue to impress editors and critics who subject this remarkable domestic tragedy to close scrutiny.

The distinctiveness of Shakespeare's later style allows more confident judgement on two plays in which, at the close of his career, Shakespeare almost certainly collaborated with John Fletcher, whose verse is also highly individual: *Henry VIII* (or *All Is True*), which was admitted to the Folio, and *The Two Noble Kinsmen*, which belonged to the King's Company and first appeared in a Quarto of 1634 with the names of both men on the title-page. Each play divides up into scenes exhibiting one or other dramatist's characteristics – of metre, vocabulary, turn of phrase, imagery, syntax, and use of colloquial contractions. A dozen or so objective tests have confirmed the traditional allocations of scenes, and there is evidence of further collaboration between Fletcher and Shakespeare about 1613 in a lost play called *Cardenio*.[2] Poetically the opening and closing acts of *The Two Noble Kinsmen* have a complex magniloquence that no 'clever imitator' of Shakespeare – such as some have postulated – could ever have achieved.

Canonical and textual problems are closely intertwined in another late play, *Pericles*, which was omitted from the First Folio, despite having been published as Shakespeare's in a Quarto of 1609 and bearing unmistakable signs of his handiwork throughout the last three acts. The Quarto is a 'bad' one (the term is fully explained below) and the question arises whether the un-Shakespearian qualities of the first two acts are due to anomalies in the transmission of the text – corruption having distorted a Shakespearian original beyond recognition in acts one and two but less drastically in acts three to five – or whether, as most scholars believe, Shakespeare incorporated into his play two acts by one or more other dramatists.[3]

A textual explanation has also been advanced for the uneven verse and disjointed structure of *Timon of Athens*, which might not have appeared in the Folio had not the printers needed to fill a gap left by suspension, because of copyright difficulties, of work on *Troilus and Cressida*. Theories of multiple authorship, still proliferating in the early decades of the twentieth century, gave way to the notion that *Timon* was wholly Shakespeare's but unfinished, the Folio text having been printed from a rough draft that juxtaposed properly developed passages with mere jottings. However, although the manuscript behind the Folio could no doubt have benefited from revision and ampli-fication, recent studies confirm the presence of a second author, Thomas Middleton having written about one-third of the play.

Modern editions of Shakespeare's complete works also print the non-dramatic poems: *Venus and Adonis*, *The Rape of Lucrece*, the *Sonnets*, *A Lover's Complaint* – printed with the *Sonnets* in 1609 and sometimes dismissed as spurious, but authenticated by recent scholarship – and *The Phoenix and the Turtle*. And Shakespeare is probably the famous Hand D that wrote (as author) a scene of 147 lines in a multi-author play called *Sir Thomas More*, preserved in a British Library manuscript.

Few Folio plays are without speeches that have at some time been pronounced non-Shakespearian, but behind most such pronouncements lies little more than a wayward impressionism. The Hecate passages are probably Middletonian intrusions into *Macbeth*, which has, as the Folio presents it, also been abridged. The likelihood that Shakespeare's plays contain unauthorized interpolations and alterations depends, of course, on the nature of the manuscripts from which they were printed.

Since, except for *Sir Thomas More* and some seventeenth-century tran-scripts of a few of the Sonnets, the Shakespearian manuscripts themselves – autographs and scribal copies – have all perished, we are reliant on printed texts.[4] Nineteen of the plays in the First Folio had already been published separately in small Quarto books,[5] and for several plays Quarto and Folio versions differ considerably. The textual scholar's job is to puzzle out the relationship between them and their respective degrees of authority – to discover in each case what processes of transmission, with their accompanying kinds of error, have intervened between the author's original and the printed text. Admittedly, to invoke 'the author's original' is to beg certain questions. Plays are textually the least stable of all literary forms, achieving their true realization in performance. Scripts evolve as they are appraised by the players, tested in rehearsal, and performed or revived in changing theatrical circum-stances. Authors' attitudes to the modifications that their initial scripts undergo in the course of this communal endeavour to present them on stage run the gamut from gratitude to ferocious indignation. Shakespeare was fortunate in writing most of his plays for an established company of which he was a key member, but he would not have thought of his own completed draft as in any sense a final text. A twentieth-century playwright usually has the chance to establish for publication a version incorporating only those theatre changes that are acceptable to him on artistic grounds. Since Shakespeare, as Heminges and Condell lamented, did not live 'to have set forth and overseen his own writings', the First Folio lacks this kind of explicit authorial sanction, and there is no evidence that Shakespeare saw the Quartos of his plays through the press, either.[6] What we are trying to reconstruct are hypothetical texts that Shakespeare 'would have' approved.

In his last speech Othello, who now knows that Desdemona was innocent of the adultery for which he killed her, refers to himself as

> one whose hand,
> Like the base *Indian*, threw a pearle away,
> Richer than all his Tribe. (5.2.349–51)

'Indian' is the reading of the Quarto of *Othello* published in 1622. In the Folio, Othello speaks of 'the base Iudean'. What did Shakespeare intend? The matter has been hotly debated. Both words make sense, but the implications differ. If 'Indian' is right, Othello is accusing himself, at worst, of crass gullibility: he is referring to what for the Elizabethans was the American Indian's proverbial ignorance of the value of gold and gems. If 'Iudean' is Shakespeare's word (capital 'I' was used in the seventeenth century where we would use 'J'), Othello is likening himself to Judas, *the* base Judean, who, in betraying Christ, threw away 'the pearl of great price' – as, in a sense, Othello has betrayed an ideal of love, incarnate in 'the divine Desdemona'. 'Iudean' would fit in with the biblical references and the religious imagery running through the play. Our idea of what the tragedy is about, and of Othello's state of mind at this moment before he performs his own judicial execution, will affect and be affected by our decision as to whether 'Indian' or 'Iudean' is what Shakespeare intended. The early texts of *Othello*, as of other major Shakespeare plays, offer hundreds of variants – few of such crucial importance, but all confronting an editor with the need to make a choice. Until this century, editors tended to choose solely according to literary-dramatic criteria, as they perceived them. We realize now that textual facts must also be taken into account.

Shakespeare wrote his plays not to be printed for readers but to be performed by his theatrical company, whose property they became.[7] The first manuscript of a completed play was known as the author's 'foul papers' – his working draft, whose degree of 'foulness' would depend on the facility with which the dramatist composed and on whether he made clean copies of his messier leaves, discarding the originals. Heminges and Condell claimed that Shakespeare's 'mind and hand went together', so that 'what he thought, he uttered with that easiness that we have scarce received from him a blot in his papers'. This conventional tribute to authorial fluency implies that Shakespeare normally handed over to the company his foul papers, but it is possible that for some plays, at least, he needed to write out a complete fair copy. A sufficiently 'fair' autograph might, with some annotation, be usable as a prompt-book; from the rougher sort of authorial manuscript a transcript especially designed to serve as a prompt-book would have been prepared by a scribe, perhaps with some help from Shakespeare himself.

There are clear indications that foul papers served as copy for several printed texts of Shakespeare plays. The clues are inconsistencies, ambiguities, redundancies, lacunae, and loose ends that would scarcely have survived into a fair copy or been tolerable in a prompt-book. For instance, in the second Quarto of *Romeo and Juliet* (1599) the designations of certain characters, in speech prefixes and directions, vary from scene to scene, as their changing functions become uppermost in the playwright's mind; most notably, Lady Capulet is 'Lady', 'Lady of the house', 'Mother', and 'Capulets Wife' in stage directions and 'Wife', 'Mo.', 'M.', 'La.', 'Capu. Wi.', 'Ca. Wi.', and 'Old. La.' in speech prefixes. In the same Quarto, a direction such as 'Enter three or foure Citizens with Clubs or partysons', to take a typical example, is not specific enough to be serviceable in the theatre, especially since the short speech thus heralded is assigned to an 'Offi[cer]'. Numbers of minor characters are often left indeterminate in this way in Q2: 'fiue or sixe', 'others', 'two or three', or 'all'. *Titus Andronicus* Q1 (1594) asks in one entry for 'others as many as can be', but we must go outside the Shakespeare canon for the more picturesquely 'permissive' or 'petitory' authorial directions, such as the following from *Alphonsus of Aragon* (1599): 'Exit Venus. Or if you can conueniently, let a chaire come downe from the top of the stage, and draw her vp'; the playwright hopes that the company can get Venus off stage as befits a goddess, but recognizes that she may have to walk through a door like everybody else. Texts printed from foul papers may lack many necessary entrances and exits, or provide entrances for 'ghost' characters who are given names but remain mute and without evident function on stage; we must assume that the playwright has changed his mind, but forgotten to adjust the stage direction.

More interesting are duplications signalling authorial changes of mind within the dialogue itself. In *Romeo and Juliet* Q2 these range from the briefest of false starts, inadequately deleted, as in 'I will beleeue, Shall I beleeue that vnsubstantiall death is amorous', to the repetition, with slight variations, of four lines that at the end of 2.2 and beginning of 2.3 are first assigned to Romeo and then to Friar Lawrence. The 1596 Quarto of *Love's Labour's Lost* even prints consecutively Shakespeare's first and second versions of Berowne's great defence of love in 4.3. The amplifications include the series of analogies proclaiming love's power to sharpen the senses and animate the whole personality, among them the quintessentially Shakespearian lines, 'Loues feeling is more soft and sensible, / Then are the tender hornes of Cockled Snayles'; and where the new and old versions run most closely parallel, the alterations create a neater rhetorical pattern and a livelier play of images, as when Berowne contrasts the 'leaden contemplation' of book-learning with 'Such fierie Numbers as the prompting eyes / Of beautis tutors haue inricht you with', or when the rephrasing has women's eyes 'sparcle' so as to clinch the comparison with 'the right promethean fier'. It is a lucky accident that has allowed us this glimpse of Shakespeare as conscious artist working up the texture of a major speech. The 1600 Quarto of *A Midsummer Night's*

Dream, also bearing signs of having been set from foul papers, affords a further kind of evidence of Shakespeare as reviser. John Dover Wilson was the first to point out that the opening eighty-four lines of Act 5 contain eight separate patches of mislined verse, and that these can be detached to leave fifty-six lines of coherent dialogue. Later scholars have accepted his deduction that Shakespeare augmented his normally set-out first draft with lines so cramped in the margin that their pentameter structure was obscured. The insertions contain the famous account of poetic creation which 'giues to ayery nothing, a locall habitation, / And a name'. In the correctly printed original lines Theseus laughingly compares the lunatic and the lover; the poet's kinship with these servants of the imagination was asserted as an afterthought, which may, however, have closely attended the initial conception.

Most texts showing authorial irregularities contain a sprinkling of idiosyncratic spellings, presumably Shakespeare's own, since scribes and compositors were apt to normalize rather than introduce oddities and there is considerable overlap between plays, which together present an old-fashioned orthographical pattern shared by the Hand D pages of *Sir Thomas More*. One spelling in the *More* manuscript, 'scilens', has been discovered nowhere else, except in the 1600 Quarto of *2 Henry IV*, a typical foul papers text, where the name of Master Justice Silence is spelt eighteen times in this curious way. The compositor would doubtless have normalized 'scilens' as a common noun, but he accepted the peculiar Shakespearian form when it appeared as the name of a character.

When two expert paleographers independently transcribed the putatively Shakespearian three pages of *Sir Thomas More*, which are written in the common Elizabethan secretary script, they differed over a handful of readings, W. W. Greg seeing 'or sorry', 'ordere', 'momtanish', and 'Shrewsbury' where E. Maunde Thompson saw 'a sorry', 'orderd', 'mountanish', and 'Shrowsbury'. The disputable letters are among those which caused most difficulty for Elizabethan–Jacobean compositors faced with Shakespeare's autograph. Dover Wilson listed as particularly frequent kinds of misreading in the 'good' Quartos minim errors and confusions between 'a' and minims ('m, n, u, i, c, r, w'), and confusions of 'e' and 'd', 'e' and 'o', and 'a' and 'o' (or 'a' and 'oi' or 'or'); also common, and explicable if Hand D of *Sir Thomas More* is Shakespeare's, are confusions involving 't', especially between 't' and 'l', 'k', or 'b' (which may all be mistaken for one another).[8] In *Romeo and Juliet* Q2 Mercutio, trying to tease a response from the hidden and lovesick Romeo, asks him to 'Crie but ay me, prouaunt, but loue and day'. The line is nonsense.[9] Quarto 1 (1597), though generally inferior, clearly preserves the Shakespearian wording, misread by the Q2 compositor: 'cry but ay me. Pronounce but Loue and Doue'. Since Hand D affords such spellings as 'insolenc', 'obedienc', and 'offyc', Q2's 'prouaunt' is probably a misreading of 'pronounc' ('n' misread as 'u', 'o' as 'a', and 'c' as 't'), and 'day' due to misreading of 'doue' as 'daie'. Many convincing emendations of the early prints have been suggested by the *ductus litterarum* – the graphic outline, in a secretary hand such as Shakespeare's, of the suspect words as Shakespeare might have spelt them. Another feature of Hand D's penmanship – his occasional tendency to leave gaps within words (as in 'fo rbid') – would explain several Quarto mistakes of the kind exemplified by 'hellie spout' in *Edward III*, though mechanical error in typesetting and subsequent miscorrection provide an alternative explanation.

Shakespeare's own draft, then, often served as printer's copy. It is generally believed that after the prompt-book and the actors' parts had been prepared, the theatre company held the authorial papers in safe-keeping as a precaution against loss of the prompt-book, which was, in normal circumstances, less likely to be released to a printer than the foul papers, because to the company the theatre document was much the more precious.[10] The prompt-book, or official 'book of the play', would exhibit a fair measure of consistency and completeness, the ideal being a curt functionalism. Speech-prefixes would be regularized and virtually all entrances marked. Some slight laxity in the provision of exits would be tolerable, as most of these are clearly implicit in the dialogue, and an actor 'can be trusted to get himself off the stage when he is no longer required'.[11] Shakespeare's 'descriptive' directions might be pruned, while properties, noises, and numbers of minor characters entering would be specified. Warnings that actors or properties should be ready for imminent entry strongly suggest the hand of the book-keeper, who would resolve the dialogue's tangles and loose ends and make cuts for performance. A prompt-book would incorporate both inadvertent and deliberate alterations to Shakespeare's original text, and might well benefit from his own second thoughts. As all plays had to be licensed by the Master of the Revels, who ensured that they were politically innocuous, it might also carry the scars of censorship.

Actors' names in a stage direction may point to prompt-copy if they duplicate those of minor characters: they may be the book-keepers' annotations towards casting. On the other hand, Shakespeare himself, writing a character-part with a particular member of his company in mind, might substitute the player's name for the fictional one: in the 1600 Quarto of *Much Ado About Nothing*, Dogberry and Verges become Constable and Headborough and then Kemp and Cowley, whom Shakespeare evidently imagined as personating his comic police.

Since the book-keeper sometimes annotated an author's draft as a preliminary to having it transcribed as a prompt-book, while authorial irregularities and superfluities were sometimes carried over into prompt-books, the nature of the copy for a given printed text is not always obvious. Moreover, other types of manuscripts existed – transcripts, either of Shakespeare's papers or of the prompt-book, made for some special purpose. Five Folio comedies, *The*

Tempest, The Two Gentlemen of Verona, The Merry Wives of Windsor, Measure for Measure, and *The Winter's Tale,* were set from tidy transcripts prepared, presumably for the printer, by the professional scrivener Ralph Crane. Documents in his hand survive, and his habits have been carefully studied. Crane's peculiarities included a passion for parentheses, apostrophes, and hyphens, and the use of 'massed entrances' listing at the beginning of a scene all the characters to appear in it, irrespective of their point of entry.

One further class of manuscripts must be described. In the preface to the Folio Heminges and Condell claimed that readers had in the past been 'abused with divers stolen and surreptitious copies, maimed and deformed by the frauds and stealths of injurious imposters'. In the eighteenth and nineteenth centuries this was taken as a blanket condemnation of all Shakespearian Quarto editions. We now recognize that the reference is to a distinct group of 'bad Quartos', of which many non-Shakespearian examples also survive. These Quartos were evidently set from manuscripts that preserved the attempts by one or more actors to reconstruct from their memories a text of a play they had performed. Plague years were particularly productive of these unauthorized 'memorial reconstructions' or 'reports,' which may have been concocted by and for out-of-work small-part players as they formed scratch troupes to tour the provinces; or actor–reporters may have planned from the start to relieve hard times by pirating plays for publishers.

Naturally, texts filtered through fallible memories are seriously corrupt. Normally an actor recalled quite accurately his own speeches and much of the dialogue surrounding them, but floundered when he tried to reproduce scenes in which he had not appeared: these may degenerate into mere collage of words and phrases misappropriated from other sections of the play, or even from other plays in the repertory. Reporters' memories betrayed them into substituting trite or imprecise expressions for imaginative ones, into inserting extrametrical exclamations and connectives, into running separate speeches together, forgetting that somebody else was supposed to speak in between, into misplacing words, lines, and even whole episodes. They omitted material without which the remembered fragments were at times unintelligible. They mangled metre and garbled sense.

The reporter of the 1603 Quarto of *Hamlet* managed the first six words of Hamlet's 'To be, or not to be' soliloquy, but completed the opening line with 'I [Ay] there's the *point*', which he proceeded to lose in a jumble of verbal oddments. Variations in the quality of his reporting indicate that his main role had been Marcellus, who is entirely absent from the portion of the play enclosing Hamlet's soliloquy. Figure 8 shows the bad Quarto (1600) and good Folio versions of the beginning of the long speech in which the Archbishop of Canterbury assures King Henry V of his right to France. Q reduces the rest of the monologue from thirty-six lines to fifteen, partly by confusing the Lady

(i) The Quarto, 1600

> There is no bar to ſtay your highneſſe claime to *France*
> But one, which they produce from *Faramount*,
> No female ſhall ſucceed in ſalicke land,
> Which ſalicke land the French vniuſtly gloze
> To be the realme of *France*:
> And *Faramont* the founder of this law and female barre:
> Yet their owne writers faithfully affirme
> That the land ſalicke lyes in *Germany*,
> Betweene the flouds of *Sabeck* and of *Elme*,
> Where *Charles* the fift hauing ſubdude the Saxons,
> There left behind, and ſetled certaine French,
> Who holding in diſdaine the Germaine women,
> For ſome diſhoneſt maners of their liues,
> Eſtabliſht there this lawe. To wit,
> No female ſhall ſucceed in ſalicke land:
> Which ſalicke land as I ſaid before,
> Is at this time in *Germany* called *Meſene*:
> Thus doth it well appeare the ſalicke lawe
> Was not deuiſed for the realme of *France*,
> Nor did the French poſſeſſe the ſalicke land,
> Vntill 400. one and twentie yeares
> After the funƈtion of king *Faramont*,
> Godly ſuppoſed the founder of this lawe:

8   *Henry V*, Act 1, scene 1, lines 35–59

Lingare with the Lady Ermengare (as the names appear in F) and so missing out the eight lines between the references to these two women and making the first, instead of the second, 'Daughter to Charles, the foresaid Duke of Lorain'. The Archbishop's speech is closely paraphrased from Holinshed's Chronicle, and the primacy of the Folio text is confirmed by its being consistently closer than Q to Holinshed in such trivial variants as F 'barre . . . against', Q 'bar to stay'; F 'is in Germanie', Q 'lyes in Germany'; F 'at this day', Q 'at this time'. The reporter turned Sala, Elue (Elbe in Holinshed), and Meisen into Sabeck, Elme, and Mesene, misnamed 'Charles the Great' as 'Charles the fift', and ludicrously misheard 'After defunction of King Pharamond, / Idly suppos'd the founder of this Law' as 'After the function of king Faramont, / Godly supposed the founder of this lawe'. Q omits the Latin tag, and translates it as 'No female shall succeed in salicke land', replacing F's 'Woman' (Holinshed's 'women') with 'female', in anticipation of 'No Female / Should be Inheritrix in Salike Land', which it renders by an exact repetition of its earlier formulation, so leaving 'Establisht there this lawe.

(ii) The First Folio, 1623

To this Imperiall Throne. There is no barre
To make against your Highnesse Clayme to France,
But this which they produce from *Pharamond*,
In terram Salicam Mulieres ne succedant,
No Woman shall succeed in *Salike* Land :
Which *Salike* Land,the French vniustly gloze
To be the Realme of France, and *Pharamond*
The founder of this Law, and Female Barre.
Yet their owne Authors faithfully affirme,
That the Land *Salike* is in Germanie,
Betweene the Flouds of Sala and of Elue :
Where *Charles* the Great hauing subdu'd the Saxons,
There left behind and settled certaine French :
Who holding in disdaine the German Women,
For some dishonest manners of their life,
Establisht then this Law ; to wit,No Female
Should be Inheritrix in *Salike* Land :
Which *Salike* (as I said) 'twixt Elue and Sala,
Is at this day in Germanie,call'd *Meisen*.
Then doth it well appeare, the *Salike* Law
Was not deuised for the Realme of France :
Nor did the French possesse the *Salike* Land,
Vntill foure hundred one and twentie yeeres
After defunction of King *Pharamond*,
Idly suppos'd the founder of this Law,

To wit' as an eight-syllable line. Paraphrase damages the metre again in 'Which salicke land as I said before'. In misremembering F's (and Holinshed's) 'their owne Authors' as 'their owne writers' the reporter was influenced by 'their Writers' in a nine-line passage which in F follows the extract illustrated, but which he failed to recover for Q. 'Anticipation' and 'recollection' of later or earlier lines are marked features of these memorially reconstructed texts.

An old hypothesis about the bad Quartos was that pirates in the audience used shorthand to obtain texts. Its weakness is not so much that Elizabethan systems of stenography were inefficient – even longhand might have sufficed, if the pirate attended several performances to compile a script by piecemeal accumulation – as that so much evidence points unequivocally to faulty memories and particular culprits. The even older idea that the bad Quartos are essentially Shakespeare's first drafts or source plays and preceded the familiar full versions has even less to recommend it, though one or two of the latter may preserve traces of an earlier stage of evolution than the corresponding Folio text records.

There are other ways in which 'memorial error' might infiltrate a text. An experienced compositor carries whole clauses in his head as he sets type, and in doing so may inadvertently make substitutions, and a scribe is similarly vulnerable. Indeed, it is possible that sometimes an authoritative manuscript was copied by a theatre person familiar enough with the play as performed to trust here and there to his memory of it; he may even have been forced to draw on his memory if the manuscript from which he was copying was in places defective or illegible.[12] Some texts have been thought to suffer from light or isolated memorial contamination without being positively 'bad'.

The undoubted bad Quartos are *The Contention* (1594), *Richard Duke of York* (1595), *Romeo and Juliet* Q1 (1597), *Henry V* (1600), *The Merry Wives of Windsor* (1602), *Hamlet* Q1 (1603), and *Pericles* (1609) – the last being the sole authority for that play, though a 'novel of the play' as the King's Men had acted it helps piece out the Quarto's imperfections. Editors use the other bad texts to correct a handful of obvious errors in the corresponding good ones. In the speech we have been examining, F *Henry V* has the Archbishop declare that the usurper Hugh Capet made specious claims in order 'To find his Title with some shewes of truth'; though 'find' has been defended, it is probably a simple misreading of 'fine', which Q gives. And the fact that the duplicated speech assigned to both Romeo and Friar Lawrence in the good Quarto of *Romeo and Juliet* is given to the Friar in the bad Quarto virtually proves that this is how the confusion in Shakespeare's working draft was resolved in the prompt-book, and that Shakespeare at the very least acquiesced in the assignment. Moreover, in their stage directions the actor–reporters often recorded vivid impressions of Elizabethan theatre business or costuming, telling us, for instance, that Juliet's Nurse enters 'wringing her hands', or that the Ghost of Hamlet's father haunts Gertrude's chamber 'in his night gowne'.

In the Oxford edition (1982) of *Henry V* Gary Taylor demonstrates that at least one reported text has been under-utilized, even so. Showing that Q (1600) was printed from a reconstruction, by the actors whose chief roles had been Gower and Exeter, of a version abridged and adapted for a cast of nine adults and two boys, he argues that although many of Q's divergences from F (printed from foul papers) are due to the reporters' forgetfulness, others, including major omissions and misplacements, arose in the course of the theatrical adaptation, and can be discounted in an estimate of the reporters' reliability, which is high for scenes in which they had both participated. Taking full account of the fluctuations in Q's quality, Taylor postulates close on forty occasions on which it preserves a true Shakespearian reading corrupted in F through compositorial error, and a dozen in which it transmits

Shakespearian afterthoughts that had been introduced into the original prompt-book, including several highly significant reassignments of speeches in the scenes at Agincourt. It remains to be seen whether other reported texts can yield such a harvest.

A bad Quarto of a different kind is *The Taming of a Shrew* (1594). The belief that *A Shrew* (customarily identified by the indefinite article) was Shakespeare's source is in this case superficially credible, for there is little verbal identity with *The Shrew* as the Folio presents it, but the derivative nature of *A Shrew* has by now been firmly established. This meagre rewrite, cobbled up from an erratic plot outline of *The Shrew*, half-remembered patches of Shakespeare's dialogue, plagiarized lines from Marlowe, and the issue of a theatre hack's own dull mother-wit, is nevertheless of some textual interest, since it completes the Christopher Sly framework, left incomplete in F, from which it may have been cut. E. A. J. Honigmann's theory that *The Troublesome Reign of John King of England* (1591) similarly derives from *King John* has not supplanted the traditional view that Shakespeare was indebted to an anonymous predecessor.

The undoubted good Quartos are *Titus Andronicus* (1594), *Richard II* (1597), *Love's Labour's Lost* (1598), *1 Henry IV* (1598), *Romeo and Juliet* Q2 (1599), *2 Henry IV* (1600), *A Midsummer Night's Dream* (1600), *The Merchant of Venice* (1600), *Much Ado About Nothing* (1600), *Hamlet* Q2 (1604, some copies dated 1605), *Troilus and Cressida* (1609), *Othello* (1622), and *The Two Noble Kinsmen* (1634). Behind most of these lay foul papers, though in the case of *Richard II*, *1 Henry IV*, and *Othello* a scribal transcript probably intervened. There is still disagreement as to whether *The Two Noble Kinsmen* was set from the official prompt-book or from authorial papers that had been annotated by the book-keeper and perhaps in part transcribed.

The Quartos of *Richard III* (1597) and *King Lear* (1608) pose special problems. Though superior to acknowledged reports, they manifest some of the same symptoms; yet the *Lear* Quarto often brings to mind foul papers. The copyist who introduced memorial error is a convenient scapegoat in such circumstances, and most modern editors of *King Lear* have resorted to modified forms of Alice Walker's theory that the two boy actors who had played Goneril and Regan gained access to the foul papers and made a surreptitious copy. But the manuscript from which *Richard III* was printed is now widely believed to have been compiled by an entire acting company, who delivered their lines from memory to a scribe, in a corporate attempt to reconstruct a missing prompt-book while on a provincial tour.[13]

Most of the Quartos were several times reprinted, as was the Folio in 1632, 1663/4, and 1685.[14] *Richard II* Q4 (1608) restored, in a memorially corrupt version, the previously unpublished deposition (4.1.154–318), but otherwise the reprints have no textual authority, each normally deriving from its immediate predecessor and adding fresh mistakes, along with conjectural corrections. When a good Quarto of a play had already been published, F sometimes reproduced it, or one of its derivatives, with little alteration. *Titus Andronicus* Q3 (1611), *1 Henry IV* Q5 (1613), *Love's Labour's Lost* Q1 (1598), *Romeo and Juliet* Q3 (1609), *A Midsummer Night's Dream* Q2 (1619), *The Merchant of Venice* Q1 (1600), and *Much Ado About Nothing* Q1 (1600) served as Folio copy in this straightforward way. However, F *Titus Andronicus* added the notorious fly-killing episode (3.2), generally regarded as authentic, and though annotation of Quartos to serve as Folio copy for these Quarto-dependent plays was perfunctory in the extreme, some casual reference was demonstrably made to the prompt-book in most cases, and recent investigators have credited authority to a handful of variants even in *Romeo and Juliet* and *Love's Labour's Lost*, where changes, mainly to stage directions and speech prefixes, are minimal; and if in these plays *any* F variant has its source in an authoritative manuscript or in accurate recollection of stage tradition, then *all* F variants must be considered as potentially authoritative.

Far more complex are the issues raised by plays in which the divergence of Folio from good or 'doubtful' Quarto is greater: *Richard III, Richard II, 2 Henry IV, Troilus and Cressida, Hamlet, Othello*, and *King Lear*.[15] Behind the Folio variation – which may include substantial additions and omissions – lies in each case an authoritative manuscript, probably the company's prompt-book, but it is sometimes difficult to determine whether F was set directly from manuscript or from a Quarto that had been marked up with reference to it; and where the prompt-book influence was certainly exerted via a Quarto, doubt may remain over which edition or editions were used. Answers to these questions of physical relationship are urgently needed, because anyone marking a Quarto to bring it into conformity with a manuscript would inevitably have performed the task imperfectly, allowing some errors to stand; since the earlier print might have contaminated F, their agreement over a dubious reading would increase suspicion of its authenticity rather than allay it.[16] The distinction is like that between corroborative and collusive testimony in a court of law. Of course, slips and irregularities in Shakespeare's foul papers – and in Hand D of *More* these minor defects are numerous – could have independently provoked two scribes, or Quarto compositor and prompt-book scribe, into making identical errors, so that evidence of direct dependence of F upon a Quarto must come mainly from F's perpetuation of Quarto anomalies arising out of the actual printing process. Minor deviations from the first Quartos of *Richard II* and *Richard III* accumulated in the two series of reprints, and the fact that many of these changes were passed on to the Folio enables us to see that *Richard II* Q3 (1598) and *Richard III* Q3 (1602) were used in the printing of F. However, it has been shown that a surprising amount of coincidental agreement over 'indifferent' variants (where the sense is not affected) can be expected between totally independent prints, and apparent Folio links with *Richard II* Q5 and *Richard III* Q6 have proved harder to interpret. *King Lear* is a special case, as will appear shortly, and of the other four plays only *Hamlet* was reprinted (once) before 1623, so that evidence from derivative Quartos is not available.[17]

Another subject of debate about most of these plays is whether any QF variation results from revision by Shakespeare. *King Lear* is the *cause célèbre*. Q contains some three hundred lines not in F, and F some one hundred lines not in Q, and there are over a thousand verbal variants between the two texts. The Quarto has recently been subjected to painstaking bibliographical investigation, which suggests that some of its aberrations can be blamed on the inexperience of its printer, Nicholas Okes, in dealing with play-scripts. Several scholars now believe that Q was set straight from untidy foul papers, and that F gives us Shakespeare's reshapings of the tragedy – perhaps undertaken four or five years after original composition. The most contentious part of this theory concerns the material peculiar to one or other text. Editors have traditionally conflated Q and F on the assumption that Q's omissions are accidental and F's due to the book-keeper's cuts. But if, as is now argued, the passages absent from Q are Shakespeare's expansions, belonging to the same process of revision as the cutting by which he himself purposefully accelerated the play's progress in Acts 3 and 4, then conflation makes for redundancy and misrepresents both the initial and subsequent authorial intentions: though Q and F may legitimately be used to correct each other's errors, we need separate modern editions of two *King Lears*.

In *Othello* and *Troilus and Cressida* cutting by the playwright is not a feature of putative revisions in F, and the editorial custom of preparing a single text remains appropriate. What we can fairly ask, however, of editors of these plays is that their textual decisions vindicate and be governed by their theories about the relationships between Q and F. The editor who, for instance, decides to adopt Theobald's 'distinct' for QF 'defunct' in Othello's allusion to 'the young affects / In my defunct, and proper satisfaction' (as F prints the lines at 1.3.263–4) cannot reasonably hold, as part of his textual theory, that Q and F derive from separate holographs, with no contamination of F by Q, since two different inscribings of 'distinct' could hardly each be misread as the less intelligible, though meaningful, 'defunct'. Nor should an editor who believes that F *Troilus and Cressida* contains Shakespeare's second thoughts, and that at 1.3.92 both Q's 'the influence of euil planets' and F's 'the ill Aspects of Planets euill' are authorial, accept Q's version in his own edition, unless he can defend a policy of consistently presenting the unrevised text.[18]

Where we have two texts of a play, variants produced by authorial revision in one may closely resemble variants produced by corruption in the other. The point may be illustrated by a brief discussion of the lines from *More* Hand D shown in Figure 9. Shakespeare himself changed 'warrs' in the seventh of these lines to 'hurly', and thus eliminated repetition of 'warrs' from line 5. If there existed two texts of the passage, one with Shakespeare's first thought

wash your foule mynds with teares and those same hands   1
that you lyke rebells lyft against the peace   2
lift vp for peace, and your vnreuerent knees   3
make them your feet to kneele to be forgyven   4
is safer warrs, then euer you can make   5
                  in in to your obedienc   6
whose discipline is ryot, why euen your ~~warrs~~ hurly   7
cannot proceed but by obedienc what rebell captaine   8
as mutynes ar incident, by his name   9
can still the rout who will obay ~~th~~ a traytor   10
or howe can well that proclamation sounde   11
when ther is no adicion but a rebell   12
to quallyfy a rebell, youle put downe straingers   13

Wash your foul minds with tears; and those same hands
That you like rebels lift against the peace,
Lift up for peace; and your unreverent knees,
Make them your feet. To kneel to be forgiven
Is safer wars than ever you can make
Whose discipline is riot. Why even your hurly
Cannot proceed but by obedience.
What rebel captain,
As mutinies are incident, by his name
Can still the rout? Who will obey a traitor?
Or how can well that proclamation sound
When there is no addition but a rebel
To qualify a rebel? You'll put down strangers,

9   Lines from *Sir Thomas More*, Hand D. The transcription (abbreviations expanded) shows the passage as left by the author; a playhouse scribe crossed out everything from 'is' in line 5 to 'obedienc' in line 8, substituting 'tell me but this'. The modernized text is edited by C. J. Sisson

'warrs' in line 7, and the other with his second thought 'hurly', it would be easy to suppose mistakenly that 'warrs' in line 7 was the 'recollection' of a faulty memory. More significantly, Shakespeare's neglect of punctuation and capital letters, his interlineation of the phrase 'in in to your obedienc', his affixing of the words 'what rebell captaine' to an already complete pentameter, and the generally convoluted nature of More's rhetoric combined to leave the intended metrical and syntactical structure of the lines so wholly obscure that the playhouse scribe struck out everything from 'is safer warrs' to 'but by obedienc', replacing it with 'tell me but this'. A compositor faced with the passage as Shakespeare left it could hardly have avoided printing some metrically irregular lines, and a scholar who suspected that such a printed text suffered from memorial corruption could point not only to the irregularity of the verse but also to the clumsy repetition of the word 'obedienc', so suggestive of an actor's 'anticipation' or 'recollection'. A Shakespearian fair copy would doubtless have cleared up the anomalies. Had a text been printed from it, a text printed from this working draft would appear corrupt by comparison. Discrimination may, however, be aided by study of Shakespeare's source material. Evidence of the degenerate nature of Q *Henry V* is afforded by F's closer adherence to Holinshed. So it is an important argument against the view that Q *Lear* merely corrupts the play restored, with some excisions, in F, that in details of wording and situation Q is closer than F to the sources available to Shakespeare in 1605/6.

Our present understanding of the Shakespearian Quartos and Folio rests on the findings in the first half of this century of Alfred W. Pollard, R. B. McKerrow, W. W. Greg, E. K. Chambers, J. Dover Wilson, G. I. Duthie, Peter Alexander, Alice Walker, and others. In the last few decades, under the auspices of Fredson Bowers, new techniques of analytic bibliography have been employed in a sustained effort to find out more about the treatment of Shakespeare's plays in Elizabethan–Jacobean printing-houses. Twin peaks of achievement are Charlton Hinman's study of the First Folio and Peter Blayney's of the First Quarto of *King Lear*.

We know now that the First Folio and several Quartos were set 'by formes' rather than 'seriatim'. The forme is the combination of type-pages that, locked up in a chase, prints one side of a sheet of paper, which is 'perfected' when a second forme prints the other side. The First Folio consists of sewn gatherings (or quires) in which three sheets, each folded once, are placed one inside the other, giving six leaves or twelve pages. Hinman showed that the Folio compositors set type for the pages of a gathering not in the numerical order in which we read them but starting with the inner forme of the inner sheet and working outwards; they would thus begin on the sixth and seventh pages, progress to the fifth and eighth, fourth and ninth, and so on, till they reached the first and twelfth. This meant that their copy had to be 'cast-off' in advance, exact amounts of copy being allotted to individual Folio pages, since the pages of the first half of the gathering were to be set in reverse order. Any miscalculation forced the compositor to expand or contract the text. Expedients for saving space included setting verse as prose and even leaving something out.

Another feature of printing in Shakespeare's day was a ready resort to stop-press correction.[19] The passage of sheets through the press was interrupted and adjustments were made to the type, but uncorrected sheets already printed off were not discarded. Rather, corrected and uncorrected sheets were bound indiscriminately, so that extant copies of a single edition may contain different mixes and be significantly variant. *King Lear* Q1 (1608) is especially notable for the quality and quantity of press-variants among the twelve surviving copies. The press-corrector sometimes consulted and deciphered the compositor's manuscript and sometimes guessed at the emendation required. In its uncorrected state Q, at 3.4.6, has Lear speak, impossibly, of 'this crulentious storme'. The corrector substituted the pleonasm, 'this tempestious storme'. F exposes this as a guess by printing the word behind the Q compositor's misreading: 'this contentious storme'. But it must have been from the manuscript that the corrector retrieved the words 'and appointed guard' at 5.3.48. Their absence from F is crucial to the case for F's dependence in some way upon a copy of the printed Quarto – one that was uncorrected at this point. There are other agreements between F and Q1 in its uncorrected state.

Much energy has been devoted to determining – through analysis of spelling preferences and typographical peculiarities – the stints of the various compositors who set Shakespeare's plays. Folio compositors 'A' and 'B', first distinguished by Thomas Satchell in 1920, have split and multiplied into at least nine workmen, whose stints can, at last, be fairly confidently defined. By examining their workmanship in straight reprints, we can gain some idea of the amount and kind of corruption they are likely to have introduced into other Folio texts. Much work remains to be done in this area. Though the main Folio compositor, B, treated his copy less high-handedly than once feared, both he and Compositor C perpetrated substitutions, omissions, and other errors at the rate of up to half-a-dozen per Folio page. Compositor D seems to have been prone to literal errors, as was the inexperienced Compositor E, who had a marked tendency to omit or add a final '–s'. Compositor E's elementary errors are, on the whole, easier to detect than Compositor B's sophistications, and E's invariable conservatism in reproducing the punctuation and spelling of known Quarto copy allows us to infer that he cannot have set his share of Folio *Othello* and *Hamlet* from the Quartos, which are spelt and punctuated too differently from F, and that his copy for F *King Lear* was marked-up Q2 (1619), not Q1.[20]

Orthographical patterns unrelated to compositorial divisions may point to heterogeneity in the manuscript underlying a printed text. Compositor B was responsible for all Folio *Timon of Athens* except a single page, set by E. Both men habitually spelt the exclamation 'O' or 'Oh' as it appeared in their copy. Within sections of *Timon* attributable to Middleton, 'Oh' occurs thirteen times, 'O' ten; 'Oh' is absent from the rest of the play, but 'O' occurs fourteen times. The 'Middletonian' and 'Shakespearian' portions of *Timon* thus reflect a Shakespearian preference for 'O' and a Middletonian liking for 'Oh' that can be deduced from good Quarto editions of their plays, from Hand D, and from Middleton's holographs of *A Game at Chess*. And the disposition of 'O' and 'Oh' spellings in Folio *1 Henry VI*, *King John*, and *Cymbeline* suggests that these plays were set from manuscripts of composite origin. Compositor studies have also challenged some cherished notions: clear indications that the Quarto of Shakespeare's *Sonnets* (1609) was set by two men, who punctuated the text in very different ways, warrant extreme scepticism of the more extravagant claims for the authority and rhetorical significance of Q's 'accidentals' (punctuation, spelling and use of capitals).

Finally, let us revert to Othello's Indian or Judean. Debate on this crux has strayed into almost every field of Shakespearian scholarship: lexicography, sources and influences, metre, characterization, associative clusters of words and images, proverb lore, theological interpretation.[21] What of the *textual* considerations? Both Q and F suffer from compositorial and scribal error, but F is on the whole superior. Q seems to have been based on a private transcript of the original foul papers, F on the official prompt-book. Unless the transcript behind Q was exceptionally 'licentious',[22] the prompt-book must have incorporated some of Shakespeare's own readjustments to the dialogue. F's use of the prompt-book was probably direct, rather than by way of a marked-up exemplar of Q. Work on Folio *Othello* was shared almost equally by Compositors B and E. Though the word 'Iudean', so spelt, existed in the early seventeenth century, it was rare, and even the place-name 'Iudea' (as it appears several times in the Geneva Bible of 1560, as well as in the King James version of 1611) was sufficiently unusual for at least two compositors of the time to misread it as the better known 'India'.[23] If Q's 'Indian' is wrong, it is a simple misreading of the less familiar as the more familiar word, in a text that contains many such errors. The proverbial association of Indians with precious stones would have facilitated the mistake. F's 'Iudean' is harder to explain as erroneous. F contains only half as many probable misreadings as Q, and nearly all fall into Compositor E's stint. 'Iudean' is on a page set by Compositor B. Psychologically, the misreading, by some agent in the transmission of F, of 'Indian' as the more difficult 'Iudean' would be much less natural than the opposite process. Yet Compositor B almost certainly set 'Iudean' deliberately, not accidentally: a simple foul-case error – causing B unwittingly to pick up a 'u' from the 'n' box – could have turned an intended 'Indian' into 'Iudian', but the 'e' spelling proves that this did not happen.[24] Nowhere in the Folio, or in the Quartos, does the word 'Indian', which Shakespeare used seven times,[25] occur in any but its modern form, and *OED*'s only two seventeenth-century citations of the spelling 'Indean', in over fifty examples of the word, both come from American archives (of 1635 and 1644), not British print. So, if Compositor B did not mean to set 'Iudean', he combined foul case 'u' with a highly abnormal spelling (or a second misprint). There are eight instances of foul case 'u' for 'n' in F *Othello*, but every one appears within the unskilled Compositor E's stints. Despite the similarity in graphic outline of 'Indian' and 'Iudean', both words might conceivably be authorial; an editor who believed this to be the case would be obliged to print 'Iudean', as originating in the text supposed to contain Shakespeare's second thoughts.

The textual probabilities tend, therefore, to favour 'Iudean', but they are no more than probabilities: a just assessment of the crux must take them into account, but other factors might outweigh them. An editor persuaded of the superiority of 'Indian' could best defend it on textual grounds by positing that Shakespeare himself, an erratic speller, used the anomalous spelling 'Indean', which was normalized in Q and by its rarity provoked minim misreading in F.

The history of Shakespearian textual studies, from the early eighteenth century onwards, is one not only of increasing willingness to investigate the primary sources and to ponder how Shakespeare's intentions can best be inferred from the evidence they provide, but also a history of critical taste.[26] Pope tried to turn Shakespeare into a strict Augustan metrist, and his care for metaphorical propriety shows in his proposal that Hamlet's 'sea of troubles' should, in view of 'arms', 'slings', and 'arrows', be a 'siege'. Johnson's sensitivity to Shakespeare's poetry is attested by his brilliant paraphrases and explanations of difficult lines, yet while conceding that 'grunt and sweat' in *Hamlet*, Q1, Q2, and F is 'undoubtedly the true reading', he found 'grunt' intolerable and changed it to 'groan'. In the nineteenth century Henrietta Bowdler and her brother Thomas expurgated obscenities from their *Family Shakespeare* (1807, 1818). Perhaps some present preoccupations will come to seem no less bizarre. The twentieth-century drive towards the establishment of 'Shakespeare's true text' coincided with the rise of the New Criticism, with its scrupulous attention to 'the words on the page'. Recent stress in Shakespeare criticism on the plays as scripts for performance has perhaps brought to textual studies a greater awareness of theatrical values. This is reflected in the new series of editions from Oxford (under the general editorship of Stanley Wells) and Cambridge (under the general editorship of Philip Brockbank).

These editions, like virtually every edition since Shakespeare's own time, present the plays in texts whose spelling and punctuation have been modernized, and in which the original stage directions have been variously amplified and adjusted. The editorial presentation of Shakespeare's texts is no less of an index to critical taste than the substantive changes to the dialogue.

Shortly before he died, John Dover Wilson, chief editor of the New Shakespeare (1921–66), wrote: 'A few years ago I spent twelve months or more examining, under the microscope so to speak, the marvellous texture of the masterpiece we call *Macbeth*. And to do that, if one has any poetic sensibility at all, is to become so enchanted by the music of it, so shaken by the horror of it, so penetrated by the pity of it, that the experience is almost overwhelming – and it's an experience one can always repeat in a different form, by editing another play.'[27] We cannot all be editors, but an interest in determining 'what Shakespeare wrote' remains a sure key to an intimate knowledge of the plays.

Notes

1. Algernon Charles Swinburne, *A Study of Shakespeare* (new edition 1918), p. 264. Swinburne quotes from Edward Capell's text, which prints 'Arrive that' in place of Q's 'To arriue at'. Q spells 'hellie', and misprints 'through' in the same line as 'throng'.
2. E. K. Chambers, *William Shakespeare*, 2 vols. (Oxford, 1930), I, 539–42.
3. The textual solution was proposed by Philip Edwards, 'An Approach to the Problem of *Pericles*', *Shakespeare Survey* 5 (Cambridge, 1952), pp. 25–49, and reaffirmed in his New Penguin edition of the play (1976). But he avoids concluding outright that Shakespeare was solely responsible for the uncorrupted *Pericles*.
4. But there exist several autograph and scribal manuscripts of Elizabethan–Jacobean plays by other authors.
5. This figure includes *The Taming of a Shrew* (1594), but not *The Troublesome Reign of John King of England* (1591).
6. And after his retirement to Stratford around 1610 he would have had little control over the evolution of his plays at the hands even of the King's Men. He may have supervised the printing of *Venus and Adonis* (1593) and *The Rape of Lucrece* (1594).
7. Author copyright, as we know it, did not exist in Shakespeare's day. A publisher who acquired the manuscript of a play needed only to enter it in the Stationers' Register, paying a small fee, in order to gain the exclusive right to print it.
8. See J. Dover Wilson's essay in the volume on *Sir Thomas More* (see Reading list) and his *The Manuscript of Shakespeare's 'Hamlet'* (Cambridge, 1934), 2 vols.
9. In Elizabethan printing 'u' was used medially, 'v' initially, regardless of phonetic value. The compositor doubtless imagined that the first 'u' of 'prouaunt' was sounded as 'v'; his comma after the word is a desperate attempt to give plausibility to the unintelligible.
10. Another Elizabethan theatrical document prepared by the book-keeper is the 'plot', a skeleton outline of the play's action, listing exits and entrances, describing dumb shows, and indicating properties and sound effects. An actor's 'part' consisted of his own lines plus necessary cues.
11. Agnes Latham, ed., Arden *As You Like It* (1975), p. xv.
12. *Titus Andronicus* Q2 (1600) was printed from a copy of Q1 (1594) that had been damaged at the foot of the last three leaves. Somebody supplied blank-verse patchwork.
13. A version of this theory was also advanced for Q *King Lear* by G. I. Duthie in his important old-spelling edition of the play (Oxford, 1949).
14. F3 (1664 issue) added *Pericles* (reprinting Q6 of 1635) and six spurious plays.
15. In the quantity and kind of QF variants *Richard II* occupies an intermediate position between plays with which it has been listed and those listed in the previous paragraph.
16. Similarly, in the case of both *Romeo and Juliet* and *Hamlet* the bad Q1 was apparently used in the printing of the good Q2, though the nature and extent of the dependence is in doubt; perhaps for each play the compositor, besides setting

limited passages from marked-up Q1 pages, consulted the corrupt Quarto as an aid to the decipherment of a difficult manuscript. Short sections of the Folio *2 and 3 Henry VI* were set from reprints of *The Contention* and *Richard Duke of York*, and more extensive use of these two bad Quartos has been postulated.

17. In *Quarto Copy* (see Reading list), J. K. Walton tackles these problems through analysis and classification of substantive readings. For an approach by way of 'accidentals' (punctuation, spelling, capitalization) see Gary Taylor, 'The Folio copy for *Hamlet, King Lear,* and *Othello*', *Shakespeare Quarterly* 34 (1983), 44–61.

18. Cf. the Oxford *Troilus and Cressida* (1982), ed. Kenneth Muir, and the Cambridge *Othello* (1983), ed. Norman Sanders.

19. Blayney (see Reading list) has disproved the dogma that this was the *only* form of correction undertaken in printing houses of the late sixteenth and early seventeenth centuries, but earlier stages of proof-correction, before presswork began, were often perfunctorily performed.

20. At 5.3.48, Q2 contains the phrase 'and appointed guard', omitted from uncorrected copies of Q1 and from F, which was set by Compositor E at this point. So a theory concerning the copy for F *Lear* must reconcile evidence for the influence on Compositor E's stints of both Q1 and Q2. Taylor unravels this complexity in the article cited in note 17 and in *The Division of the Kingdoms* (see Reading list).

21. There is a recent assessment by Richard Levin, 'The Indian/Iudean crux in *Othello*', *Shakespeare Quarterly* 33 (1982), 60–7, but his textual and lexical data require modification.

22. Alice Walker, ed., New Shakespeare *Othello* (Cambridge, 1960), p. 125.

23. See *Shakespeare Survey 37* (Cambridge, 1984), p. 218, and the Collier citation in H. H. Furness, ed., New Variorum *Othello* (Lippincott, Philadelphia, 1886), p. 331.

24. Mis-setting of 'Indian' as 'Iudian', followed by miscorrection to 'Iudean', is unlikely, because correction to the familiar 'Indian' would more readily have suggested itself.

25. There is another F instance in a Fletcherian scene of *Henry VIII.*

26. There are brief accounts by Evans in the Riverside Shakespeare and Walton in *Quarto Copy* (see Reading list).

27. *The Living Shakespeare* (1960), ed. Robert Gittings, p. 43.

Reading list

Allen, Michael J. B. and Kenneth Muir, eds., *Shakespeare's Plays in Quarto: A Facsimile Edition of Copies Primarily from the Henry E. Huntington Library* (Berkeley, California, 1981)

Blayney, Peter W. M., *The Texts of 'King Lear' and their Origins,* 1 vol. (at present), 1 Nicholas Okes and the First Quarto (Cambridge, 1982)

Bowers, Fredson, *Bibliography and Textual Criticism* (Oxford, 1964)
On Editing Shakespeare (Charlottesville, Virginia, 1966)
Textual and Literary Criticism (Cambridge, 1959)

Evans, G. Blakemore, ed., *The Riverside Shakespeare* (Boston, Massachusetts, 1974)

Gaskell, Philip, *A New Introduction to Bibliography* (Cambridge, 1972)

Greg, W. W., *The Shakespeare First Folio: Its Bibliographical and Textual History* (Oxford, 1955)

Hart, Alfred, *Stolne and Surreptitious Copies: A Comparative Study of Shakespeare's Bad Quartos* (Melbourne, 1942)

Hinman, Charlton, ed., *The Norton Facsimile: The First Folio of Shakespeare* (New York, 1968)

The Printing and Proof-Reading of the First Folio of Shakespeare 2 vols. (Oxford, 1963)

Honigmann, E. A. J., *The Stability of Shakespeare's Text* (1965)

Howard-Hill, T. H., *Ralph Crane and Some Shakespeare First Folio Comedies* (Charlottesville, Virginia, 1972)

Jenkins, Harold, ed., *Hamlet* (1982), Arden Shakespeare

McKerrow, R. B., *Prolegomena for the Oxford Shakespeare* (Oxford, 1939)

Pollard, Alfred W. and others, *Shakespeare's Hand in the Play of 'Sir Thomas More'* (Cambridge, 1923)

Prosser, Eleanor, *Shakespeare's Anonymous Editors: Scribe and Compositor in the Folio Text of '2 Henry IV'* (Stanford, California, 1981)

Shand, G. B. and Raymond C. Shady, eds., *Play-Texts in Old Spelling: Papers from the Glendon Conference* (New York, 1984)

Stone, P. W. K., *The Textual History of 'King Lear'* (1980)

Taylor, Gary and Michael Warren, eds., *The Division of the Kingdoms: Shakespeare's Two Versions of 'King Lear'* (Oxford, 1983)

Urkowitz, Steven, *Shakespeare's Revision of 'King Lear'* (Princeton, New Jersey, 1980)

Walker, Alice, *Textual Problems of the First Folio* (Cambridge, 1953)

Walton, J. K., *The Quarto Copy for the First Folio of Shakespeare* (Dublin, 1971)

Wells, Stanley, *Re-Editing Shakespeare for the Modern Reader* (Oxford, 1984)

Wells, Stanley and Gary Taylor, *Modernizing Shakespeare's Spelling with Three Studies in the Text of 'Henry V'* (Oxford, 1979)

11 Shakespeare on the stage from 1660 to 1900

I

AFTER the monarchy was restored, in 1660, London's theatre companies were re-established in a way that determined their organization until the radical changes of the 1843 Theatres Act. Two companies, Sir William Davenant's (the 'Duke's') and Thomas Killigrew's ('The King's') were licensed for regular performances. These royal patents, passing from Davenant and Killigrew to their heirs and assignees, were the instruments of governmental control over theatrical performance.

Staging methods in the Restoration theatre differed considerably from Elizabethan and Jacobean practice. Movable scenery formed a background to the play's action, women replaced boys and young men in female roles, and the companies suited their repertoire and performance style to the tastes of an audience more uniformly courtly and fashionable. The changes made to Shakespeare's plays reflect all this. At the same time, there were important continuities between Restoration theatre and its forebears. Many of the old plays were given in texts more or less approximating to the original: *Hamlet*, *Othello*, *Julius Caesar*, *1 Henry IV* and, possibly, *Henry VIII* seem to have been acted without major alterations of the kind made in *Macbeth* and *The Tempest*. Representational scenery, made up of painted wings and shutters running in grooves parallel to the front of the stage, was now a pleasing and significant part of theatrical entertainment, but it was placed in a scenic stage behind the forestage on which most of the action took place. Scenery commonly indicated generalized rather than specific location, and movement from scene to scene was still rapid. The forestage gave actors a degree of intimacy with their audience; and lighting, although necessarily artificial in these indoor theatres, was provided for both auditorium and stage. The audience had not yet lost its sense of identity as a social assembly within which the actor needed to command attention. Theatre, as in Shakespeare's day, continued to be a self-conscious medium. Acting, especially in tragedy, preserved the values of ideal and decorous behaviour, musical speech and rhetorical finish.

We have tantalizing evidence of a continuing tradition in performance, and glimpses, at several removes, of Elizabethan interpretations. John Downes,

'Book-keeper and prompter' to Davenant's company, noted in his *Roscius Anglicanus* (1708) that when Hamlet was performed by Thomas Betterton, 'Sir William (having seen Mr Taylor of the Black-Fryars Company act it, who being intructed by the author Mr Shakespear) taught Mr Betterton in every particle of it.' This Hamlet was recalled by the actor and playwright Colley Cibber. In his interview with the Ghost, Betterton

> open'd with a Pause of mute Amazement! then rising slowly to a solemn, trembling Voice, he made the Ghost equally terrible to the spectator, as to himself! and in the descriptive Part of the natural Emotions which the ghastly Vision gave him, the boldness of his Expostulation was still govern'd by Decency, manly but not braving; his Voice never rising into that seeming Outrage or wild Defiance of what he naturally rever'd.

Cibber emphasizes the dignity of Betterton in his other roles. As Brutus in the quarrel with Cassius, 'his Spirit flew only to his Eye; his steady Look alone supplied that Terror which he disdained an Intemperance in his Voice should rise to'. Brutus 'with a settled Dignity of Contempt, like an unheeding Rock, . . . repelled upon himself the Foam of Cassius'.[1]

Sir William Davenant energetically manufactured revisions of Shakespeare's plays to accommodate current theatrical and literary tastes. *The Law Against Lovers* (1661–2) combines *Measure for Measure* and *Much Ado About Nothing; Macbeth* (?1664) and *The Tempest; or, the Enchanted Island* (?1667) provide greater opportunities than their originals for music and what Samuel Pepys called 'divertissement'. Davenant also produced a version of *The Two Noble Kinsmen* (as *The Rivals*) and his company played a tragicomic version of *Romeo and Juliet*, now lost. It was Davenant's *Macbeth* which impressed Pepys as 'one of the best plays for a stage, and variety of dancing and music, that ever [he] saw'.[2] In it the witches sang, flew, and danced, the Macduffs were developed as a virtuous counterpart to the Macbeths (a meeting with the Witches was arranged) and Macbeth had a dying speech of commendable brevity: 'Farewell, vain World, and what's most vain in it,/ Ambition. (*Dies*.)'[3] Shakespeare's language was smoothed out, and his imagery simplified. In Davenant's version of the dagger speech it is the 'hilt', not the 'handle' of the weapon that Macbeth tries to 'grasp' (not 'clutch'); the 'heat-oppressèd brain' becomes 'the brain, oppress'd by heat'; wicked dreams 'infect the health' of Sleep, rather than 'abuse / The curtained Sleep'; and at the end of the speech Macbeth's ambition replaces the destination of Duncan's soul as a matter of concern:

> O Duncan, hear it not, for 'tis a bell
> That rings my coronation, and thy knell.

There is no crowding of image upon image, no jostling of the commonplace by the lofty to perplex Davenant's Macbeth, whose language loses in energy what it gains in dignity. Confronted with the desperate messenger, he asks 'Now friend, what means thy change of countenance?' – a hopelessly bland substitution for 'The devil damn thee black, thou cream fac'd loon.'

In *The Tempest; or, the Enchanted Island*, prepared in collaboration with John Dryden and later rendered more operatic by lesser hands, Miranda, who has never seen a man, is given a male counterpart, Ippolito, who (despite living on the same island) has been kept by Prospero in a corresponding state of innocence concerning women. Miranda has a sister, Dorinda; Ariel has a soul mate called Milcha; even Caliban is provided with company in the shape of a sister, named Sycorax in honour of their mother. Ippolito, being rightful heir to Mantua (usurped by Alonso), is qualified for a final scene in which rank and marriage are conferred on two couples. This increase in the island's population allows for scenes of comic misunderstanding among the lovers, treated with a worldly cynicism absent in the original. There is no place here for Miranda's exclamation, 'O brave new world . . . ' The comic scenes are augmented, not unskilfully, with a mate (Mustacho) and a mariner (Ventoso). In its more elaborate version (1674) this new *Tempest* begins with a spectacular representation of the storm, in which 'the Scene . . . represents a thick cloudy Sky, a very Rocky Coast, and a Tempestuous Sea in perpetual agitation'.

This Tempest (suppos'd to be rais'd by Magick) has many dreadful objects in it, as several Spirits in horrid shapes flying down amongst the Sailers, then rising and crossing in the Air. And when the Ship is sinking, the whole House is darken'd and a shower of Fire falls upon 'em. This is accompanied with Lightning, and several Claps of Thunder, to the end of the Storm.

Subsequent producers of *The Tempest* would also find the storm an irresistible challenge to the skill of the scenic artist.

With the attractions of music, song and scenery, *The Tempest; or, the Enchanted Island* must have been a splendid show, but it lacks the ambiguities and mystery of the original play. The new Prospero takes leave of the audience not with the Shakespearian reminder of his dual identity as player and dramatic character, and the reference to sin and forgiveness ('as you from crimes would pardoned be . . . '), but with an unqualified promise of felicity:

Henceforth this isle to the afflicted be
A place of refuge, as it was to me:
The Promises of blooming spring live here,
And all the blessings of the ripening year.
On my retreat, let Heav'n and Nature smile,
And ever flourish the enchanted Isle.

It is left to the Epilogue spoken in the theatre to bring the audience back to the realities of life. It comes as something of a surprise to modern readers to be told in the prologue to this *Tempest* that

Shakespeare's magick could not copied be,
Within that circle none durst walk but he

and to learn from Dryden that Davenant's 'high veneration' for Shakespeare had inspired his own respect for the dramatist. Dryden's preface to his version of *Troilus and Cressida* (1679) shows that he had no doubt that the language of the plays needed improvement:

> the tongue in general is so much refin'd since Shakespear's time, that many of his words, and more of his Phrases, are scarce intelligible. And of those which we understand some are ungrammatical, others course; and his whole style is so pester'd with Figurative expressions, that it is as affected as it is obscure.

The honest desire to do service to an outmoded and obscure original informs one of the most enduring Restoration versions of Shakespeare, Nahum Tate's *History of King Lear* (1681). Tate tells the reader that he found the tragedy 'a heap of jewels, unstrung and unpolish't; yet so dazzling in their disorder, that I soon perceiv'd I had seiz'd a treasure'. His improvements incorporated a love-plot between Edgar and Cordelia ('that never chang'd word with each other in the original'), omitted the Fool, and allowed Lear, Cordelia and Gloster to survive. Tate supplied incidents appropriate in kind and quantity to his audience's tastes, including Edgar's rescue of Cordelia and her confidante from two ruffians sent by Edmund, and a scene in which the Bastard and Regan are discovered in a grotto, 'amorously seated, listening to musick'. The language throughout is neater and the drift more moralizing than Shakespeare's, culminating in an absurdly optimistic prospect of the future as Lear and Gloster go off to 'some cool cell' to pass their time in 'calm reflections on our fortunes past'. Cordelia and the prosperity of Britain are neatly joined in Edgar's final speech:

> Divine Cordelia, all the gods can witness
> How much thy love to empire I prefer!
> Thy bright example shall convince the world
> (Whatever storms of fortune are decreed)
> That truth and vertue shall at last succeed.

The bathos of this is apparent – perhaps unfairly – to those acquainted with the bleakness of Shakespeare's ending, but it incorporates one of the stock dilemmas of Restoration heroic drama (love *versus* empire), much as Davenant's Macbeth returns to the topic of ambition in his dying speech. Another persistently popular adaptation, Colley Cibber's workmanlike *Richard III*, simplifies the career of its central character into a melodrama of ambition, with all the dynastic politics filleted out.

Other Restoration versions of Shakespeare assimilate their originals to current enthusiasms for classical subjects (Otway's *Caius Marius*, 1680, after *Romeo and Juliet*) or political themes (Tate's *Sicilian Usurper*, 1681, after *Richard II*) or the capabilities of individual performers (Lacy's *Sauny the Scot*, 1667, uses parts of *The Taming of the Shrew* rewritten to favour Grumio). In *The Fairy Queen* (1685) Henry Purcell and an anonymous librettist take *A Midsummer Night's Dream* as pretext for a spectacular opera-ballet. It is possible to argue that some of these uses of Shakespeare are more 'legitimate' than others, in so far as they sacrifice his work to literary rather than theatrical gods, but, given a choice between the chance to see a performance of *The Sicilian Usurper* or *The Fairy Queen*, it would be absurd to opt for Tate over Purcell. Compelling, beautiful entertainments and displays of fine acting were created out of the plays in this period. Shakespeare served a vigorous and developing art.

II

The eighteenth century began gradually restoring to the stage the original texts, or at least discarding most of the additions and verbal alterations perpetrated in the Restoration. The movement was engendered partly by an increased awareness of the plays in their original published form (through such editions as Rowe's of 1709 and Warburton's of 1747), partly in response to changing fashions in drama. Emphasis on pathos and sentiment and influence of the novelists' example in detailed realistic characterization augmented an ever-present desire on the part of artists to improve on works of the preceding generation. Acting shifted from a formal to a more 'natural' style, although the use of these terms must be qualified by the reminder that 'nature' was dressed to advantage before she was placed before the public. In serious drama, actors were praised for marking the successive physical signs of the 'Passions', a process more closely allied to the expression of known quantities than to the exploration of unconscious motivation. By the 1740s exponents of the old style seemed excessively stiff and unnatural, grandiloquent in tone and artificial in movement.In Charles Macklin (*c.* 1700–97) and David Garrick (*c.* 1717–79), audiences encountered a freshness of study and realism in marking the effects of the passions absent in the tragic performances of such actors as James Quin (1693–1766), of whom Tobias Smollett complained that his utterance was 'a continual sing-song, like the chanting of vespers' and his action resembled that of 'heaving ballast into the hold of a ship'. After Quin's deposition from the tragic roles, his Falstaff was still celebrated: 'his comely countenance, his expressive eye, his happy swell of voice, and his natural importance of deportment, all united to make up a most characteristic piece of acting'.[4]

Quin appeared as Antonio when Charles Macklin played Shylock at Drury Lane on 14 February 1741. The text was nearer to the original than *The Jew of Venice* (1701) in which Thomas Doggett had made Shylock a comic figure, with red hair and a grotesquely hooked nose. Macklin's Jew was villainous, realistic, and passionate. Macklin recalled how the 'pull' of the part came in the third act, in Shylock's scene with Tubal:

At this period I threw out all my fire; and as the contrasted passions of joy for the Merchant's losses, and grief for the elopement of Jessica, open a fine field for the actor's powers, I had the good fortune to please beyond my warmest expectations – the whole house was in an uproar of applause – and I was obliged to pause between the speeches, to give it vent, so as to be heard.

'During this scene of alternate elation and despair,' wrote a witness, 'he breaks the tones of utterance, and varies his countenance admirably.'[5] (Fig. 10)

Later in the same year, on 19 October at the theatre in Goodman's Fields, David Garrick made his London début, playing Richard III. Like Macklin, he astonished his audience with his vivid and realistic portrayal of character in moments of crisis. Thus, in his tent on the eve of the battle, Garrick's Richard started from his dream in 'a spectacle of horror'. (Fig. 11)

He called out in a manly tone, 'Give me another horse.' He paused, and, with a countenance of dismay, advanced, crying out in a tone of distress, 'Bind up my wounds;' and then, falling on his knees, said in the most piteous accent, 'Have mercy Heaven.' In all this, the audience saw an exact imitation of Nature.[6]

Although a modern audience might well have found him too studied, contemporary observers were thrilled by the rapid succession of physical illustrations of the character's state of mind. The German traveller Georg Christoph Lichtenberg gave a memorable account of Garrick's Hamlet, in his first encounter with the Ghost:

Suddenly, as Hamlet moves towards the back of the stage slightly to the left and turns his back on the audience, Horatio starts, and saying: 'look, my lord, it comes', points to the right, where the ghost has already appeared and stands motionless, before any one is aware of him. At these words Garrick turns sharply and at the same moment staggers back two or three paces with his knees giving way under him; his hat falls to the ground and both his arms, especially the left, are stretched out nearly to their full length, with the hands as high as his head, the right arm more bent and the hand lower, and the fingers apart; his mouth is open: thus he stands rooted to the spot, with legs apart, but no loss of dignity, supported by his friends, who are better acquainted with the apparition and fear lest he should collapse. His whole demeanour is so expressive of terror that it made my flesh creep even before he began to speak. The almost terror-struck silence of the audience, which preceded this appearance and filled one with a sense of insecurity, probably did much to enhance this effect. At last he speaks, not at the beginning, but at the end of a breath, with a trembling voice: 'Angels and ministers of grace defend us!' words which supply anything this scene may lack and make it one of the greatest and most terrible which will ever be played on any stage.[7]

Garrick acted Shakespeare's plays in versions more 'authentic' than those used in the Restoration, but he still made alterations that favoured either his talents or the audience's taste for spectacle and pathos. His version of *Macbeth*, like Davenant's, had no Porter and allowed the Witches their full quota of singing, dancing and flying, but the development of the Macduffs was cut, and Shakespeare's language was restored. Like Davenant, Garrick gave Macbeth an on-stage encounter with Macduff and a dying speech (in this case, eight lines long, admitting of more elaborate death throes). In *Romeo and Juliet*

10   Charles Macklin as Shylock: painting (*c.* 1768) by Johann Zoffany

(1748) Garrick followed Otway's *Caius Marius* in having Juliet wake in the tomb before her husband dies, an opportunity ignored by Shakespeare: (Fig. 12)

Romeo. . . . Eyes look your last;
      Arms take your last embrace; and lips do you
      The doors of breath seal with a righteous kiss.
      Soft! soft! She breathes and stirs!
        Juliet wakes.
Juliet. Where am I? Defend me, powers!

11   David Garrick as Richard III: engraving (1746) after a painting (1745) by William Hogarth

Romeo. She speaks, she lives! And we shall still be blessed!
    My kind propitious stars o'erpay me now
    For all my sorrows past. Rise, rise, my Juliet,
    And from this cave of death, this house of horror,
    Quick let me snatch thee to thy Romeo's arms.
    There breathe a vital spirit in thy lips,
    And call thee back to life and love! (*Takes her hand.*)[8]

Garrick's *Romeo and Juliet* is passably faithful to its original, but it clears away Rosaline (Romeo is in love with Juliet from the very beginning) and includes a spectacular funeral for the heroine. A comparison of the rival productions, which ran concurrently for twelve consecutive evenings in the 1750–51 season, demonstrates the opportunities afforded by alterations in the final scene. The reviewer noted that Mrs Cibber (with Spranger Barry, at Covent Garden) spoiled the 'tombscene' by rising at once, 'which prevents a great part of that alarming distraction which *Romeo* discovers in finding life returning to *Juliet* by slow degrees'. At Drury Lane, with Mrs Bellamy and David Garrick, Romeo's 'astonishment' rose in proportion as Juliet's awakening was protracted, and gave the actor a chance to impress by more of his 'attitudes'.[9]

    Some of Garrick's Shakespearian versions were less reverent than this: his *Catharine and Petruchio* makes an agreeable three-act farce out of the principal 'taming' plot of Shakespeare's comedy, and *Florizel and Perdita* uses the 'pastoral' scenes of *The Winter's Tale*. Towards the end of his career as manager of Drury Lane (he retired in 1776) Garrick staged a curious version of *Hamlet* which brings matters to an early conclusion by having Hamlet fight Laertes as soon as Ophelia has gone mad, thus cutting out both the gravediggers and the fencing match. *The Fairies* (1755) continued the operatic career of *A Midsummer Night's Dream*, furnishing the composer John Christopher Smith with a libretto from the lovers' plot as pretext for settings of some twenty-seven songs by various authors.

As a manager, Garrick effected a number of important reforms in organization of the theatre on both sides of the curtain: members of the audience were no longer suffered to sit on the stage, costume and scenic design were improved, and better stage lighting allowed the actor to perform effectively within the scenic picture – a move towards the eventual separation of stage and auditorium. But in many plays costume was still modern (as the engraving of *Romeo and Juliet* shows) and scenery was improved by making it handsome and consistent with the play's action rather than introducing historical accuracy or specifically interpretative effect. The continuing presence of heavy oak doors on either side of the proscenium arch, the fully lit auditorium, and such conventional signals as the green cloth laid on the stage for tragedy maintained

12   David Garrick and George Anne Bellamy in *Romeo and Juliet*: engraving (1765) by
S. F. Ravenet, after a painting (?1753) by Benjamin Wilson

the theatre's sense of formality. Tradition and custom still dominated the institution, and the hierarchy of the company's members reflected the relative dignities of the roles they played on stage. Garrick was careful in his presentation of the entertainment he offered, but this was a repertory theatre where plays might be revived and set from stock at a few days' notice, where actors had to carry an immense number of roles in their head, and where a new actor or a visitor could be coached at short notice by the prompter in the moves necessary for performing with the company. The 'giving out' of plays by announcing them for repetition at the end of a performance provided the theatre's patrons with a chance to enforce the drama's laws. The pit, a powerful critical assembly, could dominate the theatre and 'damn' a play or an actor with little chance of appeal.

Garrick's achievements as actor and manager were remarkable and his championship of Shakespeare, though not without an eye to his own reputation, did much to further the cause of 'Shakespeare Idolatry'. In 1769 he organized a grand Jubilee celebration at Stratford-upon-Avon, and may be claimed as a prime mover in the launching of the Stratford tourist industry.

III

Between 1780 and 1820 Shakespearian performance in Britain was dominated by discussion as to the rival merits of an 'ideal', neo-classical style of acting, exemplified in Mrs Sarah Siddons and her brother John Philip Kemble, and the more vigorous, 'realistic' acting of Edmund Kean. Siddons shared with her brother an enthusiasm for the models provided by classical statuary but she seems to have been more imaginative and expressive in performance. In Kemble's acting, restraint often prevailed over passion, making him stiff and unconvincing as a lover or a romantic hero. In Roman characters – Brutus, Cato in Addison's tragedy, and Coriolanus – Kemble excelled. Sir Walter Scott, writing in the *Quarterly Review* in 1826, attributed this to the presence in these roles of 'an assumed character, which qualified, if it did not master, that which nature had assigned to the individual'. The element of suppressed impulse gave power to parts 'peculiarly suited to his noble and classical form, his dignified and stately gesture, his regulated yet commanding eloquence'. Those with a taste for the 'antique' were afforded such pleasures as that of the 'Ovation' scene inserted in *Coriolanus*:

The exquisite beauty of the statue struck even the most uncultivated mind, and although no word was spoken, the spectators were in an absolute ecstasy of delight, and could have willed him ever to remain so, as the *chef d'oeuvre* of nature and of art.

Sarah Siddons, like her brother, offered 'a gallery of splendid statues . . . Images of beauty and feeling'. She 'directed her attention to the antique' for lessons 'as to simplicity of attire and severity of attitude'.[10] One consequence of this was her refusal to dress tragic characters in contemporary high fashion.

For all the general sense of classical dignity and deliberation – insisted on by contemporaries in comparing the 'Kemble school' with their rivals – descriptions of individual performances reveal an impressive emotional range and responsiveness to the text. Mrs Siddons's Lady Macbeth was both powerful and minutely detailed. In reading Macbeth's letter (I, 5) she made a slight pause before the word 'air': 'When I burn'd in desire to question them further, they made themselves — air, into which they vanish'd.' The playwright Sheridan Knowles recalled: 'In the look and tone with which she delivered that word, you recognised ten times the wonder with which Macbeth and Banquo actually beheld the vanishing of the witches.' Of the sleep-walking scene, Knowles could find 'a plain blunt phrase' to sum up his reaction: 'Well, sir, I smelt blood! I swear that I smelt blood!'[11] John Philip Kemble's Macbeth was recalled by Alexander Dyce:

In the murder scene he was more frozen with terror, more bewildered, and less noisy, than his successors in the part . . . At the banquet on the vanishing of the Ghost, he exclaimed, 'So, being gone, I am a man again', like one who had really been delivered suddenly from some intolerable burden that weighed down his very soul. In the recitation of 'tomorrow and tomorrow', etc., his voice sounded like a soft and mournful music; and his horror on hearing that Birnam Wood was on its way to Dunsinane – the vain effort of his terror-palsied arm to draw his sword and stab the bearer of such dreadful tidings – and his tremulous tones when he recovered the use of speech – all showed the consummate artist.[12]

Edmund Kean's life rivalled Lord Byron's in furnishing occasions for salacious gossip. His brilliant London début as Shylock, in 1814, the career wrecked by self-indulgence, and the pathetic death after breaking down on stage with his son, have made Kean a representative of the romantic, self-destructive artist. Kean is often characterized by quoting Coleridge's brief comment in his *Table-Talk*:

KEAN is original; but he copies from himself. His rapid descents from the hyper-tragic to the infra-colloquial, though sometimes productive of great effect, are often unreasonable. To see him act, is like reading Shakespeare by flashes of lightening.

The remarks have to be understood in the light of Coleridge's concern as a critic with an individual's intensity of response to circumstances that momentarily bring the whole sensibility into play, rather than as a comprehensive description of Kean's methods. Kean himself insisted on the deliberate and careful preparation necessary for achievement of his effects, and William Hazlitt, one of his most sympathetic critics, observed that 'Mr Kean's style of acting . . . is throughout elaborate and systematic, instead of being loose, off-hand and incidental.' Hazlitt's description of Kean as Shylock recalls accounts of Macklin, some seventy years earlier:

In giving effect to the conflict of passions arising out of the contrast of situation, in varied vehemence of declamation, in keenness of sarcasm, in the rapidity of his transitions from one tone and feeling to another, in propriety and novelty of action, presenting a succession of striking pictures, and giving perpetually fresh shocks of delight and surprise, it would be difficult to single out a competitor.[13]

Hazlitt describes many of Kean's 'points' as though they were studies for illustrations to Shakespeare – a comparison that recurs in theatrical criticism throughout the nineteenth century and which was stimulated partly by enthusiasm for grand, historical paintings of scenes from history, the Bible, or literary works, partly by such enterprises as Boydell's Shakespeare Gallery (begun in 1790) and the succession of illustrated editions of the *Works*. In descriptions of Kean, it is the actor himself rather than the whole stage picture that receives attention. Thus, as Richard III,

His manner of bidding his friends 'Good-night', after pausing with the point of his sword drawn slowly backward and forward on the ground, as if considering the plan of the battle next day, is a particularly happy and natural thought.

In the combat with Richmond,

He fights at last like one drunk with wounds; and the attitude in which he stands with his hands stretched out, after his sword is wrested from him, has a preternatural and terrific grandeur, as if his will could not be disarmed, and the very phantoms of his despair had power to kill.[14]

Another reviewer contrasted Kean's performance in the role with that of his contemporary George Frederick Cooke, who had emphasized the sarcasm and venom of Richard. In the wooing scene with Lady Anne, Cooke was 'harsh, ungentlemanly, coarse'. Kean 'made it all probable and perfectly natural. An enchanting smile played on his lips, while courteous humility bowed his head . . . he presented an object by which the mere human senses must from their very constitution be subjected and entranced.'[15] (Fig. 13)

   Kean did not show to advantage in comedy or in parts that gave no scope for 'tenderness, wrath, agony and sarcasm'.[16] As Othello, Iago, Macbeth, Richard III, and Shylock he excelled, and he made Massinger's Sir Giles Overreach, in *A New Way to Pay Old Debts*, a necessary part of the repertoire of any actor who wished to emulate him. Unlike Kemble and Garrick, he never had management of a major theatre, and his legacy was a series of 'points' rather than a shelf of acting editions. Kemble's versions of the Shakespearian plays in the repertoire, mostly improving on Garrick's in faithfulness to the original texts, became part of the nineteenth-century actor's stock-in-trade. Kemble's improvements in state-management and scenery were seen as the beginnings of a movement towards historical accuracy and pictorial realism. Kean was perceived as a legendary and (in a negative sense) exemplary figure by his colleagues and successors. William Charles Macready, whose work as actor and manager dominates the British theatre in the 1830s and 1840s,

13   Edmund Kean as Richard III: anonymous 'penny plain' print

despised Kean's morals and longed for the stage to take its rightful place among dignified, rational artistic amusements, but he acknowledged the power of Kean's acting: 'one of my highest delights was the playing of Iago to Kean's Othello – the life of my own Iago gained intensity, while that Othello stood living before me in all his noble passion'.[17]

IV

The ascendancy of Macready and his style of acting – in which domestic pathos and heroic dignity were brought together – marks the beginning of a distinctively Victorian approach to Shakespeare production. Macready was actor–manager of both the 'Patent Theatres' in turn: for the seasons of 1837– 9 (at Covent Garden) and 1841–3 (at Drury Lane). He retired from the stage in 1851, but his influence as a producer of Shakespeare was greater than these limited periods of actual management might suggest. The population of London had grown from 900,000 in the late eighteenth century to three million by 1850: in 1880 it would be almost four million. The patent houses had attempted to accommodate this greatly expanded audience by enlarging the size of their auditoria and by altering the entertainment on offer. Spectacle, music, and dance were lavished on the public in an attempt to counter the rivalry of theatres that had begun to flourish in suburbs outside the Lord Chamberlain's jurisdiction. The 'legitimate' (that is, spoken) drama was under threat at the only two theatres fully licensed for its presentation. As Covent Garden and Drury Lane courted new playgoers, their regular patrons drifted away: the two huge theatres became white elephants, expensive to run, difficult to act in, and deserted by fashionable society.

One solution to the problems facing management can be seen in the operatic medleys based on Shakespeare by Frederick Reynolds, who created a series of adaptations between 1816 (*A Midsummer Night's Dream* at Covent Garden) and 1824 (*The Merry Wives of Windsor* at the Haymarket). Reynolds's *A Midsummer Night's Dream* makes savage cuts in the lovers' part of the play, brings the performance of 'Pyramus and Thisbe' into the wood, and offers a pageant of Theseus's triumphs at the expense of Shakespeare's concluding fairy scene. Similar alterations were visited on the other comedies used by Reynolds. In 1840 *A Midsummer Night's Dream* was staged by Madame Vestris at Covent Garden, using a text more or less Shakespearian – but still allowing for more singing than the original. Vestris had staged *Love's Labour's Lost* in the preceding season, and had revived the 'operatic' *Merry Wives of Windsor* of H. R. Bishop. The priorities of her joint management (with Charles Mathews) were unequivocal: tasteful settings for the display of her considerable talents as singer, dancer, and comedienne. Only with generosity could her régime be seen as a return of the 'legitimate' to the West End. The anxious support given to Macready's efforts to reform the theatre was partly a reaction against the attractions of these shows, in a desire to re-establish at least one of the patent theatres as a 'National Theatre'. Endowment was not discussed as a realistic possibility until the end of the century: the object in view was an adjustment of the commercial theatre in favour of 'legitimate' drama.

Legitimacy came to be identified not merely with the spoken, as distinct from sung, drama, but with social respectability and improved production values. The standing of the institution, the actor, and (most important of all) the actress had to be raised. The directly social expressions of this spirit ranged from enlisting royal patronage to the expulsion of prostitutes from the lobbies and staircases of the theatres. In artistic terms, the instruments of legitimacy were 'restored' texts, realistic stage pictures and an appropriate acting technique. Macready's productions served as models to his successors, Samuel Phelps (1804–78) and Charles Kean (1811–68). In their respective managements at Sadler's Wells (1843–62) and the Princess's (1851–9), Phelps and Kean followed Macready's example. Sadler's Wells benefited from the 1843 Theatres Act, which effectively took away the Patent Theatres' monopoly of spoken drama. It has some claim to be considered a 'people's theatre', addressing itself to the middle and lower class and offering a full repertoire of established classics. Charles Kean sought a more fashionable clientèle, offering a combination of spectacular Shakespeare and the kind of 'gentlemanly melodrama' in which he himself excelled.

In acting, the Macready values were summed up by a commentator in the *Spectator*:

> If we say that naturalness (an ugly but useful word) is at the basis of all Mr Macready's impersonations, we do not conceive we shall widely err. To seize on an emotion, to make it perfectly comprehensible to every capacity, to familiarize the creations of the dramatist to the spectator, rather than to hold them in a state of august elevation, seems to be his constant aim.[18]

Macready had learned (as he himself put it) 'to measure a player by the conception of his part and by the severe truth of nature', guarding himself 'from being misled by any adventitious or false effects'. When Edmund Kean made his début as Shylock, Macready was already twenty-one years old, and in a position to judge the changes in acting that were taking place. He noticed a new emphasis in the interpretation of women's roles that foreshadows later, more sentimental treatment of Shakespeare's heroines:

> The noble pathos of Mrs Siddons's transcendent genius no longer served as the grand commentary and living exponent of Shakespeare's text, but in the native elegance, the feminine sweetness, the unaffected earnestness and gushing passion of Miss O'Neill the stage had received a worthy successor to her.[19]

Macready's friend John Forster summed up the difference between Kemble's Coriolanus and that of the younger actor as one between 'an ideal picture of one intense sentiment' and 'the reality of various and conflicting passion' – a comparison in terms familiar from every successive comparison of an 'old' school with its successor. In descriptions of Macready's acting – especially in productions over which he had artistic control – the reader commonly encounters tributes to his sense of the powerful emotive effect. In *King John* (Drury Lane, 1842) the scene in which John tempts Hubert to kill Arthur showed the vividness and subtlety of Macready's acting:

It was a foreboding look that John cast on Arthur. For a moment the tongue faltered as the horrible mission was entrusted to Hubert. For a moment the countenance of the king beamed as he said 'Good Hubert,' but the gloom returned when he said 'Throw thine eye on yonder boy.' That he did not look Hubert in the face when he proposed 'death' was a fine conception.[20]

In Macbeth's fight with Macduff, Macready gave 'a rich succession of gladiatorial pictures expressive of the sublime will and imagination of Macbeth', culminating in a terrifying death, described vividly in a review by John Forster:

Mr Macready's attitude in falling, when he thrusts his sword into the ground, and by its help for one moment raises himself to stare into the face of his opponent with a gaze that seemed to concentrate all Majesty, Hate and Knowledge, had an air of the preternatural fit to close such a career![21]

When he had responsibility for the production of a play, Macready expected to be able to base every element on his close study of the text, coaching actors and actresses, rehearsing crowd scenes, supervising the costumes and music. Among his innovations was the use of limelight, and he employed the finest scenic artists. He reinstated parts of the original plays long omitted in performance – most notably, in 1838, the role of the Fool in *King Lear* – and dispensed with the additional scenes and characters that had survived, via Garrick's and Kemble's editions, from the Restoration. Although he cannot be credited with having invented the historically accurate production of Shakespeare's plays – Charles Kemble's 1823 staging of *King John* has some claim to that honour – Macready consolidated the efforts of like-minded contemporaries. The décor, like the acting, had moved from the generalized and conventional to the 'real' and particular. At the same time, there was a sense in which such productions turned all plays into histories.

In some of Charles Kean's productions at the Princess's Theatre, between 1851 and 1859, the conversion of fantasy into history was developed to the point of absurdity. In *The Winter's Tale* (1856) geographical accuracy was maintained by converting Bohemia to Bithynia. The trial of Hermione took place in a Grecian amphitheatre, and the chorus establishing a lapse of sixteen years was accompanied by a 'classical allegory, representing the course of *Time*'. The pastoral scenes included 'the *Dionysia* or grand festival of the vintage, in honour of Bacchus, executed by an overpowering mass of satyrs, men, women and children'.[22] For *A Midsummer Night's Dream* (1856) Kean ignored the 'real' period of Duke Theseus (1200 B.C.) and offered instead a view of Periclean Athens, which gave way to a magic wood populated with beings too reminiscent (for some critics) of Christmas pantomime (Fig. 14). Henry Morley, writing in the *Examiner*, took particular exception to 'a shadow dance of fairies': this was 'as great a sacrifice of Shakespeare to the purposes of the ballet-master, as the view of Athens was a sacrifice of poetry to the scene-painter'. Morley had been better pleased by Samuel Phelps's production of the play at Sadler's Wells (in 1853) in which a gauze placed between the actors and the audience 'subdued the flesh and blood of the actors into something more nearly resembling dream-figures'.[23] Phelps did not make as much fuss about 'archaeology' as Charles Kean, and his production avoided too direct an appeal to the taste for ballet and spectacle.

Charles Kean's acting in his 'revivals' of Shakespeare elicited little praise, partly because it formed so subordinate a part of the general effect, partly because he seems not to have been a very impressive Shakespearian actor – although there is evidence of a critical conspiracy against him which makes it difficult to judge his true worth. Kean's biographer and apologist, J. W. Cole, introduced his account of *King John* (1852) with the observation that 'The days had long passed when audiences could believe themselves transported from Italy to Athens by power of poetical enchantment without the aid of scenic appliances' – a state of affairs that he considered entirely satisfactory.[24] These production methods were imitated in the provinces – notably by Charles Calvert in Manchester and Edward Saker in Liverpool – and in America. The Duke of Saxe-Meiningen, whose company was to make such a stir when it visited London in 1881, was influenced by the example of Kean's stage management and historical detail.

14 The confrontation of Oberon and Titania in Charles Kean's production of *A Midsummer Night's Dream*, Princess's Theatre, 1856: watercolour illustration from scene design of Frederick Lloyds

After Charles Kean left the Princess's in 1859, Phelps continued at Sadler's Wells for a further three years, but his retirement from the management of that theatre was the beginning of a period which one historian has called 'the interregnum'. Until Irving took over the Lyceum in 1879 there was no London management of any standing whose principal claim on the public's respect and money lay in Shakespearian production. Many actors, actresses, and managers put on an occasional Shakespeare play – at the Gaiety Theatre John Hollingshead presented *The Merry Wives of Windsor* and *A Midsummer Night's Dream*, both with Samuel Phelps; Falconer and Chatterton, managers of Drury Lane, staged showy versions of *The Winter's Tale* and *Antony and Cleopatra*, and both Phelps and Helen Faucit appeared there briefly; *The Merchant of Venice* was given by the Bancrofts at the Prince of Wales's Theatre (1875) with Ellen Terry and Charles Coghlan in a production designed by the architect E. W. Godwin. Despite these efforts, London was without a 'legitimate', Shakespearian management. The problem was partly an economic one: productions in the Charles Kean style were costly, and needed long runs to recoup their costs; the death of the stock system meant that actors no longer gained experience in the variety of plays that made up the old repertoire; improvements in transport made it possible to tour complete productions; the custom of 'stars' touring on their own, fitting into the local 'stock' production of (say) *Hamlet* or *Othello*, was discontinued. Some critics doubted whether actors trained in domestic realism or modern melodrama (less self-consciously 'poetic' than earlier work) could tackle the demands of Shakespearian verse, or achieve the dignified, romantic breadth of manner his plays were held to require. Others looked to the Irish actor Barry Sullivan (1821–91) for maintaining of the old standards. He had acted with Phelps at Sadler's Wells, and his subsequent wide touring made him a favourite in the provinces, in Ireland and abroad, but he never gained acceptance in London as a leading tragedian. George Bernard Shaw admired Sullivan as 'an actor of superb physical vigour, who excelled in the impersonation of proud, noble and violent characters'.[25]

Some lessons were to be learned from abroad. The American actor Edwin Booth (1833–93) set a high standard of personal interpretation and *mise-en-scène* in the eight major 'revivals' he staged at his own theatre in New York between 1869 and 1874. English actors had been working in the United States since the beginning of the century (and, of course, during the colonial period) and some American performers had appeared in Britain. In the 1840s Charlotte Cushman played in London and the provinces, including in her repertoire Lady Macbeth and Romeo (with her sister as Juliet). Edwin Forrest (1806–72), an actor noted for energy rather than finesse, had played in competition with Macready, but the rivalry became a feud which, stirred by anti-British political agitation, resulted in a riot in New York. Meanwhile, Charles Kean and his wife, Macready, and numerous lesser actors and actresses toured in America. In the age of full-scale scenic revivals, few American performers gained a foothold on the London stage. Booth's season (1880–1) was for the most part a *succès d'estime*, and neither Lawrence Barrett nor Richard Mansfield was able to establish himself in London in the 1880s. Mary Anderson seems to have understood that a series of expensive productions at the Lyceum was the only way to succeed. In the 1860s and 1870s a number of distinguished European actors and actresses – Ernesto Rossi, Tomasso Salvini, Adelaide Ristori – gave influential and admired performances, but there was no way in which they could be said to establish a regular Shakespearian theatre of the kind critics called for. So long as the assumptions behind Charles Kean's productions prevailed, massive investment, continuity, and dynamic leadership of a big organization would be needed, together with the ability to attract and hold the allegiance of audiences who habitually associated Shakespearian performance with the disappointment of expectations formed in reading the plays. This obstacle in the path of would-be Shakespearian managers was a legacy from the days of the Romantic reviewers. Charles Lamb had objected that *King Lear* could not be adequately acted, and Hazlitt, in a famous review of the 'operatic' *Midsummer Night's Dream*, had asserted that 'The boards of a theatre and the regions of fancy are not the same thing.' The challenge could only be met by skilled deployment of massive resources or alteration of the rules of engagement. In 1844 and 1847 Benjamin Webster had given 'Elizabethan' performances of *The Taming of the Shrew* at the Haymarket, and in 1881 William Poel directed an authentic production of the 'bad' Quarto of *Hamlet*; but the 1880s and 1890s brought a consolidation of the pictorial method by two leading managements. It seemed that the Charles Kean tradition was, after all, to be perpetuated.

V

From the late 1870s to the end of the century Shakespearian production was dominated by the work of two London managements, Henry Irving's at the Lyceum (1878–1901) and Herbert Beerbohm Tree's at the Haymarket (1887–96) and Her Majesty's (from 1896). Both actor–managers were knighted, Irving in 1895 and Tree in 1909; both took their place at the centre of fashionable and artistic life; both were internationally famous as exponents of the pictorial style. Unlike Charles Kean, neither Irving nor Tree made a parade of the 'archaeology' of their productions, but historical accuracy of scenery and costumes was carefully attended to. Without ostentatiously courting the 'decadent' movements in art and literature, both Irving and Tree catered for the sensibilities of the *fin-de-siècle*. Irving excelled in parts which gave scope to his talent for the sinister–grotesque: Shylock, Macbeth, Iago, Richard III. His haunted, intellectual Hamlet was unusual in his repertoire for its lack of this element. Othello, Romeo, Lear, and (late in his career)

Coriolanus provided too little opportunity for his peculiar genius. A fine comic actor, he adapted well to Benedick, but poorly to Malvolio. Tree was an astonishingly versatile character-actor, his creative exuberance often showing in elaborate make-up and minutely observed physical detail.

Henry Irving (1838–1905) had his first Shakespearian success as Hamlet, at the Lyceum in 1874 under H. L. Bateman's management. His reputation had been made in comic and melodramatic roles, and in 1871 he had rescued the failing management with his acting as Mathias in Leopold Lewis's melodrama *The Bells*. In 1878 he became manager of the theatre, a position he held until 1899, when control of financial affairs passed to a committee: he continued to be tenant until 1901. Irving and Ellen Terry (1847–1928), his leading lady during the years of his management, were acknowledged as 'picturesque' interpreters of Shakespeare in their own right, and Irving was a fine judge of their effect in terms of the whole stage picture. At the Lyceum, settings, costumes, lighting, and music were brought to a high standard of artistic unity. The darkened auditorium was conducive to an exceptional degree of concentration of the audience's attention. The stage lighting was subtle and expressive, and Irving had a leaning towards 'dark-scenes' – effects of twilight and mysterious gloom – achieved with a lower intensity of light than would have been possible in an undarkened auditorium. Electrical lighting was available from the mid 1880s, but Irving preferred to use gas, together with a battery of limelights and (from 1891) electric footlights.[26]

Descriptions of Lyceum productions often bring out the impact of Irving's pictures, and the haunting effect of his visual characterizations. Gordon Crosse, writing in 1952 from notes made in the 1890s, remembered his King Lear entering on the cue 'The King is coming' in the first scene: 'a striking figure with masses of white hair. He is leaning on a huge scabbarded sword which he raises with a wild cry in answer to the shouted greeting of his guards. His gait, his looks, his gestures, all reveal the noble, imperious mind already degenerating into senile irritability under the coming shocks of grief and age.'[27] Irving made a noble figure of Shylock – a part he played for twenty-four years from 1879. After the abduction of Jessica, 'amid a whirl of masquers with tabors and pipes', the curtain fell quickly, then rose again on a deserted, moonlit stage. The 'wearied figure of the Jew' came over a bridge and was about to enter his house as the act-drop fell. In the scene with Tubal, Irving was 'ferocious and pathetic by turns', and at the end of the trial scene he was unequivocally a tragic victim.[28] The final scene of *Romeo and Juliet* (1882) shows Irving's method of conceiving a play's crisis in pictorial terms. Insisting that Romeo must descend into the tomb, he divided the scene into two pictures. When Romeo opened the gates of the vault, the scene changed to the interior, with two flights of stone steps leading some twenty-five feet down to the stage floor and Juliet's bier (Fig. 15) After the death of the lovers the tableau curtains fell, then rose again to reveal a crowd bearing torches; the act-

"ROMEO AND JULIET" AT THE LYCEUM THEATRE, Act V., Scene IV
Fri: Laurence "Romeo!" O pale! Who else? What! Paris too?

15   Henry Irving and Ellen Terry in *Romeo and Juliet*, Lyceum Theatre, 1882

drop fell after Prince Escalus had joined the hands of Montague and Capulet
and spoken a four-line curtain speech. Irving's version of the catastrophe used
an added tableau where Garrick had required new speeches to improve the
pathos.

In this kind of theatre the appearance and presentation of the leading actors
would carry much of the interpretative burden, but the performance was still
limited by the peculiar strengths and weaknesses of the principals. It was not to
be expected that the Lyceum should fail to present Henry Irving and Ellen
Terry in leading roles, even ones to which they were not well suited. Thus,
Irving staged *Twelfth Night* (1884) for the benefit of Ellen Terry's Viola, but
his own Malvolio was disappointing. In *Macbeth*, given a new production in
1888, his own performance was in his familiar vein of the conscience-tortured
victim–villain typified by Mathias in *The Bells*; as Lady Macbeth Ellen Terry
was considered insufficiently hard and wicked. As, seated picturesquely in the
light from a large open fireplace, she read Macbeth's letter, she suggested 'a

gentle, affectionate wife, wrapped up in her husband' (*The Times*, 31 December, 1888). The production was one of Irving's finest, but opinion was divided on the merits of the acting. Irving was often accused – especially in George Bernard Shaw's notices – of assembling a company of second-raters who would fill out his pictures without getting in his way. Shaw had his reasons – including a bundle of his own plays that the Lyceum ought to be producing – but his apprehensions were shared by others. Irving's modern repertoire was old-fashioned, consisting principally of melodramatized history plays. His approach to Shakespeare amounted to what Shaw called 'costly bardicide', in which the author's work was tailored to serve Irving and the Lyceum style.

Like Irving, Tree (1853–1917) saw Shakespeare's plays as a series of impressive tableaux, which moved in picturesque, pathetic, and stately manner towards the celebration of one character or idea. His acting editions were more ruthlessly cut. *Julius Caesar*, presented by Tree at Her Majesty's in 1898 and revived frequently, exemplifies many aspects of his approach. There were three acts: Act 1, in five scenes, took events up to the aftermath of the assassination; Act 2, 'The Forum', was given over to the orations; Act 3 dispatched the rest of the play in two scenes, 'Brutus' Tent, near Sardis', and 'The Plains of Phillipi'. The first act concluded with Antony's preparations for the funeral. By the introduction of the grieving Calphurnia, Antony was presented as both Caesar's avenger and the champion of his widow. Act 2 ended with Antony's

> Now let it work. Mischief, thou art afoot,
> Take thou what course thou wilt,

answered by the 'great Distant shout' of the citizens, off-stage. Three 'pictures' satisfied demands for curtain calls:

First picture. Antony crosses to head of body and kneels. Citizens with torches and weapons cross from right to left and from left to right and upstage, left.
Second picture. Body of citizens crosses from left dragging Senator with them and exit right. Antony rises, sees Senator being dragged across and makes gesture of revenge.
Third picture. Antony standing at head of body with arms extended as though praying – then slowly places hands on the forehead of Caesar.[29]

After this, it is not surprising that the remainder of the play was uncompelling. The evening ended with Antony's elegy on Brutus and two more solemn 'pictures' for the curtain calls.

In Tree's *Julius Caesar* it was intended that Rome herself should be felt as a character, and the settings were designed by Sir Laurence Alma-Tadema, the period's foremost painter of classical subjects. Like Alma-Tadema, Tree hoped that his figures would be perceived as living a 'real', individually characterized life, and he directed them accordingly. The imposing, static *tableaux vivants* were counterpointed with a sense of life and movement, and the frenzy of the crowd in the Forum scene was compellingly real. But the result, although a finely conceived and executed work of art, was quite inappropriate to the theatrical methods of the original. Tree's imaginative development of his own roles would have seemed doubly gratuitous in a production approximating to Elizabethan stagecraft, but even transposed into what was effectively a new medium his eccentricities were often misjudged. His *Tempest*, again in three acts, managed to make Caliban (played by Tree) the focus of the play, ending with a 'picture' of Prospero's ship sailing off and Caliban, alone on the island, waving to it. The prompt-books of his comic parts – such as Falstaff – show interpolated lines and business making his character's reactions the focus of attention. When one piece of stage business is compared with an earlier, 'traditional' action it is common to find Tree adding new sentiment to what was already sentimental. At the end of the 'nunnery' scene in *Hamlet*, he improved the traditional gesture of Hamlet returning to kiss Ophelia's hand by having Ophelia collapse on a couch: unseen by her, Hamlet stole back and kissed one of the tresses of her hair.[30] Tree's penchant for exuberant physical detail often marred productions that were handsomely staged and which followed a well-defined artistic plan. The example for such production values can be traced back through Irving and the Saxe-Meiningen troupe to Charles Kean. By the turn of the century the right of such productions to be considered 'traditional' was being challenged, and the supremacy of the commercial organization that produced them was also under attack.

Late Victorian and Edwardian 'pictorial' Shakespeare represents the culmination of a movement that began in the Restoration. The actors now moved entirely within the picture-frame of the proscenium arch, and were fully integrated into the graphic interpretation of the play. Any self-conscious theatricality in the texts, and any indulgence of the actors' ability to play *with* an audience, were suppressed in the interests of a theatre that imposed its visions on the audience and displayed the leading actor as ruler of a finely organized machine. Reaction against this state of affairs came not merely from veneration for Shakespeare's violated and heavily cut texts, but from a desire, diversely motivated and expressed, for a less dictatorial and expensive theatre. The museum and the Academy painting no longer satisfied as models for a living stage. There is a sense in accounts of some great performances of the nineteenth century that if energy and intelligence succeeded it was in spite of the demands of the newly perfected realistic staging techniques. Ada Rehan's powerful Katharina was undoubtedly aided by 'the gorgeous mahogany-red brocade and the fiery wig in which she made her first tiger-like entry', but Augustin Daly's lavish production was in retrospect useful only in that its oppressively 'authentic' Renaissance setting gave *The Taming of the Shrew* belated admission into the 'legitimate' world.[31] Irving and Tree used Shakespeare to explore and express valuable, exciting qualities in themselves, but at some cost to Shakespeare and their fellow actors.

The history of Shakespearian production between 1660 and 1900 can seem to be an account of 240 years of lost labours, in which a succession of actors and managers wrenched the plays into a shape basically unsuited to their meaning – or to most of the meanings we might wish to release from them. But it is also the history of two and a half centuries of theatre, in which Shakespeare's plays – or a good selection of them – remained on stage and gave cause for countless artistic achievements by actors, scenic artists, and stage managers. The emergence of the unified production, requiring by its elaboration the supervision of one artist, prepared the way for the independent director. Even Reynolds's 'operatic' *Midsummer Night's Dream* and Daly's pompous *Taming of the Shrew* entertained crowded theatres. 'People,' said Dickens's Mr Sleary, 'mutht be amused'.

Notes

1. Colley Cibber, *An Apology for the Life of Mr. Colley Cibber*, ed. Robert W. Lowe, 2 vols. (1899). II, 101; 103–4.
2. Samuel Pepys, *Diary*, 19 April 1667.
3. Davenant's *Macbeth*, *The Tempest; or, the Enchanted Island* and Tate's *History of King Lear* are quoted from Christopher Spencer's editions in his *Five Restoration Adaptations of Shakespeare* (Urbana, Illinois, 1965)
4. Tobias Smollett, *Peregrine Pickle* (1751), chapter 55; Francis Gentleman, *The Dramatic Censor*, 2 vols. (1770), II, 396–7.
5. Quoted by William Appleton, *Charles Macklin, an Actor's Life* (Oxford, 1961), p. 49.
6. Arthur Murphy, *The Life of David Garrick* (Dublin, 1801), p. 17.
7. Translated by Margaret L. Mare and W. H. Quarrell, *Lichtenberg's Visits to England* (Oxford, 1938), p. 10.
8. Quoted from the edition of Garrick's *Plays* by Harry William Pedicord and Frederick Louis Bergman (Carbondale and Edwardsville, 1981).
9. Kalman A. Burnim, *David Garrick, Director* (Pittsburgh, 1961), p. 132.
10. William Robson, *The Old Playgoer* (1846), pp. 20, 23, 35.
11. Quoted by Dennis Bartholomeusz, *'Macbeth' and the Players* (Cambridge, 1969), pp. 104, 121.
12. Alexander Dyce, *Reminiscences*, ed. Richard J. Schrader (Ohio, 1972), p. 76.
13. *The Examiner*, 9 October and (on Shylock) 27 January 1814.
14. William Hazlitt, *Characters of Shakespeare's Plays* (1817; World's Classics edition, 1955), pp. 179–80.
15. Thomas Barnes, review in *The Examiner*, 27 February 1814.
16. George Henry Lewes, *On Actors and the Art of Acting* (1875), p. 20.
17. Lady Pollock, *Macready, as I Knew Him* (1884), p. 33.
18. Quoted by Alan S. Downer, *The Eminent Tragedian: William Charles Macready* (Cambridge, Mass., 1966), p. 73.
19. *Macready's Reminiscences, and Selections from his Diaries and Letters*, ed. Sir Frederick Pollock, 2 vols. (1875) I, 62.
20. *The Times*, quoted by Charles H. Shattuck, *William Charles Macready's 'King John'. A Facsimile Promptbook* (Urbana, 1962), p. 49.
21. William Archer and Robert W. Lowe, eds., *Dramatic Essays* (1896), pp. 6–7.

22. The production is discussed by Dennis Bartholomeusz, *'The Winter's Tale'* in *Performance in England and America, 1611–1976* (Cambridge, 1982).
23. Morley's reviews of both productions were reprinted in his *Journal of a London Playgoer, 1851–1866* (1866).
24. J. W. Cole, *The Life and Theatrical Times of Charles Kean*, 2 vols. (1859), II, 26.
25. Edwin Wilson, ed., *Shaw on Shakespeare* (Harmondsworth, 1969), p. 99.
26. The technical resources of the Lyceum are described by Alan Hughes, *Henry Irving, Shakespearean* (Cambridge, 1981).
27. Gordon Crosse, *Shakespearean Playgoing, 1890–1952* (1953), p. 12.
28. Description of Irving's Shylock from Hughes, *Henry Irving, Shakespearean*, chapter 9.
29. Stage directions adapted from those cited by John Ripley, *'Julius Caesar' on Stage in England and America, 1599–1973* (Cambridge, 1980), p. 167.
30. A. C. Sprague, *Shakespeare and the Actors: the Stage Business in his Plays, 1660–1905* (Cambridge, Mass., 1944), p. 155.
31. G. C. D. Odell, *Shakespeare from Betterton to Irving*, 2 vols. (New York, 1920) II, 439.

Reading list

Bartholomeusz, Dennis, *'Macbeth' and the Players* (Cambridge, 1969)
'The Winter's Tale' in Performance in England and America, 1611–1976 (Cambridge, 1982)
Booth, Michael M., *Victorian Spectacular Theatre, 1850–1910* (1981)
Burnim, Kalman A., *David Garrick, Director* (Pittsburgh, 1961)
Donohue, Joseph W., Jr, *Dramatic Character in the English Romantic Age* (Princeton, 1970)
Foulkes, Richard, ed., *Shakespeare and the Victorian Stage* (Cambridge, 1986)
Haring-Smith, Tori, *From Farce to Metadrama. A Stage History of 'The Taming of the Shrew,' 1594–1983* (Westport, Connecticut, 1985)
Hughes, Alan, *Henry Irving, Shakespearean* (Cambridge, 1981)
Lamb, Margaret A., *'Antony and Cleopatra' on the English Stage* (Cranbury, New Jersey, 1980)
Lelyveld, Toby, *Shylock on the Stage* (1961)
Mander, Raymond and Joe Mitchenson, *Hamlet through the Ages. A Pictorial Record from 1709* (1952; second edition, 1955)
Mazer, Cary M., *Shakespeare Refashioned: Elizabethan Plays on Edwardian Stages* (Ann Arbor, 1981)
Merchant, W. Moelwyn, *Shakespeare and the Artist* (Oxford, 1959)
Nicoll, Allardyce, *The Garrick Stage. Theatres and Audience in the Eighteenth Century* (Manchester, 1980)
Odell, G. C. D., *Shakespeare from Betterton to Irving*, 2 vols. (New York, 1920)
Price, Cecil, *Theatre in the Age of Garrick* (1973)
Rosenberg, Marvin, *The Masks of Othello* (Berkeley and Los Angeles, 1961)
The Masks of King Lear (Berkeley, 1972)
The Masks of Macbeth (Berkeley, Los Angeles and London, 1978)
Salgādo, Gāmini, ed., *Eyewitnesses of Shakespeare. First Hand Accounts of Performances, 1590–1890* (1975)
Shattuck, Charles H., *The Shakespeare Promptbooks: a Descriptive Catalogue* (Urbana, 1965)

Shakespeare on the American stage: from the Hallams to Edwin Booth (Washington, D.C., 1976)

Speaight, Robert, *Shakespeare on the Stage. An Illustrated History of Shakespearian Performance* (1973)

Sprague, Arthur Colby, *Shakespeare and the Actors: the Stage Business in his Plays, 1660–1905* (Cambridge, Massachusetts, 1944)

Shakespearian Players and Performances (Cambridge, Massachusetts, 1955)

12 Critical approaches to Shakespeare from 1660 to 1904

THE greatest masterpieces, according to Marcel Proust, exist for many years before they come properly to be understood. This is not merely because it takes an accumulating endeavour to discern and appreciate their richness in full detail. It is mainly because they must emerge through zones of preconception unfavourable to their very originality. Therefore, in a sense, they must prepare their own way; gradually the artist must communicate not only his novel perceptions but, to some extent, his unique mode of perceiving them. Then there is also the lag – or the limbo – that he encounters when, ceasing to be a contemporary, he is put on probation before posterity. The transition was handsomely managed in Shakespeare's case by the First Folio, and given special support by the eulogy from Ben Jonson, his strongest rival and the most judicious critic of his age. This may have helped to resolve an additional complication: the fact that Shakespeare had addressed his work primarily to theatrical audiences, rather than to the reading public, in a day when the latter was still reluctant to regard popular drama as serious art. While his plays continued to be acted more and more widely, they would be further tested and approved by twelve generations of devoted readers. The body of critical writing that bears witness to that collective experience is the largest that any single writer has ever attracted.

Much of this was bound to prove redundant. Some of it, being quite far-fetched, would at least indicate to what lengths the Shakespearian field of discussion had been expanded. The divergent range of responses attested the varied multiplicity of the respondents. Since they so often saw their own concerns in Shakespeare's mirror, it could be used to illustrate a good many other subjects. Other writers, as remote from him and from one another as John Keats and Herman Melville, can be studied in the light of his formative influence. Through his recognition and reception Shakespeare has played a cosmopolitan role in the history of taste. With the passing centuries the defects that had traditionally been held against him tended to become aesthetic virtues in newer schools of thought. Such considerations, of course, are incidental to the substantive problems of interpreting what he wrote. Nor can interpretation be divorced from evaluation: a given work must be viewed in a certain light before it can be accorded any standing; and, once it is accepted over an interval of time, it will be open to continual reinterpretation. Its meaning for us, moreover, will hinge upon the state of scholarship – which, as the years have passed, has brought us nearer to the texts by removing encrustations and reconstructing conditions. Our criticism of Shakespeare may not be progressive, but it has been cumulative in its enlarging awareness.

Lists, allusions, and commendatory verses sketch a rough outline of how he must have struck his contemporaries. Among Elizabethan and Jacobean playwrights, his position was evidently a central one, though not necessarily predominant. His reputation persisted visibly after his death through quotation, republication, and performance, though it was more or less evenly matched by the parallel records of Jonson and John Fletcher. They would all be evoked together repeatedly, in Sir John Denham's phrase from the Fletcher Folio (1647), as 'the triumvirate of wit'. That indefatigable playgoer of the Restoration, Samuel Pepys, seems to have preferred the plays of Jonson. It was not until the last decade of the seventeenth century that Shakespeare would be decisively promoted from *primus inter pares* to *facile princeps*. He is singled out for preferential treatment in the pioneering history, Gerard Langbaine's *Account of the English Dramatic Poets* (1691). He could still be subject to the polemics of Thomas Rymer, whose *Short View of Tragedy* (1693) made an object-lesson out of *Othello* through a dogmatic and brutally facetious reduction to absurdity. Rymer, who is better remembered as an assiduous antiquarian than as a would-be playwright himself, drew his neo-classical authority from his translation of René Rapin's prescriptive commentary on Aristotle's *Poetics*. Essentially he was fighting a rearguard action on behalf of an obsolescent system of critical values.

The larger controversy re-enacted the 'Querelle des Anciens et des Modernes', those continental campaigns in the Battle of the Books which English courtiers had witnessed during their French exile. Not that England had lacked a native tradition of classicism, as defined and demonstrated by Jonson. He had been the first, in praising Shakespeare, to apply the double standard of nature and art – though, having worked with the same conventions himself, he allowed Shakespeare some credit for artistry. Later critics would sharpen and personify the dichotomy: Richard Flecknoe, in his *Short Discourse of the English Stage* (1664), characterizes the contrast between Shakespeare and Jonson as 'the difference between Nature and Art'. Consequently Jonson stood much closer to prevailing canons of propriety. Shakespeare broke 'the rules'; his spontaneities were irregularities; he expressed the passions in an age of reason. The great debate in their names was most fairly and squarely argued by John Dryden through his *Essay of Dramatic Poesy* (1668). The essay is shrewdly framed as a dialogue on the related issues of Ancient versus Modern, French versus English, and Elizabethan versus Restoration dramatists. Four recognizable spokesmen present their respective viewpoints with comparable eloquence and elegance, leaving the argument in a kind of dialectical compromise. Starting from the neo-Aristotelian unities, and moving through the *liaison des scènes*, it shows French contemporaries outdoing their Greco-Roman predecessors in a rigid adherence to mechanical dogmas of decorum.

But Dryden (alias Neander) assigns himself the last word, speaking in vindication of his compatriots. This gives him the advantage of having Jonson, as well as Shakespeare, on his side. Significantly, it is *The Silent Woman* that he chooses to examine, in the manner of Corneille, as 'the pattern of a perfect play', inasmuch as 'Shakespeare . . . did not perfectly observe the laws of Comedy.' Neither did Beaumont and Fletcher, though their entertaining collaborations were currently being performed twice as often as Shakespeare's or Jonson's – such was Dryden's impression, at any rate, noted along with his comment that Shakespeare had been ranked highest during his lifetime. In concentrating for tactical reasons on Jonson, Dryden acknowledges Shakespeare to have been 'at least his equal, perhaps his superior'. Pointing up the inevitable comparison, he terms Jonson 'the more correct poet, but Shakespeare the greater wit'. Thus the former is rated in more professional terms, transcended by the term for the latter, *wit*, which signifies imagination here. Shakespeare is thereupon likened to Homer, and Jonson to Virgil. What follows is the forthright testimonial: 'I admire him, but I love Shakespeare.' Dryden's prose had uncharacteristically taken an exalted tone when, in the epistle dedicatory to his earliest play, *The Rival Ladies* (1664), he declared that 'Shakespeare . . . had undoubtedly a larger soul of poesy than ever any of our nation.' Neander goes on to elaborate that approach:

He was the man who of all modern, and perhaps ancient poets, had the largest and most comprehensive soul. All the images of Nature were still present to him, and he drew them, not laboriously, but luckily; when he describes any thing, you more than see it, you feel it too. Those who accuse him to have wanted learning, give him the greater commendation: he was naturally learn'd; he needed not the spectacle of books to read Nature; he looked inwards, and found her there.

Samuel Johnson called this part of the *Essay* 'a perpetual model of encomiastic criticism; exact without minuteness, and lofty without exaggeration'. True to the balance of his own phrasing, Johnson was impressed by the equipoise of Dryden's views. His encomium is counterbalanced by stylistic strictures on degenerate puns and swollen bombast. Another shift brings the discourse to Neander's concluding defence of rhyme against blank verse. Later, after having 'undertaken to correct' *Troilus and Cressida*, which he mistook for an apprentice effort, Dryden attacked its 'blown puffy style'. He criticized the Player's speech in *Hamlet* for smelling 'a little too strongly of the buskin', not realizing that Shakespeare had aimed precisely at that histrionic effect. Contemplated from a distance, Shakespeare displays 'an universal mind, which comprehended all characters and passions'. But more immediate scrutiny, disclosing 'a carelessness, and . . . a lethargy of thought, for whole scenes together', prompts technical censure. 'He is the very Janus of poets', or so we read in Dryden's *Defence of the Epilogue* (1672), 'he wears almost everywhere two faces; and you have scarce begun to admire the one, ere you despise the other'. The despicable aspect is attributed, with condescending sympathy, to the barbaric age in which he lived. Language had not yet been polished to that degree of refinement which it would attain, the Poet Laureate tells us, through the conversation at the court of Charles II.

In longer retrospect, and with due cognizance of his own imperfections as a playwright, it might well be Dryden who seems two-faced. So indeed it seemed to some of his contemporaries, who – like Langbaine – counted the solecisms in Dryden's dramaturgy. When critical estimates were reckoned as audits, the Earl of Mulgrave, touching on Shakespeare and Fletcher in his *Essay upon Poetry* (1682), could advise: 'Their Beauties Imitate, avoid their faults.' But Shakespeare's beauties outnumbered, and soon eclipsed, his faults. Charles Gildon excerpted 'The Most Beautiful Topics, Descriptions, and Similes that occur throughout Shakespeare's Plays' in his *Complete Art of Poetry* (1718), and William Dodd's anthology, *The Beauties of Shakespeare* (1752), would be reprinted in countless editions. This would do much to spread the attitude, cited by Dryden from John Hales of Eton, that whatever any other poet had written on any subject could be outmatched by an extract from Shakespeare. The first book devoted to Shakespearian criticism, *An Essay on the Genius and Writings of Shakespeare*, was published by John Dennis in 1712. Dennis, as a stringent neo-classicist, deplored Shakespeare's lack of art, which he ascribed to 'a want of being conversant with the ancients'. Nonetheless he considered him 'one of the greatest geniuses that the world e'er saw for the tragic stage', and speculated on how much greater he would have become with a classical education.

During that same year Joseph Addison, even then engaged in providing a model for tragic correctness with his forthcoming *Cato*, expatiated upon 'the Pleasures of the Imagination' in a well-remembered sequence of *Spectator* papers. More sensitive than Dryden to the Gothic supernaturalism of 'the Fairy Way of Writing', he instanced Shakespeare as excelling all others in 'that noble extravagance of Fancy which he had in so great perfection'. Addison too had elsewhere faulted Shakespeare for 'forced expressions', but had more severely criticized Nahum Tate for imposing a happy ending upon his sentimentalized adaptation of *King Lear*. The next generation could ask rhetorically, with Joseph Warton (echoing Milton on Shakespeare as 'fancies childe', and on how he would 'Warble his native Wood-notes wilde'):

> What are the lays of artful Addison,
> Coldly correct, to Shakespeare's warblings wild?

And Warton would be registering change when, in a periodical paper on *The Tempest* (1753), he employed such expressions as 'romantic' and 'creative imagination'. Shakespeare had been winning admiration and gaining ground all through the Augustan period. His plays actually contributed one fourth of all productions at the two official London theatres in 1740 – an all-time record, although the high proportion owes something to recent legislation, which had made it harder for new plays to get licensed. He had been treated as the great exception to the established rules; but now the rules were changing, responsive in some measure to his impact. His first editor, Nicholas Rowe (1709), excused his faults on the familiar assumption that 'Shakespeare liv'd under a kind of mere Light of Nature ... in a State of almost universal License and Ignorance.' His second editor, Alexander Pope (1725), saluted him as 'an *Original*', and legalized the usual dispensation by arguing that 'To judge ... of *Shakespear* by *Aristotle*'s rules is like trying a man by the Laws of one Country, who acted under those of another.' It was a prescient insight from an observer whose vantage-point had been so distant from that other country.

Rowe and Pope could count upon few principles or precedents to guide them in re-editing an earlier English author. Both were fellow authors, esteemed and assured through their own literary successes, but not especially qualified for the task. They respected Shakespeare's image more than his text, which they emended and abridged and underscored high-handedly. It was partly in reaction to such amateurish undertakings that the techniques of scholarship would be brought to bear upon Shakespeare by such editors as Lewis Theobald (1733), Edward Capell (1768), and Edmond Malone (1790). Dr Johnson was, of course, an all-round man of letters and also – on the basis of his *Dictionary* – a well grounded scholar. His long-meditated *Proposals* (1756) laid down a method of textual collation, and undertook to deliver the eight volumes to subscribers within a year or two. Having miscalculated the demands of the project, he was less than steady in his application to it; finally completed in 1765, it turned out to be less authoritative than expectation had promised (though it would be strengthened and supplemented, in later editions, through the cooperation of George Steevens). Johnson was more effective as a commentator than as an editor. Footnotes, he admitted, were necessary evils, and he was adept at facing necessity. Annotation – like conversation – stimulated those peculiarly Johnsonian talents for the pertinent phrase, the aphoristic sentence, and the pithy judgement.

Johnson's glosses are richly informed by his lexicographical expertness, though he had taken surprisingly little interest in Shakespeare's dramatic coevals and forebears. He is at his most lucid and lively when he paraphrases such an intricate passage as Hamlet's 'To be, or not to be ... ' Previous commentators are freely referred to, and frequently set right, notably the bumbling William Warburton (1747). Johnson almost seems to stand at the shoulder of the impressionable reader, whom he nudges now and then with adjectives like 'interesting' or 'pleasing'; oddly enough, he recommends *Coriolanus* as 'one of the most amusing of the author's performances'.

Summarizing comments are usually offered in the final notes to the various plays, where he sometimes draws the explicit moral that Shakespeare has refrained from overstressing. Thus, after his memorable paragraph on Falstaff, so playfully ambiguous in its appreciation, Johnson sternly warns us 'that no man is more dangerous than he that with a will to corrupt, hath the power to please'. In summing up *King Lear*, he recoils before the blinding of Gloucester, 'an act too horrid to be endured in dramatic exhibition'. This could be the recoil of a classicist. Yet his revulsion from the death of Cordelia – a scene which, he confesses, he could scarcely bear to read – carries him to an unclassical extreme: an attempt to rationalize the concept of poetic justice by defending Tate's version against Addison's critique.

Johnson's most important contribution, not less important for the progress of criticism at large than for the understanding of Shakespeare, was his *Preface*. Marking within a year the two-hundredth anniversary of Shakespeare's birth, it reconciled the apparent discrepancies between the critics and their outstanding author by the blunt expedient of broadening the rules. Johnson had anticipated himself in *The Rambler* (14 September 1757) when, discussing the evolution of drama, he had distinguished 'the accidental prescriptions of authority' from 'the laws of nature'. The preface still allows for the 'deformities' interspersed among the Shakespearian 'graces': anachronisms, loose constructions, obscurities of style, and – from a didactically moralistic standpoint – 'no just distribution of good or evil'. Worst of all, it would seem, was Shakespeare's addiction to the pun; and yet the paragraph leading up to the hyperbolic metaphor ('A quibble was to him the fatal *Cleopatra* for which he lost the world, and was content to lose it') suggests that Johnson himself was by no means immune to a weakness for wordplay. He invokes the habitual excuse for writing these cavils off: 'the father of our drama' had to catch 'the attention of a rude people'. But Johnson differs from most of the other interpreters, and reveals a surprising blind spot, in assuming that Shakespeare's 'natural disposition' was better suited to comedy than to tragedy.

That stricture is softened, however, by Johnson's decisive appeal 'from criticism to nature'. He realizes that life itself can never be purely comic or purely tragic, save by the arbitrary and selective arrangements of art. Hence Shakespeare's 'mingled drama' can fulfil the common end of all poetry, which is 'to instruct by pleasing'. Having delivered this telling blow against the pedantries of Rymer and Voltaire, and recalled 'the principles of drama to a new examination', Johnson is somewhat aghast at his own temerity. Yet he proceeds, 'not dogmatically but deliberately', to question an equally fundamental doctrine of neo-classicism, the Three Unities. The common sense that led him to kick a stone, in remonstrance against the metaphysical idealism of Bishop Berkeley, now leads him to redraw the crucial line between reality and fiction. Here he appeals to imagination, pointing out that 'delusion' (or dramatic illusion) is presupposed from the outset, and prefiguring what Coleridge would define as 'that willing suspension of disbelief for the moment, which constitutes poetic faith'. Once an audience has imagined itself in another time or place, there can be no limits; it may, 'by the authority of Shakespeare', do so again and again. 'Nothing is essential to the fable, but unity of action', which – except in the histories – he well enough preserves; 'the unities of time and place are not essential to a just drama'.

The procedures of critical revaluation, as premised by Johnson, had been 'gradual and comparative', rather than 'absolute and definite'. The passing of a century and a half since Shakespeare's death had freed his work from ephemeral or accidental considerations, and had conferred upon it 'the dignity of an ancient'. Retrospectively viewing him as a classic in his own right, Johnson sought to classicize him further by generalizing about his generality: his plays were 'just representations of general nature', his characters were species rather than individuals, 'the genuine progeny of common humanity'. But classical traditions were giving way to other approaches meanwhile; and the Johnsonian critique formed a watershed, subsuming much that had preceded it and preparing the ground for what was to follow. Shakespeare's pre-eminence became a matter of public celebration soon afterward, when Johnson's former pupil, David Garrick, stage-managed the inaugural festival at Stratford-upon-Avon in 1769. The speech he gave on dedicating a monument, which may have been written for him by Edmund Burke, went farther than hailing Shakespeare as 'the poet of nature' *par excellence*. That was by now a commonplace, which the speaker surpassed by declaring: 'He was another nature.' This idea reverts to a conception, held by Sir Philip Sidney and some of the Italian humanists, which envisions the poet as a demiurge (a lesser God) creating a heterocosm (a world of his own).

The apotheosis of Shakespeare had long been foreshadowed, and its choric fortissimo drowned out such reservations as could still be voiced by Oliver Goldsmith and David Hume. Idolatry had already been mentioned as a potential excess by such early classicists as Ben Jonson and John Dennis. The actor–playwright–critic Arthur Murphy, in his open letter to Voltaire (1753), could profess: 'With us islanders Shakespeare is a kind of established religion in poetry'. As a creator he could best be apprehended through his creatures; from the beginning he had been noted for the substantiality, the particularity, and the variety of his characterization. Garrick's jubilee became a landmark in his own theatrical career; but it likewise encouraged masqueraders to carry on their favourite roles off-stage; and it signalized a shifting venue from the theatre to the library. Enthusiastic amateurs were taking up Shakespeare as a hobby, subjectively identifying with his *dramatis personae*. Thomas Whately, who died in 1772, had planned a series of *Remarks on some of the Characters of Shakespeare*. The surviving fragment was posthumously published, a comparison between Richard III and Macbeth. William Richardson brought out a full-fledged *Philosophical Analysis and Illustration of some of Shakespeare's Characters* in 1774. It approaches Shakespeare as 'the Proteus of the drama; he changes himself into every character, and enters easily into every condition of human nature'.

This must mean that salient quality which has been designated by the Keatsian formulation, 'negative capability', and it might have been traced to the actor's empathy with the many parts he is called upon to enact. But Richardson's ulterior intention, as a classical pedagogue, was 'to make poetry subservient to philosophy', and accordingly to derive ethical lessons from Shakespeare's lifelike archetypes. Many of his characters, popularized through frequent allusion, had virtually assumed a proverbial status: their names were now bywords. Whereas they were commonly praised for their naturalness, the exceptional Caliban had been commended – by Dryden and Rowe – as a sheer invention, 'not in nature'. Falstaff, the best-known figure of all, set the example for notions of English humour, as they were being fixed by critics like Sir William Temple and Corbyn Morris. It seems therefore fitting that the whimsical *tour de force* of character study should have been Maurice Morgann's *Essay on the Dramatic Character of Sir John Falstaff* (1777). If 'this singular buffoon' had wound up by becoming 'the most perfect comic character that perhaps ever was exhibited', then the focus on him could be extended 'to the arts and genius of his Poetic-Maker', and 'even to the principles of human nature itself'. Morgann's tone is frankly that of 'an Advocate' rather than 'an Inquirer', and his panegyric was admittedly 'a mere Experiment . . . attended with all the difficulties and dangers, of *Novelty*'.

The paradox it exuberantly sustains is that the runaway of Gadshill must somehow not have been 'a constitutional coward'. On such occasions it concedes that 'appearances' may stand against him, and one might have thought appearance was what mattered on the stage. But, for the supersubtle reader, that is only 'part' of a latent 'whole', which can be ingeniously rationalized into yielding 'secret Impressions . . . of Courage'. Having originally charmed the Prince, having all but run away with the show itself, Falstaff has evidently persuaded Morgann that Shakespearian characters possess 'a certain roundness and integrity', and that this should differentiate them from the two-dimensional constructs of other writers. Insofar as Falstaff amounts to a great deal more than the stock *miles gloriosus*, it is possible to agree. Morgann had chanced upon a vein of vitalistic impressionism which would be profusely exploited by evocative and facile English critics. He himself was moving towards romanticism when he affirmed: 'True Poesy is *magic*, not *nature*.' His explication would still be reverberating when a twentieth-century editor and teacher, George Lyman Kittredge, rallied to the defence of Falstaffian bravery. But Johnson, as Boswell records, would have none of it, putting Morgann down with reductive irony: 'Why, Sir, we shall have the man come forth again; and as he has proved *Falstaff* to be no coward, he may prove *Iago* to be a very good character.'

Morgann's American associations, as a government official, coloured his counter-attack against the Voltairean epithet 'drunken savage'. When the name of Voltaire and his very language would be forgotten, he prophesied, the Appalachian Mountains and the banks of the Ohio River would 'resound with the accents of this Barbarian'. Johnson had never believed that Voltaire's aspersions were worth answering, and had frowned upon the spirited vindication by one of the original bluestockings, Elizabeth Montagu (1769). Shakespeare had been a preoccupation of Voltaire's throughout his long lifetime, and had become increasingly – as he would later with Tolstoy – an obsession, a rivalry, and a *bête noire*. Yet Shakespeare had been one of those liberating interests which a younger Voltaire had acquired during his political expatriation to England, and he could claim with some warrant to have publicized Shakespeare on the continent. *La Mort de César* is clearly indebted to *Julius Caesar*, and there are other links. Year by year the proponent of toleration seems to have built up his intolerance; it might have had something to do with the Seven Years War; at all events, it pitted the literary loyalties of academic France against the alleged infractions of unruly Britain. The controversy came to a head with the publication of the first translations by Pierre Letourneur. The translator's introduction, venerating Shakespeare as 'le dieu créateur de l'art sublime du théâtre', went on to import a strategic anglicism, the adjective *romantique*.

Voltaire lodged his shrillest protest in a letter to the French Academy (1776), symbolically composed not long before his death. That was an appeal, reversing Johnson as it were, from nature to criticism. Ever the satirist, he had grossly synopsized the plot of *Hamlet* and had caricatured its most celebrated soliloquy by adapting it into fancy alexandrines. He concluded by writing off Shakespeare's plays as 'farces monstrueuses'. Possibly there might have been a few residual pearls in that dunghill, occasional flashes of lightning in those obscure clouds – such chary concessions reiterate the earlier waverings of the more doubtful English critics. The other side of this ambivalence, echoing the less offensive Voltairean metaphor, was emphasized by the article of genius in Diderot's *Encyclopédie* (1757): 'Le sublime et le génie brillent dans Shakespeare comme des éclairs dans une longue nuit.' The pattern of Shakespeare's acceptance had its delayed repetition in France, where the rules were so much more deeply entrenched and the challenge to them had to be launched from abroad. There the dialectic of art versus nature would be symbolized by the two antagonists in Stendhal's controversial pamphlets, *Racine et Shakespeare* (1823–5). As it happened, Stendhal was less interested in the dramatists than in the classic–romantic issue that they personified for him. In awarding the palm to Shakespeare, he was furthering the causes of modernity, flexibility, and ultimately realism.

The cultural cross-fertilization took place when a troupe of English actors, featuring a Shakespearian repertory, performed in Paris during the late 1820s. Its consequences came to be felt in the music of Berlioz and the painting of Delacroix, as well as in the drama of Victor Hugo. Hugo's manifesto, the dynamic preface to his hardly actable *Cromwell* (1827), hit upon a peculiarly Shakespearian intermixture as a formula for modern art, the grotesque and the sublime. An older Hugo would rhapsodize diffusely in *William Shakespeare* (1864), while his son François would bring out a standard French translation. Yet it cannot be said that Shakespeare was ever naturalized in France as he has been in Germany – where, in the boast of Heinrich Heine and others, Shakespeare was better appreciated than he was in England. The foremost German critic, G. E. Lessing, though he never focused on Shakespeare in any detail, constantly held up his naturalism as a favoured alternative to the artificial French models which then set the style. His example, imitated crudely by the Storm-and-Stress playwrights and more effectively by Friedrich Schiller, aided German literature in finding its sense of national identity. That stimulus might have been a deterrent, Goethe would confide to his interlocutor Eckermann, if he had been writing in the language that Shakespeare himself had so exhaustively utilized for the exploration of human nature.

Goethe's endless devotion is implicit in the exclamatory title of his essay, 'Shakespeare und kein Ende!' (1815; translated as 'Shakespeare *Ad Infinitum*'), wherein he discriminated the motivation of Greek and Shakespearian tragedy by an antithesis between Fate and Will. The protagonist of his *Bildungsromane*, Wilhelm Meister, is doubly Shakespeare's godson, since his forename stands for William and his surname denotes mastery. His apprenticeship to a band of strolling players is consummated by a production of *Hamlet*, in the course of which he reinterprets both the character and the play (1795). Through his running commentary Goethe works out an ultraromantic rendering: 'a great deed laid upon a soul unequal to the performance of it'. This would be the *locus classicus* for versions stressing the introspective and neurotic personality, 'without the strength of nerve which makes the hero', inhibited from action by the pale cast of thought. Goethe's deconstruction would be seen as a reflection of Germany in its mood of divisiveness, passivity, and intellectualism, so that the poet Ferdinand Freiligrath could declaim: 'Deutschland ist Hamlet' (1844). Shakespeare's works constituted a family bible for Karl Marx, whose writings are salted with Shakespearian quotations and references. In a letter about a historical play by Ferdinand Lassalle, he cautioned the socialist playwright against becoming too overtly ideological (1859). For the treatment of character he offered a piece of un-Marxian advice: not to Schillerize but to Shakespearize.

By the time Gustav Freytag had compiled his influential handbook on playwriting, *Die Technik des Dramas* (1863), Shakespeare's practice had become a paradigm from which new rules evolved. But the event that did most to establish his international position, and to place his work in comparative and systematic perspective, had consisted of five lectures in a series of thirty, delivered at Vienna in 1808 by A. W. Schlegel, *Vorlesungen über dramatische Kunst und Litteratur* (1809–11). Schlegel, who was Shakespeare's chief German translator, combined wide learning with an active involvement in the romantic movement. Surveying the development of European drama, he championed the seminal Greeks against their derivative Roman successors and deprecated the conventional French vis-à-vis the more liberal situation of the English and Spanish theatres. Shakespeare could at last be fully vindicated as 'a profound artist and not a blind and wilfully luxuriant genius'. To have superciliously misconceived him for so long, as Fancy's child at best and at worst as a drunken savage, was to have been misguided by the precepts of mechanical form. This was the point at which Schlegel resolved old dilemmas, and reaffirmed the linkage between art and nature, by postulating a theory of organic form. Samuel Taylor Coleridge, on the lecture platform himself, would be the first to discuss that contradistinction in English, but not until shortly after he had read Schlegel's printed lectures.

Coleridge's efforts to disentangle his ideas from certain Germanic priorities have made for a touchy episode in the history of intertextuality. He goes out of his way, with a footnote in the *Biographia Literaria*, to claim a precedence over Schlegel in the pronouncement that Shakespeare's judgement equalled his genius. But, in the only manuscript that he left on this topic, there seem to be echoes from Schlegel; and his poetic collaborator Wordsworth, in the prose supplement to *Lyrical Ballads* (1815), notes that the Germans had arrived at that view. Certainly they had been more explicit in dealing with the classic–romantic polarity, and Schlegel had set the two modes of drama within a historical framework which Coleridge had welcomed, with side-remarks disparaging English critics. We must not expect consistency, any more than order, in a collection of critical utterances which has come down to us through stenographic transcriptions, journalistic reports, notebooks variously dated, and hearsay emanating from table-talk. The wonder is that this has added up to so esteemed and received a set of opinions. William Hazlitt, not the friendliest witness, doubted whether Coleridge was sufficiently well read in the subject to lecture upon it. The circumstance of having read so extensively in so many other subjects posed the continuous obstacle of digression. And, though in passing he touches on all the plays, his detailed analyses are centred upon no more than eight of them.

First-hand description of Coleridge as a lecturer, by his loyal friend Crabb Robinson, reports a bewildered reaction on the part of his auditors. He could be 'brilliant; that is, in passages', often extemporizing his finest insights. More often he would ramble on or repeat himself in a plaintive voice. As a course of instruction, these 'pretended lectures' sounded like 'immethodical rhapsodies'. This did not deter him from composing an essay on method (1818); rather, it may have spurred him on to do so, with expectably mixed results. Shakespeare again would be his salient exemplar, and it is in this connection that Coleridge alludes to 'our "myriad-minded bard"'. Here too, even more suggestively, in distinguishing two methods pursued by Shakespeare, the 'poetical' and the 'psychological', it was Coleridge who introduced the latter adjective. In a footnote explaining that the English language needed a term for 'the philosophy of the human mind', he apologized for what was then a neologism. He remained more at ease with the poetical method than with the psychological, which had fostered so much 'motive-mongering'. But his problematic marginal note on Iago, 'the motive-hunting of motiveless malignity', was neutralized by lectures that laid some weight on Iago's resentment and envy. Hamlet, who confessedly brought out Coleridge's 'turn for philosophical criticism', was bound to be self-consciously related to his own psychologizing – as Coleridge cheerfully admits in his *Table Talk*.

His disquisition on *Hamlet*, protracting the introvert's delays, was ticketed by one hearer as 'a satire on himself'. For the more sympathetic Robinson it was 'an elegy'. Enervated by drugs and disappointments, no longer an active poet and never quite a philosopher, a famous talker reduced to talking for all-too-slight material gain, Coleridge had turned to Shakespeare more and more for a vicarious self-realization. Through these *disjecti membra poetae* he retraced an ideal of organic wholeness. No one could have improved upon the intensive and comprehensive approach that he had laid down in this sentence from a letter to his patron, Sir George Beaumont (1804):

Each scene of each play I read, as if it were the whole of Shakespere's Works – the sole thing extant. I ask myself what are the characteristics – the Diction, the Cadences, and Metre, the character, the passion, the moral or metaphysical Inherencies, & fitness for theatric effect, and in what sort of Theatres – all these I write down with great care & precision of Thought & Language – and when I have gone thro' the whole, I shall then collect my papers, & observe, how often such & such Expressions recur & thus shall not only know what the Characteristics of Shakespere's Plays are, but likewise what proportion they bear to each other.

Certainly this was the way to read the plays, and probably it was how he was reading them – but, alas, without any care or precision in setting his observations down. Subsequent generations of scholars have filled the gap, as carefully and precisely as they could, by collecting and going through these disjointed remains. If their very fragmentation has lent them an oracular look, it has also brought the student closer to the moods and changes, the decisions and revisions of the interpretative process. We have no fuller or richer account of the interplay between Shakespeare and a mind of high poetic sensibility, reacting to his style and structure and representation of life. And since that mind was steeped in wide-ranging philosophy, it could frame those aesthetic particularities with broader formulations and more speculative definitions. But critics tend to reveal their own limitations whenever they bridle at Shakespeare, as Coleridge did when he groundlessly sought to rule out the

Porter's scene in *Macbeth* as a vulgar interpolation. Behind his humourless disgust lay a solemn refusal to enter into the Shakespearian arena of comic relief, together with a lingering reluctance to be amused by wordplay.

Shakespeare's plays were set, for Coleridge, in a context of perusal rather than of performance, which he austerely distrusted. His old schoolmate, Charles Lamb, was more at home in the theatre – and, for that matter, with the Elizabethan repertory, from which he had extracted and published *Specimens* (1808). Yet it was Lamb who propounded the critic's distrust of the actor in his paradoxical essay, 'On the Tragedies of Shakespeare, considered with reference to their fitness for Stage Representation' (1811). These transcendent works, he contended, are diminished by the makeshifts of staging. The pensive Hamlet turns into an exhibitionist, while Lear – in his weakness, if not in his grandeur – simply 'cannot be acted'. It was quite consistent for Lamb, with his sister Mary, to transpose the dramas into children's *Tales* (1807). Hazlitt, though he too engaged in theatrical criticism, also harboured doubts about performing such lyrical fantasies as *A Midsummer Night's Dream*. The essayist becomes the spectator, responding with gusto and acumen, in his *Characters of Shakespeare's Plays* (1817), dedicated to Lamb. The preface underlines its divergence from Johnson's by paying its respects to Schlegel's lectures and quoting them at length ('the best account . . . that has hitherto appeared'). Falstaff elicits another superlative, with a touch of paronomasia: 'perhaps the most substantial comic character that ever was invented'. As for Hamlet, his ultimate identification is with the reader's mind: 'It is *we* who are Hamlet.'

But the playhouse could not long be overlooked. Fitness for theatric effect – in Coleridge's terms – was tersely exemplified by the atmospheric essay of Thomas De Quincey 'On the Knocking at the Gate in *Macbeth*' (1823), which ignores the Porter to concentrate upon the stage direction that summons him. The article on Shakespeare by De Quincey, contributed to the Seventh Edition of the *Encyclopaedia Britannica* (1838), made a notable point by emphasizing Shakespeare's depiction of womanhood, 'the possible beauty of the female characters'. Some of these maidens and wives were being sketched by Heine in Germany, with wit and tenderness, in *Shakespeares Mädchen und Frauen* (1839). But such male notice had been anticipated in Dryden's time, and had been more strongly authenticated, by the testimony of a gifted woman, Margaret Cavendish, Duchess of Newcastle. A letter in her published correspondence (1664), dwelling upon the diversity of Shakespeare's personages, testifies to his empathy with his heroines: 'nay, one would think that he had been Metamorphosed from a Man to a Woman, for who could Describe *Cleopatra* better than he hath done?' A more deliberate feminist approach would be put forward by the Anglo-Irish 'lady-authoress' (her epithet), Anna Jameson, under the rather general title, *Characteristics of Women* (1832).

It appears to me that the condition of women in society, as at present constituted, is false in itself, and injurious to them, – that the education of women, as at present conducted, is founded in mistaken principles, and tends to increase fearfully the sum of misery and error in both sexes; but I do not choose presumptuously to fling these opinions in the face of the world, in the form of essays on morality or treatises on education. I have rather chosen to illustrate certain positions by example, and leave my readers to deduce the moral themselves, and draw their own inferences.

So, in an introductory dialogue, the authoress states her emancipatory purpose, which should likewise redeem her 'threadbare subject'. Shakespeare's casts could furnish modern women with role-models clearer than those of history or contemporary actuality: Portia for Intellect, Juliet for Passion, and so on (not including Katharina). Looking backward, Mrs Jameson would have found precedent for her own role in such feminine scholar–critics as Charlotte Lennox, whose *Shakespeare Illustrated* (1753–4) had canvassed his sources and demanded a fairly strict accounting from Shakespeare for his handling of them.

Scholarship on Shakespeare, which has accrued with his successive editors, was regularized by Richard Farmer's sceptical inquiry into his own scholar-ship, *An Essay on the Learning of Shakespeare* (1767). That, in turn, had been conditioned by the critical assumptions and uncertainties involving natural genius and ignorance of the classics. So idiosyncratic a thinker as Walter Whiter, starting from the theories of John Locke, could try to trace recurrent metaphors through the association of ideas. But his *Specimen of a Commentary on Shakespeare* (1794) would have to wait until the twentieth century before it bore ripe fruit in the study of images. The organization of learning in the nineteenth century was mapped out according to the guidelines of historicism. Cultural background and personal biography had to be reconstructed, if they were to throw light upon the plays. Shakespeare the man was an elusive and enigmatic idol for Carlyle and Emerson. The *Sonnets*, his sole text written in the first person, counted as many readings as readers. Edward Dowden's *Shakespeare, his Mind and Art* (1875) attempted to deduce the man from his work by treating the plays as chapters in a sort of spiritual autobiography, whose hero gave vent to tragic expression when sad and to late romance in a mellower mood. This is circular logic, reading the dramaturgy back into the personality. It would be emulated by conjectural biographers like Georg Brandes and Frank Harris – not to mention Stephen Daedalus.

Factual documentation had been accumulating, and would be con-solidated. Sir Sidney Lee, as editor of the *Dictionary of National Biography*, would produce a pedestrian but quasi-official *Life of Shakespeare* (1898), which would eventually run into fourteen editions. Since so many of the facts are trivial and all of them are external, some admirers have been put off by a seeming disparity between the man and his work, and have striven zealously to connect the authorship with more colourful figures. Some have rejoiced, with

Matthew Arnold, in the visage of Shakespeare's apparent inscrutability: 'Others abide our question. Thou art free . . .' Arnold, the premier English critic of his era, though he sometimes conjured with the name of Shakespeare, never ventured to criticize his writings in any depth. He paid no tribute, except for his youthful sonnet, to the uncritical cult that was inspiring such impressionistic rhapsodies as A. C. Swinburne's *Study of Shakespeare* (1880). Shakespeare was by now an established orthodoxy; and it was against this 'bardolatry' that Bernard Shaw, whose moderns were Ibsen and Wagner, broke many an iconoclastic lance in his dramatic reviews of the 1890s. It was their merit that, in shooting down the Bard from the empyrean, they resettled him in his own milieu, the theatre. When Shaw moved on to promote himself tongue-in-cheek as the rival playwright, his criticism is dated, even as most of his own plays have dated.

The more literary trends of interpretation, from Coleridge and the romantics through the century, culminated in A. C. Bradley's *Shakespearean Tragedy* (1904). Having been presented as Oxford lectures, and figuring ever since in university examinations, that solid volume may be said to have marked Shakespeare's assimilation into the curriculum. It subjects four tragedies – *Hamlet, Othello, King Lear,* and *Macbeth* – to the most thoughtful and painstaking reconsideration. These had already formed an inner canon for Coleridge and Hazlitt, and the choice of three would go unquestioned by anyone else. But *Othello*, though Bradley makes out a good case for its 'masterly . . . construction', seems appreciably smaller in scale than the others – or than *Antony and Cleopatra*, which was 'the most wonderful' for Coleridge. (Bradley would endeavour, in a separate lecture, to do justice to it while justifying its exclusion.) *King Lear*, on the other hand, is pronounced to be Shakespeare's 'greatest achievement' but 'not his best play'. And Bradley agrees with Lamb in maintaining that it is 'too huge for the stage'. He looks beyond the stage to reach this verdict, invoking such extra-dramatic criteria as Michelangelo's statues and Beethoven's symphonies. In so synaesthetic an atmosphere, tragedy itself is mitigated, and the King's dying emotion is 'an unbearable *joy*'. If an indifferent Nature and the capricious gods oversee no resolution from conflict, Hegel does. Suffering, at so far a remove, is sublimated into cosmic optimism.

Characterization being what it is for Shakespeare, all of his critics have had to preoccupy themselves with character study in greater or lesser degree, but none has been so thoroughgoing as Bradley. 'The centre of the tragedy,' he writes, '. . . may be said with equal truth to lie in action issuing from character, or in character issuing in action.' So much for 'mere "plot" ' – 'Iago's plot is Iago's character in action.' This could also solve the pseudo-problem of motiveless malignity. The action of Iago is simple enough, since it originates with himself; the action of *Hamlet* is highly complex, because it is forced upon Hamlet; and it is the breakdown of his resistance, the train of his ensuing states of mind, that makes his case the showpiece for Bradleian dialectic. In either instance, and in the others, the stress is on motivation, and psychology unites with ethics in the examination of motives. Nearly a hundred pages of supplementary notes, descending from the grandly general to the minutely particular, bring up queries, work out time-schemes, rationalize inconsistencies, and investigate special topics. Literal-minded as some of these may be, Bradley is capable of correcting Shakespeare by his own standards of verisimilitude: he asserts that Kent must be much older than his acknowledged forty-eight years. We should be reminded, by the lengthening norms of longevity, that Shakespeare himself retired at about that age and died not very long afterward.

In the vast area of secondary studies that have grown up around Shakespeare, no single book has gained wider acceptance than Bradley's. Yet, from the first, it has not gone unchallenged. A critique appeared in the *Times Literary Supplement* (7 April 1905), two weeks after its laudatory review, from the anonymous pen of the prominent dramatic critic A. B. Walkley. Speaking for that *optique du théâtre* which Bradley had slighted, Walkley could expose the fallacy of approaching theatrical roles as if they were flesh-and-blood people with off-stage biographies. For the next generation L. C. Knights issued his polemical pamphlet, *How Many Children Had Lady Macbeth?* (1933) – the very title parodies Bradley's Notes. Joining Coleridgean imagination to Johnsonian common sense, Knights insisted that Shakespeare was not a novelist but a poet after all, and that his animadversions on human nature might have been over-emphasized at the expense of his poetic idiom and the conventions of his craft. The 're-orientation of Shakespeare criticism' heralded by Knights has been proceeding, with innumerable and invaluable consequences, both in the direction he pointed and in that indicated by Walkley. Our century has renewed its appreciation of Shakespeare's language, his stylistic devices, his patterns of imagery, and above all the interaction between his words and his ideas. And it has restored our perception of him to his genre, the drama, enhanced by increasing historical knowledge alongside the live tradition of the performing arts.

Reading list

Andrews, W. T., ed., *Critics on Shakespeare* (1973)
Babcock, R. W., *The Genesis of Shakespeare Idolatry* (Chapel Hill, North Carolina, 1931)
Bentley, G. E., *Shakespeare and Jonson: Their Reputations in the Seventeenth Century Compared*, 2 vols. (Chicago, 1945)
Bradley, A. C., *Shakespearean Tragedy* (1904); reprinted with an introduction by John Russell Brown (1985)
Coleridge, S. T., *On Shakespeare: The Text of the Lectures of 1811–12*, ed. R. A. Foakes (1971)
Shakespeare Criticism, ed. T. M. Raysor, 2 vols. (1960)

Writings on Shakespeare, ed. Terence Hawkes, with an introduction by Alfred Harbage (New York, 1959); reprinted as *Coleridge on Shakespeare* (Harmondsworth, 1969)

Dryden, John, *Essays*, ed. W. P. Ker, 2 vols. (Oxford, 1900)

Eastman, A. M., *A Short History of Shakespeare Criticism* (New York, 1968)

Elledge, Scott, ed., *Eighteenth Century Critical Essays* (Ithaca, 1961)

Gundolf, Friedrich, *Shakespeare und der deutsche Geist* (Berlin, 1911)

Hazlitt, William, *Characters of Shakespeare's Plays* (1817, many times reprinted)

Johnson, Samuel, *On Shakespeare*, ed. Arthur Sherbo, with an introduction by B. H. Bronson, 2 vols. (New Haven, 1968)

Jusserand, J. J., *Shakespeare in France under the Ancien Régime* (1899)

Knights, L. C., *How Many Children Had Lady Macbeth?* (1933)

Levin, Harry, 'The primacy of Shakespeare', in *Shakespeare and the Revolution of the Times* (1976)

LeWinter, Oswald, ed., *Shakespeare in Europe* (Cleveland, 1963; Harmondsworth, 1970)

Pascal, Roy, ed., *Shakespeare in Germany, 1740–1815* (Cambridge, 1937)

Ralli, Augustus, *A History of Shakespeare Criticism*, 2 vols. (Oxford, 1932)

Schlegel, A. W., *Lectures on Dramatic Art and Literature*, translated by John Black, revised by A. J. W. Morrison (1909)

Shaw, G. B., *Shaw on Shakespeare: An Anthology*, ed. Edwin Wilson (New York, 1961; Harmondsworth, 1969)

Smith, D. Nichol, *Eighteenth Century Essays on Shakespeare*, 2 vols. (Oxford, 1963)
Shakespeare Criticism: A Selection (1916, etc.)

Spingarn, J. E., *Critical Essays of the Seventeenth Century*, 3 vols. (Oxford, 1908–9)

Vickers, Brian, ed., *Shakespeare: The Critical Heritage, 1623–1801*, 6 vols. (1974–81)

13a Twentieth-century Shakespeare criticism: the comedies

SHAKESPEARE'S critics in the twentieth century have served his comedies less well than his tragedies. The imbalance, while deplorable, is understandable: comedy's critics labour under a cultural disadvantage. We know that tears are important, but we think that laughter is a mark of triviality; suffering is real, but happy endings are the products of wishful thinking; wishful thinking is an indulgence, while great art (we believe) should be hard work. Comedy flouts the fundamental bias tragedy confirms, that the individual is the measure of all things and that, as a consequence, death is the central fact about life.

Shakespeare probably did not share these assumptions in favour of tragedy. It is likely that he began his career writing comedy, and the elements that compound the early *Comedy of Errors* – the dispersal and eventual reunion of a family, imagery of perilous voyages over distant waters to mysterious lands, magical deeds approaching the realm of miracle – are the elements that compound *The Tempest* as well. Criticism in the twentieth century has had to invent or rediscover a point of view that can take Shakespeare's comedy seriously but on its own, not tragedy's, terms. The emphasis on character that was productive for criticism of the tragedies has been less productive for the comedies; other emphases had to be found. Criticism also had to relate the early romantic comedies to the problem plays of the middle period, and all of these to the late romances. It has had, in other words, to rediscover the genre of comedy itself. In that effort it has worked most successfully from the late romances forward to the beginning and middle of Shakespeare's career. Several critics and trends in criticism since the 1930s have hastened that project remarkably, and this brief conspectus therefore emphasizes the half-century of achievement.

Northrop Frye provided the single most important impetus. Frye is a systems-builder. He is interested more in the relations among plays than in the details of the individual play. Though Shakespeare has been at the centre of his criticism, even Shakespeare exists for him as a series of instances of a larger whole. The most extensive elaboration of Frye's system comes in *Anatomy of Criticism* (1957); his writing specifically on comedy and Shakespeare includes the influential essay 'The Argument of Comedy'

(1948), and *A Natural Perspective* (1965), *The Secular Scripture* (on romance, 1976), and *The Myth of Deliverance* (problem plays, 1983). Frye's work is kaleidoscopic: sharply symmetrical and ever-changing. It provides no easily applicable formula for comedy but, more valuably, a point of view congenial to comedy's needs and productive for future criticism.

In a stroke Frye reverses the cultural bias in favour of tragedy: 'tragedy is really implicit or uncompleted comedy ... comedy contains a potential tragedy within itself' ('Argument', p. 65). Together, the genres form a cycle that imitates the natural cycle of birth-death-and-rebirth. This is the rhythm of the seasons and it is the basis of our enduring myths. Frye's strategy makes comedy the more capacious form because it points beyond death to intimate the cycle's fullness. In a daring move of cultural subsumption, Frye assimilates the Bible itself (as a literary form) to the plot of comedy: 'From the point of view of Christianity, tragedy is an episode in that larger scheme of redemption and resurrection to which Dante gave the name of *commedia*' ('Argument', p. 66). The comic way through death to rebirth is found as significantly in (say) *Much Ado About Nothing* as in the gospels. In the play, however, the underlying myth has been displaced towards the pole of conventional realism; part of the critic's job, then, is to uncover the mythic potential in the purposefully 'shrunken' play. But Shakespeare, even at his most conventionally realistic, is never far from the putative mythic origins of comedy. To Frye, Falstaff in *The Merry Wives of Windsor*, with horns on head, beaten and ducked, has 'done about all that could reasonably be asked of any fertility spirit' ('Argument', p. 69). In the late romances Shakespeare approaches the comic archetypes in their least displaced form.

Several of Frye's local observations have been especially influential. 'Comedy, like all forms of art that are presented in time, is primarily an impetus to completing a certain kind of movement', writes Frye, and he defines the comic impetus as 'a drive toward identity' (*Perspective*, p. 118). The marriages that end Shakespeare's comedies are the signs of achieved identity, individual or social or both. 'The normal action of a comedy,' he writes, 'moves from irrational law to festivity' (*Perspective*, p. 115). In some Shakespearian comic plots that action drives the characters from their normal social world into a 'green world' where liberating potentialities are explored and finally takes them back to a social world transformed now by its contact with the 'green world'. (An interesting elaboration of Frye's scheme is offered by Sherman Hawkins in 'The Two Worlds of Shakespearean Comedy', *Shakespeare Studies* 3 (1968).) Frye must 'stand back' from the individual play in order to discover the archetypal structure it shares with other plays. Such a stance obviously entails optical risks, and Frye has been criticized for dissolving the many comedies into one *Ur*-comedy. The benefits, however, are also great.

Frye's most important immediate precursor is G. Wilson Knight, who also approaches comedy from the direction of the late romances where the informing myths are least rationalized by demands of conventional realism. Knight's earliest work, the brief 'Myth and Miracle' (1929), stressed the final plays as 'the furthest limit of direct representation': it is reprinted in *The Crown of Life: Essays in Interpretation of Shakespeare's Final Plays* (1947). Knight also deals with comedy in *The Shakespearian Tempest* (1932). *The Wheel of Fire* (1930, revised 1949), though mainly on tragedy, contains influential essays on '*Measure for Measure* and the Gospels' and on *Troilus and Cressida*. Unlike the wittily epigrammatic Frye, Knight can descend to tedious image-cataloguing or, with equally disastrous results, ascend the heights of Christian mysticism. But while his style now seems more odd than interesting, many of his revaluations of the plays, as well as the techniques that produced those revaluations, have been absorbed almost wholly into contemporary critical thinking.

Knight's approach is symbolic and systematic: the Shakespearian canon forms a consistent, mutually informative whole. Knight typically interprets Shakespeare's symbols in terms of binary oppositions; in the comedies he stresses the opposition of 'tempest-symbolism' to music, and 'the hate-theme' to love. The critical technique Knight developed independently was simultaneously becoming a basic technique of structuralism. The symbolic configurations he finds in the plays suggest aspects of human personality. In that regard, too, Knight (for all his idiosyncrasy of expression) is in the critical mainstream, specifically in the development of psychological criticism. His work helped criticism move beyond an atomistic concern either with character or imagery or plot towards a conception of the play as an integral structure governed by self-generated rules.

Frye and Wilson Knight see the late romances not as aberrations but as the development of elements inherent in Shakespearian comedy from the beginning. In a related area, William Empson sees pastoral (in his seriously playful *Some Versions of Pastoral*, 1935) not as an occasional decorative mode but as an enduringly significant form. Historical scholarship has also influenced ideas about romance and pastoral: G. E. Bentley (*Shakespeare Survey 1* (1948), for instance), makes a case for the effect of theatrical conditions (the acquisition of the Blackfriars Theatre by the King's Men) on the development of the romances; Carol Gesner writes about possible connections between *Shakespeare and the Greek Romances* (1970); Frank Kermode's introduction to the Arden edition of *The Tempest* (1954) helpfully makes available some of the philosophical concerns of the late plays, including the opposition of 'nature' to 'nurture'. More broadly speculative work has also had its effect: Susanne Langer's *Feeling and Form* (1953) described a special 'rhythm of comedy' in terms analogous to Frye's. (Langer's theory is briefly summarized in Helen Gardner's graceful essay '*As You Like It*', 1959.)

Criticism is not an art that steadily improves, but criticism of the romances (and of comedy from the romantic-pastoral point of view) genuinely *has* improved. Its increased sophistication can be seen by comparing E. M. W. Tillyard's slight *Shakespeare's Last Plays* (1938), which asserts that the romances complete a tragic pattern of destruction leading to regeneration, with such later, more substantial studies as David Young's *The Heart's Forest* (which incorporates even *King Lear* in the pastoral ambit; 1972), Thomas McFarland's *Shakespeare's Pastoral Comedy* (1972), Douglas Peterson's *Time, Tide, and Tempest* (1973), and Howard Felperin's *Shakespearean Romance* (1972). Felperin's book is especially interesting, among other things for its encounter with the historical and theoretical objection that romance is inherently an escapist mode.

Anthropology, which invests myth and folk tale with significance, privileging the common over the culturally extraordinary, has been a great stimulus to interest in comedy. Frye's 'theory of archetypes' as well as Knight's reverence for the 'symbol' derive in part from studies of myth and ritual by the Cambridge school of anthropologists. Among Shakespearians, C. L. Barber has been the most successful at drawing upon anthropological insights; and he is, along with Frye and Knight, one of the most influential Shakespeare critics of the century. In *Shakespeare's Festive Comedy* (1957) Barber connects 'the saturnalian pattern' of comedy to actual English holidays and social customs, especially those involving May games and the topsy-turvy reign of a 'Lord of Misrule'. Barber's criticism has affinities with Frye's, but it lays relatively more stress on the anarchic, or at least anti-authoritarian, impulse in comedy than it does on the concomitant impulse towards reconciliation and renewal. Falstaff of the *Henry IV* plays emerges in Barber's account as a great comic figure because he is a great mocker of authority, the perfect embodiment of holiday licence. Barber's profound influence on other critics may be attributed to various factors including, not incidentally, the gracefulness of his style and the easy availability of his comic formula, 'Through release to clarification'. But perhaps most importantly, Barber's book suggests (although it does not itself fully explore) a useful direction for future criticism: outwards from literary formalism towards a kind of anthropological historicism. In Frye's criticism, by contrast, literature and drama (including Shakespearian comedy) inhabit a world of their own making, one cognate in certain respects with the world unformed by literature, but not vitally affected by it. Barber's work suggests that anthropological as well as historical and psychoanalytic insights can help to exfoliate the intricate interdependencies of literature and society.

Barber deals with comedies up to *Twelfth Night* – with, that is to say, the so-called romantic comedies. This was the subject also of H. B. Charlton's *Shakespearian Comedy* of 1938. Charlton appropriately disclaims any comparison between his book and A. C. Bradley's *Shakespearean Tragedy* – although Charlton's book, relatively belated and insubstantial as it is, is the best that criticism of the comedies had at that time produced. Unlike most critics of the post-Frye era, Charlton drew a sharp distinction between comedy and romance – and 'The whole history of Elizabethan comedy is a tale of the reluctance of comedy to compromise itself with romance' (p. 23). Romance, according to Charlton, was the people's unfortunate choice, against which Shakespeare had to learn to assert himself. This view of Shakespeare at odds with his audience is unconvincing. And the distinction between comedy and romance is vitiated by the historical naïvety of Charlton's conception of medieval romance. Charlton takes a developmental view of Shakespeare's career: each of the earlier comedies is struggling to attain the form of the consummate works in the genre, *Much Ado About Nothing, As You Like It*, and *Twelfth Night* – three plays about which Charlton has little to say in his anti-climactic final chapter. Despite its limitations, however, Charlton's book is historically significant for its attempt to fashion a genre criticism – what Charlton calls 'the idea of comedy' – that can help define Shakespeare's special achievement.

The romantic comedies have received considerable attention since Charlton. John Russell Brown's *Shakespeare and His Comedies* (1957) was published in the same year as Barber's *Shakespeare's Festive Comedy*. Like Charlton, Brown attempts to uncover the comic 'idea' – what he calls the 'implicit judgement' – variously expressed through dramatic action and language rather than in discursive statement. Shakespeare gives 'the impression of an artist seeking to express a vision which was always eluding a completely satisfactory presentation' (p. 27), and Brown therefore stresses the variety of Shakespeare's experiments with comic form. Peter Phialas's *Shakespeare's Romantic Comedies* (1966) is another helpful, modest introduction to the subject. Ruth Nevo's *Comic Transformations in Shakespeare* (1980) is written with a lively awareness of recent trends in critical theory. Possibly the best discussions of the individual plays are by Alexander Leggatt, in *Shakespeare's Comedy of Love* (1974). Leggatt's readings allow each comedy to establish its own special world, but with the interesting twist that Leggatt seeks 'not the internal unity of each play but its internal variety' (p. xii). In *The Merchant of Venice*, for instance, he stresses the unsettling combination of 'conventionalized action with human reality, naturalistically conceived' (p. 149). Stylistic variety becomes inherently meaningful: 'The comic device of juxtaposing different styles, and ultimately different kinds of experience, has led Shakespeare increasingly to set two kinds of art against each other: an art that orders life into self-consciously formal designs, and an art that conveys an image of experience as disordered and uncontrollable' (p. 255). These two kinds of art, both of them accommodated in Shakespeare's romantic comedy, also suggest two tendencies among Shakespeare's critics: either to emphasize the formal coherence of the play or the energies that work to subvert that coherence. Leggatt is unusual in his even-handed awareness of both tendencies, in the plays and in criticism.

Leggatt's interest in stylistic and dramatic conventions is characteristic of the best Shakespearian comic criticism. Tragedy's critics can proceed a short distance with the assumption that the plays are direct reflections of 'real life'; comedy's critics can take that assumption nowhere. Frye's position may be extreme: 'In comedy and in romance the story seeks its own end instead of holding the mirror up to nature'; but his corollary is demonstrably true: 'Consequently comedy and romance are so obviously conventionalized that a serious interest in them soon leads to an interest in convention itself' (*Perspective*, p. 8). L. G. Salingar, in *Shakespeare and the Traditions of Comedy* (1974), has this to say to a critic who regrets 'impediments' which comedy's 'artificial' conventions put in the way of his response to the play's 'human content': 'a stage convention, such as a familiar twist in a plot, is an expressive sign, a means of communication between the playwrights who use it and the audiences who enjoy or at least accept it – until time has reduced it to a dead convention, or a bad habit. A writer who allows convention to obstruct the human content of his plays either has little human content to communicate or should not be writing for the stage' (p. 5). Salingar's copious study of theatre-historical backgrounds, both medieval and classical, and of Shakespeare's use of them in the creation of character and plot, is an indispensable aid in understanding the comic conventions through which Shakespeare communicates to us. M. C. Bradbrook is another author who brings us in touch with the history of theatre, which is in large part the history of dramatic conventions. Especially relevant from her prolific career are *Shakespeare and Elizabethan Poetry* (1951) and *The Growth and Structure of Elizabethan Comedy* (1955). The system of genre is itself an aspect of convention: Susan Snyder's *The Comic Matrix of Shakespeare's Tragedies* (1979) provides an excellent account of comic theory in the Renaissance, as prelude to a practical demonstration of Shakespeare's habitual mixing of the genres in his tragedies.

Comic convention can be approached from other directions than theatre history or genre theory. Some critics stress the medieval inheritance of Shakespearian comedy, hence the specifically Christian aspects of the comic plot. Robert G. Hunter's *Shakespeare and the Comedy of Forgiveness* (1965) engages the interpretative problem posed by comedies where the conventional happy ending requires an audience to forgive an erring or indeed criminal character. Hunter historicizes Frye's plot of comedy and finds Shakespeare working in a tradition 'originally medieval and didactically Christian' (p. 8), one which reflects the theological pattern of sin, repentance, and forgiveness. For some other critics, to medievalize is to allegorize. Nevill Coghill's 'The Basis of Shakespearian Comedy' (*Essays and Studies* 3 (1950)) distinguishes Shakespeare's mode, which is in the tradition of medieval Christian romance, from Ben Jonson's, which is classical and satiric. Shakespeare's mode, according to Coghill, is amenable to an exegesis which can discern behind the courtroom scene in *The Merchant of Venice* the biblical scene, developed in various medieval sources, of the debate and reconciliation of The Four

Daughters of God. John Weld's *Meaning in Comedy* (1975) gracefully analyses possible theological affinities of romantic comedy, while R. Chris Hassel, Jr, in *Faith and Folly in Shakespeare's Romantic Comedies* (1980), draws an 'analogy between romantic and religious faith' (p. 53), and ties (more tightly than evidence warrants) Shakespeare's comic dialogue to passages in St Paul and Erasmus.

Shakespeare is a great comic playwright not because he uses comic conventions but because he extraordinarily varies and extends their possibilities. One way of describing the problem with the so-called 'problem plays' is to say that in them Shakespeare has dealt so unconventionally with his comic conventions that we are left more than usually unsure how to respond. *Measure for Measure*, for instance, is virtually explicit in its references to certain Christian doctrines, but distressingly inexplicit about the applicability of those doctrines to its characters. *All's Well that Ends Well* has as conventionally comic a title as could be imagined, but its happy ending is remarkably precarious. *Troilus and Cressida* is often grouped with the two previous plays though it might as well be grouped with (say) *Hamlet* and *Timon of Athens* as a 'problem tragedy'. Critics have tried in various ways to explain the peculiar qualities of these plays from the middle of Shakespeare's career. F. S. Boas (*Shakespeare and His Predecessors*, 1896) in effect invented the category 'problem plays', and it has been revaluated by W. W. Lawrence, *Shakespeare's Problem Comedies* (1931), E. M. W. Tillyard, *Shakespeare's Problem Plays* (1949), Ernest Schanzer, *The Problem Plays of Shakespeare* (1963), and Northrop Frye, *The Myth of Deliverance* (1983). Terence Hawkes groups the problem comedies with the tragedies in a study of *Shakespeare and the Reason* (1964); while R. A. Foakes connects them with the late romances in an analysis that stresses 'dramatic structure rather than . . . thematic patterns' (*Shakespeare, The Dark Comedies to the Last Plays*, 1971). Qualities that have made the problem plays both theatrically and critically marginal – their emphasis on unpleasant social phenomena like prostitution, their analysis of gender relationships in terms of power relationships, their exposure of the precariousness of the very theatrical conventions they are exploiting – are likely to make these plays increasingly attractive to critics inclined towards either deconstructive or Marxist theory, or to some combination of those tendencies.

Richard Wheeler's study of *Shakespeare's Development and the Problem Comedies* (1981) draws on post-Freudian psychoanalytic theory. He is one of several critics who have interestingly applied psychology to the comedies – a delicate task since comedy's characters tend more openly to proclaim themselves as dramatic types than do the relatively more individualized characters of tragedy. But recent psychoanalytic criticism has been less interested in a character's putative unconscious than in tensions that exist within the play as a whole. The plot, as a system of relationships where sexual and familial tensions are played out, can be illuminated by psychoanalytic concepts without the need to invent a psychological prehistory for characters who remain, after all, bundles of dramatic conventions. Shakespeare's persistent focus on the family – on the dispersal and reunion of parents, children, and siblings, and on the concomitant drive towards personal identity through relationship – invites exploration in terms of psychoanalytic ego psychology. Here the work of D. W. Winnicott and Erik Erikson has been especially suggestive. Some of the new psychological criticism is simultaneously informed by feminist perspectives, with the result that both the psychologism and the feminism attain finer degrees of critical sophistication. Norman N. Holland's extensive psychological criticism (including *Psychoanalysis and Shakespeare*, 1964) has been influential. More recent work is available in the collection *Representing Shakespeare: New Psychoanalytic Essays* (1980), edited by Murray M. Schwartz and Coppélia Kahn: several of its essays discuss comedy and romance, as Kahn does in chapters of her book *Man's Estate: Masculine Identity in Shakespeare* (1981). (A related idea is treated from an anthropological slant by Marjorie Garber, *Coming of Age in Shakespeare*, 1981.) There have been few very successful efforts to discuss Shakespeare's comic heroines. But the relation of genre to gender is the interesting subject of Linda Bamber's *Comic Women, Tragic Men* (1982): in comedy, a male Self is complemented by a nurturing female Other.

Of course, the 'Comic Characters of Shakespeare' (to borrow the title of John Palmer's book (1964)) have always engrossed attention, pre-, post-, or even anti-Freudian. Larry S. Champion's *The Evolution of Shakespeare's Comedy* (1970) proceeds on the assumption that Shakespeare's 'development as a comic playwright is consistently in the direction of complexity or depth of characterization' (p. 9) – an assumption that prejudices the case against the early comedies while creating false expectations for the late romances. Champion, like many other critics, believes that the characters are given a chance to 'know themselves'; he is optimistic about their therapeutic prospects. Ralph Berry, in his challenging and often original *Shakespeare's Comedy* (1972), is extraordinarily pessimistic. Berry assumes that the behaviour of the characters is 'explicable in terms of naturalistic psychology' (p. 19) – as opposed, presumably, to the conventions of comedy or the insights of psychoanalysis – and on that assumption he describes an alarmingly unattractive and unself-aware group of ostensible heroes and heroines.

Bertrand Evans, in *Shakespeare's Comedies* (1960), focuses on discrepancies of awareness between the audience's knowledge of the plot and that of the characters. His approach combines an interest in structure with an attempt at audience-response criticism. The latter is only one of many areas in which there is more work to be done. Under the influence of Frye and Wilson Knight, criticism has concentrated on the mythic dimensions of the comic plot, on the richness of image and symbol, on the quest for identity and self-knowledge. Psychoanalytic and feminist theories extend those emphases. But such theories also point to areas that can complement the pervasive formalism of the last half-century. Critics will want to ask about the relation of Shakespeare's comedy to his contemporary audience and to the life of his society as a whole: sociological theory informed by history can help. They will want to pay more attention to the theatrical dynamics of the plays, from the points of view both of audience and of actor. And while they continue to explore Shakespeare's comedies, they will also continue to explore the relation of the comedies to the histories and tragedies. In Plato's *Symposium*, after a long night of talk and drink, Socrates is overheard discoursing to Aristophanes the comedian and Agathon the tragedian, compelling them 'to acknowledge that the genius of comedy was the same with that of tragedy, and that the true artist in tragedy was an artist in comedy too. To this they were constrained to assent, being drowsy, and not quite following the argument.' Their befuddlement is appropriate: only once in the history of Western drama, not in fifth-century Athens but in late sixteenth- and early seventeenth-century England, has a playwright given living warrant to the proposition. The present brief survey has mentioned only a few approaches to the comic part of Shakespeare's genius. It has concentrated on books, unfairly neglecting many indispensable article-length studies. It has neglected several valuable books about individual plays, as well as the contributions of editions such as the Arden, Oxford, and Cambridge. It closes only with the certainty that what's past is prelude, even on the crowded scene of Shakespearian criticism.

13b Twentieth-century Shakespeare criticism: the tragedies

A. C. BRADLEY'S *Shakespearean Tragedy* (1904), based on lectures delivered earlier, was both the culmination of nineteenth-century criticism of the tragedies, and the point of departure for critics of the present century. For a generation it was regarded as the best book on the subject, though there were some dissentient voices. It was said that Bradley glossed over Shakespeare's faults, that he concentrated too much on character, that he was ignorant of stage conditions, and that he read subtleties and philosophical profundities into the plays. It was not realized by his critics that Bradley was a keen playgoer, and that he thought of his work as advice to the players.

The first significant counterblast came from Edgar Elmer Stoll who, in a series of books of which the best is *Art and Artifice in Shakespeare* (1935), tried to demonstrate the inconsistency of Shakespeare's characters and the over-valuing of his psychological penetration. He extolled him instead as a great illusionist, using poetry to persuade audiences into believing impossibilities. Levin L. Schücking, in a book translated as *Character Problems in Shakespeare's Plays* (1922), stressed the 'primitive' technique of the dramatist by which, for example, characters informed the audience about their motives or commented chorically on the action. The criticism by Lily Bess Campbell in *Shakespeare's Tragic Heroes* (1930), and in the postscripts to the 1961 edition, was that Bradley was imprisoned in nineteenth-century ideology, whereas he ought to have considered the tragedies in the light of Elizabethan philosophy and psychology. Campbell's own interpretations, however, are reductive, and much less convincing than her early chapters in which she outlines the Elizabethan world picture.

The critics associated with *Scrutiny* attacked Bradley for different reasons, and F. R. Leavis proclaimed that the dethronement of Bradley was a major achievement of his journal. L. C. Knights in *How Many Children Had Lady Macbeth?* (reprinted in *Explorations*, 1946) complained that Bradley, by regarding character as more important than poetry, had distorted the meaning of the tragedies, and both he and Leavis argued that Bradley had whitewashed the characters of the heroes, who were all seriously flawed. G. Wilson Knight, a major influence on Knights, was avowedly a disciple of Bradley, though he diverged from him in nearly every respect. His 'spatial' method subordinated character to theme, though his experience as actor and director protected him from the delusion that character was unimportant. *The Wheel of Fire* (1930) and *The Imperial Theme* (1931) had chapters on nine of the tragedies. Although it would be easy to list those points which have failed to win general acceptance (e.g. his defence of Claudius, his valuation of *Timon of Athens*), for two generations Knight's work has proved to be a dominating influence, though fiercely resisted by H. B. Charlton in *Shakespearian Tragedy*, and by John Holloway in *The Story of the Night* (1961). Ruth Nevo in *Tragic Form in Shakespeare* (1972) also fought the prevailing trend.

Meanwhile, in the 1930s, Caroline Spurgeon was systematically card-indexing all Shakespeare's images. She maintained that the preponderance of imagery drawn from a particular field threw light on Shakespeare's own interpretations. This method was most successful with regard to the tragedies: the sickness images in *Hamlet*, the man in ill-fitting garments in *Macbeth*, the tortured body in *King Lear* are clearly significant, though Spurgeon's own interpretations are questionable. Her method of classification and the distortion caused by her concentration on one or two iterative images in each play have also been criticized.

W. H. Clemen in *Shakespeares Bilder* (1936) – enlarged as *The Development of Shakespeare's Imagery* (1951) – demonstrated the necessity of considering images in their context and in relation to the other dramatic and poetic characteristics of the plays. Robert B. Heilman in *This Great Stage* (1949) and *Magic in the Web* (1956) gave detailed analyses of the imagery of *King Lear* and *Othello*. Maurice Charney's *Shakespeare's Roman Plays* (1961) and *Style in Hamlet* (1969), Brents Stirling's *Unity in Shakespearian Tragedy* (1956), Kenneth Muir's *Shakespeare the Professional* (1973), Madeleine Doran's *Shakespeare's Dramatic Language* (1976), D. A. Stauffer's *Shakespeare's World of Images* (1949), Cleanth Brooks's 'The Babe and the Cloak of Manliness' in *The Well-Wrought Urn* (1949), and Maynard Mack's 'The World of Hamlet' (*Yale Review* 41, 1952) are also concerned with imagery.

Another field of criticism is that of Shakespearian quibbles, deplored by Dryden and Johnson, but defended in William Empson's *Seven Types of Ambiguity* (1930) and his later essays in *The Structure of Complex Words* (1951) in which he discusses *Othello*, *King Lear*, and *Timon of Athens*. Empson's most distinguished follower, M. M. Mahood, has chapters on *Hamlet*, *Macbeth*, and *Romeo and Juliet* in her *Shakespeare's Wordplay* (1957).

Other critics have concentrated on Shakespeare in the theatre. A. C. Sprague in *Shakespearian Players and Performances* (1953) provided vivid accounts of Mrs Siddons's Lady Macbeth, Edmund Kean's Othello and Edwin Booth's Iago. Marvin Rosenberg in *The Masks of Othello* (1961), *The Masks of King Lear* (1972), and *The Masks of Macbeth* (1978) traced in great detail not merely how the parts have been played, but also the interaction of literary interpretation and stage performance. Earlier, Harley Granville-

Barker, after his lamented retirement from the stage, had written short prefaces to *Julius Caesar, King Lear, Macbeth*, and *Antony and Cleopatra* and long ones to *Hamlet, Othello*, and *Coriolanus*. His main purpose was to advise directors on how to produce plays on the modern stage, with the minimum of distortion, and to suggest how the parts could be performed. To do this he had to interpret the plays; and if, in the opinion of some critics, he relied too heavily on Bradley, he defends the actability of *King Lear*, and makes shrewd comments on the characters, on the speaking of the verse, and on the structure of the plays.

The question of structure was one to which Emrys Jones addressed himself in *Scenic Form in Shakespeare* (1971) and Mark Rose in *Shakespearian Design* (1972). Both these critics argue that the plays were constructed in scenes rather than in acts. Rose produces an effective analysis of the structure of *Hamlet* and Jones discusses four other tragedies. Yet the critic who has contributed most to our understanding of dramatic form is Muriel Bradbrook in her numerous works on Shakespeare and Elizabethan drama. She claims that she learnt from T. S. Eliot how to read the Elizabethans, and this was doubtless true of their dramatic poetry, but her own distinctive contribution was to absorb and metamorphose the views of Stoll and Schücking on the 'primitive' nature of Shakespeare's art. She demonstrates the positive value of his use of the primitive, of icons, and of pageantry, and she never forgets the historical, social, and theatrical backgrounds of the plays. Scattered through her many books and especially in *Shakespeare the Craftsman* (1969) and *Shakespeare the Poet in his World* (1978), are memorable interpretations of all Shakespeare's tragedies.

A number of critics have written books covering all Shakespeare's tragedies, sometimes including *Richard III* and *Richard II* in the genre. Irving Ribner's *Patterns in Shakespearian Tragedy* (1960) and Larry S. Champion's *Shakespeare's Tragic Perspective* (1976) are sensible and useful, though without adding greatly to previous criticism. Others, such as John Holloway's (see p. 242) and Harold S. Wilson's *On the Design of Shakespearean Tragedy* at times sacrifice the uniqueness of individual plays to fit a general thesis. Others again, such as Roy Battenhouse's *Shakespearean Tragedy* (1969) and Paul N. Siegel's *Shakespearean Tragedy and the Elizabethan Compromise* (1957), are too theological for most modern tastes; and the same may be said of three eloquent books by G. R. Elliott – *Scourge and Minister* (1951), *Flaming Minister* (1953), and *Dramatic Providence in 'Macbeth'* (1958) – in which he seeks to prove that all Shakespeare's tragic heroes fall through pride. Virgil K. Whitaker is less open to such objections, but *The Mirror up to Nature* (1965) was thought by many to be inferior to *Shakespeare's Use of Learning* (1953).

On the whole, the most interesting books have been written by critics with more limited objectives. M. W. MacCallum was not a profound or exciting critic, but his *Shakespeare's Roman Plays and their Background* (1910) provided the standard work on the subject for half a century and was not wholly superseded by D. A. Traversi's *Shakespeare: The Roman Plays* (1961) or by J. L. Simmons's *Shakespeare's Pagan World* (1973). Nicholas Brooke confined his attention to *Shakespeare's Early Tragedies* (1968) and Willard Farnham in *Shakespeare's Tragic Frontier* (1950) dealt only with the last four.

Another kind of deliberate restriction is illustrated by *Shakespeare and the Nature of Man* (1943) in which Theodore Spencer suggested that the poet's tragic period was prompted by the shock he received from the impact of Copernicus, Machiavelli, and Montaigne; or by Matthew N. Proser's *The Heroic Image in Five Shakespearean Tragedies* (1965), or by William Rosen's *Shakespeare and the Craft of Tragedy* (1960) which deals with only four; or, again, by Ernst Honigmann's discussion of the dramatist's manipulation of response in *Shakespeare: Seven Tragedies* (1976).

There are, of course, more general works which contain interesting comments on several of the tragedies. One thinks, for example, of Alfred Harbage's *Shakespeare and the Rival Traditions* (1952), A. P. Rossiter's *Angel with Horns* (1961), D. G. James's *The Dream of Learning* (1951), and Philip Edwards's *Shakespeare and the Confines of Art* (1968). Some books on still wider topics contain valuable comments on Shakespeare's tragedies, too many to enumerate, but Robert Ornstein's *The Moral Vision of Jacobean Tragedy* (1960) and Bernard Beckerman's *Shakespeare at the Globe* (1962) may serve as examples.

At the other end of the scale, many critics have turned away from the wide approach, believing that it was more profitable to consider individual plays in their 'minute particulars'. There has been a substantial number of books on nearly every one of the tragedies, there have been many on the acknowledged masterpieces, and scores on *Hamlet*. The remainder of this essay will therefore be concerned with each of the tragedies in chronological order, and since much of the best criticism is to be found in chapters and periodicals, these will also be considered.

The most useful criticism of the early play *Titus Andronicus* is to be found in H. T. Price's defence of Shakespeare's authorship (*JEGP* 42, 1943), modern editors being too ready to suspect an alien hand. There is a good chapter in Nicholas Brooke's study of the early tragedies (see above), an article by Eugene M. Waith, 'The Metamorphosis of Violence in *Titus Andronicus*' (*Shakespeare Survey 10*, 1957), and another by Alan Sommers, 'Wilderness of Tigers' (*Essays in Criticism* 10, 1960).

Romeo and Juliet is discussed by Brooke, by A. C. Hamilton in *The Early Shakespeare* (1967), and in essays by John Lawlor (*Early Shakespeare*, edited by J. R. Brown and B. Harris, 1961), by E. C. Pettet on the imagery of the play (*English 8*, 1950), by Harry Levin, 'Form and Formality in *Romeo and Juliet*' (*Shakespeare Quarterly* 11, 1960), by Paul N. Siegel, 'Christianity and the Religion of Love in *Romeo and Juliet*' (*Shakespeare in his Time and Ours*, 1969), and by T. J. Cribb, 'The Unity of *Romeo and Juliet*' (*Shakespeare Survey 34*, 1981).

Julius Caesar was included by Ernest Schanzer as one of *The Problem Plays of Shakespeare* (1963) because of its apparent ambivalence with regard to the assassination. Adrien Bonjour in *The Structure of 'Julius Caesar'* (1958) had likewise argued that the play demands a divided response from the audience. J. I. M. Stewart in *Character and Motive in Shakespeare* (1949) offers a brilliant interpretation of the presentation of Caesar's character, with its self-imposed persona. R. A. Foakes in 'An Approach to *Julius Caesar*' (*Shakespeare Quarterly* 5, 1954) urged that the real subject is the conspiracy and its ultimate defeat rather than the question of character. John Palmer in *Political Characters of Shakespeare* (1945) analyses the idealist illusions of Brutus, and L. C. Knights discusses 'Personality and Politics in *Julius Caesar*' in an article reprinted in his *Further Explorations* (1965).

Hamlet has aroused more controversy than any other play, some of it justifying Oscar Wilde's query 'are the critics mad or only pretending to be so?' Morris Weitz showed in *Hamlet and the Philosophy of Literary Criticism* (1964) that even the better critics differed from each other because they started from different critical principles. C. S. Lewis, perturbed by conflicting assessments of the hero's character, argued in *Hamlet: the Prince or the Poem* (1943) that the differences resulted from undue concentration on the character of the hero who was, in fact, Everyman, burdened by original sin. To some critics – Madariaga in *On Hamlet* (1948) and Rebecca West in *The Court and the Castle* (1957) – Hamlet was an evil man. Others regard him as immature, neurotic, or perverted. Knight, however, modified his early judgement in the 1949 edition of *The Wheel of Fire* and Knights was gentler in his condemnation in *An Approach to Hamlet* (1960) than he had been in 'Prince Hamlet', reprinted in his *Explorations* (1946). Hamlet's defenders have included Peter Alexander who in *Hamlet Father and Son* (1955) argued that he was heroic, tough, and sensitive, and T. J. B. Spencer, G. K. Hunter and Patrick Cruttwell in Stratford-upon-Avon Studies 5, edited by J. R. Brown and B. Harris (1963). Playgoers almost unanimously support the favourable view of Hamlet's character.

Several critics, and more directors, have followed Freud in crediting Hamlet with incestuous desires, notably Ernest Jones in *Hamlet and Oedipus* (1949) and Frederic Wertham in *Dark Legend* (1947). John Dover Wilson in *What Happens in 'Hamlet'* (1935) gave a detailed account of the action of the play, with particular reference to its meaning for its original audience, who would have been aware of the conflicting views on ghosts which different characters express. To Eleanor Prosser in *Hamlet and Revenge* (1967) the Ghost was the devil in disguise, whose purpose was to damn the hero by tempting him to commit murder. John Lawlor in *The Tragic Sense in Shakespeare* (1960) provides a plausible explanation of why Hamlet, curiously, never discusses the morality of revenge; and Roy Walker in *The Time is Out of Joint* (1948) regards the play as a portrait of moral man in immoral society. Harry Levin explored in *The Question of Hamlet* (1959) the irony and questioning which pervades the play; and Nigel Alexander in *Poison, Play and Duel* (1971) examined in a wide-ranging study its central symbols. There are good essays by Francis Fergusson in *The Idea of a Theater* (1949) and by H. D. F. Kitto in *Form and Meaning in Drama* (1956). *Aspects of Hamlet*, edited by Kenneth Muir and Stanley Wells (1979), contains a collection of articles from *Shakespeare Survey*, including Clifford Leech's retrospect on recent criticism and Inga-Stina Ewbank's 'Hamlet and the Power of Words'. It should be mentioned, finally, that Harold Jenkins's edition of the play (1982) does not merely subsume his previous writings on the subject, but acts as a filter for all his predecessors. It may prove to be the standard interpretation for the last quarter of the twentieth-century, though the editions of Philip Edwards (Cambridge) and George Hibbard (Oxford) show that there can be no definitive solution of the play's manifold problems.

Othello has also aroused considerable controversy. The scathing attacks on the hero by T. S. Eliot and by F. R. Leavis for his lack of self-knowledge and brutal egotism, and the uneasy feeling expressed by Bradley and Granville-Barker that the play was depressing, have been answered by Helen Gardner, both in *The Noble Moor* (1956) and in her retrospect on recent criticism, reprinted in *Aspects of Othello* (edited by Kenneth Muir and Philip Edwards, 1977). They have been answered also by John Bayley in *Characters of Love* (1960) and by John Holloway.

The tension between the metaphysical and psychological treatment of character has been analysed by Bernard Spivack in *Shakespeare and the Allegory of Evil* (1958). Stanley E. Hyman's *Iago: Some Approaches to the Illusions of his Motivation* (1970) brings out the conflicting impressions we derive from the text of the play, and Elinor S. Shaffer showed in 'Iago's Malignity Motivated' (*Shakespeare Quarterly* 19, 1968) reasons why Coleridge should have retracted the word 'motiveless'. G. K. Hunter's *Othello and Colour Prejudice* (1968) demonstrates how Shakespeare used and overturned the association of black with evil; and in the *Aspects* volume Nigel Alexander brilliantly refutes Rymer's criticisms. Reuben A. Brower's *Hero and Saint* (1972) contains a good chapter on the play.

King Lear is now the most popular tragedy with the critics, though not with audiences. Yet there have been critics who have seriously doubted whether the play is really a masterpiece. Tolstoy notoriously thought it inferior to its source, *King Leir*. George Orwell's 'Lear, Tolstoy and the Fool' (*Selected Essays*, 1957) is an interesting reply. J. Middleton Murry in *Shakespeare* (1936) thought that *King Lear* was lacking in control and inferior to *Coriolanus*. André Gide, after seeing Olivier in the title role, commented in his journal on the badness of the play – 'How Hugo would have loved it!' A number of critics have shared Bradley's belief that, notwithstanding its greatness as a dramatic poem, it was not a good stage play. The greatness of *King Lear* has been celebrated in Helen Gardner's lecture (1967), in Maynard Mack's *King Lear in Our Time* (1965), in several contributions to *Some Facets of 'King Lear'* (edited by Rosalie L. Colie and F. T. Flahiff, 1974), in two of Knight's best chapters, and in an essay by L. C. Knights in his *Some Shakespearean Themes* (1959).

The other contention is between those critics who regard the play as essentially Christian, though set in a pagan world, and those who regard it as agnostic. In *King Lear and the Gods* (1966) W. R. Elton argued that the more intelligent members of the audience would pick up Shakespeare's suggestion that the world was not providentially governed. Nicholas Brooke in his short book on the play (1963) and in his essay on its ending in *Shakespeare: 1564– 1964*, edited by E. A. Bloom (1964), came to a similar conclusion. But Kenneth Myrick, in the same volume, writing on 'Christian Pessimism in *King Lear*', supports a Christian interpretation. So did John Danby in *Shakespeare's Doctrine of Nature* (1949) and *Poets on Fortune's Hill* (1952), Oscar J. Campbell in 'The Salvation of Lear' (*ELH* 15, 1948), and Enid Welsford in *The Fool* (1935), who remarked that the metaphysical comfort of the scriptures, though absent, is not necessarily denied. Perhaps the superiority of Kozintsev's film to Peter Brook's was partly due to his refusal to regard the play as Shakespeare's *End Game*. *Aspects of King Lear*, edited by Kenneth Muir and Stanley Wells (1982), contains a retrospect of criticism by G. R. Hibbard and eight other articles.

Macbeth has aroused less controversy, though not everyone agrees with W. C. Curry's view that Lady Macbeth was literally possessed by the spirits that tend on mortal thoughts (*Shakespeare's Philosophical Patterns*, 1937) or with W. Moelwyn Merchant's 'His fiend-like Queen' (*Aspects of Macbeth*, edited by Kenneth Muir and Philip Edwards, 1977). In the same collection there is a retrospect on recent criticism by G. K. Hunter and an article by Glynne Wickham in which he traces the influence of medieval drama on the Porter scene. H. N. Paul in *The Royal Play of Macbeth* (1950) discusses not merely the witchcraft and the topicality of the play but also King James's special interests. H. L. Rogers's *Double Profit in 'Macbeth'* (1964) makes a number of acute observations.

Timon of Athens was Wilson Knight's favourite play, but most critics are more concerned with finding the source of its weaknesses. Una Ellis-Fermor (*Review of English Studies* 8, 1942) suggested that it was left unfinished and others have argued that it was a work of collaboration. L. C. Knights, in *The Morality of Art* (edited by D. W. Jefferson, 1969), is highly critical of the play. There are useful discussions by E. A. J. Honigmann (*Shakespeare Quarterly* 12,

1961), by W. M. Merchant (*Shakespeare Quarterly* 6, 1955), and by J. C. Maxwell (*Scrutiny* 15, 1948). Rolf Soellner's *Timon of Athens* (1949) is the better of the two full-length studies.

Antony and Cleopatra, Franklin Dickey assures us in *Not Wisely But Too Well* (1957), would have been regarded by Jacobeans as a play about people who sacrificed duty to sensuality. He quotes from many condemnations of the lovers, but two poets read by Shakespeare, Chaucer and Daniel, took a different view. L. C. Knights in *Some Shakespearean Themes* (1959) argued that Shakespeare in the end condemned the lovers. J. Dover Wilson, in his edition of the play (1950), Knight in *The Imperial Theme*, and Robert Speaight in *Nature in Shakespearian Tragedy* (1955), all defend the lovers. The conflict of views led Ernest Schanzer to class the play as one of *The Problem Plays of Shakespeare* and John Danby in *Poets on Fortune's Hill* argues that Shakespeare is deliberately ambivalent. Robert Ornstein discusses 'The ethic of the imagination' in *Later Shakespeare*, edited by J. R. Brown and B. Harris (1966). Bradley's essay in *Oxford Lectures* (1909) is still one of the best things written on the play.

Bradley also wrote on *Coriolanus* (1912). Other criticism of continuing interest includes a chapter by Una Ellis-Fermor in *Shakespeare the Dramatist* (1961), J. Middleton Murry's 'A forgotten heroine of Shakespeare' (*Countries of the Mind*, 1922), and R. F. Hill's article in *Essays and Studies* 17 (1964). Some of the most interesting criticism has centred on political content – Brents Stirling's *The Populace in Shakespeare* (1949), E. C. Pettet's '*Coriolanus* and the Midlands Insurrection of 1607' (*Shakespeare Survey 13*, 1960), Norman Rabkin's '*Coriolanus*: the Tragedy of Politics' (*Shakespeare Quarterly* 17, 1966), and John Palmer's shrewd assessment in *Political Characters of Shakespeare*.

13c Twentieth-century Shakespeare criticism: the histories

ALTHOUGH too extensive and varied to be covered adequately in a brief survey, twentieth-century criticism of Shakespeare's histories has probably been more uniform in its interests than that of other groups of plays. The central critical effort – sometimes explicit, sometimes implicit – has been to define the genre: to discover the qualities of the histories that transcend their remarkable differences in structure and tone and that distinguish them from Shakespeare's other works. The most influential critics have concentrated upon three distinctive features: the patriotism of the plays (they are all English histories), their preoccupation with politics, and their sequential nature. Although many critics have viewed the plays from all three perspectives, it may be helpful to consider these singly, for each has its own history and raises its own set of questions.

In the century's first book on the histories, *The English Chronicle Play* (1902), Felix E. Schelling takes an emphatically patriotic approach. Distinguishing the 'chronicle play', both Shakespearian and non-Shakespearian, from the Italianate and neo-classical strains in Elizabethan drama, Schelling traces its origins to such native traditions as the morality and miracle plays, folk plays on historical themes, and pageantry; its animating spirit he attributes to the surge of nationalism that accompanied the defeat of the Spanish Armada. Although critical of the genre's tendencies towards formlessness – at its best, as in Shakespeare, the chronicle achieves epic, not dramatic unity – Schelling celebrates its patriotic energy. 'The Chronicle Play', he asserts, was 'distinctively English. Its growth was indigenous, its spirit national' (p. 2).

This view of the histories as a kind of patriotic drama dominated the first half of the century and achieved its most poignant expression, as one might expect, in England during the First and Second World Wars. The patriotism of the plays is stressed by J. A. R. Marriott in *English History in Shakespeare* (1918), a work dedicated to bringing Shakespeare's message on 'national unity and social solidarity' (p. 293) to a country torn by war without and dissension within; by H. B. Charlton in a brief but rewarding lecture, *Shakespeare, Politics and Politicians* (1929); by G. Wilson Knight in *The Olive and the Sword* (1944); and by J. Dover Wilson in *The Fortunes of Falstaff* (1943) and his Cambridge editions of the histories, particularly *Henry V* (1947), in which he asserts that Henry's words before Agincourt and Churchill's after the Battle of Britain 'come from the same national mint' (p. xxxi).

The decline of the patriotic approach owes much to shifts in the political climate after World War II, in both England and the United States. It may owe something as well, paradoxically, to the century's most influential study of the histories, E. M. W. Tillyard's *Shakespeare's History Plays* (1944). Although Tillyard repeatedly acknowledges the importance of patriotism in the plays, his major concerns lie elsewhere – in their politics and unity as a series. Tillyard's view of Shakespeare's patriotism, moreover, differs widely from Schelling's. Whereas Schelling's Shakespeare is a popular dramatist, drawing his inspiration from folk plays and folk sentiment, Tillyard's is a learned dramatist, drawing, for the most part, upon political and historical doctrine. The relative indifference of critics after Tillyard to the patriotic dimension of the histories, particularly their formal links with popular traditions, has had some unfortunate effects, among them a tendency to over-intellectualize the plays, to reduce drama to dogma. The notion that the 'real hero of the English history-play is England' (p.11), as Charlton puts it, contains an important insight with wide-ranging implications, only a few of which have been developed.

Since the Second World War, the dominant approach to the histories has been political. A number of earlier critics were conscious of the political concerns of the histories – Charlton, for example, saw the Henriad as a study of kingship – but they searched the plays most often for political lessons timeless and universal in scope. In the 1940s, however, the political approach became rigorously historical. Untouched by the 'new criticism' that dominated certain fields of literary study, the most influential critics of this period assumed that Shakespeare's histories were didactic political dramas and that their messages could be decoded through a careful study of Elizabethan political thought. This faith in the capacity of historical scholarship to produce definitive interpretations of works of art pervades the writings of such critics as J. Dover Wilson but was most fully developed by L. B. Campbell and E. M. W. Tillyard, whose studies have been at the centre of critical debate on the histories since their publication.

In *Shakespeare's 'Histories'* (1947) Campbell defines Shakespeare's purpose as that of every Elizabethan historian – to use history as a mirror for contemporary politics. Campbell places each of the histories in an immediate political context, analysing *Richard II*, for example, as a topical play about the 'problem of the deposition of a king' (p. 211) and *1* and *2 Henry IV* as studies of the problem of rebellion. Tillyard's approach, in *Shakespeare's History Plays* (1944), complements Campbell's, for he is less concerned with topical issues than with political doctrine and its philosophical context, the so-called Elizabethan 'world picture' that placed so high a premium on principles of order and degree. The Shakespeare that emerges from both studies is a didactic dramatist, learned in the political and historical thought of his day, and committed to specific political doctrines, such as that of non-rebellion, promulgated by the Tudor monarchy. Although no longer widely accepted, this view held sway for many years in lecture halls and popular introductions. With some qualifications, it has influenced profoundly many important studies, among them Irving Ribner's *The English History Play in the Age of Shakespeare* (1957; 1965), the first major study of the entire genre since Schelling's; M. M. Reese's *The Cease of Majesty* (1961); and David Bevington's *Tudor Drama and Politics* (1968).

The impact of Campbell and Tillyard upon later critics can be traced in three lines of attack that gathered momentum in the 1960s and have persisted ever since. One approach has been to show that the 'world picture' they created is simplistic, because it represents either the lowest common denominator of Elizabethan thought – the *Mirror for Magistrates* rather than Bacon or Machiavelli – or, worse, Tudor propaganda. Instead of finding in the plays reflections of Tudor commonplaces or orthodoxies, these critics have found in them the scepticism, tensions, and equivocations that characterized Elizabethan debate on central political problems. Two useful studies of this kind focus on the question of rebellion in *Richard II*: Ernest William Talbert's *The Problem of Order* (1962), and Wilbur Sanders's *The Dramatist and the Received Idea* (1968), which also includes a discussion of *Richard III*. A more general and more recent study, Moody E. Prior's *The Drama of Power* (1973), provides a balanced assessment of historical approaches since Campbell and Tillyard.

Critics adopting an Elizabethan perspective towards the histories have generally assumed that they reflect the political thought of the time, whether simple or complex, orthodox or unorthodox. A second line of attack, however, has questioned this assumption, asserting the independence of Shakespeare and the difference between drama and political doctrine. In these studies one often detects the influence of the 'new criticism', with its emphasis upon imagery, tone, and ambivalence. One of the earliest of such critics, and certainly the wittiest, was A. P. Rossiter, whose widely anthologized lectures, 'Ambivalence: the dialectic of the histories' (1951) and 'Angel with horns: the unity of *Richard III*' (1953), express his need for an approach 'less Tudor-moral'. Resisting what he considers the reductive tendencies of the historical critics, Rossiter probes the plays for ironies and ambiguities that disrupt the very orthodoxies they contain; the characteristic political attitude of the plays, he contends, is ambivalence, the simultaneous acceptance of two valid but incompatible judgements. Perhaps the single most compelling argument against the 'Tudor-moral' approach is provided by Robert Ornstein, who, in *A Kingdom for a Stage* (1972), criticizes not only the over-simplifications of historical scholarship but its 'implicit refusal . . . to grant that the ultimate standard for the interpretation of art is aesthetic' (p. 8). In recent years the aesthetic dimension of the histories has attracted increasing attention, but the critical bias remains historical.

A third, complementary reaction against the 'Tudor-moral' approach has been to resist its tendency to restrict Shakespeare's political relevance to his own age, an age characterized, as Tillyard put it, by doctrines both 'remote and queer' (p. 146). Although some critics, such as Michael Manheim in *The Weak King Dilemma in the Shakespearean History Play* (1973), have claimed a special contemporary relevance for the histories, most have sought to generalize their political issues in ways that highlight their universality. Implicit in many studies of individual plays, this tendency is perhaps most fully articulated in several essays by L. C. Knights, the most recent being 'Shakespeare and History' (1978). Knights argues not only against viewing the histories as mere illustrations of Tudor political thought, and thus neglecting the universality that ensures their continuing interest, but against restricting their scope to politics. Shakespeare, he asserts, explores 'political attitudes and acts that are no more merely political than they are merely of historical interest' (p. 395). In his study of *Richard II* in *Shakespeare and the Common Understanding* (1967), Norman Rabkin takes a similar approach, arguing for the universality of Shakespeare's political themes and, in his tragic conception of political action, his ultimate transcendence of politics. The political approach to the plays has thus tended to return, with more critical sophistication and historical understanding, to assumptions common during the first few decades of the century.

Unless writing on *King John* or *Henry VIII*, all critics of the history plays, whether defining them as patriotic or political, have had to consider their third distinctive feature, their sequential nature. Although written in reverse chronological order, Shakespeare's two tetralogies span the history of England from the deposition of Richard II to the ascendancy of the first of the Tudors, Henry VII, at Bosworth Field. Early critics, such as Schelling, frequently called attention to the epic sweep of the histories, but few explored their continuities in any detail. Doubts about the authorship and order of composition of the first tetralogy precluded serious study of its unity until the 1940s, but even the second tetralogy, unaffected by such questions, provoked little sustained interest as a sequence.

The main impulse to explore the continuities among the plays came from early studies of one of Shakespeare's chief historical sources, Hall's *Chronicle*, which records the very span of history that Shakespeare dramatizes in the two tetralogies. In 'The influence of Hall on Shakespeare's English historical plays' (1936), for example, W. Gordon Zeeveld credits Shakespeare with a 'new dramatic expression of the theme by which Hall imposed unity on fifteenth-century history' (p. 319); the theme is that announced in Hall's Preface, the 'mischief' caused to kingdoms by 'intestine division'. Tillyard took this idea one step further, arguing that Hall's concern with 'intestine division' expresses not merely a political theme but a providential view of history. According to Tillyard, Hall's *Chronicle* depicts the working out of God's curse against England for the deposition and murder of Richard II – a curse lifted temporarily during the heroic reign of Henry V but not expiated until the triumph of Henry VII and the Tudor monarchy. This so-called 'Tudor myth', argues Tillyard, was the plan by which Shakespeare unified eight histories into a national epic. Tillyard's Shakespeare is thus not merely a patriot and political thinker but a historian.

Tillyard's attempt to show the epic unity of the *Richard II – Richard III* series has received far less support than his more general interpretation of the political and philosophical background. Some critics have opposed his view on the basis of the order of composition of the plays; others have criticized his simplistic treatment of Elizabethan conceptions of Providence; still others have found no unequivocal evidence of the curse he describes in the plays themselves. The question has been put to rest, it seems, by Henry Ansgar Kelly, who, in *Divine Providence in the England of Shakespeare's Histories* (1970), concludes that the scheme Tillyard attributes to Hall is 'an ex post facto Platonic Form' created by Tillyard's own 'synthesizing energy' (p. 298).

Despite its limited acceptance, Tillyard's ambitious effort has encouraged critics to look more closely at connections among the plays. Studies of a single tetralogy, particularly the second, have become increasingly common – usually with a focus upon political themes, but sometimes, if only implicitly, with an attention to underlying conceptions of historical process. An unfortunate side effect of this tendency has been a relative neglect of *King John*, usually studied as a point of transition between the first and second series, and *Henry VIII*, which, until very recently, has attracted mainly disparaging commentary or denials of complete Shakespearian authorship.

The growth at mid-century of a consensus in favour of Shakespeare's authorship of the Henry VI plays prompted critics to revalue these early histories, often condemned for their formlessness. One of the most influential of these reassessments, after that of Tillyard, has been Hereward T. Price's monograph, *Construction in Shakespeare* (1951), in which he analyses *1 Henry VI* as a completely new dramatic form, based not on Aristotle's notion of unity of action but on a distinctly Elizabethan unity of design. Appreciation of the artistry of the early histories has also been furthered by J. P. Brockbank in 'The Frame of Disorder – *Henry VI*' (1961), A. C. Hamilton in *The Early Shakespeare* (1967), and Emrys Jones in *The Origins of Shakespeare* (1977). Two studies have sought to define, from different points of view, the unity of the first tetralogy as a whole: in *Shakespeare's Heroical Histories* (1971), David Riggs interprets the series from a political perspective, as Shakespeare's testing and eventual abandonment of the conception of heroic kingship he inherited from the humanistic tradition; in *Patterns of Decay* (1975), Edward Berry traces a series of themes that define the stages of England's disintegration after the death of Henry V. The early histories have thus found a secure if modest place in the canon; their reputation has been enhanced, moreover, by widely acclaimed Stratford productions in 1963 (as *The Wars of the Roses*, heavily adapted) and 1977.

Neither the greatness nor the essential unity of the second tetralogy has ever been much in doubt, but interpretations have been so many and various as to make summary impossible. Fortunately, anthologies of criticism on these plays abound. They include William A. Armstrong's *Shakespeare's Histories: An Anthology of Modern Criticism* (1972); R. J. Dorius's *Discussions of Shakespeare's Histories: 'Richard II' to 'Henry V'* (1964); and Eugene M. Waith's *Shakespeare: The Histories* (1965). Volumes on individual plays include Casebooks on *Richard II* (ed. Nicholas Brooke, 1973), *Henry IV, Parts One and Two* (ed. G. K. Hunter, 1970), and *Henry V* (ed. Michael Quinn, 1969). Related volumes are Paul M. Cubeta's *Twentieth Century Interpretations of 'Richard II'* (1971), R. J. Dorius's *Twentieth Century Interpretations of 'Henry IV, Part One'* (1970), David P. Young's *Twentieth Century Interpretations of 'Henry IV, Part Two'* (1968), and Ronald Berman's *Twentieth Century Interpretations of 'Henry V'* (1968).

A useful touchstone for interpretations of this tetralogy – indeed, for interpretations of all the histories – is the scene in which Hal rejects Falstaff at the end of *2 Henry IV*. Every approach brought to bear on the histories, it seems, finds its severest test in this episode, which has attracted fine criticism from some of the century's major critics, such as A. C. Bradley, J. Dover Wilson, William Empson, and C. L. Barber.

Most critics have approached the second tetralogy from the double perspective of H. B. Charlton, for whom the *Henry IV–Henry V* plays were 'psychologically, studies in kings', but dramatically, 'views of kingship' (p. 14). In *Shakespeare from 'Richard II' to 'Henry V'* (1957), Derek Traversi takes a predominantly psychological approach, finding the basic question of the series to be: 'What are the personal, as distinct from the political, qualities that go to the making of a king?' (p. 4). Although refined by later critics, Una Ellis-Fermor's 'Shakespeare's Political Plays' (1945) remains a classic statement of a more complex and influential view. Ellis-Fermor traces throughout the histories the manner in which Shakespeare builds towards a 'composite figure – that of the statesman-king' (p. 47); the process culminates in the character of Henry V, whose appearance coincides, ironically, with Shakespeare's discovery of the limitations of his own ideal, a discovery that anticipates the great tragedies. Broader studies of the tetralogy have adopted a variety of perspectives. In 'The Henriad: Shakespeare's Major History Plays' (1970), Alvin B. Kernan provides an original synthesis of many unifying patterns, ranging from the historical (a shift from the Middle Ages to the modern world) to the psychological (a shift from identity as fixed to identity as a temporary role). The increasing tendency to stage the histories in series has given this kind of interpretation a lively relevance to the theatre.

By far the most controversial of the histories, *Henry V* remains at the centre of a long-standing critical debate. At one extreme are critics, such as J. Dover Wilson, who celebrate Henry V as Shakespeare's ideal king and the play as a great dramatic epic. Others, less satisfied by the play than Wilson, see Shakespeare aspiring towards a conception of heroic kingship but failing to portray it with conviction. Still others, satisfied by the play but unconvinced by Wilson's heroic idealism, detect a vein of irony in Shakespeare's treatment of Henry, either from his first appearance or upon his rejection of Falstaff, when he can be seen as turning away his full humanity for the sake of political expediency. At the opposite extreme are a substantial minority of critics who, although as satisfied by the play as Wilson, view it not as epic but as something close to satire. Probably the most influential spokesman for this approach has been Harold C. Goddard; in *The Meaning of Shakespeare* (1951), Goddard dissects Henry's flaws as both man and king, finding him 'too close for comfort to Machiavelli's ideal prince' (I, 267). The dilemma posed by these radically divergent interpretations is outlined forcefully by Norman Rabkin in *Shakespeare and the Problem of Meaning* (1981). Rabkin concludes that the division of the critics reflects Shakespeare's own profound ambivalence.

The controversy over *Henry V*, it seems, has reached the point of diminishing returns. Although more extreme than most other debates about the plays, it can be taken as illustrative, for it proceeds from assumptions that have long dominated studies of the genre. Bounded by the history of ideas on one side and the 'new criticism' on the other, for the most part, criticism of the histories has remained within a relatively narrow range of interests. If criticism of *Henry V* stands at an impasse, it is because the genre as a whole requires new approaches.

In recent years, encouragingly, new questions have been asked and old ones redirected in promising new ways. In *Threshold of a Nation* (1979), for example, Philip Edwards has resurrected the patriotic view of the histories, carefully distinguishing between patriotism and nationalism, and placing the plays, particularly *Henry V*, within the broad and illuminating context of Elizabethan expansionism. Although less original than Edwards's study, John Wilders's *The Lost Garden: A View of Shakespeare's English and Roman History Plays* (1978) and David Scott Kastan's *Shakespeare and the Shapes of Time* (1982) have also widened the context for criticism – the former by defining Shakespeare's conception of history in relation to both the English and Roman plays, the latter by defining the histories, tragedies, and romances as genres embodying different conceptions of time. Several interesting feminist approaches have appeared of late, the most revealing that of Coppélia Kahn in *Man's Estate* (1981); Kahn combines feminist and psychoanalytic perspectives to explore the problem of masculine identity in this overwhelmingly masculine genre. Although there has been no major theatrical study of the histories since

Arthur Colby Sprague's *Shakespeare's Histories: Plays for the Stage* (1964), recent critics have become increasingly concerned with theatrical questions, aided, in part, by Sally Beauman's fascinating edition of *The Royal Shakespeare Company's Production of 'Henry V'* (1976).

The closest thing to a trend in recent criticism is represented by three metadramatic studies: Joseph A. Porter's *The Drama of Speech Acts* (1979), James L. Calderwood's *Metadrama in Shakespeare's Henriad* (1979), and John W. Blanpied's *Time and the Artist in Shakespeare's English Histories* (1983). In each of these studies, political affairs become, to borrow Calderwood's words, 'metaphors of art' (p. 4). Basing his approach upon the 'speech act' theory of the British philosopher J. L. Austin, Porter examines language and speech action in the second tetralogy, concluding that the series 'figures, enacts, manifests the rise of the genre of drama out of, and in opposition to, nondramatic literature' (p. 177). Calderwood too focuses upon language as a unifying theme in the Henriad, tracing the shift in the series from a sacramental to a rhetorical view of language. Blanpied surveys both tetralogies, concentrating more generally upon 'the evolving relationship of subject to medium, history to drama' (p. 12).

Interest in the history plays thus remains strong, both in the theatre and in the study. If there are signs that the major critical issues, debated most compellingly from about 1940 to 1975, have been exhausted, there are also signs that a number of these issues are being redefined in fruitful ways. And although the histories have been relatively untouched by the more venturesome critical theories of the past forty years, some of the more recent studies are demanding that readers question established assumptions and methods of interpretation. It is hard to escape the conclusion that we have reached the end of a tradition of critical thought regarding the histories, and that the genre as a whole, if indeed genre itself remains a viable framework, requires new questions and new critical models. Given the enduring vitality of the plays, one suspects that they will come.

14   Shakespeare on the twentieth-century stage

ON 10 January 1900, Herbert Beerbohm Tree mounted an elaborate production of *A Midsummer Night's Dream* at Her Majesty's Theatre, London. The scenery was representational: on carpets of moss, among bluebell thickets, ran live rabbits. The acting was declamatory, and Oberon, played by a woman, sang the more lyrical passages. The incidental music was Mendelssohn's, the epitome of nineteenth-century romanticism. This performance was an extreme example of the late nineteenth-century manner of staging Shakespeare, which placed great emphasis on spectacular scenery, with cuts made in the text to allow time for the sets to be changed. Tree was an actor–manager in the tradition of Henry Irving at the Lyceum Theatre. The Lyceum itself, however, was occupied in early 1900 by Frank Benson.

Benson, too, was an actor–manager, though of a somewhat different kind. He ran a touring company which worked primarily in the provinces, especially at Stratford-upon-Avon, where Benson provided the annual Shakespeare season each April. In those days this season was very short, between one and three weeks, involving the minimum of rehearsals and a different play almost every night. In 1910, a short summer season was added; it was not until 1933 that the two were merged into a continuous season of nearly five months, the beginnings of the present ten-month season at Stratford. Touring and financial considerations virtually ruled out elaborate scenery like Tree's, but Benson used painted representational cloths, and added decorations of other kinds to the text. His *Richard II*, for instance, contained not only his own star performance as a conscious artist–king, described in a famous review by C. E. Montague,[1] but also the incident, derived from Froissart, where Richard's greyhound deserts him for Bolingbroke. This interpolation was also employed by Tree in his *Richard II* of 1903; Benson was clearly a man of his time.

William Poel was not. In February 1900, while Benson was performing at the Lyceum, Poel staged the First ('Bad') Quarto of *Hamlet* in the Carpenters' Hall, London. Both the text and the venue are significant. He chose the Bad Quarto because of its closeness to Elizabethan performance, particularly in its stage directions, and he tried to reproduce the conditions of those performances by using a permanent two-levelled set, an unlocalized platform stage, and Elizabethan dress. But the fact that he was working in a hall rather than in a theatre helps to underline the drawbacks of Poel's experiments: he lacked theatrical and financial resources, he engaged amateur actors whom he drilled to reproduce mechanically his own phrasing of the speeches, and he made cuts as arbitrarily as the actor–managers. It was easy, therefore, for drama critics to dismiss his experiments as the work of an unprofessional eccentric. There could be no such dismissal of Harley Granville-Barker's productions at the Savoy Theatre between 1912 and 1914.

Although Granville-Barker was an admirer of Poel and had acted for him, he did not follow Poel in attempting to recreate Elizabethan conditions; instead he sought to capture their effect. He provocatively rejected the kind of design then in vogue, substituting coloured curtains and hard white light for Tree's 'atmospheric', realistic settings. The speaking was rapid, and the action continuous on a stage built out over the conventional orchestra pit. Granville-Barker aimed to make his audience concentrate on virtually complete texts by means of startlingly original effects, notably in *A Midsummer Night's Dream*, where the fairies were painted gold, and their oriental poses, shuffling movements, and mechanical gestures suggested the exotic world of Diaghilev's Russian ballets.

Not surprisingly, Granville-Barker's productions aroused fierce controversy. Some felt that his innovations focused attention on the text, others that they were so eccentric as to distract from it. What is quite clear is that, already early in the century, it was the director rather than the actor–manager upon whom critical reaction was fixed. In the period between the wars, directors were equally influential and varied in their approach. Between 1921 and 1958, Nugent Monck directed the entire Shakespeare canon, using amateur actors, at his Maddermarket Theatre, Norwich, in simulated Elizabethan conditions. At the opposite extreme, from 1926 to 1933, Terence Gray's Cambridge Festival productions indulged in deliberately outrageous exhibitionism. The cast of *Henry VIII* appeared like the royal figures on a pack of playing cards, and at the end the baby princess Elizabeth was thrown into the audience.

Experimenting in a more intelligent way, Barry Jackson at the Birmingham Repertory Theatre in the 1920s began the vogue for presenting the plays in modern dress. The aim was to make the plays more immediate by bringing them closer, if only in terms of clothing, to the experience of the audience. The danger was that, in order to be consistent with the new period, details would take over and draw undesirable attention to themselves. The jarring contrast between the Elizabethan text and its modern 'equivalent' often trivialized the original. This happened in Jackson's *Macbeth* (1928) when the murderers climbed through a diamond-paned window to kill Lady Macduff as she took afternoon tea in her 1920s sitting-room.

A decade later at Stratford-upon-Avon, the Russian director Theodore Komisarjevsky set the same play in a modern nightmare world of steel helmets and machine-guns; Banquo's 'ghost' was a shadow on the wall. Komisarjevsky also staged several of the comedies at Stratford in a fantasticated jumble of different periods. These productions are inevitably given prominence by stage historians, because they were the ones which attracted attention at the time. But it is important to keep a sense of perspective, and to remember that they were greatly outnumbered by straightforward, workmanlike stagings which no doubt gave great pleasure at Lilian Baylis's Old Vic Theatre in London, and at Stratford-upon-Avon, several of whose directors of the inter-war years had gained their early theatrical experience with William Poel.

In the 1930s, and indeed in the forties and fifties, theatrical interpretation of Shakespeare owed as much to actors as directors, and to two actors in particular: John Gielgud and Laurence Olivier. Olivier himself usefully contrasts their styles: 'When I was playing Romeo I was carrying a torch, I was trying to sell realism in Shakespeare. I believed . . . that Johnny was . . . paying attention – to the exclusion of the earth – to all music, all lyricism, and I was for the other side of the coin.'[2] Gielgud's natural gift for speaking verse was invaluable for Hamlet and Richard II, two of his most celebrated roles in the thirties. His very fluency was sometimes a disadvantage: he could fall into a mannered delivery, a kind of 'singing' style which appeared to place sound above sense. This was what Olivier objected to; but in general Gielgud used the shape of the verse to bring out the sense, notably as Prospero in *The Tempest*. This is a dangerous part because it can tempt an actor – especially an actor as fluent as Gielgud – to treat its famous set-pieces as so many 'arias'. Gielgud successfully avoided this, stressing, by the thrilling emphasis he gave to the phrase '*Graves* at my command / Have wak'd their sleepers, op'd, and let 'em forth' (5.1.48–9), the awesome, terrifying aspect of Prospero's 'rough' magic at the moment he rejected it.

It is perhaps unfair to dwell upon Gielgud's delivery of a particular phrase, since his great achievement was to sustain the shape and flow of his speeches. It was Olivier who adopted a jagged delivery, breaking the verse into fragments, and often arbitrarily stressing single words. There is a permanent record of several of Olivier's famous roles of the thirties and forties – Hamlet, Henry V, and Richard III – in the films he subsequently made of them, as he did of his much later Othello. But the dangers and achievements of Olivier's approach are particularly well captured by Richard David in his description of what was clearly a remarkable performance, Olivier's Titus Andronicus at Stratford in 1955:

At his first entry one might almost have accused him of mugging, so hard did he work with swallowing and pursing, wrinkling and charming to build up, on the bare bones of the part, a Great Man, cantankerous, choleric and at the same time compelling . . . The great central scene, where Titus stands

> as one upon a rock
> Environ'd with a wilderness of sea . . .

so grew and proliferated in the astonishing variety of his reactions to disaster (the enormous physical agony of the severed hand was almost unbearable) that with the crowning frenzy of 'I am the sea' Olivier seemed to . . . become . . . madness itself.[3]

Although these two styles, the lyrical and the realistic – to use Olivier's over-simple but convenient terms – were the main influences on Shakespearian acting until the end of the 1950s, there were obviously many other notable performances, in particular from Edith Evans, Peggy Ashcroft, and Ralph Richardson, and also from Donald Wolfit, who formed his own touring company in which, following the tradition of the actor–managers, he himself was very much the star. As directors, Gielgud and Olivier moved with the times – so much so that Gielgud's celebrated 1949 production of *Much Ado About Nothing*, revived frequently during the following ten years, gives an excellent idea of the dominant approach to Shakespeare production in the fifties.

In his book *Stage Directions*, Gielgud says that he 'had always imagined *Much Ado* with scenery and dresses of the Boccaccio period, the action taking place, perhaps, on a terrace above the city, out of doors'. Accordingly, his set was an enclosed garden, but varied 'ingeniously so that it could be opened on hinges by attendants, and the screen walls thus became an unrealistic interior, with the trees of the garden and the sky still showing over the top . . . while the

16   *Much Ado About Nothing*, Shakespeare Memorial Theatre, Stratford-upon-Avon, 1950. Centre: Peggy Ashcroft as Beatrice, John Gielgud as Benedick

penthouse in the centre at the back was finally opened like a Chinese box by the pages and became the interior of the church'.[4] This set was a permanent structure with 'ingenious' variations. It combined a basically pictorial quality which ultimately derived from nineteenth-century spectacle with a more modern ingenuity which enabled the action to proceed without pauses. It was typical of stagings in the 1950s at Stratford, under the general direction of Anthony Quayle and Glen Byam Shaw, and also at the Old Vic under Michael Benthall, where all the plays in the First Folio were given between 1953 and 1958.

To Gielgud, *Much Ado About Nothing* was 'above all a play of the Renaissance', so he was amazed 'to find it . . . decked out in Victorian or Regency scenery and costumes'. Indeed, the great majority of productions of this play since 1958 have been set in the nineteenth or early twentieth century. As with use of modern dress, the motive for the change of period was usually to make the play seem more accessible. The argument runs that a play which depends upon distinctions of rank or class, and upon different concepts of honour, may be communicated more clearly to a modern audience in terms of nineteenth- or early twentieth-century 'officers and gentlemen', where such distinctions can be expressed visually through uniforms and so on, than in Renaissance costumes, where they cannot. In much the most successful of these updatings, at Stratford-upon-Avon in 1976, John Barton set *Much Ado About Nothing* in Imperial India. This sharpened the distinction between the military and civilian worlds: as Anne Barton put it in the programme, 'the offence done not only to his honour but to that of Don Pedro, his superior officer, is all that counts' to Claudio. It provided a genuine context in which Claudio's treatment of Hero could be understood, if not condoned, whereas Gielgud's production had deliberately glossed over such problems with 'the romantic fantasy of [his] imagination'. And the change of period in no way hampered Beatrice and Benedick: it was hard to imagine how the famous names of the past could possibly have played these parts better than Judi Dench and Donald Sinden.

A play which has been illuminated still more by similar updating is *All's Well That Ends Well*. Tyrone Guthrie in 1953 and 1959, and Trevor Nunn in 1981–3 created an extraordinarily detailed, instantly recognizable Edwardian world of rigid protocol, in which class distinctions were of paramount importance. This vividly emphasized the crucial social gulf between Bertram and Helena, and so provided the perfect context to motivate the intensity of Helena's despair. The Countess of Rossillion, grandly cast by both directors – Edith Evans by Guthrie, Peggy Ashcroft by Nunn – was the gracious representative of an elegant aristocratic society soon to disappear forever in the face of two world wars. But whereas Guthrie shattered the Edwardian world he had so fastidiously created by locating the 'Tuscan wars' amid the 'Desert Rats' of the Second World War, Nunn sustained the chosen period by setting both

Parolles's downfall and Bertram's attempted seduction of Diana in a marvellously atmospheric café close to the front, thus binding the two intrigues
closely together.

Guthrie's second version of his production, like Nunn's first (which then
moved to London and to Broadway), was at Stratford-upon-Avon; but
Guthrie's 1953 version inaugurated, with *Richard III*, the Canadian
Shakespeare Festival at Stratford, Ontario. Guthrie had directed frequently at
the Old Vic and other conventional theatres during the thirties and forties, but
when he was given the chance to launch a new theatre building, not just a new
festival, he seized the opportunity to create an open stage based roughly on the
Elizabethan model. Although modifications have been made to the Ontario
stage several times since 1953 – when it was erected inside a huge tent; the
actual theatre building dates from 1957 – the basic design has remained the
same: a huge platform juts out into the audience, at the back of which steps
lead to an upper level supported by pillars. The chief problem which this stage
presents to the actor is that, with the audience positioned in a wide arc on three
sides of him, it is impossible to address all the audience all the time. Guthrie
was aware of the problem from the start, and he advised the actor to divide up
long speeches into sections, 'turning slowly, facing now this, now that, part of
the house'.[5] This inevitably has disastrous consequences in terms of both
continuity and audibility, for as soon as the actor turns to left or right, the third
of the audience from whom he turns away lose the thread of the speech, and
often the actual words as well.

This aggressively uncompromising stage has been used in strikingly
different ways to point Shakespeare's text, notably by John Hirsch, director of
the festival from 1981 to 1985. In *The Tempest*, for instance, Hirsch exploited
the vast emptiness of the huge stage to emphasize Prospero's sense of loss
once he has renounced his magic, his feeling of isolation on 'this bare island'.
In *A Midsummer Night's Dream*, on the other hand, he completely transformed
the stark platform into a wood by filling the stage and balcony from floor to
roof with slender midsummer saplings that sprouted brown autumn leaves, an
apt visual equivalent for the seasonal chaos which Titania describes and which
mirrors the chaotic relationships among both fairies and mortals. This set still
allowed room for the human tensions to be acted out in a full-scale opening
battle fought by Theseus and his army of conquistadors against Hippolyta and
her Amazons, a conflict repeated in the quarrel between Oberon and Titania,
played by the same actors. Titania's extended account of the seasonal
confusions caused by that quarrel achieved additional impact and urgency in a
context which stressed tension so strongly, and in which the design
harmonized with her language instead of blatantly contradicting it, as in many
modern productions. The 'gentle concord' which resolves those tensions was
matched by a stroke of sheer theatrical magic: the consecrated field-dew with
which the fairies blessed the palace was reflected in shimmering light not only

over the entire acting area but over the roof of the theatre as well. This stage provides opportunities for stunning effects to directors with the skill and confidence to employ them without overwhelming the actors or distracting from the text.[6]

Numerous outstanding productions in Ontario have served to remind the British, whose attitude to Shakespearian production is frequently insular, that there is a world elsewhere, a point also vividly made by Giorgio Strehler's production of *The Tempest* with the Piccolo Teatro of Milan (1978–84). Strehler and his distinguished designer, Luciano Damiani, characteristically silhouetted important dramatic moments, such as Antonio's attempt to kill Alonso, against a cyclorama suffused with glowing light. Theatrical devices were openly paraded in order to present Prospero's magic as a series of overtly theatrical 'shows', and, as the practical executant of Prospero's art, Ariel's was the key performance. He frequently descended on an obvious, undisguised flying-wire from which at the end Prospero unhooked him and set him free. In a white skull cap, white face make-up, and billowing white costume, Ariel was part androgynous spirit, part *commedia dell'arte* pierrot. As he delicately accompanied the 'sounds, and sweet airs' of the island on his tabor, Caliban stretched himself sensuously on the floor to listen, while the clowns sat slumped in a maudlin alcoholic stupor: a strange harmony took over the stage, from which the clowns were not excluded. What distinguishes Damiani's designs and lighting from so many British productions is a technical mastery of exceptionally beautiful visual effects whose purpose is interpretative, not merely decorative. Visual distinction of a rather different kind has been achieved by another Italian, Franco Zeffirelli. Realism was the keynote of his *Romeo and Juliet* at the Old Vic in 1960. The rival gangs lounged and brawled amid peeling, crumbling Italian back streets, and Mercutio was stabbed by accident. This was the realism of the Italian cinema of the time. It served the prose well but not the verse, much of which was cut, and an original but only half-successful stage production found its true medium in Zeffirelli's subsequent film version.

There have been Shakespeare festivals at Stratford, Connecticut, and in Central Park, New York, directed by Joseph Papp, where *The Taming of the Shrew* made no concessions to modern unease regarding male chauvinism and female subjection. Petruchio's 'She is my goods, my chattels' (3.2.226) was uncompromisingly provocative, and it duly roused its audience to excited reactions both for and against such sentiments. Shakespeare was no remote classic for this audience, nor for those attending various European performances of *Coriolanus* which have provoked completely opposed ideological responses, reflecting the even-handed quality of Shakespeare's most political play. At the Comédie Française in 1932, there were right-wing protests against the democratic sentiments, while at the opposite end of the political spectrum, Brecht's adaptation for the East German Berliner Ensemble

17   *A Midsummer Night's Dream*, Stratford Festival, Canada, 1984
(i)   Patricia Conolly as Titania

presented Coriolanus objectively as a man indispensable in war but thereafter, as his mother puts it in this version, merely 'a threat, mortal to all'.

Back in England, the story of Shakespearian production since 1960 is chiefly the story of the Royal Shakespeare Company. The Old Vic Theatre was used by the National Theatre for the first thirteen years of its life, from 1963 to 1976, when the National's own building was ready. Partly because Shakespeare is only one of the many dramatists whose work is given there, the National's Shakespearian record has been unimpressive, with the arguable exception of Olivier's Othello (1964), played as an exhibitionistic self-deceiver after F. R. Leavis's analysis.

The Royal Shakespeare Company was created by Peter Hall. When he became director of the Shakespeare Memorial Theatre in 1960 (renamed the Royal Shakespeare Theatre the following year), he wanted a real company, rather than the *ad hoc* group of actors which had, until then, been assembled

(ii)　Nicholas Pennell as Oberon, Diego Matamoros as Puck

each spring in Stratford; so he engaged a group of actors, directors, and designers to form the nucleus of a long-term company, and took over a London theatre, the Aldwych, for modern works as well as transfers from Stratford. In 1968, Peter Hall handed over the running of the company to Trevor Nunn, who was joined as co-director by Terry Hands in 1977; and in 1982 the company moved its London base from the Aldwych to the purpose-built Barbican Theatre.

Realizing that the proscenium stage at Stratford, built in 1932, is essentially unsuitable for staging Shakespeare, successive directors have repeatedly attempted to remodel it, always with the aim of thrusting the action further out into the audience. With this has gone an emphasis on bare, uncluttered stages, which have acted as the starting point for many different kinds of interpretation. For *Cymbeline* in 1962, for instance, William Gaskill used an off-white surround into which solid objects – Imogen's bed, Belarius's cave, Jupiter's massive eagle on a solid steel pole – could swiftly be moved or flown. By isolating the characters' emotions, strongly projected by a company already showing the advantages of Peter Hall's policies, and by holding them literally spotlit, this staging illuminated Shakespeare's own manipulation of character and incident in this play. It also drew attention to the words, especially to those of Iachimo, played by Eric Porter, the finest exponent of Peter Hall's insistence that verse-speaking should place meaning above music. Alan Brien usefully analysed Porter's style:

Its fluid, unmannered, almost insolent, clarity and control of dramatic poetry – always tuned to wring every last syllable of sense from the lines without once losing the rhythm – begins to make the sometimes metallic, brassy resonance of an Olivier, or the occasionally disembodied, reedy fluting of a Gielgud, sound exaggerated and affected.[7]

In the same season, Peter Brook used a similarly neutral white set and hard white lighting to direct, as it were, a spotlight on to King Lear, who emerged as an arbitrary domestic tyrant, overturning Goneril's dinner-table in his rage. The sheer intensity of Paul Scofield's Lear held attention throughout his mad scenes, and the staging of 4.6, with the mad Lear and the blind Gloucester squatting, two tiny figures in rags, against a vast empty white stage, caught both the human pathos ('I know thee well enough; thy name is Gloucester') and the universal scale ('this great stage of fools') of the scene. Later in the decade (1969), Trevor Nunn's *Winter's Tale* presented another empty white set within which Leontes's sudden outburst of jealousy was paralleled by a violent change of lighting, sullying the purity of the white world, as Hermione and Polixenes acted out in weird slow motion Leontes's erotic fantasies. A logical development from stages stripped of inessentials was the studio Shakespeare presented at Stratford's small makeshift theatre, the Other Place, where the claustrophobic conditions enabled Trevor Nunn in 1976 to

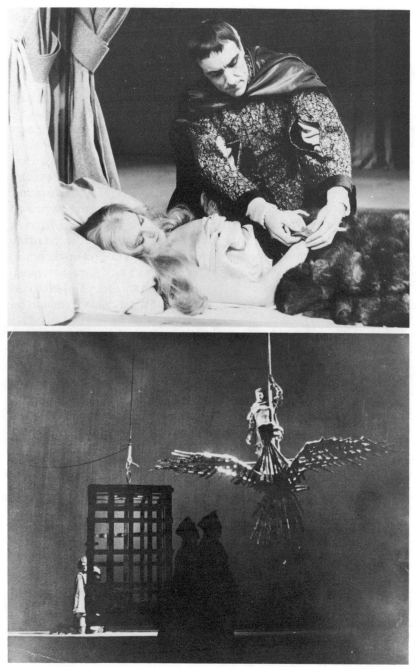

18   (i) *Cymbeline*, Royal Shakespeare Theatre, Stratford-upon-Avon, 1962. Vanessa
Redgrave as Imogen, Eric Porter as Iachimo
(ii) The descent of Jupiter (John Corvin)

focus attention upon what was going on in the mind of Ian McKellen's unrelentingly intense Macbeth, and allowed Ron Daniels in 1979 to control the wandering narrative of *Pericles* while making the most of the intimate encounters, such as Marina's conversion of Lysimachus or her reunion with her father.

As these examples show, bare, functional staging can be used to illuminate markedly different Shakespeare plays. Peter Brook's controversial *Midsummer Night's Dream* of 1970 defined its limitations. The fairies, whose costumes suggested oriental acrobats or circus clowns, used the props of the circus or the gymnasium – trapezes, swings, ropes – to 'fly' in and out of the huge white box which was the set. When Puck gave the magic flower to Oberon, he spun a plate from a plastic rod, and Oberon caught it on another rod; both characters were suspended meanwhile on trapezes in mid-air. The fiercely opposed reactions to this production closely resembled those to Granville-Barker's production of the same play in 1914. Some felt that Brook's devices freed the imagination to concentrate upon the words and the processes of magic, others that it was impossible to reconcile what was said with how it was presented, that in dispensing with nineteenth-century conventions Brook also jettisoned such essential aspects of Shakespeare's play as the wood and the combination of court and countryside.

These had been superbly presented by Peter Hall in the previous Stratford *Midsummer Night's Dream* (1959–63), which beautifully reconciled court and rural imagery by setting the play in an Elizabethan country house that could be swiftly transformed into a wholly convincing wood. This was a good example of the many satisfying productions which, as in earlier decades of the century, drew less discussion than the more sensational ones and so are unfairly neglected by stage histories, including this survey. Others were Peter Hall's 1958 and John Barton's 1969 productions of *Twelfth Night*, each with an exquisite Viola (Dorothy Tutin for Hall, Judi Dench for Barton) and Clifford Williams's *Comedy of Errors* (1962, etc.) which firmly established that play in the modern repertoire. But two achievements of the twentieth-century stage stand out above all others in their contribution to the interpretation of Shakespeare.

The first concerns the histories. Richard David's review of Stratford-upon-Avon's 1951 productions, in sequence, of *Richard II*, *Henry IV*, and *Henry V*, began: 'Shakespeare's Histories are not popular. They are generally regarded as inferior works, neither flesh nor fowl.'[8] Yet by 1955, Kenneth Tynan could write: 'I suspected it at Stratford four years ago, and now I am sure. For me the two parts of *Henry IV* . . . are the twin summits of Shakespeare's achievement, . . . great public plays in which a whole nation is under scrutiny and on trial.'[9] This view has been frequently echoed since, and the histories have often been performed together, notably at Stratford in 1964, when the entire cycle from *Richard II* to *Richard III* was staged by the Royal Shakespeare Company to celebrate the four-hundredth anniversary of Shakespeare's birth. They had not been popular earlier because a single play would be given in isolation, thus forfeiting context and continuity. When the first four plays were given as a cycle in 1951, 'no longer do we yawn while an undifferentiated crowd of blustering barons keeps us from Falstaff, for the barons are now an element in the design, of equal weight to Falstaff'.[10] This sounds obvious to us now, but performance clearly needed to establish it in 1951. Robert Speaight pointed out another notable advantage of the cyclic method of presentation: 'Boling-broke, instead of being three not-quite-star parts in three separate plays, becomes a great tragic protagonist',[11] trapped by the inevitable consequences of his own action in deposing Richard II.

The consequences of fatal actions coming home to roost are as powerfully felt in the *Henry VI* trilogy, especially when it is performed in sequence with the first four plays. In the 1964 cycle at Stratford, the trilogy was shortened to fit into two evenings, and bridge passages necessitated by the cutting were added by John Barton, who also directed the plays with Peter Hall. They saw these as an analysis of power politics, and within a menacing steel set a council

19 *Henry VI*, Royal Shakespeare Theatre, Stratford-upon-Avon, 1963–4. Around the council table: Suffolk (Michael Craig), Margaret (Peggy Ashcroft), Henry VI (David Warner), Winchester (Nicholas Selby), Exeter (Clifford Rose), York (Donald Sinden), Warwick (Brewster Mason)

table was constantly employed to focus the sharply differentiated personalities of the squabbling barons who sat around it. These plays need precisely the kind of ensemble acting that Peter Hall had created, and he and his company subsequently used the insights gained during the history cycle to present a *Hamlet* in which Elsinore was a busy administrative and political centre; David Warner's Hamlet was as unable to cope with this society as his gentle Henry VI had been unable to cope with those barons.

Just as Bolingbroke emerges as a major protagonist when *Richard II* and *Henry IV* are played in sequence, so too does Queen Margaret in *Henry VI* and *Richard III*. Hers then becomes the longest, and perhaps the most challenging, woman's part in Shakespeare. In 1964, Peggy Ashcroft developed from the young princess of *1 Henry VI* to the cursing old woman of *Richard III*, and was at her finest in the astounding scene in which Margaret ritually slaughters her enemy, York (*3 Henry VI*, 1.4.66–176). Her speech had extraordinary variety. '*Where* is your darling Rutland?' was taunting, as she produced the napkin stained with the boy's blood, before she violently slapped him across the face with it. When York refused to 'grieve' even at this, she shifted into mockery with the paper-crowning: 'York cannot speak (*ironic pause; slower speed:*) unless he wear a *crown!*' When York finally replied, she laughed cruelly at first, but slowly fell silent; then, in the act of stabbing him, she briefly burst into hysterical tears, thus releasing her pent-up tension and evincing a human response to the inhuman cruelty of what she had done. This was an amazing performance from the greatest actress of our time.

The other main achievement of the modern stage has been to establish *Love's Labour's Lost* as one of Shakespeare's major plays. That this has been done on stage rather than in the study is recognized by one of the play's editors, John Dover Wilson. After struggling with its topical jokes which loom so large on the page but pass by so rapidly in the theatre, Wilson saw Tyrone Guthrie's production at the Old Vic in 1936:'I have had many memorable and revealing evenings . . . in the theatre . . . but none to equal this.' Guthrie not only showed him 'a new play, the existence of which I had never suspected' but also suggested how 'the whole of Shakespearian comedy might be reviewed in a new light'. The shattering of the revels by Marcade, the black-clad messenger of death, emphasized how, in Shakespearian comedy, 'tragedy is always there, *felt*, if not seen', and that, 'for all its surface lightness and frivolity, the play had behind it a serious mind at work'.[12]

That entry of Marcade has had a comparable impact in numerous subsequent productions, but John Barton at Stratford in 1965 and 1978 characteristically probed much further than other directors into 'the relationships of the characters beneath the highly jewelled surface'. The King and the Princess were very human, both obviously embarrassed by their sudden mutual attraction; the original oath was taken very seriously, so that 'when the King and the rest break it at the first sight of a woman's eyes, the girls are

20 *Love's Labour's Lost*, Royal Shakespeare Theatre, Stratford-upon-Avon, 1978. Berowne (Michael Pennington), Dumaine (Paul Whitworth), the King (Richard Griffiths), the Princess (Carmen du Sautoy), Rosaline (Jane Lapotaire), Maria (Sheridan Fitzgerald), Katherine (Avril Carson)

justified in questioning their oaths of love' and in imposing those harsh penances at the end. The long dying fall began earlier than in most productions, with Armado's elegiac reference to Hector whom he plays in the village pageant, 'The sweet war-man is dead and rotten' (5.2.652–3); this modulated into Marcade's entry without diminishing its impact. After the concluding dialogue between the owl and the cuckoo, a real owl hooted above the actors' heads. This is a typical Barton touch. What makes him such a satisfying director of Shakespeare is that he can bring out Shakespeare's combination of gaiety and sadness, his ability to present affairs of state, of the heart, and of the countryside, all at the same time. As Penelope Gilliatt put it, 'When it is done this way, the play can become a marvellous testament of a great writer finding himself; . . . and the soaring generosity of the play as it climbs to its sombre ending . . . has the grasp of a genius who has suddenly found his life work under his hands.'[13] To have restored this masterpiece after centuries of neglect is an achievement of which the twentieth-century theatre may justly feel proud.

Notes

1. Quoted in T. C. Kemp and J. C. Trewin, *The Stratford Festival* (Birmingham, 1953), pp. 39–40.
2. Quoted in Richard David, *Shakespeare in the Theatre* (Cambridge, 1978), p. 232.
3. *Shakespeare Survey 10* (Cambridge, 1957), p. 127.
4. *Stage Directions* (1963), pp. 42–3, 39–40.
5. *Shakespeare Survey 8* (Cambridge, 1955), p. 129.
6. My visit to Stratford, Ontario for the 1984 season was made possible by a Research Award from the British Academy.
7. *The Sunday Telegraph*, 15 November 1964.
8. *Shakespeare Survey 6* (Cambridge, 1953), p. 129.
9. *The Observer*, 1 May 1955.
10. Richard David, *Shakespeare Survey 6*, p. 131.
11. *The Tablet*, 8 September 1951.
12. *Shakespeare's Happy Comedies* (1962), pp. 64, 73.
13. *The Observer*, 11 April 1965.

Reading list

Barton, John, and Hall, Peter, *The Wars of the Roses* (1970)
Berry, Ralph, *On Directing Shakespeare* (London and New York, 1977)
David, Richard, *Shakespeare in the Theatre* (Cambridge, 1978)
Gielgud, John, *Stage Directions* (1963)
Kemp, T. C., and Trewin, J. C., *The Stratford Festival* (Birmingham, 1953)
Shakespeare Survey and *Shakespeare Quarterly*: annual account of Shakespeare productions
Speaight, Robert, *Shakespeare on the Stage* (1973)
Trewin, J. C., *Shakespeare on the English Stage 1900–1964* (1964)
Warren, Roger, *Text and Performance: A Midsummer Night's Dream* (1983)
Wells, Stanley, *Royal Shakespeare* (Manchester and Furman, South Carolina, 1976)
Wharton, T. F., *Text and Performance: Henry IV* (1983)
Wilson, J. D., and Worsley, T. C., *Shakespeare's Histories at Stratford 1951* (1952)

15 Shakespeare on film and television

THERE is something expansive about Shakespeare's dramatic genius. His plays reach out to audiences in a profoundly popular way that makes film and television seem congenial media for their performance today. One suspects that if he were writing now, he would be writing scripts for these forms, just as in his own day he wrote his plays for the venue – the public theatre – that afforded the broadest possible audience for his work. The difference is that where the Elizabethan audiences for his plays numbered in the thousands, film and television versions can reach millions.

These enormous twentieth-century audiences have of course been primarily attracted to film and television productions of Shakespeare because of their intrinsic appeal as entertaining works of art. As these productions have accumulated and (especially in the United States) become more and more readily available for private and classroom viewing, they have also become an important educational resource. For beginning readers of the plays, they are useful 'audio-visual aids'. They provide help in overcoming the initial difficulties of the language and immediate access to the human interests of the text, a stepping-stone for those who are learning to 'see' and 'hear' what they read. For more advanced students of literature, the productions can serve as a vivid form of interpretative commentary, especially when more than one version of a given play can be compared in detail. Is the text better served when Claudius and Polonius are taken at Hamlet's estimate of them (as in Olivier's film) or at their own estimates (as in the Shakespeare Plays television version)? Is Richard III's wooing of Lady Anne more credible when divided in two and separated by the scene with Clarence (as in Olivier's film) or when enacted without a break (as in the Shakespeare Plays version)? At what point and for what reasons does Anne capitulate? The two treatments differ in provocative ways that send one back to the text for a closer look.

Students of theatre can watch videotapes and films repeatedly with an eye for fine points of acting or design. A number of television shows have taken viewers backstage to rehearsal situations. Students of performance history can see first-hand the styles of the recent past (some already seem very remote) and thereby develop educated eyes and ears for their values. No Shakespeare library can any more be considered complete without a collection of films and videotapes and facilities for viewing them.

The history of Shakespeare on film begins in the earliest period of silent film, with a brief portion of Beerbohm Tree's stage production of *King John* (1899). Shakespeare's heyday in the silent era was between 1908 and 1914, when numerous excerpts and versions appeared in England and the United States and on the Continent. Thereafter, World War I and then the promise of 'talkies' contributed to a sharp decline. These productions must have had an attraction for their original audiences, but today it is hard to see why. Those that have survived have some historical value (stage historians are glad to have a record of Forbes-Robertson's 1913 Hamlet), but, otherwise, silent Shakespeare is of interest only as a curiosity. He demands to be heard.

Among the first of the sound films was *The Taming of the Shrew* (1929), starring Mary Pickford and Douglas Fairbanks. It failed and is remembered only for the vanity of its credit: 'Written by William Shakespeare with additional dialogue by Sam Taylor.' There were several more efforts in the 1930s; of them only *A Midsummer Night's Dream* (1935), directed by Max Reinhardt and William Dieterle and with James Cagney as Bottom and Mickey Rooney as Puck, has much interest today. The first Shakespeare film to be both a popular and an artistic success was Olivier's *Henry V* (1944). Olivier also directed and starred in *Hamlet* (1948) and *Richard III* (1955). His has been the largest individual contribution to Shakespeare films. The 1950s saw a total of seven Shakespeare films, including Joseph Mankiewicz's *Julius Caesar* (1953) with Marlon Brando as Antony, and Kurosawa's film based on *Macbeth*, *Throne of Blood* (1957), the one version of Shakespeare sometimes referred to as a 'great film' in its own right. Between 1960 and 1970, no fewer than thirteen Shakespeare films were produced. Among them was an 'electronovision' record of Richard Burton's Broadway *Hamlet* (1964), shown briefly in theatres and then destroyed. In 1965 Orson Welles directed and starred in the most successful of his Shakespeare films, *Chimes at Midnight* (1965), an adaptation of the Falstaff plays. This was the period of Zeffirelli's *Taming of the Shrew* (1966) and his Top Ten box-office success *Romeo and Juliet* (1968). 1970 brought a pair of *King Lear*s, directed by Peter Brook and Kozintsev. Since then, the only considerable films have been Polanski's *Macbeth* (1971), Derek Jarman's *The Tempest* (1980), and Kurosawa's *Ran*, a version of *King Lear* (1985). The making of Shakespeare films is currently on the wane.

It is televised Shakespeare that is on the increase. Again Shakespeare's plays were important in this medium from its infancy. As early as 1937–9, the BBC showed a variety of scenes and full-length plays, and since World War II hardly a year has gone by without producing a Shakespeare play or two. In the 1960s came 'An Age of Kings' (1960), a rendering of the English history plays from Richard II to Richard III; 'The Spread of the Eagle' (1963), the Roman plays excluding *Titus Andronicus*; 'Hamlet at Elsinore' (1964), *All's Well that Ends Well* (1968), and 'The Wars of the Roses' (1965, John Barton's adaptation of the Henry VI plays and *Richard III*). In 1970 Ian McKellen played Richard II and in the early 1970s the 'Play of the Month' series usually included a play by Shakespeare, notably *Macbeth* (1970) with Eric Porter and Janet Suzman and *The Merchant of Venice* (1972) with Maggie Smith as Portia. BBC-TV has in its archives tapes of almost all its productions since 1955, but those made before 1979 are regrettably not currently available for purchase or rental.

On English commercial television, the first Shakespeare was the live Peter Brook/Paul Scofield *Hamlet* (ATV, 1956) whose conclusion was cut by a commercial announcement! Other noteworthy presentations were the Jonathan Miller/Olivier *Merchant of Venice* (ATV, 1974) and Royal Shakespeare Company productions of *Antony and Cleopatra* (ATV/RSC, 1974), the musical *Comedy of Errors* (ATV/RSC, 1978), and *Macbeth* (Thames/RSC, 1979). RSC performers have also appeared in acting and verse-speaking demonstrations on the South Bank Show (LWT, 1979) and in the nine-part series presented by John Barton ('Playing Shakespeare', LWT, 1983). In 1983 Olivier starred in *King Lear* (Granada).

In the United States, Shakespeare on television was synonymous in the 1950s with Maurice Evans and the Hallmark Hall of Fame, in which ten ninety-minute productions were performed; the most memorable featured Richard Burton as Caliban (1960). Since then, productions have been sporadic, chiefly under the aegis of Joseph Papp. The Canadian Broadcast Company has recently begun televising productions at the Stratford Festival Canada.

The most ambitious single project is the Shakespeare Plays series of the complete plays (produced by BBC-TV/Time-Life 1979–85). Although the project was originally conceived as offering 'standard' productions suitable for libraries and likely to last for 'a quarter of a century', this unlikely goal has not been realized. Limited mostly to a few weeks each for rehearsal and taping, its shows have had a journeyman air about them, offering not absolute artistry but the work of competent craftsmen fulfilling an agenda of six plays a year. Although not definitive, the series has had its share of successes and relatively few out-and-out failures (*Romeo and Juliet* being the worst). Aside from performing half-a-dozen plays never before produced for television, the series' most distinctive contribution has been in the area of design, in the use where appropriate of settings that resemble paintings: by Vermeer for *All's Well that Ends Well*, by Veronese for *Antony and Cleopatra*.

As this historical sketch illustrates, many of Shakespeare's plays have a proven adaptability for film and television. Shakespeare of all dramatists has had by far the largest number of his plays filmed;[1] the same is even more true of television. His prestige as the pre-eminent dramatist is one reason for this. Another, more basic reason is the colourfulness and complexity of his characters, despite the few roles he gives to women. Most important, his plots read like scripts for motion pictures and television, with their continuous action, free changes of scene, rhythmic cutting from one plot-line to another, strong situations, and satisfying climaxes. In some ways, indeed, the camera seems even better suited to his purposes than was the thrust stage of his own time. The Elizabethan public stage was remarkable for allowing both intimate effects (as in the soliloquies) and large crowd scenes, often in sharp juxtaposition. Yet the camera (with its close-ups) can allow even greater intimacy while at the other extreme affording panoramic views, shot on location.

Nevertheless, the affinity of Shakespeare's texts with film and television is far from complete. Although the modern theatre (with its elaborate lighting effects and elite audiences) is itself very different from the Globe, its stage is still the most natural medium for Shakespeare since it provides the opportunity for live interaction between player and playgoer. Only in the legitimate theatre can spectators join with actors in living the life of a Shakespeare play – all in the same place and at that very moment.

It does not follow, however, that film and television versions of Shakespeare should seek to become as much like live theatre as possible, at least not in a literal way. Styles of acting that suit the stage may not suit film and television. The film based on Olivier's *Othello* (1965) is valuable as a record of his stage performance. But as cinema his 'grand manner' gestures that told so powerfully in the theatre seem stagey while Frank Finlay's subtle Iago, who seemed underplayed in the theatre, steals the film. On the stage Vanessa Redgrave's Rosalind was enchanting; on television, she appeared mannered and as if she were acting in slow motion. On the other hand, if tactfully employed, theatrical styles can be effective on camera. Gielgud's elocutionary style is apt for his filmed Clarence and Henry IV and televised John of Gaunt.

Sometimes live theatrical performances have been videotaped, with the inclusion of laughter and applause from the audience. When the camera-work is well-rehearsed and a zoom lens used to advantage, this approach can be effective, particularly when the performance itself is presentational in style. The American Repertory Theater's *A Midsummer Night's Dream* (1981), with interpolated music and songs from Purcell's *The Fairy Queen*, is a good example. It remains, however, simply the record of a stage performance. An interesting extension of this approach is a half-hour treatment of Joseph Papp's *Taming of the Shrew*. This offers not only episodes shot in live performance but backstage interviews. Meryl Streep, for example, justifies Kate's final advice to wives 'to place your hands below your husband's foot' by analogy with the unconditional devotion of a parent towards a child, for whom no necessary abasement is too great. We then see her, in performance, convincingly suit her action to these words, at which Raul Julia as Petruchio tenderly responds in kind, stooping no less low to raise her up. There are also lively interviews with members of the audience. The result provides a fresh perspective on the play, yet the half-hour remains essentially a documentary evocation of Shakespeare's work rather than a performance of it.

Whatever the approach, the special needs and proclivities of film and television must be respected. The performer must mediate between their pull towards the visual and Shakespeare's pull towards the verbal, a tug-of-war that is of course most crucial in the treatment of his dialogue. Heavy cutting of lines has been common; Olivier cut a third of *Henry V* and half of *Hamlet*, Zeffirelli more than half of the lines in *Romeo and Juliet*, Jarman two-thirds of *The Tempest*. It is not simply that full-length versions of many of the plays would run longer than the two-and-a-half hours ordinarily allotted to films and television productions. Shakespeare's style has a Renaissance copiousness and explicitness that can make it seem long-winded in forms where much is often left unspoken. The camera's capacity for close-ups can make speeches that have a full-throated, public character seem overblown. The device which Olivier discovered in *Henry V* of moving the camera progressively away during the king's exhortations to his troops is effective, but it cannot be effective often. Shakespeare's language, especially the verse, has its own rhythms. Michael Birkett, the producer, writes:

Peter Hall and I found in *A Midsummer Night's Dream* that there were several passages where, looking at the picture on a movieola, without any sound, the cutting pattern seemed to be perfect. Hearing the sound track on its own, the rhythms of the speech also seemed to be fine. When the two were run together, however, the result seemed unsatisfactory. We had to evolve a style of cutting which was equally fair to the rhythm of the verse and to the rhythm of the pictures.[2]

Hall's solution was to 'create a picture rhythm by cutting to the verbal pattern – that is, on the caesura, or at the end of the line' (pp. 124–5). In the opening scenes, this rhythm seems mechanical and jerky; but in the scene in which all four of the young lovers quarrel, Hall employs it with virtuosity and comic effect.

As different as both film and television are from the stage, they are also essentially different from one another. Often their differences are ignored. Sometimes films (such as Olivier's *King Lear* and Hall's *A Midsummer Night's Dream*) have been made for first showing on television; a number of films have been made available on video-cassettes. The differences remain nonetheless. For a film Hall uses too many of the close-up head-shots that come so naturally to television. Zeffirelli's Shakespeare films seem tamed when reduced to videotape: their riotous energy has a sweep that requires a full-sized screen. The larger-than-life figures projected on a movie screen make for a more engulfing experience for the audience than do the miniature figures on television. The address of a film to a large audience in a motion-picture theatre also invites a broader style of performance than when a few viewers sitting in a living room are addressed. Where televised Shakespeare is concerned this last difference has often been exaggerated, resulting in an excessively subdued style, more restrained than suits the text or indeed would suit plays originally written for television. Jeremy Kemp's portrayal of Leontes in the Shakespeare Plays *Winter's Tale* is an instance. At the finale, his grief is so restrained that there is no point in the dozen lines of consolation that the other characters offer him.

Because of such differences between the two media, and marked differences among the plays themselves, certain of Shakespeare's plays have proved better suited to the one medium or the other. The English history plays seem most at home on television. Their concern with matters of state appears apropos in a medium so much given over to political news and events. Their language – more colloquial than in other Shakespearian genres – is less removed from the mundane language ordinarily spoken on the television. Their episodic structure within a grand historical sweep is especially suited to television as we know it, with its hour and half-hour patterns. The plays thrive on consecutive performance, which television is especially able to provide. 'An Age of Kings', which rendered the two historical tetralogies in fifteen parts over a period of weeks, was in effect the first 'mini-series'. In it the fall of Duke Humphrey in *2 Henry VI* became a distinct episode (it was a *Mirror for Magistrates* tragedy complete in itself), a treatment that arguably better served its text than did its original context. Apart from their leading roles, the histories do not require casts of such quality as to exceed the usual low level of television budgets. For the leading roles, on the other hand, they afford rich opportunities to develop a character through a sequence of plays. Over the two parts of *Henry IV* in the Shakespeare Plays series, Anthony Quayle exuberantly traces Falstaff's descent from innocent merriment to malicious rascality. Perhaps the greatest single performance of a Shakespearian role on television is that of Dame Peggy Ashcroft as Margaret in the 'Wars of the Roses' trilogy: before our eyes she changes from a young French princess through a battlefield fiend to a prophetic wraith.

More than anything else, television has an air of fact about it that enhances Shakespeare's vision of the past. The televised 'Wars of the Roses' improved on its stage original in precisely this respect. On the stage, the production had an intrusive theoretical element; scholar–critics Tillyard and Kott were all but visible in the wings. On television, the presentation struck the viewer as not so much a theory of history as history itself. That, one felt, was very likely 'the way it was'. Since the medium is not engulfing like film but cool and detached, one could watch history unroll itself with an almost Brechtian dispassion. In this context, an assertive directorial line seems out of place, like an editorial on the front page of a newspaper. A case in point is the Shakespeare Plays *1 Henry VI*. Its director, Jane Howells, found its characters fundamentally childish and worked with her designers to produce a set suggestive of a brightly coloured playground, with Playcraft props, 'dressing up' costumes, and armour inspired by the shoulder pads of American football; Gloucester and Winchester at one point rode hobby-horses. This approach did liberate the actors to give a livelier and more demonstrative rendering of the lines than is usual in this series, but at the cost of historicity. On the other hand, realism can be pushed too far. In the Shakespeare Plays *Henry IV* the naturalism of showing the dying Hotspur with a mouthful of blood and the dying king with leprous sores on his face did not sort with their high-flown diction. The best of the Shakespeare Plays histories have been enlightened costume dramas, at ease with their historical ambience yet not at the expense of such dramatic strengths as Claire Bloom's movingly dignified Katherine in *Henry VIII* and the endlessly fascinating interplay between Jon Finch's strong, silent, enigmatic Bolingbroke and Derek Jacobi's effete and self-destructive yet eloquent and finally piteous Richard II.

The cinema has, of course, also had its successes with the histories. Olivier's *Henry V* and *Richard III* both project a quintessential value belonging to all Shakespeare's English histories: that the real protagonist is the realm itself, whether in the throes of foreign war or of civil dissension. It is as if Olivier set out to demonstrate what true royalty is (in Henry V) and what it is not (in Richard III). When at the end of the *Richard III* film false royalty has at last been destroyed, the final image of Lord Stanley bearing the crown aloft and striding forward to the stirring music of William Walton sums up the

21 Peggy Ashcroft as Queen Margaret in *The Wars of the Roses*
(i)   The Queen when young (with Suffolk, played by William Squire)

(ii)   The Queen when old

patriotic feeling at the heart of the two films. *Henry V* indeed is less a history play than a national anthem. Its authenticity is undercut by the deliberate artifice of its format, moving from the recreation of an Elizabethan performance to a two-dimensional Book of Hours backdrop to the movie-realism of Agincourt on location and back again. Little visible blood is shed at Olivier's Agincourt, which is more a tournament than a battle. A sense of the past is not truly Olivier's concern in *Richard III* either, as evidenced by his cutting of Queen Margaret and the tie with disastrous past events which she recalls. Olivier's Richard at heart derives from stage melodrama, updated to cool, sly black comedy.

Orson Welles's flawed masterpiece, *Chimes at Midnight*, is a special case. His conflation of the two *Henry IV* plays, including portions of *Henry V*, encompasses in a single film much of Shakespeare's sweeping vision of this era. His treatment of the Battle of Shrewsbury has a realism – with its brutal violence and ultimate slogging of combatants in the mud – that Olivier chose to avoid at Agincourt. Olivier's picturesque shots of the armoured French being dropped from hoists on to their steeds are in fact recalled, and put down, by Welles's quick shot of armoured Falstaff plopping to the ground from his comically overloaded hoist. Its point of view, however, is not that of a simple historical present but of the past recalled, often as if from a distance. It begins with the reminiscence between Shallow and Falstaff about hearing 'the chimes at midnight' in their youth, to which it later returns. Profoundly retrospective, this film is at heart less a history than an elegy.

In general it is on film that Shakespeare's tragedies have appeared most at home. A key factor has been their strong directors, who by their mastery of the film medium impart to their work what amounts to an implied narrative voice, setting the pace, sustaining the mood, choosing the perspective, highlighting the detail, pointing the contrast that most enhances the unfolding action. At best we are not even conscious of their contribution. The director's 'voice' strikes one as intrusive when it is too audible. This is literally the case when Olivier simplistically announces at the beginning of his filmed *Hamlet* that 'This is the tragedy of a man who could not make up his mind.' The intrusion is no less blatant when Polanski at the end of his *Macbeth* claims a too-easy irony, showing Donalbain limping towards the witches' lair, taking up where Macbeth left off.

These are abuses, however, of a necessary function. What happens when this function is not served may be seen in the television versions of the tragedies, which have not attracted strong directors. What one remembers from them are not satisfying complete works but outstanding individual performances: Nicol Williamson and Jane Lapotaire as Macbeth and Lady Macbeth, Janet Suzman as Lady Macbeth and Cleopatra, Alan Howard as Coriolanus, Robert Shaw as Claudius, Jonathan Pryce as Timon. Olivier and Anna Calder-Marshall remain in the memory because her Cordelia is the prime reason for his King Lear to go on living. When they are together he glows – with paternal affection at the very beginning and at their reunion with an ethereal aura, his white hair hanging straight to his shoulders, as if he had indeed passed on to another existence. In other respects, however, the production lacks a controlling vision; each member of the all-star cast goes his or her own way in a hodge-podge of acting styles.

Almost without exception, the television treatments have failed to create the unique, imagined 'worlds' that the tragedies require. The television version of Trevor Nunn's *Macbeth* with Ian McKellen and Judi Dench as Macbeth and Lady Macbeth is an exception that points this rule. When performed in the Other Place studio theatre, the play had the quality of a communal rite. It was like a seance in which an inner circle of actors (present even when not required by the action) and an outer circle of spectators together conjured up in their midst an enactment of the 'dreadful deed'. On television, even though many features of the original were retained, the social context gave way to a disturbing psychological one. All backgrounds were blacked out. Watching it alone, with the action cabined, cribbed, confined in the television box, is like suffering a nightmare or going insane. Judi Dench's long moan in the sleep-walking scene is so powerful because her anguish expresses one's own. An inner 'world' has replaced the outer one.

The impression of an outer world is a key strength of filmed Shakespeare. Again it is the director who chiefly creates this impression. Polanski's Inverness, for example, is not only a chamber of bloody horrors but a place where ordinary life goes on – where fowls roam the courtyard and servants move furniture, run errands, catch a pig for the night's banquet. The domestic details serve at once to lend authentic balance to the horrors, and by contrast to intensify their effect when they come. Often this outer world serves as a metaphor for the inner world of the play. So in *Chimes at Midnight* the Prince's choice between his father and Falstaff is made visible by the contrast between the high-vaulting but cold stone of the court and the low-ceilinged but warm wood of the tavern. This kind of visual metaphor can go too far. Kozintsev's *Hamlet* is less an enactment of Shakespeare's play than a lyric meditation upon it, rendered in visual symbols of stone, iron, fire, sea, earth. The balance is better in his powerful *King Lear*; in it the King's enlightenment results from wanderings across his land during which he becomes outwardly indistinguish-able from his people. Peter Brook's film of *King Lear* is probably too tendentious an exposition of the inexorable cruelty and absurdity of life *à la* Artaud and Beckett, heavy-handedly reinforced by wintry landscapes and characters who are animal-like in more ways than their fur coverings. Yet it yields the most memorable single scene in Shakespearian film to date, when mad Lear (Paul Scofield) and blind Gloucester (Alan Webb) meet on the sands of Dover. They are like the two tramps in *Waiting for Godot*, it is true; yet unlike them they are fully humanized. Especially in this bleak context, what hard heart is not touched by the tender camaraderie of these two tough old losers?

In Kurosawa's *Throne of Blood*, directorial interpretation has gone all the way to free adaptation. It is the treatment of Shakespeare most admired by other directors – Kozintsev, Brook, Hall – and with good reason. Not only does Kurosawa create scenes of painterly beauty; his work has a purity that is unique among the films in this survey. There is something inescapably hybrid about a 'Shakespeare film'; it is almost a hyphenated sub-genre of its own. Unhampered by Western loyalties to Shakespeare's text and drawing boldly on the traditions of Noh drama and samurai film, Kurosawa takes great liberties with the plot (Lady Macbeth, for example, becomes pregnant, then miscarries), the characters (the Weird Sisters become a man-eating hag from a Noh play), and the language (which is not Shakespearian at all). Yet its rendering of the irony of a man's fated self-destruction (summed up in the original Japanese title 'Castle of the Spider's Web') is profoundly Shakespearian and comes across with a power that has escaped the other filmed versions of *Macbeth*.[3]

For the most part Shakespeare's comedies have not been well served either

22 The reunion of blind Gloucester (Alan Webb) and mad Lear (Paul Scofield) in Peter Brook's *King Lear*, 1970

by film or television. Only the comic moments in Zeffirelli's films evoke the
hearty laughter that the plays can still excite in the theatre. He is at his funniest
in the encounter between the Nurse and Mercutio and in the first meeting of
Kate and Petruchio. Both express high spirits in fast-paced physical action.
Zeffirelli extravagantly magnifies the text yet does so in a way that is
masterfully to scale. The success of other filmed comedies tends to the
grotesque, as in the woods and fairies of the 1935 *A Midsummer Night's Dream*
and in Derek Jarman's controversial *The Tempest*, where Prospero is a
magician out of a horror-flick and Ariel very possibly one of the living dead he
once released ('graves at my command / Have waked their sleepers, oped, and
let 'em forth'). Making an outrageous musical pun, the wedding masque
features 'Stormy Weather', sung beautifully by the jazz singer Elisabeth
Welch.

On television, one might have thought that Jonathan Miller, himself so
clever in 'Beyond the Fringe', would excel with the comedies put on during his
tenure as a producer of the Shakespeare Plays series. Instead he has gone out
of his way to make them *un*funny. With the comic talent of John Cleese at his
disposal as Petruchio, he chose to regard *Taming of the Shrew* as a Calvinist
tract on the text: 'To me, she's married, not unto my clothes.' It ends with the
singing of a Psalm. Of the televised 'happy' comedies, *Much Ado About Nothing*
has fared best, in a television version of Zeffirelli's stage success, starring
Maggie Smith and Robert Stephens as Beatrice and Benedick; and in A. J.
Antoon's 1973 musical treatment set in turn-of-the-century America and
featuring Charleston-style dancing.

The best of Jonathan Miller's efforts remains the televised version of the
Edwardian *Merchant of Venice* he directed at the National Theatre, with Olivier
as Shylock in a top hat. Not laughter but the off-camera howl of his broken
Shylock is what stays in one's memory. And among the comedies it is with the
dark ones that the Shakespeare Plays series has had most success. *All's Well
that Ends Well* has received the most praise. It does have a strong supporting
cast, and its Helena (Angela Down) is touching. Yet like so many of the comic
heroines in this series, she lacks vitality: her staunch endurance of deprivation
is emphasized rather than her resilience and resourcefulness. At her return
from presumed death, we are encouraged to substitute the reflected joy of her
companions (underlined by background music) for our direct enjoyment of
her own radiance. *Measure for Measure* is preferable. Its conflicts may be
somewhat polarized: Kate Nelligan is a very virtuous Isabella (in her white
habit) and Tim Pigott-Smith a very devil-like Angelo (with his black garb and
pointed beard). Yet there is more than a little such soap-opera in the original,
and their twin scenes together are skilfully choreographed and beautifully
played.

Although the past fifty years have achieved some remarkable successes in
presenting Shakespeare's plays on film and television, future performance

historians will doubtless see this as a very early and highly exploratory era in which many very different approaches were tried. It is still an open question as to how best a camera may be used to put Shakespeare on a screen. The difficulty is not primarily that the texts are dated and need by various means to be made more accessible to modern audiences. It is more that they present a perennial challenge that has still to be fully met. Peter Brook has had the keenest perception of this challenge. In *The Empty Space* he observes that the Elizabethan theatre 'not only allowed the playwright to roam the world, it also allowed him free passage from the world of action to the world of inner impressions'. Through his mastery of language Shakespeare was able to capitalize on this opportunity and thus to succeed 'where no one has succeeded before or since in writing plays that pass through many stages of consciousness'.[4] Elsewhere Brook concludes: 'the problem of filming Shakespeare is one of finding ways of shifting gears, styles, and conventions as lightly and deftly on the screen as within the mental processes reflected by Elizabethan blank verse onto the screen of the mind'.[5] That challenge still stands.

23 Elizabeth Taylor as Kate bashing Richard Burton as Petruchio in Zeffirelli's *Taming of the Shrew*, 1966

Notes

1. Roger Manvell, *Theatre and Film* (Fairleigh Dickinson, N.J., 1979), pp. 370–9.
2. Roger Manvell, *Shakespeare and the Film* (1971), p. 142.
3. Kurosawa's *Ran* ('chaos') was released after this article was set in type. Although cut from the same cloth as *Throne of Blood*, it is less successful in catching the essence of its original, *King Lear*. Certainly it lacks none of Shakespeare's savagery. If anything the film is more violent than the play. Its Great Lord is guilty of many atrocities, and its most memorable character is one of his surviving victims, a woman whose parents he had slaughtered and who – by cunning and sexual wiles – exultantly destroys his royal line, turning his three sons against one another and himself. Made up to suggest a Noh mask, this woman is part Goneril, part Edmund, part demon, part Samurai – a remarkable creation. The contemplative part of the tragedy, however, is less freshly imagined; Kurosawa relies too much on traditional forms from Buddhism and Noh, and – if the subtitles are a fair translation – his dialogue lacks eloquence (Great Lord: 'I'm lost'; Fool: 'It is the human condition'). In the end even the film's pessimism seems pat: its final image is of a blind man on the extreme verge of a cliff, 'the human condition' in italics.
4. Peter Brook, *The Empty Space* (1968), pp. 79, 80.
5. Geoffrey Reeves, 'Finding Shakespeare on film: from an interview with Peter Brook', *Focus on Shakespearean Films*, ed. C. Eckert (Englewood Cliffs, 1972), p. 38.

Reading list

Ball, Robert Hamilton, *Shakespeare on Silent Film* (New York, 1968)
Barry, Michael, 'Shakespeare on television', *BBC Quarterly* 9 (1954), 143–9
Eckert, Charles W., ed., *Focus on Shakespearean Films* (Englewood Cliffs, 1972)
Hallinan, Tim, 'Interview with Jonathan Miller', *Shakespeare Quarterly* 32 (1981), 134–45
Jorgens, Jack J., *Shakespeare on Film* (1977)
Kozintsev, Grigori, *Shakespeare: Time and Conscience* (Durham, 1967)
　'*Hamlet* and *King Lear*: stage and film', in *Shakespeare 1971*, ed. Leech and Margeson (Toronto, 1972), pp. 190–9
　'*King Lear*': the Space of Tragedy (1977)
Manvell, Roger, *Shakespeare and the Film* (1971)
　Theatre and Film (Fairleigh Dickinson, N.J., 1979)
Wells, Stanley, 'Television Shakespeare', *Shakespeare Quarterly* 33 (1982), 261–77
　For BBC-TV productions: precise dates are given in the *BBC Programme Index* (Chadwyck-Healey, Cambridge); credit lists appear in the *Radio Times*; productions are always reviewed in *The Listener* and in recent years often in other periodicals, such as the *Shakespeare Quarterly*, *TLS*, etc. Useful introductory materials for the Shakespeare Plays series are given in the individual companion editions published by the BBC. *Shakespeare on Film Newsletter* includes television in its purview. *Literature/Film Quarterly* has devoted four special issues to Shakespeare: I, 4, 1973; IV, 2, 1976; V, 4, 1977; XI, 3, 1983. *Shakespeare Survey 39* has Shakespeare on film and television as its principal theme.

16   Shakespeare and new critical approaches

I Old and new: the question of expression

THE newness of any critical approach can only be a relative matter; one which requires us initially to settle what we mean by the 'old'. In the case of modern Shakespearian criticism, the latter role is fulfilled by the approach established in A. C. Bradley's monumental *Shakespearean Tragedy* of 1904. That views proposed in the first quarter of the twentieth century still stand firmly enough to require challenging in its final quarter is certainly a surprising circumstance. An appropriate sifting of its implications would need to take into account a number of factors which lie beyond the province of what we have tended to think of as criticism itself.

But of course the notion of criticism 'itself' would be an early victim of such probing. The rise, in our century, of a new and fully professionalized field of study known as 'English' emerges as a major aspect of this situation, and any explanation of its causes and consequences would reach deep into the roots of our way of life, to embrace the concerns of politics and history as well as of literature. At stake is what we mean by the term 'criticism'.

Bradley's enduring influence, despite the cogency of attacks made upon his work from many quarters, thus itself becomes a current area of complex critical interest, and the presuppositions of that work form the background against which 'new' critical approaches must define themselves. A theory of reading and a theory of character are centrally involved, and they raise two important questions: what happens when we read a play by Shakespeare, and of what sort of materials is it composed?

Bradley's theory of reading may be said to rest on a particular concept of language as a transparent and directly expressive medium. Reading, in this view, takes the reader *through* the text to make contact with the mind of the author whose contents the text expresses. The theory assumes, as a first principle, that the text functions as a reasonably straightforward pathway to that mind, and as a second that there exists a fully expressive 'fit' between the text and its author's mental processes. The one, therefore, is capable of giving full expression to the other. The concern of reading is to follow the path indicated by the text as closely as possible and so to recreate in the reader's mind the original process of composition, as it occurred in the poet's mind. In a letter to Gilbert Murray in 1901 Bradley makes the point directly: 'Reading or understanding' the poem, he says, will involve readers in 'making the same process occur in themselves as occurred in the poet's head'. In a lecture on the general nature of poetry, he is no less explicit. We should study poetry, he recommends, 'in order to reproduce in ourselves more faintly that which went on in the poet's mind when he wrote'.[1]

According to Bradley, Shakespeare's tragedies indicate that the 'main interest' of their author's mind was in character: the inner nature of human beings which determines their deeds and their fate. Thus the centre of *Hamlet* 'may be said with equal truth to lie in action issuing from character, or in character issuing in action'. The dictum that, with Shakespeare, 'character is destiny' may, he tells us, be an exaggeration, but it is the 'exaggeration of a vital truth'.[2]

Bradley's concern with Shakespearian character has of course been challenged by a number of critics on the grounds that it is reductive. It scales emblematic, non-realistic dramas down to the level of quasi-realistic portrait galleries of interesting human specimens: it turns the plays into second-rate novels. But the challenges offered by a wide variety of newer critical approaches are perhaps more radical, since they take issue not only with Bradley, but also with some of his subsequent detractors and revisers on the central issues of the nature of language, the capacity of writing to express the operations of the writer's mind or to present 'character', and indeed the nature of characters, of reading and of the written text. The most fundamental challenge is that offered by what has come to be known as 'structuralism'.

II Structuralism

The term is a broad one, referring rather generally to a number of roughly related critical positions which emerged in France and America during the 1950s and 1960s. The roots of structuralism lie in studies of the nature of language made by the Swiss linguist Ferdinand de Saussure, and by American linguists such as Edward Sapir, Benjamin Lee Whorf, and Leonard Bloomfield. Its fundamental arguments are difficult to summarize, but central to them is a denial of the sort of transparency in language which Bradley's notion of reading requires. The world certainly appears to consist of independently existing things which our language transparently presents to us. However, it is relatively easy to demonstrate that this is an illusion, albeit one in which certain societies make a considerable investment.

It would be much closer to the truth, linguistic studies indicate, to view language not as a pane of transparent glass through which we perceive the world, but as a pane of stained glass, which imposes its own shapes, colours, and formations on the world we see. The very words which seem transparently to conduct us to the world are themselves part of a vast and complex system of signs which is far more likely to be obeying its own laws than to be reflecting any actualities beyond it. The word *dog*, to put the matter crudely, has no essentially dog-like qualities. There is nothing tree-like about the word *tree*. These words 'mean' whatever it is that they mean not because of anything essential in themselves or in those things to which they refer, but because the structure of the language in which they occur provides that function for them. They mean what they mean only because they do not mean other things. *Dog* means dog not because of what it is but because of what it is not: because it is not *bog* and it is not *god* or *log*. Thus, the meaning of words lies not in the words themselves but in the relationships which language establishes *between* words.

Since human beings are creatures of language, wholly immersed in and formed by that one feature which distinguishes them from the rest of Creation, then the fundamental characteristics of language can be said, so far as human beings are concerned, to invest the whole of reality. The true nature of things can be said to lie, that is, not in things themselves, but in the relationships which we construct, through language, between them. This notion, that the world is made up of relationships rather than things, constitutes the first principle of a way of thinking which can properly be called 'structuralist'. And its first conclusion must be that the full significance of any entity or experience cannot be perceived unless and until it is integrated into the structure of which it forms a part.

In respect of literary criticism, the first casualty of this kind of thinking will be the simple, straightforward concept of realism: the idea that language makes actual, unmediated contact with a 'real world' beyond itself, which it describes with greater or less accuracy. The second, related casualty will be a no less simple, straightforward concept of 'expression': the notion that language directly and in an unmediated fashion expresses the thoughts that occur in the head of the utterer. The nature of language as a structure, and as a structuring process, clearly denies the transparency on which these notions depend. In effect, structuralism argues, both the 'real world' and our own thoughts about it are determined by the language through whose agency we exist in and encounter the world. It follows, even from the dangerously skimpy outline given above, that the foundations of Bradleian criticism of Shakespeare will be severely shaken by any such approach.

There is, such an approach would be bound to say, no immediate access available from one mind to another through language. The idea that we can experience in our own minds a version of what went on in Shakespeare's is therefore groundless. There is also, clearly, no basis for the kind of psychological 'realism' on which Bradley's notion of character rests. Shakespeare's texts, composed of language, offer us self-referring, self-supporting structures, rather than psychological analyses of real people in real situations. The uncomplicated reaching out, through language, to the concrete world beyond it, on which Bradleian analysis depends, is frustrated from the outset by structuralism's first principles.

There is no large body of self-announced structuralist criticism specifically devoted to Shakespeare's plays. Indeed, in Anglo-American terms, the fundamental stance of structuralism and its subsequent development has been diagnostic as much as remedial: concerned to show why and how an older sort of criticism is misconceived rather than positively to replace it. But there does exist a bulk of anti-Bradleian Anglo-American criticism which might reasonably be called quasi-structuralist: that is, its commitment lies wholly against Bradleian 'realism' and very much in favour of a view of the plays as structures deploying depersonalized 'themes' in which opposed concepts (such as appearance and reality, disorder and order, death and life) present a moral or political scheme in general rather than particular psychological terms.

The major exemplars of this sort of untheorized 'structuralism' in English would be L. C. Knights and G. Wilson Knight. The work of Northrop Frye, which sees Shakespearian comedy, for instance, in terms of the working out of particular plot or mythic structures, falls into a rather different category, but it is one which could also with some justification be called 'structuralist', albeit *avant la lettre*. Given this, the French critic Roland Barthes's account of the work of Racine, in which the plays appear not as vehicles for a moral or historical view of their contemporary world, but as the basis of a 'Racinian anthropology' whose complex and highly patterned system of thematic oppositions looks inward rather than referring directly outward, would not appear wholly foreign to Anglo-American readers familiar, say, with Wilson Knight's concept of the 'Lear universe'.[3]

But perhaps the classic 'structuralist' reading of a Shakespearian text remains that undertaken by Roman Jakobson and Lawrence Jones in their analysis of Shakespeare's Sonnet 129 'Th' expense of spirit in a waste of shame'.[4] The complex patterning which such a reading claims for the text will not of course be immediately obvious to all readers. Indeed, one critic complained they would have to be 'superreaders' to cope. But it stands as a powerful and exhilarating exercise in pushing one kind of structuralism to its virtual limits, and it has found a not unappreciative audience in I. A. Richards, whose piece on 'Jakobson's Shakespeare: the subliminal structures of a sonnet' provides a valuable commentary on the process.[5]

The major gain of this sort of reading lies in its recognition of the Shakespearian text as precisely that: a *text*. It is not claimed as a guide to the author's state of mind, or to the psychological make-up of the characters involved, to the extent of wishing a 'real life' dimension upon them. In fact, structuralism in its early days roundly pronounced the 'death' of the author, in the sense that it denied any possibility of an untrammelled, unmediated passage from the text to its presumed authorial 'source'. The target of such a stratagem was of course the 'authority' that seems to derive from the author as source, because that can claim to limit the meanings which a text may have. *Macbeth*, seen thus, could only mean what Shakespeare, its author, authoritatively meant it to mean. On the contrary, the structuralist case claims that since, to use Heidegger's notion, it is language that speaks rather than man, then the written word, independent of the 'authority' of its author, can be said to enjoy an autonomous productivity: writing, not the author, writes. As *texts*, in the structuralist view, Shakespeare's plays thus have a life, a structure, of their own.

III Beyond structuralism: poststructuralism or deconstruction

The major limitation of the structuralist project must lie in its commitment to fitting every aspect of a text into the overall pattern or structure which it perceives. Breaks in the pattern, indeterminate features or developments, moments when issues are clouded or ways forward only ambiguously discernible are obviously disruptive of the enterprise at large. But poststructuralism, or the activity of deconstruction which puts its principles into practice, focuses precisely on these indeterminacies, using them to mount a larger philosophical argument which ultimately aims to subvert, not only structuralism's claims, but the whole Western view of the world.

In effect, deconstruction focuses attention precisely on the reading–writing nexus and through it on the illusions which it claims hold the Western mind in thrall: that language refers to an originating 'presence' beyond itself; that writing, apparently the shadow of language, can reach and communicate meaningfully about a prior unified reality vested in its author; that reading involves the simple transference of an agreed meaning from writer to reader. The most devastating attack upon the falsifying 'metaphysics of presence' underlying these notions has been mounted by Jacques Derrida, in his *De La Grammatologie* (Paris, 1967) and subsequent volumes.

Saussure's work demonstrates, as we have seen, that language creates meaning through the differences and distinctions it manufactures within itself. Our sense of a direct, one-to-one correspondence between words and the 'real world' to which they refer beyond language is thus an illusion, albeit a compelling one. Derrida attacks the broad extension of that illusion into our conceptual presuppositions – even those of Saussure himself. Its epicentre lies in our sense that there exists somewhere, beyond all mediation, a pristine voice, an antecedent 'presence', a graspable origin towards which that mediation impels us. The grip of that illusion remains powerful and anaesthetic. In fact, Derrida sees this 'logocentric' or essentialist belief in 'presence' as a major factor limiting our apprehension of the world: a world which consists, finally, of no ultimate unmediated or original presence with which we can come face to face, but of a multiplicity of competing sign-systems referring endlessly in their 'free play' of differences one to another.

For the Shakespearian critic, the implications are vast. Clearly, such a view, like that of structuralism, requires the abandonment of anything approaching Bradley's notion of reading as a pathway to the final 'presence' of the author's mind. Bradley's sense of the capacity of the text to reveal 'character' is also doomed by it. For the deconstructive critic, the very tropes, metaphors, and images through which Bradley sees the real presence of character yielding itself in all its complexity, are nothing less than the means by which language exhibits its strategies for freedom from the constraints of 'presence'. Precisely because of its tropes, its metaphors, its images, language cannot be reduced to a series of unified, graspable, 'readable' and authorially validated meanings. It certainly cannot accurately depict character. Texts are never accurate or finished or concluded. They are endlessly, like language itself, in free play: wholly and permanently productive, referring to other texts, other uses of language, rather than to a limited range of referents imposed from outside themselves. The kind of reduced 'readability' presupposed by 'old' Shakespearian criticism is not genuinely available. As Hillis Miller puts it, all texts are unreadable 'if by "readable" one means a single definitive interpretation'.[6]

The aim of deconstructive analysis, therefore, can hardly be the reconstitution or recuperation of what the 'unreadable' text means to the reader. On the contrary, it aims to demonstrate that no such meaning, no such limited 'readability' exists. By running the readability film backwards, by unpicking or 'deconstructing' the carefully woven strands which make up the text's sense-making surface, by focusing attention on its contradictory features which the writer – unwittingly – is unable to control, and by showing that they offer, not a guarantee of a restricted presence beyond themselves, but an entry to the broad realm of language at large, the deconstructive critic puts the case that literature gives priority to the free play of language over meaning. As Geoffrey Hartman expresses it, deconstruction 'refuses to identify the force of literature with any concept of embodied meaning'. Rejecting such 'logocentric or incarnationist perspectives', it recognizes that words offer, not the restriction of presence, but the freedom of 'a certain absence or indeterminacy of meaning'.[7]

Essentially, then, a deconstructive account of a Shakespearian text would seek to undermine the illusion of character and of access to the author's mind that Bradleian criticism presupposes. It would also refuse and subvert the pattern of oppositions and tensions that structuralism discerns in the text, claiming that these are imposed on it from outside as a means of limiting its potentially endless proliferation of meaning. In seeking to show how all writing covertly resists its own reduction to unitary 'meaning' and how no such meaning can be recovered from or be made simply available to the single text confronting the reader, deconstruction would finally play havoc with the modern editor's efforts to produce a unified text of a Shakespearian play, and would regard all such enterprises as marks of the tyrannical boundaries within which the Western mind operates.

There is, as yet, no body of deconstructive analysis of Shakespeare to which a supporter or a detractor can point and so the above outline can do no more than gesture at the sort of undermining of fundamental principles which would be involved. However, Christopher Norris's introductory volume *Deconstruction: Theory and Practice* (1982) gives the central details of the theory, and his 'Post-structuralist Shakespeare: text and ideology' takes up a number of the issues at stake.[8] James L. Calderwood's extremely lively *To Be and Not To Be: Negation and Metadrama in Hamlet* (New York, 1983) also considers matters raised by poststructuralist notions in a disconcerting and provocative reading of the play.

It may of course be objected that where both structuralism and poststructuralism focus upon the *text* of the Shakespearian play, that text is only one aspect of the play's existence. A prior and major dimension of it must involve the play's performance, before an audience, in the theatre. The modern critical approach which takes this issue on board derives from the study of semiotics.

IV Semiotics

The central concern of semiotics is with the nature of signs. Although as a field of study it cannot properly be termed a science and in truth is more accurately described as a point of view, or 'way of looking' at the world, it has a long history, stretching back at least to the ancient Greeks. Semiotics is dedicated to the study of how meaning is produced in society, and thus concerns itself with the whole range of the process of signification and communication: that is, with the generation and exchange of meanings. In Keir Elam's words 'its objects are thus at once the different sign-systems and codes at work in society and the actual messages and texts produced thereby'.[9] Semiotic literary criticism certainly draws on the insights provided by structuralism, particularly with regard to its concept of the text, but it aims at a more complete investigation of the text within its own historical and cultural setting, as well as within the setting it acquires in the modern world. Seen thus, the text is far from the relatively simple object that Bradleian critical analysis makes of it. In the words of Alessandro Serpieri, it stands as the site of 'virtually all the semiotic systems at work in a given culture'.[10]

In the case of the *dramatic* text, the situation is even more complex as numbers of non-verbal semiotic systems involving dress, make-up, gesture, spatial relations, the use of props, the use of music, the use of sound effects, etc., all become involved. And even though the dominant system may be that of language, it is language designed to be uttered and not read: language that performs actions, and in doing so also refers to the context in which it is uttered.

The generation and exchange of meanings on stage and between stage and audience whilst the dramatic text is being performed thus becomes the centre of attention for the semiotic analysis of a play, and its complexities are clearly manifold. They are increased by the fact that the theatre traffics in a virtually indiscriminate 'semiotizing' process to an extent that is neatly encapsulated in Jiri Veltrusky's pronouncement that 'All that is on the stage is a sign.'[11] This makes the *semiosis* of the dramatic text impossible finally to control. If the actor playing Hamlet fortuitously turns up with a pimple on his nose, the audience is free to respond to this as part of the play's meaning, perhaps as a symbol of the corruptibility of the flesh.

Nevertheless, the semiotic analysis of Shakespeare's texts has made a number of inroads into the wilderness, and is actively involved in clearing a significant space within which it is able to operate. Something of the power of that operation can be glimpsed in a brief consideration of the issue of deixis.

Deixis refers to the process whereby language establishes the context in which it is taking place and deictics are those words, such as the personal pronouns 'I' and 'you' and the adverbs 'here' and 'now', whose meaning can only be pinned down by a specific context. The context, that is, enables such words as 'I' and 'you' and 'here' and 'now' to generate meaning. Deixis is a highly important semiotic device in drama, and indeed a play could hardly function without characters presenting themselves as 'I' and addressing other characters as 'you' in contexts in which 'here' and 'now' are clearly determined.

In the Elizabethan theatre, the structure of the playhouse and the close relation of stage to audience, to say nothing of the centrality of 'performance' in the way of life of a far from wholly literate culture, would have given the deictic thrust of words and gestures a heightened potential for including the audience within their range. Iago's

> Even now, now, very now an old black ram
> Is tupping your white ewe   (1.1.89–90)

thus had an immediacy in an Elizabethan context that a contemporary theatre cannot match. The same is true of the moment in *The Winter's Tale* when Leontes, speaking of his wife's supposed infidelity, says

> And many a man there is, even at this present,
> Now while I speak this, holds his wife by th' arm
> That little thinks she has been sluiced in 's absence.   (1.1.192–4)

The context established by the deictics 'now' and 'this' in these lines includes the whole theatre, and thus men currently holding their wives by the arm in the present audience. The Shakespearian play's capacity suddenly to reach out and include the audience in the action almost as an additional, and highly important, character is revealed clearly by this sort of analysis to be part of its complex of stratagems for the generation of meaning.

In fact, Serpieri has argued that all semiotic functions in the dramatic text derive from the deictic orientation of the utterance towards its context and that deictic words thus constitute the basic semiotic units of dramatic representation. If gesture and bodily movement as well as costume and the use of props are added to the picture, they can all be seen as means of establishing, in the deictic mode, the whole meaningful sphere in which the 'I' and 'you' who people the stage finally operate. In Serpieri's words, 'In the theatre . . . meaning is entrusted *in primis* to the deixis.'[12]

More recently, Serpieri's work has turned to the task of relating Shakespeare's texts to what the Italian semiotician Umberto Eco has called the 'global semantic field' of the era in which they were conceived. To this end he has examined the semiotic terms used to handle the 'great structural and epistemological crisis' that occurred between the sixteenth and seventeenth centuries. If the crisis is seen as a clash between two opposed 'models' of the world, two different ways of organizing reality, their semiotic dimensions can be discerned by considering them in the manner suggested by the Soviet semiotician Yuri Lotman as a *symbolic* model opposed to a *syntagmatic* model. In the former model (a product of the classical–medieval–Renaissance tradition) meaning was guaranteed by metaphor or analogy; in the latter by rational causal relationships. These two models can also be seen to reflect two opposed notions of language. The degree to which Shakespearian drama encodes the decay of the symbolic model and the encroachment upon it of the syntagmatic model can be demonstrated by an account of the semiotics of the play's language, settings, spatial relationships, and 'deictic orientations'.

Despite its complexities, forced upon it by the nature of the task, the semiotic analysis of Shakespearian texts is beginning to afford new insights as well as to confirm older ones. A good general introduction to the subject may be found in Keir Elam's *The Semiotics of Theatre and Drama* (1980) and a more specific account of its application to Shakespeare is given by Serpieri in his 'Reading the signs: towards a semiotics of Shakespearean drama'.[13] Elam's *Shakespeare's Universe of Discourse: Language Games in the Comedies* (Cambridge, 1984) breaks new ground in related areas and indicates the potential range of this sort of activity.

One of the major semiotic fields involving all of us must be that of gender. While nature may be said to divide the human species into male and female, the process which assigns the categories and roles of 'men' and 'women' belongs to the realm of culture. The ways in which culture generates meaning by means of gender has become a primary concern of that sphere of critical activity which derives from feminism.

V Feminism

In fact, the range of interests covered by this term is wide and varied, but in so far as it involves a single and central shift of social focus its different aspects can be said to manifest a unity, however flexibly jointed the connections might be.

For the feminist literary critic, two fundamental strategies immediately offer themselves. A text may be analysed in order to register details of its overt presentation of women in terms of the role and function it establishes for them or imposes on them; or the texts can be analysed from what may be termed a woman's point of view. The first strategy runs the risk of defeating feminism's ultimate, or ulterior, purpose, which presumably involves a change in the status of women in society. It does so because in effect it begins from and thus does not so much challenge as reinforce the male or phallocentric status quo. It would point out and certainly deplore the light in which a play like *The Taming of the Shrew* presents women. It would add, perhaps, that whatever a modern production might try to do to reverse its implications, it is a light which the Shakespeare canon by and large confirms. However much we admire Beatrice's spirit, say, in *Much Ado About Nothing*, or the challenges to traditional male authority implicit in *A Midsummer Night's Dream* or *As You Like It*, these plays continue to endorse a particular view of women's 'nature' which is dominated by requirements of marriage and family and which relegates women to an inevitably subordinate social position. Unfortunately, such readings leave the text very much as they find it. The play 'says', albeit more clearly, what it has always said.

On the other hand, to choose to read a Shakespeare text from a woman's point of view involves a radical re-reading of it, against its traditional male-orientated 'grain', and will produce accounts of the text that carry quite different historical implications and which might well involve an imperative for action in the present. Thus a feminist reading of *Macbeth* would produce a text crucially different from the one to which most of us are presently accustomed. The differences would obviously lie in the centrality accorded by it, first to Lady Macbeth rather than her husband, and second to the Witches. Those actions of Lady Macbeth which covertly subvert and finally annul Macbeth's manhood would, in such a reading, be seen to transfer a putative 'manly' role to herself in a specific mode: in order to succeed, she has to be 'unsexed', to become a 'man' of a particular sort. The challenge she represents to the established order would emerge precisely in those terms: she challenges that order's notion of what a man (and therefore a woman) properly is. Her subversion of propriety thus involves far more than regicide: it involves homicide in a surprisingly full sense of that term. She becomes the play's most radical murderer, perhaps embodying the sort of political ogre that a severely threatened maleness might conceive in response to a particular set of historical circumstances.

The Witches, hovering between maleness and femaleness, focus in this kind of reading on precisely the same fundamental and defining boundary. In a society whose religion is overtly male-dominated, witchcraft can be apprehended as the vehicle of a female voice forced to speak covertly of possible alternative notions of the supernatural and of an alternative set of relations to it. Elizabethan and Jacobean hysteria concerning witchcraft might then be seen as one indication of a crisis felt by society in respect of the role it assigned to women, with its consequent suppression of their counter-claims to a different degree and level of involvement. The political and religious linchpin of that society, King James, was a man whose sexual status was not easily determinable, and who might thus be said to have experienced women as to some extent threatening. He was in any case the author of a famous volume denouncing witchcraft, *Daemonologie* (1597). Read thus, a play like *Macbeth* – designed for performance before the King and focusing attention on James's own forebears in the person of Banquo – can be said at least to reproduce aspects of, even to diagnose, an otherwise occluded yet major conflict.

Such readings obviously transform texts of which we have inherited a particular view, and they do so radically. Within the range of activity labelled 'feminism' only a relatively small amount of material has so far been produced which focuses directly on Shakespeare, but its impact is potentially very powerful indeed. The work of Juliet Dusinberre in *Shakespeare and the Nature of Women* (1975), Marilyn French in *Shakespeare's Division of Experience* (1982), and Lisa Jardine in *Still Harping on Daughters: Women and Drama in the Age of Shakespeare* (Brighton, 1983), as well as the collection of essays edited by Carolyn Lenz, Gayle Green and Carol Thomas Nealy, *The Woman's Part: Feminist Criticism of Shakespeare* (Chicago, 1980) tends to fall into the first category mentioned above. The view implicit in the second category is taken, for example, in Catherine Belsey's work.[14] Valuable bibliographies are to be found in all the above volumes.

Finally, attention must be drawn to one of the oldest of 'new' critical approaches, and to a relatively recent set of developments from within it. This involves Marxism and the study of discourse.

VI Marxism and discourse

The claims of feminism to offer a 'new' critical approach to Shakespeare are indisputable. Those of Marxism are less so if only because it can hardly present itself as 'new' in the same way. Nor, in this respect, is it as readily discernible as a discrete entity. In much Anglo-American criticism, Marxist terms and concepts have to a considerable degree been absorbed, naturalized, or even (Marxists might claim) domesticated, with the result that, say, feminism, semiotic analysis, even some aspects of deconstruction, may be undertaken from a Marxist point of view. Traditional untrammelled Marxism remains nonetheless the concern of a number of critics such as Elliot Krieger, whose *A Marxist Study of Shakespeare's Comedies* (1979) offers a solid introduction to this sort of approach, and the East German critic Robert Weimann. Weimann's *Shakespeare and the Popular Tradition in the Theatre* (Baltimore and London, 1978) presents a dialectical study of the relation of Shakespeare's plays to the popular drama which preceded and was contemporaneous with them, and in whose tradition they operate. Here the Elizabethan theatre emerges as 'a national institution in which native popular traditions were enlarged and enriched in many ways by a variety of elements, most notably, Renaissance ideology' (p. 208).

That ideology's manifestations of itself, in folk plays and social customs, in mysteries, moralities, and interludes, in the shape and physical dimensions of the platform stage and the relation it fostered between *platea* and *locus*, between 'neutral, undifferentiated "place" and symbolic location' (p. 212), forms the book's central concern.

Yet probably the most significant development in Marxist theory in recent years has involved changes in the concept of ideology itself. The influence of thinkers such as Louis Althusser has required a redefinition and a broadening of its scope. As a result ideology has ceased to be thought of as involving a false apprehension of the world, something that we can elect to believe in or stand aside from. Instead it appears as a 'given', a sense of the 'natural' and the 'real' which we inherit, willy-nilly, and without which it is impossible to conceive the world we inhabit. To use the words of Jonathan Dollimore, ideology appears as 'not a set of false beliefs capable of correction by perceiving properly, but the very terms in which we perceive the world, almost . . . the condition and grounds of consciousness itself'.[15]

If some sort of ideology is inescapable, even necessary, it is nevertheless possible, even desirable, to challenge the form it takes, the 'norms' it imposes, the concepts of identity and selfhood it determines. The traditional Marxist battle in this respect between the 'falsely' ideological and the 'truly' non-ideological can hardly take place, since that distinction is dissolved. Instead, the contests for power that shape all ideologies and can be discerned to be under way in each of them, may be seen as a struggle between a number of opposed ways of using language. These antagonistic 'discourses', or discursive 'practices', compete with each other for dominance, for the right to determine what 'knowledge', and so what 'reality', is.

The major proponent of this view is the French philosopher Michel Foucault, and the impact of his 'Foucauldian' notions can be seen in the work of such Shakespeare scholars as Stephen Greenblatt and Jonathan Goldberg.[16] From this standpoint, Shakespeare's plays become instances of and arenas for the clash of different and opposed discourses, and thus of different and opposed kinds of knowledge and ultimately power. What is at stake is a quite different concept of history and in particular of the history of the Renaissance in Europe: one which directly challenges the work, say, of E. M. W. Tillyard's *The Elizabethan World Picture* (1943). The insights yielded by this sort of analysis into the construction of notions of identity, subjectivity, women and the family in Shakespeare's time are seen to carry powerful implications for similar concepts in our own.

VII New and old: the question of reception

The notion that a 'reading' undertaken from a particular political or social point of view can transform a text which pre-exists that reading, nevertheless contains a potential pitfall which it is important, finally, to confront. For it involves the idea of an essential and ultimately unchanging text which lies behind all the different readings to which it may be subjected. In confronting that idea we are led towards a major and developing area of recent critical activity which involves the study of the degree to which all texts are always read from particular points of view all the time. The 'essential' text, it seems to follow, is never genuinely available to us.

Work in this sphere forms part of a general shift of interest, characteristic of modern critical theory at large, from the author of the text to its reader. Bradley's concern with what goes on in the poet's mind is thus finally rejected and replaced by its opposite: a concern with the manner and the circumstances in which the text is responded to or received by its audience.

A number of collective names exists for critical enterprises of this general sort, and a good survey of the differences between various approaches is given in Robert C. Holub's *Reception Theory* (1984), where the intricacies of the German studies in *Rezeptionsgeschichte* (history of reception), *Wirkungsästhetik* (aesthetics of effects or response), and *Rezeptionsästhetik* (aesthetics of reception) are distinguished from Anglo-American confections such as 'transactive criticism' and 'reader-response criticism'.

The first principle of such studies must be that no text means by itself: no text has a single, essential untransformable meaning to which, when all criticism is said and done, we can finally turn. We *make* texts mean, the argument runs, and the positions from which we do so constitute a major aspect of the meanings we produce. There is even a complex sense in which, in the case of Shakespeare's plays, our culture can be said to mean *by* them. This of course implies that those plays function as an important arena in which opposed social and political forces compete to construct and promote meaning. To deny that is to deny that the plays exist within, and as part of, history. That is certainly what any argument which appeals to the text 'itself', beyond and untroubled by such competition, denies. But if there is no essential text 'itself' – able to be plucked from the historical context which defines and brings it to our attention – then the case requires a good deal of further consideration.

These are issues to which a number of recent studies have dedicated themselves and their work can be said to turn attention from Shakespeare's texts to the way in which those texts are processed. In short, it turns to the literary criticism, and indeed to the larger industry of production, packaging, and presentation which surrounds the plays. It tries to give, by an analysis of that processing, an insight into the nature of the society for which a particular set of Shakespearian meanings is constructed.

In this sense, as was said earlier, the nature, the provenance, and the durability of criticism such as Bradley's is of great interest. A new critical approach can here be seen directly to confront an 'old' approach, by making that its subject. The concern of such analysis is the use to which the plays are put, rather than the plays themselves, and it is undertaken in a context which denies that those are separable concerns and which insists that the plays have no effective existence in or as 'themselves'. One of the founding fathers of this kind of criticism must be said, perhaps surprisingly, to be Alfred Harbage, whose underrated study *Conceptions of Shakespeare* (Cambridge, Mass., 1966) was one of the first to take this as a major issue. Subsequent work, by Brian Doyle and Derek Longhurst for instance, relates the processing of Shakespeare to the establishment of 'English' itself as a subject closely involved in a drive to reinforce particular notions of national coherence and identity in times of crisis.[17] Shakespeare's part in the academic promotion of an ideal of 'Englishness' thus becomes a major factor in the persistent underwriting of his plays as components of a 'national' heritage.

If this means, in terms of the present undertaking, that the newest of the new critical approaches to Shakespeare is finally concerned with the nature and function of the older Shakespearian criticism, then that might seem to stand as only another instance of how the whirligig of time brings in his revenges. Yet that Shakespeare should be joined on the syllabus by A. C. Bradley, that the texts of Shakespearian tragedy should share the critic's attention with a text called *Shakespearean Tragedy*, is not mere perversity. It is the result of a fundamental questioning of the legitimacy of inherited polarities such as writer–reader, actor–audience, creator–critic, which it has been the achievement of modern criticism to initiate, and which it now remains its task to continue.

Notes

1. See Katherine Cooke, *A. C. Bradley and his Influence on Twentieth Century Shakespeare Criticism* (Oxford, 1972), p. 50 and p. 184.

2. A. C. Bradley, *Shakespearean Tragedy* (1904, 1964), pp. 7–8.
3. Roland Barthes, *On Racine* (*Sur Racine*, Paris, 1963); translated by Richard Howard (New York, 1964). See also G. Wilson Knight, *The Wheel of Fire* (Oxford, 1930), chapter 9.
4. Roman Jakobson and Lawrence Jones, *Shakespeare's Verbal Art in Th' Expence of Spirit* (The Hague, 1970).
5. See *The Times Literary Supplement*, 28 May 1970, pp. 589–96.
6. See Harold Bloom, Paul de Man, Jacques Derrida, Geoffrey H. Hartman, J. Hillis Miller, *Deconstruction and Criticism* (New York, 1979), p. 226.
7. *Ibid.* pp. vii–viii.
8. The essay appears in John Drakakis, ed., *Alternative Shakespeares* (1985).
9. Keir Elam, *The Semiotics of Theatre and Drama* (1980), p. 1.
10. Alessandro Serpieri, 'Reading the signs: towards a semiotics of Shakespearean drama', in *Alternative Shakespeares*, p. 120.
11. Elam, *Semiotics*, p. 7.
12. *Ibid.*, pp. 139–40.
13. See note 10.
14. This includes an essay, 'Disrupting sexual difference', in *Alternative Shakespeares*, pp. 166–90, and a book, *The Subject of Tragedy* (1985).
15. Jonathan Dollimore, *Radical Tragedy: Religion, Ideology and Power in the Drama of Shakespeare and his Contemporaries* (Brighton, 1984) p. 9.
16. See reading list.
17. Brian Doyle, 'The hidden history of English studies' and Derek Longhurst, 'Not for all time, but for an Age' in Peter Widdowson, ed., *Re-reading English* (1982). See also Terence Hawkes, *The Shakespeherian Rag* (1986).

Reading list

GENERAL
Drakakis, John, ed., *Alternative Shakespeares* (1985)
Dollimore, Jonathan, and Sinfield, Alan, eds., *Political Shakespeare* (Manchester, 1985)

STRUCTURALISM
Hawkes, Terence, *Structuralism and Semiotics* (1977, 1984)
Frye, Northrop, *A Natural Perspective* (New York and London, 1965)

POSTSTRUCTURALISM
Norris, Christopher, *Deconstruction: Theory and Practice* (1982)
  'Poststructuralist Shakespeare: text and ideology', in John Drakakis, ed., *Alternative Shakespeares*
Culler, Jonathan, *On Deconstruction: Theory and Criticism after Structuralism* (1983)
Calderwood, James L., *To Be and Not To Be: Negation and Metadrama in Hamlet* (New York, 1983)

SEMIOTICS
Elam, Keir, *The Semiotics of Theatre and Drama* (1980)
  Shakespeare's Universe of Discourse: Language Games in the Comedies (Cambridge, 1984)
Serpieri, Alessandro, 'Reading the signs: towards a semiotics of Shakespearean drama', in John Drakakis, ed., *Alternative Shakespeares*

FEMINISM

French, Marilyn, *Shakespeare's Division of Experience* (1982)
Jardine, Lisa, *Still Harping on Daughters: Women and Drama in the Age of Shakespeare* (Brighton, 1983)
Lenz, Carolyn Ruth Swift, Green, Gayle, and Nealy, Carol Thomas, eds., *The Woman's Part: Feminist Criticism of Shakespeare* (Chicago, 1980)
Belsey, Catherine, *The Subject of Tragedy* (1985)
  'Disrupting sexual difference', in John Drakakis, ed., *Alternative Shakespeares*

MARXISM AND DISCOURSE

Krieger, Elliot, *A Marxist Study of Shakespeare's Comedies* (1979)
Weimann, Robert, *Shakespeare and the Popular Tradition in the Theatre* (Baltimore and London, 1978)
Dollimore, Jonathan, *Radical Tragedy: Religion, Ideology and Power in the Drama of Shakespeare and his Contemporaries* (Brighton, 1984)
Greenblatt, Stephen, *Renaissance Self-Fashioning* (Chicago, 1980)
Goldberg, Jonathan, *James I and the Politics of Literature: Jonson, Shakespeare, Donne and their Contemporaries* (Baltimore and London, 1983)
Horowitz, David, *Shakespeare: an Existential View* (1965)
See also the essays in *Political Shakespeare*

RECEPTION, ETC

Holub, Robert C., *Reception Theory* (1984)
Harbage, Alfred, *Conceptions of Shakespeare* (Cambridge, Mass., 1966)
Doyle, Brian, 'The hidden history of English studies', in Peter Widdowson, ed., *Re-reading English* (1982)
Longhurst, Derek, 'Not for all time, but for an Age', *ibid.*
Hawkes, Terence, *That Shakespeherian Rag* (1986)

17 Shakespeare reference books

Bibliographies

THE reader who wants a more or less complete list of writings on Shakespeare up to 1958 will have to work his or her way through four volumes that attempt to provide a comprehensive and systematic record of everything written on the poet and his works.

William Jaggard's *Shakespeare Bibliography* (1911) is not very reliable or systematic, but still useful for the information it contains on early Shakespeare criticism. Its continuation by W. Ebisch and L. L. Schücking, *A Shakespeare Bibliography* (1931) and *Supplement for the Years 1930–35* (1937), is much more professional and easier to use, whereas the fourth volume, Gordon Ross Smith's *A Classified Shakespeare-Bibliography, 1936–1958* (1963), is rather too sophisticated in its classification and therefore less easy to consult.

An intelligently selective list is given in volume one of *The New Cambridge Bibliography of English Literature*, edited by George Watson (1974), and there are several helpful shorter bibliographies. Ronald Berman's *A Reader's Guide to Shakespeare's Plays: A Discursive Bibliography* (1965, revised edition 1973) gives a judicious selection with brief and sensible comment, but, as its title suggests, it covers the plays only, not more general aspects or background. A good and not too formidable survey of important titles is offered by Stanley Wells in *Shakespeare: A Reading Guide* (second edition 1970); another is provided by *A Selective Bibliography of Shakespeare Editions, Textual Studies, Commentary*, edited by James G. McManaway and Jeanne Addison Roberts (1975); published for the Folger Shakespeare Library, it lists 4,519 items, mainly from 1930 to about 1973. David Bevington's *Shakespeare* (1978) in the series Goldentree Bibliographies in Language and Literature gives an excellent selection of roughly the same scope. Helpful guidance of a more discursive kind is provided by *Shakespeare: Select Bibliographical Guides*, edited by Stanley Wells (1973). Its seventeen chapters are written by different scholars, and concise bibliographies are given at the end of each chapter.

For more recent books and the annual contributions to Shakespeare studies the reader must consult either the *Annual Bibliography of English Language and Literature*, published by the Modern Humanities Research Association, or the annual bibliography published as part of the *Publications of the Modern*

Language Association of America. There are also annual bibliographies in *Shakespeare Quarterly*, briefly annotated and available as a separate volume, and in *Shakespeare Jahrbuch*. The *Jahrbuch* of the Deutsche Shakespeare-Gesellschaft West had, between 1971 and 1983, an annual bibliography of works on Shakespeare published in German-speaking countries. From 1984 there is no bibliography and the reader is referred to *Shakespeare Quarterly*.

Equally useful for most purposes are the annual reviews of the most significant contributions in *The Year's Work in English Studies* (usually about two or three years behind) and, generally more up-to-date, in *Shakespeare Survey*, with sections on 'Life, Times, and Stage', 'Critical Studies', and 'Textual Studies'.

There are also extensive bibliographies in many of the reference books mentioned below, especially the *Shakespeare Encyclopaedia*, the *Shakespeare Handbuch*, and Bullough's *Narrative and Dramatic Sources of Shakespeare*.

Periodicals

There are several periodicals devoted to the study of Shakespeare.

Shakespeare Quarterly, started in 1950, includes reports on Shakespearian productions all over the world and reviews of important books as well as miscellaneous articles. Each volume of the annual *Shakespeare Survey* (from 1948) has a particular theme, but also includes articles on other topics. Several volumes begin with helpful surveys of critical writings on the theme of the volume (e.g. *Hamlet* in 1956 and 1965, *Othello* in 1968, *King Lear* in 1980, and 'The Ancient World in Shakespeare' in 1978). *Shakespeare Studies* (from 1965) is another annual collection of essays and reviews.

The oldest periodical is the *Shakespeare Jahrbuch*, published for the first time in 1864 by the Deutsche Shakespeare-Gesellschaft. When this association split up in 1964, the Shakespeare-Gesellschaft West renamed its annual volume *Deutsche Shakespeare-Gesellschaft West. Jahrbuch* though editors and publisher remained the same, whereas the Shakespeare-Gesellschaft with its seat in Weimar started its own annual volume under the old name. Both publications contain essays in English and German, reviews of productions and books, and reports of the annual meetings. *Shakespearean Research and Opportunities* (from 1965) reports on the annual MLA conference and provides checklists, reviews, and selected papers as well as a section 'Research in Progress'.

Dictionaries, encyclopaedias, handbooks

There are a number of good reference books on Shakespeare's plays and their background. F. E. Halliday's *A Shakespeare Companion. 1564–1964* (1964) is surprisingly comprehensive for its size and extremely useful: a dictionary with entries on a great variety of topics, from Aaron (*Titus Andronicus*) to Zuccaro, the portrait painter. It is particularly good on textual matters, theatrical companies, contemporary documents and personalities. *Shakespeare. An Illustrated Dictionary* by Stanley Wells (1978, revised 1985) is equally reliable and more pleasant to use though also more selective. Much more ambitious and comprehensive is the splendid *A Shakespeare Encyclopaedia*, edited by Oscar James Campbell and Edward G. Quinn (1966). Many of its articles are written by well-known experts. There are plenty of illustrations and long sections on each play, discussing dates, textual evidence, stage history, and interpretation, and concluding with brief excerpts from influential critics. *A New Companion to Shakespeare Studies*, edited by Kenneth Muir and S. Schoenbaum (1971) is a book of a different kind. It contains eighteen essays by different authors on general aspects, such as Shakespeare's language, his theatre, the social and historical background, and the history of Shakespeare criticism.

The German *Shakespeare-Handbuch. Die Zeit. Der Mensch. Das Werk. Die Nachwelt*, edited by Ina Schabert (second edition 1978) is a volume of nearly a thousand pages covering every aspect of Shakespeare studies, from the historical background to the history of Shakespeare criticism and adaptation, with detailed bibliographies at the end of each section. It is perhaps the most comprehensive reference book of its kind.

Among reference books proper the indispensable *Annals of English Drama 975–1700* should also be mentioned. It was first edited by Alfred Harbage and completely revised by S. Schoenbaum (1964, with supplements in 1966 and 1970). It provides, as the subtitle says, *An Analytical Record of all Plays, Extant or Lost, Chronologically Arranged and Indexed by Authors, Titles, Dramatic Companies &c.* Much fuller bibliographical information is provided by W. W. Greg's *A Bibliography of the English Printed Drama to the Restoration*, in four volumes (1939–59).

Concordances

John Bartlett's *A New and Complete Concordance or Verbal Index to Words, Phrases, and Passages in the Dramatic Works of Shakespeare with a Supplementary Concordance to the Poems* (1894) was the standard work of its kind until the appearance of Marvin Spevack's *The Harvard Concordance to Shakespeare* (1973) which is based on the monumental, computerized *A Complete and Systematic Concordance to the Works of Shakespeare* in eight volumes (1968–75) by the same editor, classified by plays, characters, and stage directions and providing all kinds of interesting statistical information on Shakespeare's vocabulary, the language of each character, and the linguistic peculiarities of each play. There are also the handy little volumes of the old-spelling *Oxford Shakespeare Concordances* by T. H. Howard-Hill (1969–73), covering one play each and useful for quick reference.

Language

E. A. Abbott's *A Shakespeare Grammar. An Attempt to Illustrate Some of the Differences between Elizabethan and Modern English* (1869, reprinted 1966) is still very useful; so is the more systematic and comprehensive *Die Sprache Shakespeares in Vers und Prosa* (1939, revised and enlarged edition of *Shakespeare-Grammatik*, 1898–1900) by W. Franz. A good modern survey is G. L. Brook's *The Language of Shakespeare* (1976); another stimulating introduction to many aspects of Shakespeare's language is provided by N. F. Blake, *Shakespeare's Language. An Introduction* (1983). Hilda M. Hulme's *Explorations in Shakespeare's Language. Some Problems of Lexical Meaning in the Dramatic Text* (1962) is good on selected aspects (use of proverbs, spelling, pronunciation, meaning).

On the more strictly practical level C. T. Onions's *A Shakespeare Glossary* (1911, repeatedly reprinted with addenda) is an invaluable little dictionary of Shakespearian meanings. On matters of pronunciation Helge Kökeritz's *Shakespeare's Pronunciation* (1953) has become a classic; it has only been partly superseded by the more systematic and comprehensive accounts of E. J. Dobson, *English Pronunciation 1500–1700*, two volumes (1957), and Fausto Cercignani, *Shakespeare's Works and Elizabethan Pronunciation* (1981). Dobson's work is, of course, not confined to Shakespeare and Cercignani is rather narrowly phonological in method and less concerned with literary aspects. There is also a useful little dictionary by Kökeritz on the pronunciation of names, *Shakespeare's Names: A Pronouncing Dictionary* (1959). Eric Partridge's dictionary of *Shakespeare's Bawdy* (1947, second edition 1968) makes entertaining reading, but occasionally tends to overestimate the indecent connotations of innocent words. More useful is the comprehensive collection by R. W. Dent, *Shakespeare's Proverbial Language. An Index* (1981), partly based on the important compilation by M. P. Tilley, *A Dictionary of the Proverbs in England in the Sixteenth and Seventeenth Centuries* (1950), which it expands considerably as far as Shakespeare is concerned. It lists 4,684 proverbial expressions in Shakespeare's work. Richmond Noble's *Shakespeare's Biblical Knowledge and Use of the Book of Common Prayer* (1935) is a useful inventory of two of the most important influences on Shakespeare's language.

Editions

Most serious students of Shakespeare will, sooner or later, want a complete edition of the plays and poems, and there are several good one-volume editions to choose from. The most widely used and most frequently quoted is still Peter Alexander's edition (*The Complete Works*, 1951) which is also available in four handy volumes; it has a sound text and a brief glossary, but not much in the way of background information or interpretation. C. J. Sisson's edition (*The Complete Works*, 1954) has a little more introductory material and includes *Sir Thomas More*. A number of American editions are more generous with glosses and commentary. Two good paperback single-play series (see below) have been gathered into one volume each, the Pelican edition (*The Complete Works*, edited by Alfred Harbage, 1969) and the Signet edition (*The Complete Signet Classic Shakespeare*, edited by Sylvan Barnet, 1972). More expensive and bulky but much more informative and useful for the student is *The Riverside Shakespeare*, edited by G. Blakemore Evans (1974); it includes background information, illustrations, and some excellent critical essays. Oxford University Press are preparing a new one-volume edition based on a complete rethinking of a number of fundamental textual issues; there will also be an old-spelling edition, a novelty that will be welcomed at least by all those readers who have been used to reading many of Shakespeare's contemporaries in the original spelling.

Many readers will prefer editions of individual plays, perhaps in addition to a one-volume edition. There is an almost embarrassing but also very helpful choice of single-play editions at various levels of sophistication and thoroughness.

The most formidable and the oldest of the series in progress is the New Variorum edition (*A New Variorum Edition of Shakespeare*), begun more than a century ago by H. H. Furness (1871) and still far from completed. It offers not only an old-spelling text with plenty of glosses, but also comment from the time of Shakespeare as well as a full anthology of criticism. The older volumes are invaluable inventories of early Shakespeare criticism and some have been reprinted in paperback form (1963). The more recent volumes are, in a way, less satisfactory, because modern criticism has grown to such an extent that it seems virtually impossible to represent it adequately within a single volume and the editors have to resort to mere bibliographical surveys or listings.

The New Shakespeare, edited almost single-handed by John Dover Wilson between 1921 and 1966, is still valuable for its influential textual innovations, for its useful stage histories, and for much stimulating comment, even though many of Dover Wilson's more daring theories concerning the genesis of the texts are no longer accepted by most scholars. The earlier volumes are, naturally, more outdated, but the later ones, especially the tragedies (partly edited by other scholars) are still very useful.

The new Arden Shakespeare began as a revision of the 'old' Arden edition (from 1899) in 1951 under the editorship of Una Ellis-Fermor, but it soon changed its policy and almost all the later volumes present a completely new text and commentary, together with full introductions, attempting to cover every important aspect of the play. By and large it is still the most impressive and helpful edition of all the plays, though it is rather uneven and in continual process of revision. Some of the latest volumes, especially those by the general editors (e.g. *A Midsummer Night's Dream*, edited by Harold Brooks, 1979, and *Hamlet*, edited by Harold Jenkins, 1982), will probably remain the most thorough and comprehensive single-volume editions for some time to come.

The American Signet Classic Shakespeare, edited by Sylvan Barnet (1963–70), is a useful paperback edition, with brief glosses on the page, good critical introductions, and excerpts from particularly stimulating critics. The individual volumes are edited by different scholars. The same applies to the Pelican Shakespeare, edited by Alfred Harbage (1956–67). It is, on the whole, more thorough and original than the Signet edition and the commentary is more scholarly.

The New Penguin Shakespeare (General Editor: T. J. B. Spencer; Associate Editor: Stanley Wells), begun in 1967 and still not quite complete, is the most widely used paperback edition in England; for some time now the Royal Shakespeare Company have based their productions on these texts. A number of the editors are the same as those for the Arden Shakespeare, but the edition obviously seeks to appeal to a wider audience. The volumes are, nevertheless, based on original scholarship and include information about text, date, sources and previous scholarship. There is a fairly long introduction to the play and a critical commentary following the text, explaining unfamiliar meanings, but also, in many cases, illuminating construction, style, and staging.

Two new series have just begun to appear and it is difficult to make a fair assessment on the basis of the first volumes. The Oxford Shakespeare (General Editor: Stanley Wells) differs sufficiently from earlier series to make it very rewarding, though the first volumes (three in 1982, two in 1984) are noticeably uneven in thoroughness and originality. The texts are freshly edited, sometimes with surprising results, as in the case of *Henry V*, edited by Gary Taylor. The commentary is particularly full on lexical matters (with an index) and on staging. Stage history (often with illustrations) plays a much larger part than in most previous editions and the critical introductions frequently pay as much attention to the theatrical qualities of the text as to literary aspects. The New Cambridge Shakespeare (General Editor: Philip Brockbank), begun in 1984 (eight volumes to date) is, perhaps, slightly less ambitious in scope and fullness; its intention, apparently, is to appeal to a wider public. The glosses at the foot of the page and the critical introductions are, to judge by the first volumes, a little more elementary than in the Oxford Shakespeare, but the principles of arrangement and commentary are very similar; in both cases the typographical design of the page is particularly successful and makes the text a pleasure to use. The Cambridge edition has an even more pronounced emphasis on problems of staging, with appealing drawings by C. Walter Hodges, illustrating possible reconstructions of Elizabethan staging. Both series are also available in paperback.

Facsimile editions are a special case; they are illuminating not just for the textual scholar, but for anyone wanting to see for themselves what the original page of a Shakespeare text looked like. This can provide a very good idea of the complex problems of modernization, emendation, and glossing that the modern editor has to face. The most sophisticated facsimile edition of the First Folio is the Norton Facsimile (*The First Folio of Shakespeare*, edited by Charlton Hinman, 1968); it is based on the best of the seventy-nine copies of the First Folio in the Folger Shakespeare Library and reproduces each page in its final and most perfect state. Most of the Quartos have also been published in facsimile editions (Shakespeare Quarto Facsimiles, edited by W. W. Greg and Charlton Hinman, from 1939), and they have been collected in a single volume (see p. 184, first item in Reading list).

Textual problems

The best introduction to the textual problems posed by individual plays is in most cases provided by the textual commentary of such critical editions as the Arden, the Oxford, or the New Cambridge. On a number of the problems which confront a modern editor Stanley Wells and Gary Taylor offer necessary and well-considered new ideas in *Modernizing Shakespeare's Spelling, with Three Studies in the Text of 'Henry V'* (1979); more general and wider in scope is Stanley Wells's *Re-Editing Shakespeare for the Modern Reader* (1984). F. P. Wilson's *Shakespeare and the New Bibliography* (revised and edited by Helen Gardner, 1970) is an expert introduction to the principles and the history of modern textual studies. A variety of textual and editorial problems are considered in E. A. J. Honigmann's *The Stability of Shakespeare's Text* (1965). Fredson Bowers, one of the most influential textual scholars of his generation, has written a useful survey *On Editing Shakespeare* (1966). One of the most thorough and sophisticated demonstrations of modern textual methods (with a touch of Sherlock Holmes, but not quite his finality) is Charlton Hinman's monumental study *The Printing and Proof-reading of the First Folio of Shakespeare* (two volumes, 1963); it supplements, but does not in all respects supersede, W. W. Greg's *The Shakespeare First Folio: Its Bibliographical and Textual History* (1955). Finally, there is a full bibliography of textual studies by T. H. Howard-Hill, *Shakespearian Bibliography and Textual Criticism: A Bibliography* (1971).

Shakespeare's life and time

Shakespeare's life has attracted all kinds of biographers and fact has often become inextricably confused with fiction and legend. One of the soundest and most useful works of reference is still E. K. Chambers's authoritative collection of all the surviving evidence relating to Shakespeare's life and his plays: *William Shakespeare: A Study of Facts and Problems* (two volumes, 1930). The condensed version, *A Short Life of Shakespeare with the Sources*, abridged by Charles Williams (1933), is a useful little compendium, even though some of the information is not quite up-to-date. A good brief survey is G. E. Bentley's *Shakespeare: A Biographical Handbook* (1961), which provides a reliable assessment of the evidence. There are a number of attractive pictorial volumes on Shakespeare's life, such as F. E. Halliday, *Shakespeare: A Pictorial Biography* (1953), and Anthony Burgess, *Shakespeare* (1970), and, of course, many more or less popular biographies, such as the sound and very readable volume by M. M. Reese, *Shakespeare: His World and His Work* (1953, second edition 1980), or Peter Quennell's reliable and informative account: *Shakespeare: The Poet and His Background* (1963). E. I. Fripp's *Shakespeare Man and Artist* (1938), in two volumes, is a useful quarry for miscellaneous information, particularly on the Stratford and Warwickshire background, but not always very reliable or easy to read. Much more factual and trustworthy, though more limited in scope, is Mark Eccles's *Shakespeare in Warwickshire* (1961).

The most authoritative and up-to-date books on Shakespeare's life are all by S. Schoenbaum. His monumental *Shakespeare's Lives* (1970) is not a biography in the usual sense, but a fascinating and entertaining history of Shakespeare biographers, biographies, the search for reliable information, and the invention of colourful legends. It is a book *about* biography rather than a straightforward account of Shakespeare's life and yet it leaves the reader with a more substantial and trustworthy image of its subject than most of the traditional biographies.

For those who wish to look at all the documentary evidence for themselves Schoenbaum's sumptuously produced collection of photographic facsimiles, *William Shakespeare. A Documentary Life* (1975), provides expert commentary and is the ideal biography. The narrative and many of the documents are included in the much cheaper and handier volume *William Shakespeare. A Compact Documentary Life* (1977; paperback edition 1978). This is easily the most reliable and best documented brief biography of Shakespeare.

Shakespeare. The Globe and the World (1977) is the catalogue of an exhibition arranged by the Folger Shakespeare Library. It is a wonderful picture book, with an excellent commentary by S. Schoenbaum, covering a wide range of subjects related to Shakespeare's life and work. The last volume, another splendidly illustrated and attractively produced book, completes the series of biographical documentation and illustration: *William Shakespeare: Records and Images* (1981), again by S. Schoenbaum. It is an invaluable supplement to the earlier works, illustrating and discussing Shakespeare's involvement in various legal disputes, his handwriting, and his portraits.

On Shakespeare's time and background there are, of course, a vast number of historical reference books and general studies that fall outside the scope of this brief survey. *Shakespeare's England: An Account of the Life and Manners of his Age*, edited by Sidney Lee and C. T. Onions (two volumes, 1916), is a still very useful collection of essays by various authors on many aspects of English culture in the age of Elizabeth. *Shakespeare Survey 17* (1964) forms a kind of supplement to it as well as an attempt to bring some of it up-to-date. *Shakespeare Survey 29* (1976) has a good review article by J. W. Lever on 'Shakespeare and the Ideas of His Time'. J. Dover Wilson's *Life in Shakespeare's England* (1911) is an informative and entertaining anthology of contemporary texts, deservedly popular and frequently reprinted.

Many books try to describe the Elizabethan world picture as a necessary introduction to the study of Shakespeare's works. This is always a risky undertaking, liable to superficial generalization, but some of the classic studies are still worth reading and considering: Hardin Craig, *The Enchanted Glass: The Elizabethan Mind in Literature* (1935) and the same author's *New Lamps for Old: A Sequel to the Enchanted Glass* (1960) are valuable introductions to crucial Renaissance concepts, as is A. O. Lovejoy's influential study *The Great Chain of Being* (1936). E. M. W. Tillyard's *The Elizabethan World Picture* (1943), frequently reprinted and quoted, offers perhaps a rather too neat view of a complex subject, but it is very readable and still one of the best introductions. J. B. Bamborough, *The Little World of Man* (1952), is particularly helpful on Elizabethan ideas on psychology. Madeleine Doran's *Endeavors of Art. A Study of Form in Elizabethan Drama* (1954) is one of the best and most influential accounts of literary conventions of the Renaissance.

Literary sources and influences

The most comprehensive account of Shakespeare's sources, together with all the more important texts, is to be found in Geoffrey Bullough's indispensable collection *Narrative and Dramatic Sources of Shakespeare* (eight volumes, 1957–75). There is a section on each play, with a substantial introduction and many complete texts or excerpts from sources and analogues. Foreign texts are given in translation. Kenneth Muir's *The Sources of Shakespeare's Plays* (1977) is a briefer survey of the same subject, without the texts.

Most critical editions of the plays give an account of the sources and (as in many volumes of the Arden edition) a selection of texts. More general questions of literary influence are discussed in T. W. Baldwin's *Shakespeare's Smalle Latine and Lesse Greeke* (two volumes, 1947) which gives useful information on the texts available in Shakespeare's time and in Elizabethan schools. John Velz, *Shakespeare and the Classical Tradition: A Critical Guide to Commentary, 1660–1960* (1968) is a comprehensive bibliography of studies on the subject (2,487 items), with brief comment.

There are many books on particular influences. V. K. Whitaker, *Shakespeare's Use of Learning* (1953), is stimulating, if rather general. R. A. Brower, *Hero and Saint. Shakespeare and the Graeco-Roman Heroic Tradition* (1972), discusses the tragedies in the light of classical influences. An extremely helpful account of the traditions of comedy and their impact on Shakespeare is to be found in Leo Salingar, *Shakespeare and the Traditions of Comedy* (1974), which covers classical, medieval and Italian influences. Emrys L. Jones, *The Origins of Shakespeare* (1976), is useful on dramatic influences on the early Shakespeare, especially the combination of popular and classical material. A wide-ranging and influential reassessment of popular traditions and their impact on Shakespeare is offered in Robert Weimann's learned as well as highly original study *Shakespeare and the Popular Tradition in the Theatre. Studies in the Social Dimension of Dramatic Form and Function*, edited by Robert Schwartz (1978), first published in German (1967). More limited, but of seminal importance, is Bernard Spivack, *Shakespeare and the Allegory of Evil* (1958). Different influences are discussed in Carol Gesner, *Shakespeare and the Greek Romance* (1970), which is more thorough and exact than the earlier study by E. C. Pettet, *Shakespeare and the Romance Tradition* (1949).

Shakespeare's stage

Most of the documents relating to Shakespeare's theatre and his company are collected in Chambers's *William Shakespeare* and in his equally indispensable *The Elizabethan Stage* (four volumes, 1923). There is a good account of playhouse structures by Richard Hosley in volume three of *The Revels History of Drama in English* which covers the period from 1576 to 1613 (1975). The whole theatrical context is presented and discussed in Glynne Wickham's stimulating and richly documented *Early English Stages 1300 to 1660*, particularly volume two, parts one (1963) and two (1972). The two most important playhouses are elaborately reconstructed by I. Smith in *Shakespeare's Globe Playhouse* (1956) and *Shakespeare's Blackfriars Playhouse: its History and Design* (1964); C. W. Hodges's *The Globe Restored* (1953, second edition 1968) is an important and beautifully illustrated book. John Orrell's *The Quest for Shakespeare's Globe* (1983) is a fascinating reconstruction of the structure and the dimensions of Shakespeare's Globe, mainly on the basis of Hollar's 'Long View of London' and related evidence. A balanced introduction to the subject is Andrew Gurr's *The Shakespearean Stage, 1574–1642* (1970, second edition 1980).

On the actual performances at the Globe B. Beckerman's *Shakespeare at the Globe 1599–1609* (1962) is most helpful; Beckerman discusses questions of production, dramaturgy, and stage conditions while T. J. King, *Shakespearean Staging, 1599–1642* (1971) gives useful information about the plays performed and the conclusions we can draw regarding staging and playhouse design. Peter Thomson's *Shakespeare's Theatre* (1983) is a sound and stimulating study of Shakespeare's company, its activities and its stage as well as the way in which these theatrical conditions can influence our reading of the texts. There are many interesting hints about possible ways of staging particular scenes in the new volumes of the Oxford Shakespeare and the New Cambridge Shakespeare (illustrated by C. W. Hodges). On Elizabethan acting Bertram Joseph's *Elizabethan Acting* (1951, revised edition 1964) is worth consulting.

Stage history

There are good and detailed sections on stage history in the volumes of the New Shakespeare, mostly by Harold Child and later by C. B. Young, and in the Oxford and New Cambridge Shakespeare. G. C. D. Odell's *Shakespeare from Betterton to Irving* (two volumes, 1920) and C. B. Hogan's *Shakespeare in the Theatre* (two volumes, 1952–7) contain a good deal of valuable material. Robert Speaight, *Shakespeare on the Stage. An Illustrated History of Shakespearean Performance* (1973) provides a spirited survey from Richard Burbage to Laurence Olivier. J. C. Trewin's *Shakespeare on the English Stage 1900–1964* (1964) will also be found quite useful. Michael Mullin's *Theatre at Stratford-upon-Avon* (two volumes, 1980) is a computerized index to performances at Stratford 1879–1978, listing productions, plays, and theatre personnel. William Halstead's *Shakespeare as Spoken* (twelve volumes, 1977–80) collates some 2,500 printed acting editions and prompt-books with the Globe text.

Some modern productions are discussed in J. R. Brown, *Shakespeare's Plays in Performance* (1966), in J. L. Styan, *The Shakespearean Revolution: Criticism and Performance in the 20th Century* (1977), and in Richard David, *Shakespeare in the Theatre* (1978). The annual reviews of performances in *Shakespeare Survey* (mainly London and Stratford) and *Shakespeare Quarterly* (more international) are important sources of information. The most detailed studies of the stage history are devoted to individual plays; particularly thorough and informative are books by Marvin Rosenberg on three of the great tragedies: *The Masks of Othello* (1961), *The Masks of King Lear* (1972), and *The Masks of Macbeth* (1978). Rosenberg's approach is a fascinating combination of stage history and close study of the text.

Shakespeare's impact and changing reputation

On Shakespeare's immediate impact and his contemporary reputation E. A. J. Honigmann's *Shakespeare's Impact on His Contemporaries* (1982) is well documented as well as boldly original in some of its conclusions. A different aspect is discussed by David L. Frost, *The School of Shakespeare. The Influence of*

Shakespeare on English Drama 1600–1642 (1968), which is more strictly confined to literary questions. On early Shakespeare criticism by far the most important source is the collection by Brian Vickers, *Shakespeare: The Critical Heritage* (six volumes, 1974–81), with long excerpts from critics up to 1801 and excellent introductions. Augustus Ralli, *A History of Shakespeare Criticism* (two volumes, 1932) discusses each critic in sequence and is a useful mine of information. The German *Shakespeare-Handbuch*, edited by Ina Schabert, has a long and intelligent chapter on the development of Shakespeare criticism. A. M. Eastman, *A Short History of Shakespeare Criticism* (1968), provides a useful sketch of the whole subject and there is a judicious brief study of twentieth-century criticism up to 1950 by Kenneth Muir, 'Fifty years of Shakespearian criticism: 1900–1950', in *Shakespeare Survey 4* (1951). Many of the reference works mentioned above also give information about the history of Shakespeare criticism; a generous selection from earlier critics will be found in the volumes of the New Variorum edition. Useful anthologies of criticism on particular plays, often with good critical introductions, have appeared in the Casebook Series (from 1968).

Music and the visual arts

Many critics have commented on the important part played by music in Shakespeare's plays. Edward W. Naylor's *Shakespeare and Music* (1896, revised edition 1931) is a classic survey of the subject. More detailed and specialized studies are F. W. Sternfeld's *Music in Shakespearean Tragedy* (second edition 1967) and Peter J. Seng's *The Vocal Songs in the Plays of Shakespeare: A Critical History* (1967). Sternfeld's book is as readable as it is learned and discusses many different aspects of its topic. It takes account of previous scholarship and gives transcriptions of early musical settings. Seng's work is a kind of Variorum edition of the songs, with much useful information on musical settings. Three books by John H. Long attempt a comprehensive survey of the available material: *Shakespeare's Use of Music: A Study of the Music and its Performance in the Original Production of Seven Comedies* (1955), *Shakespeare's Use of Music: The Final Comedies* (1961), and *Shakespeare's Use of Music: The Histories and Tragedies* (1971). *Shakespeare in Music*, edited by Phyllis Hartnoll (1964), is a particularly useful collection of essays on music in Shakespeare and Shakespeare in music. There is a long and most rewarding essay by Winton Dean on 'Shakespeare and Opera' and a seventy-eight page 'Catalogue of Musical Works Based on the Plays and Poetry on Shakespeare' which, though not complete and not entirely free from error, is the most comprehensive compilation in existence so far. There is an ambitious *Shakespeare Music Catalogue* in progress, however, edited by Bryan N. S. Gooch and David S. Thatcher at the University of Victoria. Its five projected volumes will contain a complete inventory of all music connected with

Shakespeare, including incidental music in Shakespearian productions. When completed it will be an indispensable tool for any further research on Shakespearian music.

Shakespeare in the visual arts (illustration, stage design, and paintings inspired by the plays) has been most imaginatively studied by W. Moelwyn Merchant whose *Shakespeare and the Artist* (1959) remains the most important book on the subject. *Shakespeare and Pictorial Art*, edited by Charles Holme, with a text by Malcolm C. Salaman (1971), is an instructive picture book, with 130 plates. Geoffrey Ashton's *Shakespeare and British Art* (1981) is the scholarly catalogue of an important exhibition.

Since the first edition of *The Cambridge Companion to Shakespeare Studies*, a number of important reference books and editions have appeared.

Bibliographies

The *Select Bibliographical Guides*, edited by Stanley Wells, have been thoroughly revised and updated, with some chapters rewritten by different authors, a new chapter on recent critical developments and a new title: *Shakespeare: A Bibliographical Guide. New Edition* (1990). Another useful tool is David Bergeron and Geraldo U. de Sousa, *Shakespeare: A Study and Research Guide* (1987), and Larry S. Champion, *The Essential Shakespeare* (1986). More ambitious, but limited in scope, is the compilation edited by Bruce T. Sajdak, *Shakespeare Index: An Annotated Bibliography of Critical Articles on the Plays 1959–1983*, Vol. I: *Citations and Author Index*, Vol. II: *Character, Scene and Subject Index* (1992). A very useful critical survey of editions is provided by *Which Shakespeare? A User's Guide to Editions*, edited by Ann Thompson and others (1992).

Periodicals

Since the two German Shakespeare associations reunited in 1993, the two yearbooks have also once again merged. The volumes for 1993 and 1994 bear the title *Deutsche Shakespeare-Gesellschaft. Jahrbuch*. From 1995, the traditional title *Shakespeare Jahrbuch* will be resumed. There are now, besides general articles, extensive sections on Shakespeare productions in Germany, Austria and Switzerland and reviews of new publications.

Editions

Among the one-volume editions of Shakespeare's works David Bevington's *The Complete Works of Shakespeare* (1980) offers a reliable text and brief introductions. Rather more adventurous is the new Oxford volume, edited by Stanley Wells and Gary Taylor, with John Jowett and William Montgomery: *William Shakespeare: The Complete Works* (1986). There is a modern spelling edition and a fully edited 'Original Spelling Edition'. The plays are arranged in chronological order and the texts have been more thoroughly examined and revised than perhaps in any edition since the appearance of the First Folio. The two versions of *King Lear* are both given in full. There are brief introductions to each play, but no annotation. Very full commentary on all textual issues and the individual texts is provided in the companion volume to the edition, *William Shakespeare: A Textual Companion*, by Stanley Wells and Gary Taylor, with John Jowett and William Montgomery (1987); this is easily the best and most comprehensive guide to all textual and editorial problems of Shakespeare's texts.

A complete revision of the new Arden Shakespeare, under the general editorship of Richard Proudfoot, is in preparation; the first volumes are announced for 1995. Both the Oxford Shakespeare and the New Cambridge Shakespeare have progressed steadily during the past years. More than half the plays and poems have appeared in each of the two series, and nearly every play is now available in one of them. The two projects together provide the most useful editions of many plays: e.g. the New Cambridge edition of *King Lear*, edited by Jay Halio (1993), is the first single-volume edition to give a thorough account of the two versions of the play in the Quarto and the Folio, without conflating the texts. A supplementary volume gives a critical quarto-based edition (1994). The more general reader is well served by *The New Folger Library Shakespeare*, edited by Barbara Mowat and Paul Werstine (1992–). The volumes are illustrated with material in the Folger Library collections; there are brief, up-to-date critical introductions and helpful material on sources, stage history and critical problems.

Shakespeare's life and time

Richard Dutton's *William Shakespeare: A Literary Life* (1989) offers a concise account of Shakespeare's life as an author and a man of the theatre. Samuel Schoenbaum's monumental *Shakespeare's Lives* has been reissued in a shortened and updated edition (1990). An interesting, though largely undocumented, period of Shakespeare's career is investigated in Ernest Honigmann's stimulating *Shakespeare: The 'Lost Years'* (1985).

Shakespeare's stage

Much work has been done in recent years on Shakespeare's theatre and the staging of his plays. Christine Eccles, *The Rose Theatre* (1990), offers a good account of the history and the recent archaeological findings. The third and revised edition of Andrew Gurr's *The Shakespearean Stage, 1574–1642* (1992) also includes a discussion of recent developments and discoveries. David Bradley, *From Text to Performance in the Elizabethan Theatre. Preparing the play for the stage* (1992) is very helpful on Elizabethan stage conditions, as is T.J. King, *Casting Shakespeare's Plays. London actors and their roles, 1590–1642* (1992).

Index

Note: figures in italics refer to illustrations or their captions